2007-2008

THE CAROLINA READER
Readings for Writing in English 101

EDITED BY LEE BAUKNIGHT

With
Brooke Rollins and Eme Crawford

For the University of South Carolina
First-Year English Program
Dr. Chris Holcomb, Director

D1444358

PEARSON
Custom
Publishing

Cover Art: Courtesy of PhotoDisc by Getty Images.

Editor
Lee Bauknight

Assistant Editors
Brooke Rollins
Eme Crawford

Web Addresses
English Department: *http://www.cas.sc.edu/engl*
First-Year English Program: *http://www.cas.sc.edu/engl/fye/index.html*

The Carolina Reader: Readings for Writing in English 101 is designed for use in the University of South Carolina's First-Year English Program.

Printed in the United States of America

10 9 8 7 6 5 4 3 2 1

ISBN 0-536-48979-3

2007240280

EC/TT

Please visit our web site at *www.pearsoncustom.com*

PEARSON CUSTOM PUBLISHING
501 Boylston Street, Suite 900, Boston, MA 02116
A Pearson Education Company

Copyright Acknowledgments

Table of Contents

Contents by Genre

While few essays fit neatly into a single category, this list is included to help you find examples of the kinds of papers your teacher may ask you to write. As you read the list, keep in mind that many essays contain elements of more than one genre. Thus, most of the pieces in this book appear in more than one of the categories below.

STUDENT WRITING

Available Online

Sample student essays from previous English 101 classes are posted at
    <www.cas.sc.edu/engl/fye/index.html>

PERSONAL NARRATIVES

EXPLORATORY PIECES

DEFINITIONAL ISSUES

EVALUATIVE ISSUES

CAUSAL ISSUES

POLICY ISSUES

HUMOR/SATIRE

INTRODUCTION

Why Argue?
BY PAUL G. COOK (2007)

WHAT'S THE BIG DEAL? ARGUING CULTURE

Textbooks often begin by telling you that argument is "everywhere" and that you need only glance at the nearest newspaper, blog, or cable news program to find examples of argumentative writing or of "argument-in-action." In fact, you might even hear that you can find arguments in less obvious places than these: environmental policy statements, public health announcements, scientific treatises, songs, online profiles, cartoons, advertisements, and even bumper stickers.

For all of that seeming accessibility, however, argument may still appear to be something formalized or distant—a kind of strict, rule-bound interaction that takes place in, say, Congressional hearings, organizational policy meetings, the hallowed halls of academia, or the corporate board room. According to this view, authentic or "real" argument (argument that "gets things done," so to speak) happens somewhere *out there*, in privileged spaces to which we have limited access or in forums that deal with issues over which we have little control. As you'll see, while this "C-SPAN version" of argument is prevalent, it's far from the only game in town.

If this formalized version of argument feels too distant, then its counterpoint, argument of the "knee-jerk" variety, might feel a bit too familiar. We take part in this "knee-jerk" argumentation when we react (perhaps badly) to someone trying to convince us of what we feel isn't true. We take part in "knee-jerk" argumentation when we bristle against a claim that is contrary to our own beliefs. This brand of argument, which has its precursor in our childhood disagreements with friends, siblings, or parents, is usually more informal, occurs in our everyday interactions, and often ends in shouting matches and pitched fits.

This contentious, often farcical, and easily parodied type of argument is symptomatic of what sociolinguist Deborah Tannen identifies as our "argument culture." For Tannen, the desire to "win" at all costs (even when it's unclear exactly what one "wins" in the first place) has seeped into not only journalism, but also the discourses of politics, law, and even academia—a place we tend of think of as somehow above such petty squabbling. No wonder, then, that for some it might seem best to just avoid all this mess to begin with. In fact, the popularity of *The Daily Show with Jon Stewart*, Comedy Central's satirical news program that attempts to parody this type of argumentation (among other things in the mainstream media), could be explained by the extent to which people are simply fed up with the adversarial argument culture that marks contemporary discourse.

Michiko Kakutani, in a 2002 piece for the *New York Times*, has diagnosed this apparent desire to avoid argument and dissent as characteristic of the so-called "Millennial" generation—those post-Gen X students now populating US colleges and universities (some pundits have cleverly termed this crucial demographic the "iGeneration"). According to Kakutani, a variety of factors—among them a philosophical relativism and the rise of various multiculturalist agendas—have resulted in "a reluctance to engage in the sort of impassioned argumentation that many baby boomers remember from their college days."

Quite simply, where earlier generations were eager to engage in public discourse, to disagree, and to generally shake things up, the new generation is far more reticent about fouling the air with what is largely perceived as unnecessarily agonistic, mean-spirited debate. (We might call this the "Why can't we all just get along?" syndrome.)

While I don't doubt that much of the blame for this generational hesitation concerning argument could be placed on the prevalent notion of argument as somehow unpleasant or antagonistic, I also suspect that what deters many of today's students from argument is the sneaking suspicion that the gateways to power are not as accessible as we might have been led to believe. As members of a democratic society (a fact of which we are constantly reminded by a host of different sources), decision-making powers fall to the people. Right? Isn't it our Jeffersonian duty to be informed, educated, and articulate citizens? Yes, but again, even as students we are aware that the way power works—

that is, the manner in which things get done, decisions get made, and policy gets enacted—is a far more complicated business than "We the people" implies.

WHAT IS ARGUMENT? IDENTIFYING THE CONVERSATION

At its simplest level, an argument makes a claim and provides reasons to support that claim. But as you've probably already guessed, it gets a bit more complicated than that, especially when you want to construct an argument that has the power to persuade or to really get people thinking about an idea or issue. In this class, you'll learn several techniques for identifying, reading, and writing arguments, but here are a few preliminary remarks about what argument is *not* that you should keep in mind as you encounter various texts. Some of these points might look familiar, as we've already mentioned a couple of them:

1. Argument is not all about winning. Ideally, the goal of argument is to discover a suitable solution or to acquire new knowledge.

2. Argument is not knee-jerk reaction. ("Yes it is!" "No it isn't!")

3. Argument that has the power to *do* things or to productively intervene in a problem doesn't always take place in privileged spaces to which most people have little or no access (i.e., on C-SPAN).

4. Argument is not a means for personal attack.

5. Argument is not all about *you*.

So, what *is* argument? At the risk of oversimplifying things, an argument is a fragmentary take on the world, a representation of a set of ideas or values, and a way of making sense of how things are or how they should be. We've already talked about how arguments can be found pretty much wherever you look, which—apart from making "argument" such a difficult term to define—also explains why the acts of reading and writing are virtually inseparable from the practice of identifying arguments. Encountering arguments—whether in the so-called "real world" or in the articles and essays presented in this textbook and in your class—requires that you develop the ability to see the often subtle forms that arguments take, even (or especially) when their "non-argumentativeness" seems self-evident.

Take something as familiar as Myspace or Facebook. If you're like the vast majority of college students, you're probably well acquainted with these popular online networks. Now think about the decisions you make as you're setting up or editing your profile: Which pictures do you include? How do you fill out the obligatory "About me" section? Should you remove Backstreet Boys from your "Favorite Music"? Why or why not?

These decisions, whether they're performed consciously or not, are instances of argument in action. In constructing—or, if you will, *writing*—your highly visible, fluid online identity, you're constantly making claims about yourself, your membership in particular groups or networks, your tastes and sensibilities, your social affiliations, and so forth. Some of these claims are obvious and explicit: "I'm a really cool guy!" Okay, sure. Some are more subtle and implicit: "I like all types of music (except Country)!" I'll leave it to you to figure out what claims are being made in this popular profile statement.

On the flipside, when you *read* the "Spaces" or "Faces" of others on the network, you deploy particular reading strategies that help you better *see* what kind of person you're dealing with, and (perhaps more importantly) whether or not you want add them as a "Friend." The point is that you weren't born with these reading or writing strategies—Myspace and Facebook have only been around for a few years. You had to learn the conventions or the languages of these sites through repeated encounters with these strange, online texts we call "Profiles." But you *did* learn them, to the extent that your ability to successfully write, revise, and edit your shifting online identity has become something close to second nature, a virtually automatic skill.

Okay, so what does Myspace have to do with this textbook or with this course? Quite simply, the point is that if you're comfortable using these sites, then you've probably already mastered one set of reading and writing strategies (and probably a few more, as well). What this class will teach you is how to master the reading and writing of other kinds of arguments: definitional essays, researched policy papers, and other writing exercises—all of which operate in similar ways and have their own sets of rules, strategies, and conventions.

READING AND WRITING THE CONVERSATION

What we're basically talking about here is what might be called "rhetorical awareness"—a necessary skill in a fast-paced, heavily mediated cultural milieu such as our own. If the sound-byte and the bumper sticker threaten to supplant reasoned discussion and informed debate as the dominant modes of argument, then learning how to read and write in an engaged manner is extremely vital to your ability to recognize arguments wherever you might encounter them.

It's no coincidence that Aristotle, the classical Greek philosopher from whose thought we have developed many of our ideas about the nature of argument, knowledge, and ethics, famously defined "rhetoric" as the "ability, in each particular case, to *see* the available means of persuasion." As you will learn, this idea of "seeing" arguments and texts is incredibly important. Indeed, you will likely hear it called by many different names, such as "close reading," "engaged reading," or "productive reading."

Most people assume that reading is an act of decoding, of translating what's there on the page into whatever it is the author meant to say. True enough, but as we've already seen, when it comes to reading arguments, you have to be aware of a lot more than what's immediately present on the page.

Let's try a different example: When someone talks about skillfully reading a piece of music, they're referring to the ability to juggle several tasks at once, to simultaneously see the notes, the key changes, the shifts in tone and tempo. Sure, you *can* read a piece of music one note at a time, cautiously plunking your way through the melody. And musicians will often give a new song a quick read-through to become more familiar with it. But at some point, the goal is to be able to read *into* the musical composition, to really get a feel for its texture and complexity—in short, to make it your own. (As we'll see, this is also a significant first step in constructing your own arguments, which is why reading and writing are so closely connected.)

But it's not enough to just be able to read the individual notes that together make up the musical composition; one also has to be in tune, aware of various musical conventions, and have some idea of how the song is to be performed or read. Reading music is tricky precisely because the musician has to be aware of so many things at the same time, while also producing a pleasant sound and either remaining true to the spirit of the original piece or improvising their own interpretation.

Similarly, reading arguments requires that you do more than just figure out the gist of the essay or the major claims, or even answer the question "What's it about?" (Though this is an excellent place to start.) You also have to understand what's going on *around* the text you're reading, what is usually referred to as the "context" of the argument. What issues are being addressed by the argument? What are the hidden assumptions or subtle implications of its major claims? What makes this argument succeed (or fail)? How can I respond to the claims being made?

Reading just to get the basics of what's being argued is a helpful tool and an important prerequisite, but there's more to being a careful and observant reader than simply understanding the skeletal framework of an argument. Superficial reading is like listening to a player piano—once the novelty of it wears off (I mean, really, when's the last time you saw a player piano?), you'd probably rather be listening to something far more interesting, like a full-scale musical performance in which all the sonic elements combine to produce something closer to an actual experience. In effect, this is what it means to read rhetorically, to be in tune (so to speak) with what's happening in a text as it unfolds.

WHAT CAN ARGUMENT DO? ENTERING THE CONVERSATION

It is vitally important that you have some sense of how your participation in the argumentative process can effect the way things work. This is not smoke and mirrors. As a student, your participation in what goes on in the world may seem pointless, and your access to the networks of power might appear to be severely limited.

However, being able to critically read the world around you or look at things in a different way is not only central to understanding how things work or how things get done, but also is key to your intervention in the critical conversation.

Literary theorist Kenneth Burke used the helpful metaphor of a "heated discussion" in a parlor to describe the kind of ongoing critical conversation to which I'm referring. For Burke, entering the critical conversation is like entering a room in which a vigorous debate is already in progress. No one there has the time, the ability, or perhaps the inclination to catch you up on what you've missed, but you're too enthralled to even think about not entering the discussion. So, you listen to the back and forth remarks until you think you've grasped the "tenor of the argument" and feel that you are ready to intervene or make your own claims. Even when it gets late and you have to leave the parlor, the debate continues on without you.

Like reading an online profile or listening to good music, encountering arguments critically is an act that invites response, and this is precisely where writing comes into play. While this class is not designed to turn you into some kind of bickering automaton or "argument-machine," it will give you the necessary tools to begin seeing arguments and asking the important questions for yourself. These questions will guide both the way you read arguments and how you'll respond to the arguments you encounter, which is why reading and writing are so closely bound up with each other, and why you'll be doing a lot of both in this class. In addition to learning the various reading strategies and the conventions of several genres, you will also be expected to fashion your own claims, to take stands on various issues, and to become intimately familiar with the conversation percolating through a particular problem or debate.

It's easy to get stymied by your perceived distance from the gateways of power, from those privileged spaces where the "real work" of the world gets done. We tend to think of argument as something that only matters if it produces immediate results, and we think our actions important only insofar as they *make things happen*. What this course will show you—in your class discussions and through the use of this textbook and other materials—is how your intervention in ongoing critical conversations can not only make you a more conscientious and critical reader of the world around you, but also has the potential to make more permeable the avenues of power themselves—if only in a gradual or even personal way.

If the Internet has taught us anything, it's that there are audiences to be had (just not always the ones you want). One of the greatest benefits of this course is that you are provided with a ready and willing audience for your writing, for your intervention in the critical conversation. In addition to your instructor, you'll also learn to depend on the insights of your classmates, friends, and others with whom you come in contact.

When you think about what you want to write about, consider those issues with which you feel a certain connection and a drive or desire to transform. But also think about what you read in the pages of this textbook. Pay attention to the conventions of the genre and learn how to hear the subtleties of the arguments. Learn to see the minute operations and to get a feel for the rhetorical maneuvers that occur in these essays; take the time to figure out what makes them work (or not work). When you read, you should always be writing. When you write, you should always be reading.

What you'll find in the pages of this anthology and in your first-year composition course is an introduction to argumentative essays (and essay-writing) that takes seriously the notion that argument is vital to not only understanding how discourse works, but also to being able to function in a world in which effective communication—reading and writing—is essential to one's well-being and success.

———

Paul G. Cook is a Ph.D. candidate in rhetoric and composition studies at the University of South Carolina, where he teaches first-year composition and advanced writing courses. His academic interests include, but are not limited to, cultural theory, the history of composition studies, classical rhetoric, Nietzsche, and so-called "critical theory." Some days (but not all) he finds time to dance.

One

READING, WRITING, AND THE POWER OF WORDS

Writing Off Reading

BY MICHAEL SKUBE (2006)

We were talking informally in class not long ago, 17 college sophomores and I, and on a whim I asked who some of their favorite writers are. The question hung in uneasy silence. At length, a voice in the rear hesitantly volunteered the name of . . . Dan Brown.

No other names were offered.

The author of "The DaVinci Code" was not just the best writer they could think of; he was the *only* writer they could think of.

In our better private universities and flagship state schools today, it's hard to find a student who graduated from high school with much lower than a 3.5 GPA, and not uncommon to find students whose GPAs were 4.0 or higher. They somehow got these suspect grades without having read much. Or if they did read, they've given it up. And it shows — in their writing and even in their conversation.

A few years ago, I began keeping a list of everyday words that may as well have been potholes in exchanges with college students. It began with a fellow who was two months away from graduating from a well-respected Midwestern university.

"And what was the impetus for that?" I asked as he finished a presentation.

At the word "impetus" his head snapped sideways, as if by reflex. "The what?" he asked.

"The impetus. What gave rise to it? What prompted it?"

I wouldn't have guessed that impetus was a 25-cent word. But I also wouldn't have guessed that "ramshackle" and "lucid" were exactly recondite, either. I've had to explain both. You can be dead certain that today's college students carry a weekly planner. But they may or may not own a dictionary, and if they do own one, it doesn't get much use. ("Why do you need a dictionary when you can just go online?" more than one student has asked me.)

You may be surprised—and dismayed—by some of the words on my list.

"Advocate," for example. Neither the verb nor the noun was immediately clear to students who had graduated from high school with GPAs above 3.5. A few others:

"Derelict," as in neglectful.

"Satire," as in a literary form.

"Pith," as in the heart of the matter.

"Brevity," as in the quality of being succinct.

And my favorite: "Novel," as in new and as a literary form. College students nowadays call any book, fact or fiction, a novel. I have no idea why this is, but I first became acquainted with the peculiarity when a senior at one of the country's better state universities wrote a paper in which she referred to "The Prince" as "Machiavelli's novel."

As freshmen start showing up for classes this month, colleges will have a new influx of high school graduates with gilded GPAs, and it won't be long before one professor whispers to another: Did no one teach these kids basic English? The unhappy truth is that many students are hard-pressed to string together coherent sentences, to tell a pronoun from a preposition, even to distinguish between "then" and "than." Yet they got A's.

How does one explain the inability of college students to read or write at even a high school level? One explanation, which owes as much to the culture as to the schools, is that kids don't read for pleasure. And because they don't read, they are less able to navigate the language. If words are the coin of their thought, they're working with little more than pocket change.

Say this—but no more—for the Bush administration's No Child Left Behind Act: It at least recognizes the problem. What we're graduating from our high schools isn't college material. Sometimes it isn't even good high school material.

When students with A averages can't write simple English, it shouldn't be surprising that people ask what a high school diploma is really worth. In California this year, hundreds of high school students, many with good grades, faced the prospect of not graduating because they could not pass a state-mandated exit exam. Although a judge overturned the effort, legislators (not always so literate themselves) in other states have also called for exit exams. It's hardly unreasonable to ask that students demonstrate a minimum competency in basic subjects, especially English.

Exit exams have become almost a necessity because the GPA is not to be trusted. In my experience, a high SAT score is far more reliable than a high GPA—more indicative of quickness and acuity, and more reflective of familiarity with language and ideas. College admissions specialists are of a different view and are apt to label the student with high SAT scores but mediocre grades unmotivated, even lazy.

I'll take that student any day. I've known such students. They may have been bored in high school but they read widely and without prodding from a parent. And they could have nominated a few favorite writers besides Dan Brown—even if they thoroughly enjoyed "The DaVinci Code."

I suspect they would have understood the point I tried unsuccessfully to make once when I quoted Joseph Pulitzer to my students. It is journalism's job, he said, to comfort the afflicted and afflict the comfortable. Too obvious, you think? I might have thought so myself—if the words "afflicted" and "afflict" hadn't stumped the whole class.

Michael Skube teaches journalism at Elon University in Elon, N.C. He wrote this piece for the August 20, 2006, edition of *The Washington Post* <www.washingtonpost.com>.

Aggressive Reading Won't Kill You (No Matter What Mark Twain Says)

BY TODD HAGSTETTE (2007)

At the beginning of his masterpiece, *Adventures of Huckleberry Finn*, Mark Twain offers the following warning to the reader:

NOTICE

Persons attempting to find a motive in this narrative will be prosecuted; persons attempting to find a moral in it will be banished; persons attempting to find a plot in it will be shot.

This comic, false-modest proclamation urges readers to glance at his text lightly, with no attempt at subsurface penetration. It urges the reader, in other words, to read passively. Though Twain is obviously being facetious, many contemporary students unfortunately seem to take this satirical injunction seriously when it comes to their own reading. They follow Twain's advice to the letter by failing to consider the overriding theme or meaning of a text (the moral), the author's intentions (the motive), or even the basics of the language itself (the plot). In short, they fail to recognize that good writing begins with aggressive reading. It is the most overlooked and disregarded step in the writing process, but without aggressive reading at the launch, papers drift as aimlessly as rafts on a river. The good news is that with a few simple (and obvious) techniques, any student can learn to read more carefully, engage with the text more thoroughly, and thus write more successfully.

THE VALUE OF DISCOMFORT

The first thing you need to do to begin the aggressive reading process is to get uncomfortable. That's right, *UN-comfortable*. One of the major problems that many students encounter in their studies is that they attempt to deal with their school reading the same way that they read for pleasure. Taking a book to bed with you to help you fall asleep or curling up in your comfy leather chair with Oprah on in the background may be great ways to enjoy the latest Nicholas Sparks novel or the new issue of *People* magazine. But, when it comes to active, retentive reading, you need to set the scene a bit more seriously. Think about it in terms of baseball: the difference between reading for pleasure and aggressive reading is like the difference between playing catch in the backyard and practicing as part of major league spring training. Playing catch can be fun, but it does nothing to improve your skills. Even the best of the best pro ball players must drill and work relentlessly to be successful in the game. And so must you in your academic reading. Play catch on your own time. Get out of the backyard hammock, and sit down at a desk or a table in a quiet room. That way you will be ready to really focus on the task at hand.

BEATING YOUR PROMISCUOUS MIND

Better focus is exactly what most inexperienced readers need. It is easy to get distracted while reading; in fact, it is a natural, understandable consequence of the reading process. We all have had the experience of drifting off into a daydream over a text and then snapping out of it to discover that we have no idea what the last several pages were about. Reading gets your mind working. It stimulates your thinking. And often it sends your mind spinning off into tangential directions. Think of it this way: reading is like Viagra(r) for the imagination. The problem is that being that mentally, um, erect leads directly to intellectual promiscuity. Aggressive reading is about learning to be monogamous. Just as it takes discipline for a married man to stay home at night, you must develop the discipline to keep your brain faithful to the text at hand. And that simply takes practice. Crank up the aggressive reading by not letting your daydreams control your comprehension of the text. As soon as you wake up, go back to the last thing you remember reading and start over. Stop believing in the virtue of plowing through a story or essay, and divest yourself of the idea that the end of the text is the finish line of the assignment. Rather, come to think of comprehension as the end point. Also, make peace with reading slowly. We are trained to believe that reading quickly is a sign of proficiency and intelligence, but speed reading is not aggressive reading. Slow down, go back when necessary, and focus on truly absorbing the material.

TEXTS ARE READ TOO PASSIVELY BY YOU

Overall, this kind of absorption is about confirming to yourself that you understand everything you have read, that you have followed along with the author every step of the way and internalized his or her arguments and themes. The best ways to accomplish that assurance is to take ample notes while you read and take the time to research anything unfamiliar to you. Vocabulary is a tricky thing, and because we are all trained to be very good at interpreting so-called context clues, most of us can glean a fairly good idea of what a word means just by noting how it is used. All words, though, have different nuances that are more complicated than what a simple deduction allows us to discern. In the previous section, for instance, I used the word "tangential." Now, you probably could figure out that I meant something like "inappropriate" or "irrelevant" based on the context of the sentence. But, why did I choose that particular word instead of some other pseudo-synonyms like "digressive," "peripheral," or "divergent"? You must know the subtleties of definition to fully grasp the specific type of wandering mind that it suggests.

You must also master allusions. If you do not know the reference, then no matter how effectively you read context clues, you will not fully grasp a writer's point. For example, in a recent political article, the author suggests that vocal anti-war liberals should spend an evening with Damocles' sword before they criticize President Bush. Though you may be able to get the general idea that this author is condemning the former and supporting the latter, without knowing the Greek story of that Sicilian blowhard you will miss the specific nature of the writer's criticism. The point is: never simply read right past elements you do not fully understand. Everything in a text is there for a conscious reason. Your job as an aggressive reader is to decode the vocabulary and allusions you encounter. So be prepared to do all of your reading with a dictionary (or Dictionary.com) and an encyclopedia (or Wikipedia) close at hand.

BREAKING THE 4TH WALL

There is more to engaging with a text than simply eliminating your physical passivity, though. Besides being diligent in incorporating writing into your reading, you must also accept the mental challenges that a text presents. Do not simply accept everything you read—question the material. Challenge an essay writer's argument, doubt a character's motivation, criticize a poem's theme. Only by bringing your own perspective into a text will you fully internalize it. Consider the theatrical world where there is an imaginary wall that separates the performers from the audience. This 4th wall (as distinct from the three actual walls that form a play's set) maintains the distance between the real world of the audience and the imaginary world of the drama. But, some playwrights opt to violate this separation by having the actors "break the 4th wall" and speak directly to the audience. Shakespeare famously does this in *A Midsummer Night's Dream*, and so do many children's plays. The purpose of breaking the wall is to get the audience members more involved in the action, to wrest them out of their passive enjoyment of the work and make them active participants. You must do the same thing in your reading. It is not enough to simply read a text. You must interact with it and thereby become an aggressive contributor to it.

REDUNDANCY, REPETITION, RE-READING

The final step in the aggressive reading process is to simply do it all over again. No matter how accomplished a reader you are, you are unlikely to fully understand a text after reading it only once. In fact, I believe that you must read most short stories *three* times before you have a solid grasp of them; argumentative essays must be read *five* times; and, poems require *ten* readings before you can feel confident in your understanding. It sounds superfluous and painful, I know, but nobody ever said that aggressive reading was easy. Only through repeated immersion in the text will you gain the kind of focus you need, ensure that your notes and research are complete, and guarantee that you have completely questioned the material in full. If you don't believe me, try it. You are almost at the long-anticipated end of this essay. Read it again. See if there isn't something you missed the first time or that you don't grasp better the second time. Go ahead—read it again. I dare you.

DODGING THE MARK TWAIN BULLET

This how we must come to think of Mark Twain's warning at the beginning of *Huck Finn*: not as a restriction but as a dare. He is not encouraging readers to approach his work passively, but rather challenging them to read it aggressively. Anyone who has read even of few pages of Twain's book can readily discern the author's mastery of language (plot), deep thematic import (moral), and socio-political ambition (motive). He is imploring you not to haphazardly miss those things in the text, and so am I. Because, ultimately, aggressive reading leads to proficient writing. So get uncomfortable, stay focused, take notes, look up unfamiliars, question the material, and re-read the text. Put your pole in the water and guide your raft confidently down the treacherous waters of the aggressive reading process. It won't kill you.

———

Todd Hagstette is a Ph.D. candidate in English at USC, where he teaches English 101 and 102 and other courses in writing and literature.

Sing

BY LISA BAILEY (2007)

"And of course there must be something wrong
In wanting to silence any song."
—Robert Frost, "A Minor Bird"

When watching the Olympics, I'm always amazed at how few of the U.S. gold medal winners actually sing our national anthem when on the podium, receiving the honor of their accomplished lives. It's not due to lack of patriotism, as far as I can tell. In fact, most times these athletes seem *exceptionally* patriotic, with tears streaming down their faces as the music plays, often having paraded around with U.S. flags after winning their events. So, why not sing loud and long as an extension of this celebratory patriotism? These are confident, passionate, successful athletes, yet they stand mute in their moment of grandest glory.

I sing it for them. Loud and with passion. My daughter is mortified, especially if she has friends over or if the windows happen to be open. Truth be told, I sing "The Star Spangled Banner" at full tilt every chance I get. At sporting events, I belt it out; I make it a point not to be late to football and basketball games so that I can give my vocal cords a go. I look forward to it, actually. Sometimes tears come to my eyes, and I have to blow my nose or put on sunglasses as a cover.

As I was growing up, my household was full of music. In those days, before dozens of cable channels to choose from, we listened to the radio more than we watched TV. When we did watch, we sang along with the commercials and theme songs—even ticked along with the *60 Minutes* stop watch. Mom, my sister Marsha, and I would sing along with music regardless of its source, dancing when moved to do so. As far as I knew, this was what the world was like. Music was a participatory experience, similar to conversation. I would no more listen passively to a favorite song on the radio than I would sit silently while a friend engaged me in conversation. Music was interactive. My family created music with our voices and various instruments (harmonica, guitar, piano, clarinet, flute), and we appreciated especially snappy numbers by moving our bodies. In church, we sang. In school, we sang. At home, we sang.

Imagine my surprise when I realized that not all households encouraged people to join in when the music was happening. I don't think I fully understood how odd my close relationship with singing was until I was living with roommates in college. After getting ready for class one morning, I left my room to get some breakfast. As I hurried down the hall toward the kitchen, I could hear a couple of my roommates quietly laughing. Candy, still giggling, looked sideways at Debbie and then somewhat snidely said to me, "I heard you singing while you were blow-drying your hair." Then they burst out laughing.

What an odd comment. Why remark on such an unremarkable thing? As I stood in our nasty, barely functional kitchen, staring at my two snickering roommates, it occurred to me that I was supposed to be embarrassed because I was overheard *singing*. I would no sooner be embarrassed for singing than I would be embarrassed for talking on the phone with my mother. It was just one of those normal, almost mundane, things that people do. *Or was it?* Come to think of it, I had never heard Candy or Debbie sing unless it was a swaying, squinting, drunken rendition of "American Pie" after an evening at the bars. *I took my Chevy to the levy / but the levy was dry.* How had I not noticed this before? My friends didn't really sing to the radio. They nodded their heads, perhaps got a distant look in their eyes, but they made no sounds. And even if they did look at me rather curiously when I sang along, no one had confronted me about it to that point. Or perhaps I was singing too loudly to notice.

A DIFFERENT KIND OF VOICE

In his introduction to *The Best American Essays 2004*, Louis Menand posits that "[t]he real basis for the metaphor of voice in writing is not speaking. It is singing." How beautiful: to consider that what writers are doing is a version of music, a humming of sorts. That could explain our love and appreciation for a well-written sentence. The rhythm, its lyricism, is a thing to treasure, to read again and again. This metaphor could also help to explain a writer's reluctance to create. In our society we classify people into groups of those who have the right to sing (the good singers) and those who should be quiet (the rest of us). We do that to writers as well.

Although school is supposed to be a place where students learn about writing and gain confidence in themselves as writers, many times they actually come away less self-assured and more reluctant to put words to paper. As a Graduate Teaching Assistant and fellow student writer, I worry about the impact of my teacherly comments on my students' papers. I want to be as helpful in their development as writers as possible. I try not to sound angry or offended (even if I am); after all, none of my students set out to taunt me with a comma splice, an awkward word choice, a repeated mistake, or a general disregard for my instructions. I struggle, wondering: what sorts of comments and advice are most useful to my emerging singers? How much is too much? How do I help to improve the quality of the music without destroying the soul of the musician, or even the substance of the song? If I explicitly tell them how to write, and then they write accordingly, who, exactly, is singing?

A few years ago my teen-aged daughter, Hannah, was involved in an after-school activity, *Written and Illustrated*. Students met on Tuesdays to compose a story, illustrate it, and eventually have it published. Hannah was excited about participating, and I was excited for her. When she was in grade school and learning to read, I was concerned that she didn't seem to love words and stories the way I had as a child. Hannah preferred activities with other people to more solitary reading or writing. Although she has always been an "A" student, she is not a passionate or excited reader or learner. She prefers acting, dancing, and cheerleading. And although she rarely misses school, it's not because she worries about lost learning opportunities; no, she insists on attending class with a cold because she doesn't want to miss out on any gossip.

So, I was excited to see Hannah interested in writing, and I was curious to read what she and the other students would create in *Written and Illustrated*. After much deliberation about her topic (from which I was excluded), Hannah wrote a draft of her story, in a great hurry, and turned it in to her teacher. We waited for a week to receive the teacher's comments and suggestions. (Yes, *we*. I asked her every evening, trying to be casual, if her story had been returned yet.) Hannah was uncharacteristically quiet one Tuesday after school. I asked whether her teacher had returned her story, and Hannah abruptly retorted, "I don't want to do *Written and Illustrated* anymore."

"Why not? You were so excited about it . . ."

"I don't like it anymore."

"Didn't your teacher like your story?"

"She said she didn't really get into it, so she couldn't really give me any comments."

"Well, maybe she didn't have time to write comments on all the stories."

"No, she gave comments to the kids who had good stories."

I understood. The teacher commented on the stories that she thought had potential, and the stories that needed the most work were dismissed. As a parent, I was enraged. As a writing teacher, I didn't understand her pedagogical approach. I always spend the most time with the struggling students on the worst papers. Those students need me most, after all. What gives a teacher the right to just abandon an emerging, or even struggling, writer? I grabbed my purse and keys and headed for the door: "That's ridiculous! I'm going to talk to that teacher and see what's going on. I may even talk to the principal."

"Mom! No! You can't—I'll have her next semester for English. Please don't!!"

"All the more reason to get this straightened out now."

"Please, Mom! I don't even want to be in *Written and Illustrated* anymore."

It *was* an extracurricular activity. I couldn't force her to go, but I still seethe. Hannah never went back to *Written and Illustrated*, and to my knowledge, she hasn't written anything that wasn't required for a class since.

BREAKING THE SILENCE

It's not just singing and writing. We silence and are silenced constantly. Many times we actually silence ourselves. We are a society of perfectionists who don't feel entitled to participate unless we are exceptional. Students fear speaking up in class because they don't want to sound unintelligent. We make fun of clumsy dancers in nightclubs. What is our society losing out on by causing people to be afraid to contribute? How many individuals stop trying before they produce something truly great because they fear either their work or they themselves are no good? Intellectually, we understand that people grow from trying, from doing, from active participation. So why do we shut down fledgling efforts if the results aren't immediately perfect, before the work and the human truly have a chance of becoming as beautiful, as wonderful as possible?

But singing still happens, despite near-constant attempts at silencing. My daughter, and 89 other eighth- and ninth-graders, showed up faithfully at 7 a.m. three to five days a week for Junior High Chorale practice. Young people queue up around giant city blocks to try out for *American Idol*. I continue to write. My students keep writing, too. Singing continues, yet I have to believe it is a bit cautious: we're holding back, looking around for nods of approval or grimaces of displeasure. What could we accomplish if we could all let loose and just sing?

Perhaps more people would contribute their unique voices to the classroom discussions, so that we don't hear the same voices each class period, or so that we aren't forced to hear yet another solo performance from the instructor. Perhaps instead of passively digesting information, students would enter into conversations with their textbooks, making notes in the margins, writing or journaling responses, or bringing up questions in class. Perhaps instead of thinking of a writing assignment as an obstacle to overcome, or something to endure, students would consider assigned papers as opportunities to belt out their passionately held convictions on a given subject matter.

The point is that people shouldn't have to be drunk in order to sing; no one needs permission. Singing, in its literal and metaphoric forms, is part of what it is to be human. It's part of what it means to live actively, to participate in what's going on instead of merely being a passive observer. Whether it's award-winning singing, or a struggling, continual effort to figure out the words of the chorus, singing is meant to be participatory. So don't just listen. Don't just read. Don't be mute. Participate. Write. Sing.

––––––

Lisa Bailey is a Ph.D. candidate in USC's English Department studying Composition and Rhetoric. She enjoys helping her students sing in English 101 and 102.

Nothing but the Facts?

BY EME CRAWFORD (2007)

Sitting at the front desk of Doug Jones's Auto Sales I closed David Brinkley's autobiography and imagined the splash I would make in college. As the editor of my high school newspaper, I had taken a recent interest in the daring young newspaper reporters who had broken the Watergate scandal, Woodward and Bernstein. Unfortunately, since the local library held nothing on those *enfants terrible* of the early 70s, I had to settle for the aging, dignified old man of ABC news. It didn't matter much. After all, what interested me most was *journalism*. I imagined the clean, clipped prose of a hard-boiled news story, written by pure-hearted newspapermen and women, notepad in hand, ever striving for the noble dream of objectivity.

As I waited on the dozen customers who came in to make car payments throughout the day, I pondered how my past had prepared me for a life of writing. For the past four years in high school I had worked on my school newspaper climbing my way up from grunt staff writer to worldly editor. I thought about how this would be great material for my own biography. *She was ready to write. She was ready to become the next Pulitzer Prize winning journalist. It was the summer of 1998 and Eme Crawford was ready for the world, but was the world ready for her brilliant prose?*

"Eme, would you put the book down and refill the coke machine?"

The monotony of a small-town summer job eventually gave way to the limitless possibility of the first week of college, and soon I found myself in my first composition course. Our assignment was on a subject I thought I knew backwards and forwards—Moses. We were to read a passage from Exodus and make an argument about his character. I had attended the requisite Sunday school classes. I knew about the miracles—the first Passover, the parting of the water, the Ten Commandments. I got it. What more was there to write about?

But I wanted to be a good student. I would utilize the writing skills of those noble journalists who populated my imagination, reporting nothing but the facts of the story. I worked all weekend on that essay. I called and consulted my mother, consulted my roommate, and consulted my Bible. By Sunday I had written an essay I felt proud of. My biographer, shuffling through the papers from my college years, would pause a moment when she reached this essay. *From her earliest days as a college freshman, Crawford's writing bore the markings of future greatness.*

But when our essays were returned, I was floored. I got a "C"! I had never gotten a "C" in my life! I knew this story! How could I have gotten a "C"?! I was more hurt than angry. And I felt more like a mournful Old Testament character than a brash young reporter. I wanted to cry right there in the classroom, tear my clothes and dump ashes on my head. Instead, I went against my prophetic instincts, slinking back to my dorm room to eat a bag of double stuffed Oreos. I imagined my biographer scrapping the first paragraph of chapter two and starting over. *Despite the success of her high school years, Crawford's first essay for English 101 turned out to be a major setback.*

The next day I was furious. I scheduled a meeting with my professor to get to the bottom of her crazy notions of what good writing should be and do. I explained to her that writing should be about the facts. It should honestly represent an event. In this case, I felt like I told the whole Moses story accurately.

"But," she pressed me, "what specifically do you find interesting about Moses as a character?"

"Why would you consider Moses heroic?"

"What characteristics constitute heroism?"

"What are some of his faults?"

I was pelted with hard questions I had no idea how to answer, or if I did answer them, I didn't know how to explain why I thought the way I thought.

"The facts," my professor told me, "are still up for debate. Knowledge isn't simply there to be discovered, but has to be created."

"Perhaps good writing," she told me, "has more to do with creatively engaging with texts and asking questions rather than summarizing the safe facts. Sure we sometimes write to accurately convey an event, but I'm asking you to write to push your thinking on what you think you know. Go back to your dorm room and think about Moses' story again. Make an argument about his character that's from you—not what someone has told you."

This, of course was heresy. The facts are still up for debate? My professor was nuts. She would have me cast aside objectivity and make up facts whole cloth. I imagined David Brinkley shaking his gray head in disgust.

I went back to my room, my head swimming from the questions and ideas fired at me. How was I going to do this? How to un-learn the things I thought I had known all my life? If I start questioning what kind of man Moses was, how can I stop from thinking about what kind of man Jesus was? By extension what do I think about God? If God were a human and did the things attributed to him in the Old Testament, what would I think about that person? For the time being I had to stop myself. I had to limit myself to only Moses.

Contemplating Moses's lot in life and my own, I began to envy Moses and his trusty burning bush. How could Moses have it so easy? My mind started to wander. I wondered what really happened during the composition of the Ten Commandments. Who was doing the actual writing? Moses or God? Was this a collaborative process? Were there drafts? Did God come up with the content and Moses help with the grammar? Did they fight over word choice? Did they spend hours arguing over "Thou shall not murder" versus "Thou shall not kill"? Moses was on Mount Sinai for forty days and forty nights, but there were no first-hand witnesses as to what happened. This was bad material for a news story.

Then again, they had to be discussing something. Why did Moses *really* break the first tablet? After walking down the mountain, away from the eye of God the Father, God the Editor, did Moses find himself unhappy with the work? It seemed a little strange that Moses would lose his cool after seeing the Israelites sinning it up. I mean, didn't he know what they were like before? Moses must have been a big believer in the collaborative and re-writing process. He just *had* to go back for another draft.

As I furiously typed away at my second draft, I realized I was straying far from my ideal of objective writing. But I also felt a rush of freedom by creating new knowledge. To be sure, Brinkley would not be pleased. I imagined my biographer in solidarity with him, trying to accommodate the stylistic shift. *Crawford's second essay, with its self indulgence and wild speculation, bore little resemblance to the first. She was teetering on the edge.*

I don't know exactly when it happened, but eventually my metaphor-hungry subconscious eventually grasped onto the Moses story as its dominant trope, leaving behind those sacred cows of my high school years. Moses patiently wandered through the desert for forty years searching for the Promised Land. For four years in college I patiently searched my writing, finding out what worked and what didn't. Unlike what I had expected when I first started college, instead of turning outward and observing and summarizing the world around me, the greatest reward of writing was turning my journalistic eye inward, observing and evaluating my own beliefs and knowledge.

Of course, Moses never actually reached the Promised Land. Would he have embarked on the journey, knowing that the land of milk and honey would forever elude him? Maybe not, but I'd like to think he eventually came to embrace his role in the process. If I ever make it there, I think I'll start my autobiography this way: *Sitting at the front desk of Doug Jones's Auto Sales I closed the book of Exodus and imagined the journey ahead of me in college.*

———

Eme Crawford, a Ph.D. candidate in composition and rhetoric at USC, teaches in the First-Year English Program and has a Boston terrier named Andi. She has yet to start her autobiography, but when she does, Andi will figure prominently in it.

Shitty First Drafts

From *Bird by Bird: Some Instructions on Writing and Life*
BY ANNE LAMOTT (1994)

All good writers write shitty first drafts. This is how they end up with good second drafts and terrific third drafts. People tend to look at successful writers, writers who are getting their books published and maybe even doing well financially, and think that they sit down at their desks every morning feeling like a million dollars, feeling great about who they are and how much talent they have and what a great story they have to tell; that they take in a few deep breaths, push back their sleeves, roll their necks a few times to get all the cricks out, and dive in, typing fully formed passages as fast as a court reporter. But this is just the fantasy of the uninitiated. I know some very great writers, writers you love who write beautifully and have made a great deal of money, and not one of them sits down routinely feeling wildly enthusiastic and confident. Not one of them writes elegant first drafts. All right, one of them does, but we do not like her very much. We do not think that she has a rich inner life or that God likes her or can even stand her. (Although when I mentioned this to my priest friend Tom, he said you can safely assume you've created God in your own image when it turns out that God hates all the same people you do.)

Very few writers really know what they are doing until they've done it. Nor do they go about their business feeling dewy and thrilled. They do not type a few stiff warm-up sentences and then find themselves bounding along like huskies across the snow. One writer I know tells me that he sits down every morning and says to himself nicely, "It's not like you don't have a choice, because you do—you can either type or kill yourself." We all often feel like we are pulling teeth, even those writers whose prose ends up being the most natural and fluid. The right words and sentences just do not come pouring out like ticker tape—most of the time. Now, Muriel Spark is said to have felt that she was taking dictation from God every morning—sitting there, one supposes, plugged into a Dictaphone, typing away, humming. But this is a very hostile and aggressive position. One might hope for bad things to rain down on a person like this.

For me and most of the other writers I know, writing is not rapturous. In fact, the only way I can get anything written at all is to write really, really shitty first drafts.

The first draft is the child's draft, where you let it all pour out and then let it romp all over the place, knowing that no one is going to see it and that you can shape it later. You just let this childlike part of you channel whatever voices and visions come through and onto the page. If one of the characters wants to say, "Well, so what, Mr. Poopy Pants?," you let her. No one is going to see it. If the kid wants to get into really sentimental, weepy, emotional territory, you let him. Just get it all down on paper, because there may be something great in those six crazy pages that you would never have gotten to by more rational, grown-up means. There may be something in the very last line of the very last paragraph on page six that you just love, that is so beautiful or wild that you now know what you're supposed to be writing about, more or less, or in what direction you might go—but there was no way to get to this without first getting through the first five and a half pages.

I used to write food reviews for *California* magazine before it folded. (My writing food reviews had nothing to do with the magazine folding, although every single review did cause a couple of canceled subscriptions. Some readers took umbrage at my comparing mounds of vegetable puree with various ex-presidents' brains.) These reviews always took two days to write. First I'd go to a restaurant several times with a few opinionated, articulate friends in tow. I'd sit there writing down everything anyone said that was at all interesting or funny. Then on the following Monday I'd sit down at my desk with my notes, and try to write the review. Even after I'd been doing this for years, panic would set in. I'd try to write a lead, but instead I'd write a couple of dreadful sentences, xx them out, try again, xx everything out, and then feel despair and worry settle on my chest like an x-ray apron. It's over, I'd think, calmly. I'm not going to be able to get the magic to work this time. I'm ruined. I'm through. I'm toast. Maybe, I'd think, I can get my old job back as a clerk-typist. But probably not. I'd get up and study my teeth in the mirror for a while. Then I'd stop, remember to breathe, make a few phone calls, hit the kitchen and chow down. Eventually I'd go back and sit down at my desk, and sigh for the next ten minutes. Finally I would pick up my one-inch picture frame, stare into it as if for the answer, and every time the answer would come: all I had to do was to write a really shitty first draft of, say, the opening paragraph. And no one was going to see it.

So I'd start writing without reining myself in. It was almost just typing, just making my fingers move. And the writing would be *terrible*. I'd write a lead paragraph that was a whole page, even though the entire review could only be three pages long, and then I'd start writing up descriptions of the food, one dish at a time, bird by bird, and the critics would be sitting on my shoulders, commenting like cartoon characters. They'd be pretending to snore, or rolling their eyes at my overwrought descriptions, no matter how hard I tried to tone those descriptions down, no matter how conscious I was of what a friend said to me gently in my early days of restaurant reviewing. "Annie," she said, "it is just a piece of chicken. It is just a bit of cake."

But because by then I had been writing for so long, I would eventually let myself trust the process—sort of, more or less. I'd write a first draft that was maybe twice as long as it should be, with a self-indulgent and boring beginning, stupefying descriptions of the meal, lots of quotes from my black-humored friends that made them sound more like the Manson girls than food lovers, and no ending to speak of. The whole thing would be so long and incoherent and hideous that for the rest of the day I'd obsess about getting creamed by a car before I could write a decent second draft. I'd worry that people would read what I'd written and believe that the accident had really been a suicide, that I had panicked because my talent was waning and my mind was shot.

The next day, though, I'd sit down, go through it all with a colored pen, take out everything I possibly could, find a new lead somewhere on the second page, figure out a kicky place to end it, and then write a second draft. It always turned out fine, sometimes even funny and weird and helpful. I'd go over it one more time and mail it in.

Then, a month later, when it was time for another review, the whole process would start again, complete with the fears that people would find my first draft before I could rewrite it.

Almost all good writing begins with terrible first efforts. You need to start somewhere. Start by getting something—anything—down on paper. A friend of mine says that the first draft is the down draft—you just get it down. The second draft is the up draft—you fix it up. You try to say what you have to say more accurately. And the third draft is the dental draft, where you check every tooth, to see if it's loose or cramped or decayed, or even, God help us, healthy.

What I've learned to do when I sit down to work on a shitty first draft is to quiet the voices in my head. First there's the vinegar-lipped Reader Lady, who says primly, "Well, that's not very interesting, is it?" And there's the emaciated German male who writes these Orwellian memos detailing your thought crimes. And there are your parents, agonizing over your lack of loyalty and discretion; and there's William Burroughs, dozing off or shooting up because he finds you as bold and articulate as a houseplant; and so on. And there are also the dogs: let's not forget the dogs, the dogs in their pen who will surely hurtle and snarl their way out if you ever stop writing, because writing is, for some of us, the latch that keeps the door of the pen closed, keeps those crazy ravenous dogs contained.

Quieting these voices is at least half the battle I fight daily. But this is better than it used to be. It used to be 87 percent. Left to its own devices, my mind spends much of its time having conversations with people who aren't there. I walk along defending myself to people, or exchanging repartee with them, or rationalizing my behavior, or seducing them with gossip, or pretending I'm on their TV talk show or whatever. I speed or run an aging yellow light or don't come to a full stop, and one nanosecond later am explaining to imaginary cops exactly why I had to do what I did, or insisting that I did not in fact do it.

I happened to mention this to a hypnotist I saw many years ago, and he looked at me very nicely. At first I thought he was feeling around on the floor for the silent alarm button, but then he gave me the following exercise, which I still use to this day.

Close your eyes and get quiet for a minute, until the chatter starts up. Then isolate one of the voices and imagine the person speaking as a mouse. Pick it up by the tail and drop it into a mason jar. Then isolate another voice, pick it up by the tail, drop it in the jar. And so on. Drop in any high-maintenance parental units, drop in any contractors, lawyers, colleagues, children, anyone who is whining in your head. Then put the lid on, and watch all these mouse people clawing at the glass, jabbering away, trying to make you feel like shit because you won't do what they want—won't give them more money, won't be more successful, won't see them more often. Then imagine that there is a volume-control button on the bottle. Turn it all the way up for a minute, and listen to the stream of angry, neglected, guilt-mongering voices. Then turn it all the way down and watch the frantic mice lunge at the glass, trying to get to you. Leave it down, and get back to your shitty first draft.

A writer friend of mine suggests opening the jar and shooting them all in the head. But I think he's a little angry, and I'm sure nothing like this would ever occur to you.

———

Anne Lamott is the author of five novels and several works of non-fiction, as well as a regular columnist for Salon.com. The 1994 book *Bird by Bird,* from which this piece is excerpted, is available in paperback from Anchor Books.

Metaphors: We Are What We Speak

From *The Argument Culture: Moving from Debate to Dialogue*
BY DEBORAH TANNEN (1999)

All language uses metaphors to express ideas; some metaphoric words and expressions are novel, made up for the occasion, but more are calcified in the language. They are simply the way we think it is natural to express ideas. We don't think of them as metaphors. Someone who says, "Be careful: You aren't a cat; you don't have nine lives," is explicitly comparing you to a cat, because the cat is named in words. But what if someone says, "Don't pussyfoot around; get to the point"? There is no explicit comparison to a cat, but the comparison is there nonetheless, implied in the word "pussyfoot." This expression probably developed as a reference to the movements of a cat cautiously circling a suspicious object. I doubt that individuals using the word "pussyfoot" think consciously of cats. More often than not, we use expressions without thinking about their metaphoric implications. But that doesn't mean those implications are not influencing us.

At a meeting, a general discussion became so animated that a participant who wanted to comment prefaced his remark by saying, "I'd like to leap into the fray." Another participant called out, "Or share your thoughts." Everyone laughed. By suggesting a different phrasing, she called attention to what would probably have otherwise gone unnoticed: "Leap into the fray" characterized the lively discussion as a metaphorical battle.

Americans talk about almost everything as if it were a war. A book about the history of linguistics is called *The Linguistics Wars*. A magazine article about claims that science is not completely objective is titled "The Science Wars." One about breast cancer detection is "The Mammogram War"; about competition among caterers, "Party Wars"—and on and on in a potentially endless list. Politics, of course, is a prime candidate. One of innumerable possible examples, the headline of a story reporting that the Democratic National Convention nominated Bill Clinton to run for a second term declares, "DEMOCRATS SEND CLINTON INTO BATTLE FOR A 2nd TERM." But medicine is as frequent a candidate, as we talk about battling and conquering disease.

Headlines are intentionally devised to attract attention, but we all use military or attack imagery in everyday expressions without thinking about it "Take a shot at it," "I don't want to be shot down," "He went off half cocked," "That's half the battle." Why does it matter that our public discourse is filled with military metaphors? Aren't they just words? Why not talk about something that matters—like actions?

Because words matter. When we think we are using language, language is using us. As linguist Dwight Bolinger put it (employing a military metaphor), language is like a loaded gun: It can be fired intentionally, but it can wound or kill just as surely when fired accidentally. The terms in which we talk about something shape the way we think about it—and even what we see.

The power of words to shape perception has been proven by researchers in controlled experiments. Psychologists Elizabeth Loftus and John Palmer, for example, found that the terms in which people are asked to recall something affect what they recall. The researchers showed subjects a film of two cars colliding, then asked how fast the cars were going; one week later, they asked whether there had been any broken glass. Some subjects were asked, "About how fast were the cars going when they bumped into each other?" Others were asked, "About how fast were the cars going when they smashed into each other?" Those who read the question with the verb "smashed" estimated that the cars were going faster. They were also more likely to "remember" having seen broken glass. (There wasn't any.)

This is how language works. It invisibly molds our way of thinking about people, actions, and the world around us. Military metaphors train us to think about—and see—everything in terms of fighting, conflict, and war. This perspective then limits our imaginations when we consider what we can do about situations we would like to understand or change.

Even in science, common metaphors that are taken for granted influence how researchers think about natural phenomena. Evelyn Fox Keller describes a case in which acceptance of a metaphor led scientists to see something that was not there. A mathematical biologist, Keller outlines the fascinating behavior of cellular slime mold. This unique mold can take two completely different forms: It can exist as single-cell organisms, or the separate cells can come together to form multicellular aggregates. The puzzle facing scientists was: What triggers aggregation? In other words, what makes the single cells join together? Scientists focused their investigations by asking what entity issued the order to start aggregating. They first called this bosslike entity a "founder cell," and later a "pacemaker cell," even though no one had seen any evidence for the existence of such a cell. Proceeding nonetheless from the assumption that such a cell must exist, they ignored evidence to the contrary: For example, when the center of the aggregate is removed, other centers form.

Scientists studying slime mold did not examine the interrelationship between the cells and their environment, nor the interrelationship between the functional systems within each cell, because they were busy looking for the pacemaker cell, which, as eventually became evident, did not exist. Instead, under conditions of nutritional deprivation, each individual cell begins to feel the urge to merge with others to form the conglomerate. It is a reaction of the cells to their environment, not to the orders of a boss. Keller recounts this tale to illustrate her insight that we tend to view nature through our understanding of human relations as hierarchical. In her words, "We risk imposing on nature the very stories we like to hear." In other words, the conceptual metaphor of hierarchical governance made scientists "see" something—a pacemaker cell—that wasn't there.

Among the stories many Americans most like to hear are war stories. According to historian Michael Sherry, the American war movie developed during World War II and has been with us ever since. He shows that movies not explicitly about war were also war movies at heart, such as westerns with their good guy-bad guy battles settled with guns. *High Noon*, for example, which became a model for later westerns, was an allegory of the Second World War: The happy ending hinges on the pacifist taking up arms. We can also see this story line in contemporary adventure films: Think of *Star Wars*, with its stirring finale in which Han Solo, having professed no interest in or taste for battle, returns at the last moment to destroy the enemy and save the day. And precisely the same theme is found in a contemporary low-budget independent film, *Sling Blade*, in which a peace-loving retarded man becomes a hero at the end by murdering the man who has been tormenting the family he has come to love.

PUT UP YOUR DUKES

If war provides the metaphors through which we view the world and each other, we come to view others—and ourselves—as warriors in battle. Almost any human encounter can be framed as a fight between two opponents. Looking at it this way brings particular aspects of the event into focus and obscures others.

Framing interactions as fights affects not only the participants but also the viewers. At a performance, the audience, as well as the performers, can be transformed. This effect was noted by a reviewer in *The New York Times*, commenting on a musical event:

> *Showdown at Lincoln Center. Jazz's ideological war of the last several years led to a pitched battle in August between John Lincoln Collier, the writer, and Wynton Marsalis, the trumpeter, in a debate at Lincoln Center. Mr. Marsalis demolished Mr. Collier, point after point after point, but what made the debate unpleasant was the crowd's blood lust; humiliation, not elucidation, was the desired end.*

Military imagery pervades this account: the difference of opinions between Collier and Marsalis was an "ideological war," and the "debate" was a "pitched battle" in which Marsalis "demolished" Collier (not his arguments, but him). What the commentator regrets, however, is that the audience got swept up in the mood instigated by the way the debate was carried out: "the crowd's blood lust" for Collier's defeat.

This is one of the most dangerous aspects of regarding intellectual interchange as a fight. It contributes to an atmosphere of animosity that spreads like a fever. In a society that includes people who express their anger by shooting, the result of demonizing those with whom we disagree can be truly tragic.

But do audiences necessarily harbor within themselves a "blood lust," or is it stirred in them by the performances they are offered? Another arts event was set up as a debate between a playwright and a theater director. In this case, the metaphor through which the debate was viewed was not war but boxing—a sport that is in itself, like a debate, a metaphorical battle that pitches one side against the other in an all-out effort to win. A headline describing the event set the frame: "AND IN THIS CORNER . . .," followed by the subhead "A Black Playwright and White Critic Duke It Out." The story then reports:

> *the face-off between August Wilson, the most successful black playwright in the American theater, and Robert Brustein, longtime drama critic for* The New Republic *and artistic director of the American Repertory Theatre in Cambridge, Mass. These two heavyweights had been battling in print since last June. . . .*
>
> *Entering from opposite sides of the stage, the two men shook hands and came out fighting—or at least sparring.*

Wilson, the article explains, had given a speech in which he opposed Black performers taking "white" roles in color-blind casting; Brustein had written a column disagreeing; and both followed up with further responses to each other.

According to the article, "The drama of the Wilson-Brustein confrontation lies in their mutual intransigence." No one would question that audiences crave drama. But is intransigence the most appealing source of drama? I happened to hear this debate broadcast on the radio. The line that triggered the loudest cheers from the audience was the final question put to the two men by the moderator, Anna Deavere Smith: "What did you each learn from the other in this debate?" The loud applause was evidence that the audience did not crave intransigence. They wanted to see another kind of drama: the drama of change—change that comes from genuinely listening to someone with a different point of view, not the transitory drama of two intransigent positions in stalemate.

To encourage the staging of more dramas of change and fewer of intransigence, we need new metaphors to supplement and complement the pervasive war and boxing match metaphors through which we take it for granted issues and events are best talked about and viewed.

MUD SPLATTERS

Our fondness for the fight scenario leads us to frame many complex human interactions as a battle between two sides. This then shapes the way we understand what happened and how we regard the participants. One unfortunate result is that fights make a mess in which everyone is muddied. The person attacked is often deemed just as guilty as the attacker.

The injustice of this is clear if you think back to childhood: Many of us still harbor anger as we recall a time (or many times) a sibling or playmate started a fight—but both of us got blamed. Actions occur in a stream, each a response to what came before. Where you punctuate them can change their meaning just as you can change the meaning of a sentence by punctuating it in one place or another.

Like a parent despairing of trying to sort out which child started a fight, people often respond to those involved in a public dispute as if both were equally guilty. When champion figure skater Nancy Kerrigan was struck on the knees shortly before the 1994 Olympics in Norway and the then-husband of another champion skater, Tonya Harding, implicated his wife in planning the attack, the event was characterized as a fight between two skaters that obscured their differing roles. As both skaters headed for the Olympic competition, their potential meeting was described as a "long-anticipated figure-skating shootout." Two years later, the event was referred to not as "the attack on Nancy Kerrigan" but as "the rivalry surrounding Tonya Harding and Nancy Kerrigan."

By a similar process, the Senate Judiciary Committee hearings to consider the nomination of Clarence Thomas for Supreme Court justice at which Anita Hill was called to testify are regularly referred to as the "Hill-Thomas hearings," obscuring the very different roles played by Hill and Thomas. Although testimony by Anita Hill was the occasion for reopening the hearings, they were still the Clarence Thomas confirmation hearings: Their purpose was to evaluate Thomas's candidacy. Framing these hearings as a two-sided dispute between Hill and Thomas allowed the senators to focus their investigation on cross-examining Hill rather than seeking other sorts of evidence, for example, by consulting experts on sexual harassment to ascertain whether Hill's account seemed plausible.

SLASH-AND-BURN THINKING

Approaching situations like warriors in battle leads to the assumption that intellectual inquiry, too, is a game of attack, counterattack, and self-defense. In this spirit, critical thinking is synonymous with criticizing. In many classrooms, students are encouraged to read someone's life work, then rip it to shreds. Though criticism is one form of critical thinking—and an essential one—so are integrating ideas from disparate fields and examining the context out of which ideas grew. Opposition does not lead to the whole truth when we ask only "What's wrong with this?" and never "What can we use from this in building a new theory, a new understanding?"

There are many ways that unrelenting criticism is destructive in itself. Our most creative thinkers can waste time and effort responding to critics motivated less by a genuine concern about weaknesses in their work than by a desire to find something to attack. All of society loses when creative people are discouraged from their pursuits by unfair criticism. (This is particularly likely to happen since, as Kay Redfield Jamison shows in her book *Touched with Fire*, many of those who are unusually creative are also unusually sensitive; their sensitivity often drives their creativity.)

If the criticism is unwarranted, many will say, you are free to argue against it, to defend yourself. But there are problems with this, too. Not only does self-defense take time and draw off energy that would better be spent on new creative work, but any move to defend yourself makes you appear, well, defensive. For example, when an author wrote a letter to the editor protesting a review he considered unfair, the reviewer (who is typically given the last word) turned the very fact that the author defended himself into a weapon with which to attack again. The reviewer's response began, "I haven't much time to waste on the kind of writer who squanders his talent drafting angry letters to reviewers."

The argument culture limits the information we get rather than broadening it in another way. When a certain kind of interaction is the norm, those who feel comfortable with that type of interaction are drawn to participate, and those who do not feel comfortable with it recoil and go elsewhere. If public discourse included a broad range of types, we would be making room for individuals with different temperaments to take part and contribute their perspectives and insights. But when debate, opposition, and fights overwhelmingly predominate, those who enjoy verbal sparring are likely to take part—by calling in to talk shows, writing letters to the editor or articles, becoming journalists— and those who cannot comfortably take part in oppositional discourse, or do not wish to, are likely to opt out.

This winnowing process is easy to see in apprenticeship programs such as acting school, law school, and graduate school. A woman who was identified in her university drama program as showing exceptional promise was encouraged to go to New York to study acting. Full of enthusiasm, she was accepted by a famous acting school where the teaching method entailed the teacher screaming at students, goading and insulting them as a way to bring out the best in them. This worked well with many of the students but not with her. Rather than rising to the occasion when attacked, she cringed, becoming less able to draw on her talent, not more. After a year, she dropped out. It could be that she simply didn't have what it took—but this will never be known, because the adversarial style of teaching did not allow her to show what talent she had.

POLARIZING COMPLEXITY: NATURE OR NURTURE?

Few issues come with two neat, and neatly opposed, sides. Again, I have seen this in the domain of gender. One common polarization is an opposition between two sources of differences between women and men: "culture," or "nurture," on one hand and "biology," or "nature," on the other.

Shortly after the publication of *You Just Don't Understand*, I was asked by a journalist what question I most often encountered about women's and men's conversational styles. I told her, "Whether the differences I describe are biological or cultural." The journalist laughed. Puzzled, I asked why this made her laugh. She explained that she had always been so certain that any significant differences are cultural rather than biological in origin that the question struck her as absurd. So I should not have been surprised when I read, in the article she wrote, that the two questions I am most frequently asked are "Why do women nag?" and "Why won't men ask for directions?" Her ideological certainty that the question I am most frequently asked was absurd led her to ignore my answer and get a fact wrong in her report of my experience.

Some people are convinced that any significant differences between men and women are entirely or overwhelmingly due to cultural influences—the way we treat girls and boys, and men's dominance of women in society. Others are convinced that any significant differences are entirely or overwhelmingly due to biology: the physical facts of female and male bodies, hormones, and reproductive functions. Many problems are caused by framing the question as a dichotomy: Are behaviors that pattern by sex biological or cultural? This polarization encourages those on one side to demonize those who take the other view, which leads in turn to misrepresenting the work of those who are assigned to the opposing camp. Finally, and most devastatingly, it prevents us from exploring the interaction of biological and cultural factors—factors that must, and can only, be understood together. By posing the question as either/or, we reinforce a false assumption that biological and cultural factors are separable and preclude the investigations that would help us understand their interrelationship. When a problem is posed in a way that polarizes, the solution is often obscured before the search is under way.

WHO'S UP? WHO'S DOWN?

Related to polarization is another aspect of the argument culture: our obsession with ratings and rankings. Magazines offer the 10, 50, or 100 best of everything: restaurants, mutual funds, hospitals, even judges. Newsmagazines tell us Who's up, Who's down, as in *Newsweek*'s "Conventional Wisdom Watch" and *Time*'s "Winners and Losers." Rankings and ratings pit restaurants, products, schools, and people against each other on a single scale, obscuring the myriad differences among them. Maybe a small Thai restaurant in one neighborhood can't really be compared to a pricey French one in another, any more than judges with a vast range of abilities and beliefs can be compared on a single scale. And timing can skew results: Ohio State University protested to *Time* magazine when its football team was ranked at the bottom of a scale because only 29 percent of the team graduated. The year before it would have ranked among the top six with 72 percent.

After a political debate, analysts comment not on what the candidates said but on the question "Who won?" After the president delivers an important speech, such as the State of the Union Address, expert commentators are asked to give it a grade. Like ranking, grading establishes a competition. The biggest problem with asking what grade the president's speech deserves, or who won and who lost a campaign debate, is what is not asked and is therefore not answered: What was said, and what is the significance of this for the country?

AN ETHIC OF AGGRESSION

In an argument culture aggressive tactics are valued for their own sake. For example, a woman called in to a talk show on which I was a guest to say, "When I'm in a place where a man is smoking, and there's a no-smoking sign, instead of saying to him, 'You aren't allowed to smoke in here. Put that out,' I say, 'I'm awfully sorry, but I have asthma, so your smoking makes it hard for me to breathe. Would you mind terribly not smoking?' Whenever I say this, the man is extremely polite and solicitous, and he puts his cigarette out, and I say, 'Oh, thank you, thank you!' as if he's done a wonderful thing for me. Why do I do that?"

I think this woman expected me to say that she needs assertiveness training to learn to confront smokers in a more aggressive manner. Instead, I told her that there was nothing wrong with her style of getting the man to stop smoking. She gave him a face-saving way of doing what she asked, one that allowed him to feel chivalrous rather than chastised. This is kind to him, but it is also kind to herself, since it is more likely to lead to the result she desires. If she tried to alter his behavior by reminding him of the rules, he might well rebel: "Who made you the enforcer? Mind your own business!" Indeed, who gives any of us the authority to set others straight when we think they're breaking rules?

Another caller disagreed with me, saying the first caller's style was "self-abasing" and there was no reason for her to use it. But I persisted: There is nothing necessarily destructive about conventional self-effacement. Human relations depend on the agreement to use such verbal conventions. I believe the mistake this caller was making—a mistake many of us make—was to confuse *ritual* self-effacement with the literal kind. All human relations require us to find ways to get what we want from others without seeming to dominate them. Allowing others to feel they are doing what you want for a reason less humiliating to them fulfills this need.

Thinking of yourself as the wronged party who is victimized by a lawbreaking boor makes it harder to see the value of this method. But suppose you are the person addicted to smoking who lights up (knowingly or not) in a no-smoking zone. Would you like strangers to yell at you to stop smoking, or would you rather be allowed to save face by being asked politely to stop in order to help them out? Or imagine yourself having broken a rule inadvertently (which is not to imply rules are broken only by mistake; it is only to say that sometimes they are). Would you like some stranger to swoop down on you and begin berating you, or would you rather be asked politely to comply?

As this example shows, conflicts can sometimes be resolved without confrontational tactics, but current conventional wisdom often devalues less confrontational tactics even if they work well, favoring more aggressive strategies even if they get less favorable results. It's as if we value a fight for its own sake, not for its effectiveness in resolving disputes.

This ethic shows up in many contexts. In a review of a contentious book, for example, a reviewer wrote, "Always provocative, sometimes infuriating, this collection reminds us that the purpose of art is not to confirm and coddle but to provoke and confront." This false dichotomy encapsulates the belief that if you are not provoking and confronting, then you are confirming and coddling—as if there weren't myriad other ways to question and learn. What about exploring, exposing, delving, analyzing, understanding, moving, connecting, integrating, illuminating . . . or any of innumerable verbs that capture other aspects of what art can do?

THE BROADER PICTURE

The increasingly adversarial spirit of our contemporary lives is fundamentally related to a phenomenon that has been much remarked upon in recent years: the breakdown of a sense of community. In this spirit, distinguished journalist and author Orville Schell points out that in his day journalists routinely based their writing on a sense of connection to their subjects—and that this sense of connection is missing from much that is written by journalists today. Quite the contrary, a spirit of demonography often prevails that has just the opposite effect: Far from encouraging us to feel connected to the subjects, it encourages us to feel critical, superior—and, as a result, distanced. The cumulative effect is that citizens feel more and more cut off from the people in public life they read about.

The argument culture dovetails with a general disconnection and breakdown of community in another way as well. Community norms and pressures exercise a restraint on the expression of hostility and destruction. Many cultures have rituals to channel and contain aggressive impulses, especially those of adolescent males. In just this spirit, at the 1996 Republican National Convention, both Colin Powell and Bob Dole talked about growing up in small communities where everyone knew who they were. This meant that many people would look out for them, but also that if they did something wrong, it would get back to their parents. Many Americans grew up in ethnic neighborhoods that worked the same way. If a young man stole something, committed vandalism, or broke a rule or law, it would be reported to his relatives, who would punish him or tell him how his actions were shaming the family. American culture today often lacks these brakes.

Community is a blend of connections and authority, and we are losing both. As Robert Bly shows in his book by that title, we now have a *Sibling Society*: Citizens are like squabbling siblings with no authority figures who can command enough respect to contain and channel their aggressive impulses. It is as if every day is a day with a substitute teacher who cannot control the class and maintain order.

The argument culture is both a product of and a contributor to this alienation, separating people, disconnecting them from each other and from those who are or might have been their leaders.

WHAT OTHER WAY IS THERE?

Philosopher John Dewey said, on his ninetieth birthday, "Democracy begins in conversation." I fear that it gets derailed in polarized debate.

In conversation we form the interpersonal ties that bind individuals together in personal relationships; in public discourse, we form similar ties on a larger scale, binding individuals into a community. In conversation, we exchange the many types of information we need to live our lives as members of a community. In public discourse, we exchange the information that citizens in a democracy need in order to decide how to vote. If public discourse provides entertainment first and foremost—and if entertainment is first and foremost watching fights—then citizens do not get the information they need to make meaningful use of their right to vote.

Of course it is the responsibility of intellectuals to explore potential weaknesses in others' arguments, and of journalists to represent serious opposition when it exists. But when opposition becomes the overwhelming avenue of inquiry—a formula that *requires* another side to be found or a criticism to be voiced; when the lust for opposition privileges extreme views and obscures complexity; when our eagerness to find weaknesses blinds us to strengths; when the atmosphere of animosity precludes respect and poisons our relations with one another; then the argument culture is doing more damage than good.

. . .

I do not believe we should put aside the argument model of public discourse entirely, but we need to rethink whether this is the *only* way, or *always* the best way, to carry out our affairs. A step toward broadening our repertoires would be to pioneer reform by experimenting with metaphors other than sports and war, and with formats other than debate for framing the exchange of ideas. The change might be as simple as introducing a plural form. Instead of asking "What's the other side?" we might ask instead, "What are the other sides?" Instead of insisting on hearing "both sides," we might insist on hearing "all sides."

Another option is to expand our notion of "debate" to include more dialogue. This does not mean there can be no negativity, criticism, or disagreement. It simply means we can be more creative in our ways of managing all of these, which are inevitable and useful. In dialogue, each statement that one person makes is qualified by a statement made by someone else, until the series of statements and qualifications moves everyone closer to a fuller truth. Dialogue does not preclude negativity. Even saying "I agree" makes sense only against the background assumption that you might disagree. In dialogue, there is opposition, yes, but no head-on collision. Smashing heads does not open minds.

There are times when we need to disagree, criticize, oppose, and attack—to hold debates and view issues as polarized battles. Even cooperation, after all, is not the absence of conflict but a means of managing conflict. My goal is not a make-nice false veneer of agreement or a dangerous ignoring of true opposition. I'm questioning the *automatic* use of adversarial formats—the assumption that it's *always* best to address problems and issues by fighting over them. I'm hoping for a broader repertoire of ways to talk to each other and address issues vital to us.

———

Deborah Tannen, a sociolinguist at Georgetown University, has published 19 books and many scholarly articles. This piece is an excerpt from her 1999 book *The Argument Culture: Moving from Debate to Dialogue.*

Is Persuasion Dead?

BY MATT MILLER (2005)

Speaking just between us—between one who writes columns and those who read them—I've had this nagging question about the whole enterprise we're engaged in.

Is persuasion dead? And if so, does it matter?

The significance of this query goes beyond the feelings of futility I'll suffer if it turns out I've wasted my life on work that is useless. This is bigger than one writer's insecurities. Is it possible in America today to convince anyone of anything he doesn't already believe? If so, are there enough places where this mingling of minds occurs to sustain a democracy?

The signs are not good. Ninety percent of political conversation amounts to dueling "talking points." Best-selling books reinforce what folks thought when they bought them. Talk radio and opinion journals preach to the converted. Let's face it: the purpose of most political speech is not to persuade but to win, be it power, ratings, celebrity or even cash.

By contrast, marshaling a case to persuade those who start from a different position is a lost art. Honoring what's right in the other side's argument seems a superfluous thing that can only cause trouble, like an appendix. Politicos huddle with like-minded souls in opinion cocoons that seem impervious to facts.

The politicians and the press didn't kill off persuasion intentionally, of course; it's more manslaughter than murder. Persuasion just isn't relevant to delivering elections or eyeballs. Pols have figured out that to get votes you don't need to change minds. Even when they want to, modern media make it hard. They give officials seconds to make their point, ignore their ideas in favor of their poll numbers or showcase a clash of caricatures, believing this is the only way to make "debate" entertaining. Elections may turn on emotions like hope and fear anyway, but with persuasion's passing, there's no alternative.

There's only one problem: governing successfully requires influencing how people actually think. Yet when the habits of persuasion have been buried, the possibilities of leadership are interred as well. That's why Bill Clinton's case on health care could be bested by savage "Harry and Louise" ads. And why, even if George Bush's Social Security plan had been well conceived, the odds were always stacked against ambitious reform.

I'm not the only one who amid this mess wonders if he shouldn't be looking at another line of work. A top conservative thinker called recently, dejected at the sight of Ann Coulter on the cover of *Time*. What's the point of being substantive, he cried, when all the attention goes to the shrill?

But the embarrassing truth is that we earnest chin-strokers often get it wrong anyway. Take me. I hadn't thought much about Iraq before I read Ken Pollack's book, *The Threatening Storm: The Case for Invading Iraq*, a platonic ideal of careful analysis meant to persuade. It worked. I was persuaded! So what should we conclude when a talent like Pollack can convince us—and then the whole thing turns out to be based on a premise (W.M.D.) that is false?

If serious efforts to get it right can lead to tragic errors, why care about a culture of persuasion at all? On one level, everyone needs a good rationalization at the core of his professional life; mine holds that the struggle to think things through, even when we fail, is redeeming.

But beyond this, the gap between the cartoon of public life that the press and political establishment often serve up and the pragmatic open-mindedness of most Americans explains why so many people tune out—and how we might get them to tune back in. Alienation is the only intelligent response to a political culture that insults our intelligence.

The resurrection of persuasion will not be easy. Politicians who've learned to survive in an unforgiving environment may not feel safe with a less scripted style. Mass media outlets where heat has always sold more than light may not believe that creatively engaging on substance can expand their audience. But if you believe that meeting our collective challenges requires greater collective understanding, we've got to persuade these folks to try.

I'm guessing Ann Coulter isn't sweating this stuff. God willing, there's something else keeping her up nights. In the meantime, like Sisyphus, those who seek a better public life have to keep rolling the rock uphill. If you've read this far, maybe you're up for the climb, too.

———

Matt Miller, a senior fellow at the Center for American Progress and the author of The 2 Percent Solution, *wrote this essay for the June 4, 2005, edition of* The New York Times *<www.nytimes.com>.*

Seeking Balance in an Either-Or World
BY KATHLEEN PARKER (2005)

"Blessed are the peacemakers for they shall catch hell from both sides."
—Sign on the wall of Justice Department attorney Burke Marshall, 1964

In today's food-fight environment, where extremes dominate debate and choice is defined by either-or, finding a comfortable place to land is increasingly difficult.

Like most people I know, I tend to run screaming from both ends of the spectrum. Too conservative for the left wing and too liberal for the right wing, I find myself scrambling for the center aisle.

Yet, people in the middle often are held in contempt as fence-straddlers. If you're an opinion columnist, you're forced to pick a side. People want to know: Are you conservative or liberal? "It depends" is considered a weak answer, morally relativistic, lacking in backbone.

Abortion provides a convenient if unpalatable example. I've written dozens of columns through the years, more or less urging a pro-life position—having a baby forces a review of one's assumptions—while clinging to a pro-choice conclusion. Abortion is a terrible thing, I say, the violent termination of a life and a decision many women (and men) regret with time and perspective.

Nevertheless, I can find no way to justify government-enforced maternity. Under penalty of what? By whom? Under what circumstances? The practical applications of the moral ideal become nightmarish as we extrapolate to the real. Thus, one might hope to seek compromise. Can't a female who's old enough to samba deduce that she's pregnant and decide within, oh, 6–8 weeks? This is, after all, not a "Gee whiz, I dunno" question.

In the spirit of compromise, I also can argue passionately in favor of tougher education standards when it comes to abortion. If we can demonstrate how to use condoms to high school students, surely we can make vivid the pros and cons of abortion as birth control. In time, given what can't be ignored when abortion is studied up close, we'd accomplish the goal supported by most Americans (64 percent, according to Luntz Research Companies, August 2003) and articulated by President Bill Clinton: to make abortion safe, legal and rare.

My middle road, of course, makes me equally contemptible to those who dwell in the peripheries—both to the pro-lifers who view all abortion as murder, and to the slippery-slopers who consider objecting to "partial-birth abortion" tantamount to embracing the Vatican's view of The Pill. Caught between extremes of community morality and individual choice—amid near-hysterical ideological partisanship from parties that have been hijacked by radicals—people like me are adrift.

Apparently, I'm not alone. Indeed, given current trends, we may declare that we have reached a perfect storm of political backlash. Americans who cleave to neither extreme— some 50 percent of whom identify themselves as "moderate"—are fed up with the Ann Coulter/Michael Moore school of debate and are looking for someone to articulate a commonsense, middle path. They may have found their voice in John P. Avlon, chief speechwriter for former New York Mayor Rudy Giuliani and a *New York Sun* columnist, whose 2004 book *Independent Nation* has just been released in paperback.

Avlon insists that centrism is the more patriotic political position because it adheres more strictly to American values and founding principles than to ideology. A balance between idealism and realism, centrism is a yin-yang proposition that rejects shrill extremes and embraces reason, decency and a practical perspective. To those who insist that centrism is the death of dissent, Avlon argues that centrism is dissent—from outdated political orthodoxies.

"Extremists and ideological purists on either side of the political aisle condemn compromise," he writes. "But inflexibility either creates deadlock or dooms a cause to irrelevance."

That's from the introduction to *Independent Nation*. The balance of the book is a compendium of short biographies of several U.S. presidents, senators and governors and their personal journeys as they illuminate the theme of centrism. Avlon says his purpose in writing the book was to give today's centrists a framework for understanding their frustration with extreme politics and a place for the politically homeless to hang their iPods. Or their heart monitors, as the case may be.

Extremists won't agree with Avlon that centrism is a patriotic position, but who cares? They've held the nation hostage long enough. Meanwhile, Independents are the fastest-growing group of voters across the country, especially among the young, hundreds of whom have e-mailed Avlon since his appearance last week on *The Daily Show* with Comedy Central's Jon Stewart. A Pew Poll published last week in *The Economist* broke down voters as 39 percent Independent, 31 percent Democrat and 30 percent Republican.

Socially liberal and fiscally conservative, Independents could be a powerful reckoning force by 2008. Politicians better wise up and tone it down.

———

Syndicated columnist Kathleen Parker is a regular contributor to TownHall.com <www.townhall.com>, where this column was published on April 20, 2005.

FROM READING TO WRITING

1. Describe your best writing experience. What made it so good? Now, describe your most frustrating writing experience. What made it so bad? Which of these experiences affected you the most? Why?

2. Using specific passages from their essays to support your response, describe how you think the following essayists would define the word "writer": Lisa Bailey, Anne Lamott, Eme Crawford, Todd Hagstette. Do you fit any of these definitions? Explain.

3. What is it about today's college students that concerns journalism professor Michael Skube? Based on your own experience in the classroom, do you think his claims are accurate? Finally, comment on how Todd Hagstette's "aggressive reading" might be of some help to the students described in Skube's essay.

4. Based on the reading you've done in this chapter, how would you define "good writing"? What does it take to become a "good writer"? Or a "great writer"? Explain, making references to the pieces you've read.

5. Considering Anne Lamott's essay, what are the advantages or disadvantages, in your mind, of short writing sessions versus getting it all out in one big effort? Can you relate to either experience or have you created your own way of writing and revising?

6. In her essay "Metaphors: We Are What We Speak," Deborah Tannen writes, "Americans talk about almost everything as if it were a war." Examine a newspaper, a magazine, or a news media website (such as CNN.com, FoxNews.com, or NYTimes.com) and count the military and battle metaphors you see. Why do you think writers use these kinds of metaphors? How do they affect the way you react to the articles? Do you agree with Tannen when she asserts that the "terms in which we talk about something shape the way we think about it—and even what we see"? Why or why not?

7. How does Matt Miller define "persuasion"? In his essay, he writes, "Ninety percent of political conversation amounts to dueling 'talking points.' . . . By contrast, marshaling a case to persuade those who start from a different position is a lost art." Do you agree with him? Explain your answer.

8. What do Tannen's and Miller's articles say about the power of rhetoric? Examine a newspaper or online news source and analyze the rhetorical choices it makes.

9. In "Seeking Balance in an Either-Or World," Kathleen Parker suggests that "centrism" is a much-needed haven from extremist politics. How would you describe the terms "centrism"

and "extremism" in terms of public discourse? Parker also writes that "Americans who cleave to neither extreme—some 50 percent of whom identify themselves as 'moderate'—are fed up with the Ann Coulter/Michael Moore school of debate and are looking for someone to articulate a commonsense, middle path." What do you think can be done to help find this middle path?

Two

COLLEGE LIFE

Debate? Dissent? Discussion? Oh, Don't Go There!

BY MICHIKO KAKUTANI (2002)

That familiar interjection "whatever" says a lot about the state of mind of college students today. So do the catch phrases "no problem," "not even" and "don't go there."

Noisy dorm and dining room debates are no longer de rigueur as they were during earlier decades; quiet acceptance of differing views—be they political or aesthetic—is increasingly the rule.

Neil Howe and William Strauss's book *Millennials Rising*—a survey of the post-Gen X generation—suggests that the young people born in the early 1980's and afterward are, as a group, less rebellious than their predecessors, more practical-minded, less individualistic and more inclined to value "team over self, duties over rights, honor over feeling, action over words."

"Much the opposite of boomers at the same age," the authors write, "millennials feel more of an urge to homogenize, to celebrate ties that bind rather than differences that splinter."

These are gross generalizations, of course, but a student's article titled "The Silent Classroom," which appeared in the Fall 2001 issue of *Amherst* magazine, suggested that upperclassmen at that college tend to be guarded and private about their intellectual beliefs. And in this writer's own completely unscientific survey, professors and administrators observed that students today tend to be more respectful of authority—parental and professorial—than they used to be, and more reticent about public disputation.

"My sense from talking to students and other faculty is that out of class, students are interested in hearing another person's point of view, but not interested in engaging it, in challenging it or being challenged," Joseph W. Gordon, dean of undergraduate education at Yale, said. "So they'll be very accepting of other points of view very different from their own. They live in a world that's very diverse, but it's a diversity that's more parallel than cross-stitched."

The students' reticence about debate stems, in part, from the fact that the great issues of the day—the Sept. 11 terrorist attacks and the war in Afghanistan—do not engender the sort of dissent that the Vietnam War did in an earlier era. It also has roots in a disillusionment with the vitriolic partisanship that held sway in Washington in the 1990's: the often petty haggling between right and left, Republicans and Democrats, during President Bill Clinton's impeachment hearings and the disputed presidential election of 2000, and the spectacle of liberals and conservatives screaming at each other on television programs like *Crossfire.*

"Debate has gotten a very bad name in our culture," Jeff Nunokawa, a professor of English at Princeton University, said. "It's become synonymous with some of the most nonintellectual forms of bullying, rather than as an opportunity for deliberative democracy." He added that while the events of Sept. 11 may well serve as a kind of wake-up call, many of his students say that "it's not politic or polite to seem to care too much about abstract issues."

"Many of them are intensely socially conscientious, caring and committed," he said. "It's just not clear precisely what they wish to commit themselves to."

In a much talked-about article in *The Atlantic Monthly* a year ago, the writer David Brooks argued that elite college students today "don't shout out their differences or declare them in political or social movements" because they do not belong to a generation that is "fighting to emancipate itself from the past," because most of them are "not trying to buck the system; they're trying to climb it." And yet to suggest that the archetypal student today is "the Organization Kid," as Mr. Brooks did, seems too simplistic, ignoring the powerful effect that certain academic modes of thinking—from multiculturalism to deconstruction—have had in shaping contemporary college discourse.

Indeed, the reluctance of today's students to engage in impassioned debate can be seen as a byproduct of a philosophical relativism, fostered by theories that gained ascendance in academia in the last two decades and that have seeped into the broader culture. While deconstruction promoted the indeterminacy of texts, the broader principle of subjectivity has been embraced by everyone from biographers (like Edmund Morris, whose biography of President Ronald Reagan mixed fact and fiction) to scholars (who have inserted personal testimony in their work to underscore their own biases). Because subjectivity enshrines ideas that are partial and fragmentary by definition, it tends to preclude searches for larger, overarching truths, thereby undermining a strong culture of contestation.

At the same time, multiculturalism and identity politics were questioning the very existence of objective truths and a single historical reality. As the historians Joyce Appleby, Lynn Hunt and Margaret Jacob observed in their book, *Telling the Truth About History*, radical multiculturalists celebrated "the virtues of fragmentation," arguing that "since all history has a political—often a propaganda—function, it is time for each group to rewrite history from its own perspective and thereby reaffirm its own past."

During the height of the culture wars of the early 90's, such views led to vociferous showdowns between academic radicals and traditionalists. It also led to the politicization of subjects like history and literature, and ideological posturing that could be reductive and doctrinaire in the extreme. Thankfully, these excesses have begun to die down, as bipolar dogmatism has started to give way to a scholarly eclecticism—less concerned with large paradigms, and more focused on narrower issues—but the legacy of multiculturalism and identity politics remains potent on college campuses.

On one hand, it has made students more accepting of individuals different from themselves, more tolerant of other races, religions and sexual orientations. But this tolerance of other people also seems to have resulted in a reluctance to engage in the sort of impassioned argumentation that many baby boomers remember from their college days.

"It's as though there's no distinction between the person and the argument, as though to criticize an argument would be injurious to the person," said Amanda Anderson, an English professor at Johns Hopkins University and the author of a forthcoming book, *The Way We Argue Now*. "Because so many forms of scholarly inquiry today foreground people's lived experience, there's this kind of odd overt actfulness. In many ways, it's emanating from a good thing, but it's turned into a disabling thing."

"A lot of professors complain about the way students make appeals to relativism today," Professor Anderson added. "It's difficult because it's coming out of genuinely pluralistic orientation and a desire to get along, but it makes argument and rigorous analysis very difficult, because people will stop and say, 'I guess I just disagree.'"

Outside the classroom, it's a mindset ratified by the PLUR ("Peace, Love, Unity and Respect") T-shirts worn by ravers (whose drug of choice is Ecstasy, which induces warm, fuzzy feelings of communion). It is also a mindset reinforced by television shows like *Oprah* that preach self-esteem and the accommodation of others, and by the Internet, which instead of leading to a global village, has created a multitude of self-contained tribes—niche cultures in which like-minded people can talk to like-minded people and filter out information that might undermine their views.

At the same time, the diminished debate syndrome mirrors the irony-suffused sensibility of many millennial-era students. Irony, after all, represents a form of detachment; like the knee-jerk acceptance of the positions of others, it's a defensive mode that enables one to avoid commitment and stand above the fray.

What are the consequences of students' growing reluctance to debate? Though it represents a welcome departure from the polarized mudslinging of the 90's culture wars, it also represents a failure to fully engage with the world, a failure to test one's convictions against the logic and passions of others. It suggests a closing off of the possibilities of growth and transformation and a repudiation of the process of consensus building. "It doesn't bode well for democratic practice in this country," Professor Anderson said. "To keep democracy vital, it's important that students learn to integrate debate into their lives and see it modeled for them, in a productive way, when they're in school."

Reporter Michiko Kakutani wrote this piece for *The New York Times* <www.nytimes.com> in March 2002.

Realistic Idealists

BY ALEX WILLIAMS (2005)

Lynn Grossman, a writer in Manhattan who is married to the actor Bob Balaban, comes from a long line of social activists. Her mother joined the civil rights movement, and she herself marched in protest of the Vietnam War. But she said that things had changed by the time her eldest daughter, Mariah, now 27, came of age.

For many in Mariah's generation, community service was little more than a requirement that private schools imposed for graduation. Some took brief working vacations in
places like Costa Rica, or the Caribbean island of Dominica, where they helped build
roads and houses. "These kids had never seen a hammer before," Ms. Grossman said with
a laugh. "I don't know what they did aside from get suntans."

Now, she said, "things are completely different."

As an eighth grader, her youngest daughter, Hazel, transformed a basement storage
room in a Brooklyn homeless shelter into a library stocked with 5,000 volumes. At 13,
she mobilized her fellow students to paint walls, hire librarians and design a functioning
library-card system linked to a computer database. "We were floored," Ms. Grossman
said. "And it's not just Hazel. A lot of kids out there are like this. They are like C.E.O.'s
of community service."

Hazel Balaban, now a freshman at Connecticut College in New London, spent her
first days on campus last week trying to organize a bake sale for victims of Hurricane
Katrina. "It's almost expected," she said. "With the Internet and 24-hour TV, you just
see all these problems. They're everywhere."

Hazel is at the leading edge of a generation whose sense of community involvement
was born four years ago on Sept. 11, 2001. The attacks spurred an unprecedented outpouring of donations and volunteerism from Americans. Since then teenagers have witnessed the deadly Florida hurricane season of 2004, the more than 150,000 killed by the
tsunami in Asia last December, and now Katrina. Encouraged by an increasing number
of high schools with community service requirements and further motivated by college
admissions offices looking for reasons to choose one honor student over another, teenagers
are embracing social activism with the zeal of missionaries and the executive skills of
seasoned philanthropists. Not only are more students participating, educators say, the
scale of ambition seems to be continually increasing.

"We've seen a shift in the zeitgeist away from what you would call 'community service'
and more into social action," said Tom Krattenmaker, a spokesman for Swarthmore
College near Philadelphia. "It's not just about working in a soup kitchen," he said, but
about "creating new programs, shooting higher."

Gregory Pyke, the senior associate dean of admission at Wesleyan University in Mid-
dletown, Conn., said that one recent applicant had started a Web-based initiative to collect eyeglasses—thousands of pairs—to be passed along to the needy in underprivileged
countries. Another created a large-scale program to collect and refurbish discarded

computers before passing them along to the poor. "The number of discussions where a dean is pulling us aside and saying, 'You have to hear about what this kid has done' has also gone up," he said.

While cynics—and not a few colleges—may question whether the young people initiating such grand projects are looking to impress admissions officers, Mr. Pyke said he thought that most of the motivation was altruistic. "These are kids who are aware of many ways in which world is a pretty lousy place," he said. "They want to exercise more authority in the world than adults give them credit for."

Educators, sociologists and parents explain the outpouring of youthful philanthropy by noting that this generation has been bombarded not only by bad news, all of which seems to demand an immediate response, but by calls to action from political leaders and celebrities. Disaster relief, unlike opposition to the Vietnam War, which stirred many in their parents' generation, is uncontroversial and encourages wide-scale participation. And once roused, young people have greater tools at their disposal, particularly the Internet, to expand projects.

More than 82 percent of high school seniors performed volunteer work, according to the 2004 American Freshman survey, a nationwide poll conducted by a graduate division of the University of California, Los Angeles, compared with just over 74 percent a decade earlier, and 66 percent in 1989.

The Collegiate Challenge program run by Habitat for Humanity in which students spend a week of their summer building housing for the poor in cities throughout the nation, has grown twelve-fold since it started in 1989, said Alynn Woodson, the manager. It has seen a 30 percent growth in participation by high school students in the last two years. "In some ways service has gotten to be kind of a trendy thing to do," Ms. Woodson said.

Katrina is the cause of the moment, and students across the country have responded like seasoned aid workers. By Sept. 2, four days after the storm came ashore in Alabama, Louisiana and Mississippi, students at Westside High School in Houston had raised more than $16,000 for the American Red Cross.

"We have 2,870 students," said Noralea Jordan, the senior class president, who helped organize the drive. "If we made $16,000 in a day, I'm sure in another week we could triple that."

That same day, students at Boiling Springs High School in South Carolina collected 6,000 gallons of bottled water. "We're not very good at our football, but it's been said by rival football teams, 'Whenever it comes to things that matter, Boiling Springs always gets the job done,'" said Jessica Gregg, 17, the student body president.

At many schools students were ready to mobilize because they have had so much practice. Cloydia Garrette, 17, the student council president at Jack Yates High School in Houston and a veteran of drives to raise money for tsunami victims, leukemia research and Ronald McDonald House, collected clothes and other essentials when evacuees from New Orleans began to reach the Astrodome. Charity is infectious, she said, "A lot of kids see us doing it, and they're following along."

Once rare, community service is now mandatory for an increasing number of schools in all 50 states, said Jennifer Piscatelli, a policy analyst at the Education Commission of the States. Maryland requires every high school student to perform 75 hours of public service to graduate, and similar requirements exist at school districts in Chicago, Los Angeles and Philadelphia. College officials have taken such activity into account when making admission decisions. Bruce Walker, the vice provost and director of admissions for the University of Texas in Austin, said the university, which is faced with an increasing number of qualified candidates, is paying more attention to applicants' public service, or as he said, "what kind of citizen they were, and are."

But even increased basic requirements do not seem to account for the grandiosity of initiatives on the part of many teenagers, educators say. "It's kind of intimidating to see what some kids have done," Mr. Walker said. In Owings Mills, Md., two high school freshman, Greg Becker and Michael Swirnow, exceeded the McDonogh School's 40-hour community service requirement by doing 500 hours. Starting when they were 14, the boys set out to raise money to build a house for a struggling family in Baltimore through Habitat for Humanity.

"Sometimes, doing everything you can isn't enough," said Greg, who initiated the effort. Through meetings with executives at various foundations and a raffle that raised $42,000 (a Mini Cooper was the top prize), the students collected $88,000.

"At first, I never really thought about it as something for college," said Michael, now 15. "As it went on, though, it suddenly hit me: this is going to be huge on my college application."

Such examples of over-the-top public service can put a competitive pressure on other families who believe colleges are watching. For those who have yet to fall into line with the trend, the anxieties can be great. "I've had three families come in today saying, 'What is this community service thing?'" said Howard Greene, a private college admissions consultant in Manhattan.

But some college admissions counselors have already grown skeptical about what's known in the trade as the "How I Saved the World" essay, as well as about projects that just happen to commence early in a student's junior year. "There are two sides, to me," said Jim Bock, dean of admissions and financial aid at Swarthmore, which this past year received 300 more freshman applications than the previous year. "One is the jaded side—is it a strategy? The other side is, is it part of a new generation of students who really are committed to making a better world?"

Mr. Bock noted that his college put a high premium on public service: it highlights Swarthmore students' antigenocide initiatives in Sudan alongside its main features on its Web home page. Two weeks ago Mr. Bock watched a colleague ask nearly 400 freshman at an orientation seminar how many had done community service projects in high school.

"I'll have to admit I was moved," Mr. Bock said. "Ninety-five percent of the freshmen stood up."

Katherine Cohen, a college admissions consultant who has discussed community service with many high school students in Manhattan, noted that admitting such candidates was in the colleges' self-interest. "Colleges love to see fund-raisers, of course," Ms. Cohen said. "Ding-ding-ding, the bell goes off, because they want to see money raised in the future" for their own endowments.

Teenagers who pull off outsize projects shrug off suspicions that their aims were other than altruistic. Michael Swirnow, the Maryland youth who helped raise $88,000 for Habitat for Humanity, said the motivating factor was to "give back" to the less fortunate. "I think the most important thing is learned I'm capable of doing something this big," he said. "It's about confidence."

Several educators said that it didn't really matter in the end whether teenagers were expending effort out of self-interest or altruism so long as good deeds were done. Some level of self-interest, after all, is why kids read books and do homework.

"This is a generation that was born after the consciousness revolution" of the 1960's and 70's, said William Strauss, the co-author with Neil Howe of *Millennials Rising: The*

Next Great Generation, a portrait of Americans born after 1982. "A lot of them are now children of baby boomers, and they look at them as a generation that looked at the self instead of the community. Now they've turned that around. Generations set themselves apart by correcting the mistakes they perceive their parents to have made."

Alex Williams wrote this article for the September 11, 2005, edition of *The New York Times* <www.nytimes.com>.

Gen Y's Ego Trip Takes a Bad Turn

A new report suggests that an overdose of self-esteem in college students could mean a rough road ahead.
BY LARRY GORDON AND LOUIS SAHAGUN (2007)

No wonder YouTube is so popular.

All the effort to boost children's self-esteem may have backfired and produced a generation of college students who are more narcissistic than their Gen X predecessors, according to a new study led by a San Diego State University psychologist.

And the Internet, with all its MySpace and YouTube braggadocio, is letting that self-regard blossom even more, said the analysis, titled "Egos Inflating Over Time."

In the study being released today, researchers warn that a rising ego rush could cause personal and social problems for the Millennial Generation, also called Gen Y. People with an inflated sense of self tend to have less interest in emotionally intimate bonds and can lash out when rejected or insulted.

"That makes me very, very worried," said Jean Twenge, a San Diego State associate professor and lead author of the report. "I'm concerned we are heading to a society where people are going to treat each other badly, either on the street or in relationships."

She and four other researchers from the University of Michigan, University of Georgia and University of South Alabama looked at the results of psychological surveys taken by more than 16,000 college students across the country over more than 25 years.

The Narcissistic Personality Inventory asks students to react to such statements as: "If I ruled the world, it would be a better place," "I think I am a special person" and "I like to be the center of attention."

The study found that almost two-thirds of recent college students had narcissism scores that were above the average 1982 score. Thirty percent more college students showed elevated narcissism in 2006 than in 1982.

Twenge said she and her coauthors are not suggesting that more students today have a pathological narcissistic personality disorder that needs psychiatric treatment. Still, traits of narcissism have increased by moderate but significant amounts, said Twenge, who last year published a book titled "Generation Me: Why Today's Young Americans Are More Confident, Assertive, Entitled—and More Miserable Than Ever Before."

The narcissism report is under review for publication in a scholarly journal, which would give it the stamp of academic recognition it now lacks.

It was released, Twenge said, in connection with the upcoming paperback edition of her book and with a student affairs workshop today at the University of San Diego at which she and another speaker will discuss how today's college students approach education.

Some of the increase in narcissistic attitudes was probably caused by the self-esteem programs that many elementary schools adopted 20 years ago, the study suggests. It notes that nursery schools began to have children sing songs that proclaim: "I am special, I am special. Look at me."

Those youngsters are now adolescents obsessed with websites, such as MySpace and YouTube, that "permit self-promotion far beyond that allowed by traditional media," the report says.

Other trends in American culture, including permissive parenting, increased materialism and the fascination with celebrities and reality TV shows, may also heighten self-regard, said study coauthor W. Keith Campbell, psychology professor at the University of Georgia. "It's part of a whole cultural system," he said.

The researchers seek to counter theories that current college students are more civic-minded and involved in volunteer activities than their predecessors. Because many high schools require community work, increases in volunteering "may not indicate a return to civic orientation but may instead be the means toward the more self-focused goal of educational attainment," the report says.

An annual survey of U.S. college freshmen by the Higher Education Research Institute at UCLA has found growing interest in public service and social responsibility, presumably in response to Hurricane Katrina and other disasters around the world.

But that survey also showed that current freshmen are much more interested in financial success and less in "a meaningful philosophy of life" than students were in the 1970s.

At Cal State Long Beach on Monday, an informal survey produced divided opinions about Gen Y personality traits.

Students and teachers said they often see examples of inflated egos on campus: students who converse in the computer center while others are trying to concentrate, preen in front of the reflecting windows of the economics building or expect good grades simply for showing up at class.

Laura Rantala, 26, a sociology major, said the phenomenon got in the way of a survey she conducted last semester on the attitudes of men and women about jury duty.

"It took about three minutes to complete the survey," she recalled. "But many students were so self-absorbed they didn't want to participate.

"I think it's because we all have our own cellphone and iPod with which we're doing our own thing in our own little world," she mused.

Some students seeking degrees in finance and management said, however, that they had good reason to stress confidence and esteem.

James Coari, a lecturer in the College of Business Administration, agreed, to a point. In an interview in his office, Coari said, people looking for jobs "have to be concerned about image because competition is fierce."

Marc Flacks, an assistant professor of sociology, said that he believed that narcissism was too harsh a description for current students and that it was more important to discuss why "we have a society in which narcissistic behavior is a good quality to have."

"This is a bottom-line society, so students are smart to seek the most direct route to the bottom line," he added. "If you don't have a me-first attitude, you won't succeed."

Flacks summed up the attitudes he often encounters in students, who expect a tangible payoff from their education:

"The old model was a collegial one in which students and professors alike sought knowledge for knowledge's sake. The new model is 'I paid my money, give me my grade and degree.' It makes me want to ask [students], 'Want fries with that order?'"

———

Larry Gordon and Louis Sahagun wrote this piece for the February 27, 2007, edition of the *Los Angeles Times* <www.latimes.com>.

LOOK@ME: Generation Next Is Living Out Loud and Online

BY MELISSA LUDWIG (2007)

Jackie Davis knows people talk trash about her.

On her MySpace.com page, the self-described party girl, club promoter and 22-year-old student at the University of Texas at San Antonio has photos of herself dressed to the nines out on the town and on the beach clad in an orange bikini. In one photo, Jackie is wearing a skin-tight black leather Catwoman costume, two triangles of vinyl struggling to cover her silicone-enhanced breasts.

"People have said stuff about it," Davis said of the Web page. "I think in part it is because I have fake boobs. It doesn't mean I'm like a porn star. I mean, give me a break. In 10 years, I am not going to look like this. I want to remember that I used to be hot."

Her message to the trash talkers?

"I just am who I am. I am not going to apologize for it," Davis said. "Everyone who really knows me knows I am a good person. Other than that, why do I care?"

That could be an anthem for Davis' generation, a group of 18- to 25-year-olds who have been dubbed Millennials, Generation Next or the "Look at me" generation.

In these kids, a combination of self-confidence and technological savvy has led to the explosion of Web sites such as YouTube, which allows users to upload homemade videos, and social networking sites such as MySpace and Facebook, where anyone can create a personalized Web site to message friends and post pictures, blogs, videos and music.

Much of the stuff floating around in cyberspace is tame, mundane even. But there also is plenty that's racy, embarrassing or squeamishly intimate. Bad or good, Generation Next is living out loud and doing it online, before a global audience, in a medium where digital archives may linger for a long, long time.

Young and old alike tout the positive aspects of the communication revolution: It empowers regular folks to create, innovate or mobilize around a cause. But there's also fear, especially among parents, that Nexters just now crossing over into "real life" still are too young to fully grasp the permanence of their online actions, and the possible consequences down the road.

"It is scary," said Jeanne Culver, a mother from Dallas whose daughter Katy is a freshman at Trinity University. "It is uncharted waters for the parents and the children. We are all experiencing it for the first time together."

Already, there are famous examples of how the Internet can come back to bite you: the Paris Hilton sex tape; Miss Nevada USA, Katie Rees, who lost her crown over risqué pictures that showed up on MySpace; Frenchie Davis, an "American Idol" contestant booted off the show after posing topless for an adult Web site.

In their own lives, college students say they know people who have been stalked, had their identities stolen or had relationships go sour after a revealing picture or message surfaced online.

So why do they do it?

Because it's part of life, Davis said.

"I have to be aware that those pictures will be there forever. People can copy that, it can be on Google someday. I can be married to a senator and that stuff will come up," she said.

"And like, I know that, but at the same time, I don't feel like not living life because of the chances of something happening."

Brooke Johnson, a 20-year-old UTSA student who blogs on her own Web site, agreed.

"I think it's pretty neat that people can know things about me," Johnson said. "Technology is allowing us to do amazing things and communicate in totally different ways. People abuse it, but people abuse anything."

GENERATION ME

Wednesday, 11:30 a.m., Starbucks.

Davis's reddish-brown hair is stuffed into a corduroy pageboy cap and her lightly freckled cheek still bears the indent of her pillow. She sits down with an iced coffee and later digs into a gold quilted bebe bag for her cigarettes.

Davis says she got on MySpace about a year ago, when she started doing club promotions. Before that, she thought it was a bunch of "punk rock kids and creeper guys," people who found it easier to talk online than in person.

Now, she checks her MySpace page every day. She has upward of 800 friends, an array of photos and ads for sexy-sounding clubs like Bliss Ultra Lounge.

She doesn't disown the popular party girl portrayed on the site. As a club promoter, she gets paid to be that person. But the inner Jackie stays offline, she said.

"I don't want people to feel like they intimately know me," she said.

She never would blog about her personal life under her own name, isn't interested in meeting men online and never would pose nude.

Other college students do: At Boston University, an edgy sex magazine called Boink employs fellow students as models to exemplify the publication's tagline: "College Sex by the People Having It."

The closest thing at UTSA is Study Breaks, a lightweight entertainment magazine where the student models often are scantily clad, but not nude.

For Davis, the Internet is about marketing.

"This is the information age. They had industrialism where it's like, 'What can you build?' Now, it's like, 'Who do you know and what do you know?' It's the world we live in and MySpace is free marketing."

Brooke Johnson also is marketing herself online, but in a totally different way.

Johnson writes poetry and blogs about her life on a Web site she created. Many of the posts are abstract, but some get specific about her upbringing, her struggles moving to San Antonio from a small town and inner conflicts over character flaws like bossiness.

Johnson wouldn't be caught dead online in a Catwoman suit, but her blog has the kind of soul searching that would make Davis squirm.

Granted, her audience isn't wide. It's mostly for parents and friends to understand how she feels without "getting out a bongo drum and turning down the lights," Johnson said.

But she wouldn't mind a larger readership.

"We all do it for attention, I guess," Johnson said. "In the least vain way possible, I think I have valid things to say and I want people to know."

That attitude is more common among college students these days, said Jean Twenge, a psychology professor at San Diego State University in California.

Twenge, the author of "Generation Me," said her research shows about one-third more college kids today are narcissistic than college kids were in the 1980s, a trend she believes grew out of the self-esteem movement of the 1970s and '80s.

"Since birth, their generation has heard you need to put yourself first, that loving yourself is the most important thing, you shouldn't care what anyone thinks about you," Twenge said. "This is not something the baby boomers heard in the '50s."

Facebook, MySpace and YouTube provide an outlet to a generation of voices competing to be heard, she said. The sites have gone beyond touching base with friends to an arena where people vie for the most digital friends, the best videos, the coolest sites, and biggest audience.

"Now it all becomes a competition, seeking attention and seeking status rather than a true connection between people, or a meaningful connection," Twenge said.

In addition, many young people believe MySpace will launch them to stardom. In a recent poll conducted by the Pew Research Center, half of all 18- to 25-year-olds listed being famous as an important goal for their generation.

"I know some girls who are modeling or actresses and think they are going to get on Maxim and all that off of their MySpace," said Liz Bernardo, a 20-year-old student at UTSA and 2004 Miss Austin Teen USA.

Bernardo, who grew out of her own teenage modeling dreams, laughs at the notion.

"I never thought by having a profile I would become famous."

GET USED TO IT

For every self-promoter, however, there is someone like Charity Pierce or Samantha Schoenfeld, two UTSA students who use social networking sites strictly for communication with friends and family.

Both have profiles on MySpace and Facebook, but they are closed to any user who hasn't been accepted as a friend. Because they are in a sorority, they are required to keep their sites clean: no sloppy drunk photos.

Yet they spend hours on the sites.

"If you don't want to do homework, just get on Facebook. It's addicting," Pierce said.

Pierce is pretty typical. According to the Pew poll, 54 percent of Generation Nexters said their peers spent too much time on social networking sites, and 72 percent feel others post too much personal information on the Internet.

Pierce freaked out when a friend told her—after the fact—that she met someone online and gave him her address to come pick her up for a date.

"And that's just creepy," Pierce said. "It's so. . . ."

"Scary," Schoenfeld finished.

"Bizarre," Pierce added.

In addition to her sorority, Pierce believes employers and college officials are keeping tabs on these sites.

There are stories like that of a New York journalist who, after discovering her 26-year-old nanny was blogging about life in their household, fired her. Or three students at the University of Mississippi who were investigated for creating a Facebook group composed of students who wanted to have sex with a particular professor.

"I am graduating soon and I can't risk anyone getting a misconception about me," Pierce said.

But spying on social networking sites isn't yet widespread among employers.

"I have not heard of employers actively using it," said Becky Woods, vice president of human resources at the Doherty Employment Group, a Minneapolis company that does staffing and human resources outsourcing. "The buzz is about, should we or should we not?"

Woods said trying to judge applicants' work performance by what they put on a Web site is tricky.

"It is like putting on a stage show, and I am not sure that stage show is what employers should look for," Woods said.

Matthew Williams, a student at San Antonio College, agreed.

"A lot of stuff you put on there is not what you would say or do in real life. It is more extreme or more dopey than normal stuff," Williams said.

Still, once you hit go, you lose control of information, said Alan Weinkrantz, the 53-year-old owner of a high tech public relations firm and an avid blogger.

"It is like giving a car to a 16-year-old kid," Weinkrantz said. "Hey, it's freedom, it's neat, but you can also run over and kill someone."

Time and space shrink very fast in cyberspace, he said.

"With all the goodness of speed, you have to teach the kids to say: 'Stop. Do you really want to say this?' If you don't care, then you don't care. But realize there are consequences of not caring. You are putting an imprint of yourself that could linger for years on end that you could not take down."

For instance, Williams, the SAC student, blogs on MySpace about his view that Sept. 11, 2001, attacks may have been the work of the U.S. government. He wants to run for public office some day, and isn't sure whether those views may hurt or help him.

"If it's true, someone might pull up my MySpace and say, 'Look at this guy, he knew the truth,'" Williams said. "If it is before the government acknowledges they took part in it, it could very well hurt my run for president."

Despite the cautionary tales, it's likely trial and error that will shape how people behave in this new social media.

"Lots of the rules that I grew up with are not rules anymore," said Cyndi Taylor Krier, a regent for the University of Texas System. "Lots of new ways of communicating have taken their place. (Young people) view (the Internet) the way we viewed picking up a phone and calling somebody when we were their age."

Old notions of privacy also have changed. In an age where you can Google people and find their address and phone number, where the government can drop in on your calls and where every carton of ice cream you buy is logged into a database, what does privacy mean anymore, many kids ask.

"The government and everyone else knows everything about you anyway," Davis said. "It's done, the Internet is here, the Internet broadcasts everything, what can you do about it? Get used to it."

———

Melissa Ludwig wrote this piece for the March 25, 2007, edition of the *San Antonio Express-News* <www.mysanantonio.com>.

Generation Me Does Plenty for Others
BY DANIEL T. SWANN (2007)

A recent study concluded that my generation is narcissistic. It was based on a nation-wide survey of college students called the Narcissistic Personality Inventory. The higher the NPI score, the more narcissistic the subject. Two-thirds of my peers had above-average scores, a 30 percent increase since the NPI was first conducted in 1982. The study was led by a researcher who has written a book called "Generation Me."

Generation Me. That label implies that college students lack empathy and value themselves much more than relationships. Jean Twenge, the San Diego State University professor who headed the study, argued that technology is a driving force of this neo-narcissism. Websites such as MySpace and Facebook are all about drawing attention to ourselves.

It's true that we love our online profiles, but we aren't that simplistic. Narcissism and altruism can exist in the same generation.

I saw it in the young woman in my residence hall at Northeastern University who helped build schools in Haiti and Mexico before she came to college. I heard it when I listened to two international affairs majors named Aly Brennan and Hannah Robertson-Forrest talk about Invisible Children, a program of Uganda-CAN, an organization working to end the war in northern Uganda.

Invisible Children is a reason to believe in my generation. I joined Uganda-CAN last fall after watching a DVD about the Invisible Children program. Three filmmakers from Southern California, all in their early 20s, formed the group in 2004 after they traveled to Uganda and documented a disturbing chapter in the 21-year war between the Lord's Resistance Army rebels and the Ugandan government. The refugee camps set up 10 years ago have been housing 1.8 million people, including children who are trying to avoid being abducted by the LRA and used as child soldiers.

Invisible Children spreads awareness of the displaced children by showing the documentary at college campuses nationwide. The nonprofit also boasts a variety of grass-roots campaigns to improve conditions in the refugee camps and encourage peace talks.

The Schools for Schools campaign designed to provide schools in northern Uganda with clean water, books, teachers, and technology raised $150,000 in a month and a half.

What does all of this have to do with Generation Me? Everything. It was all Generation Me.

"I would say 75 percent of people [in Invisible Children Inc.] are under 25," said Chris Zwakenberg, 24, a national tour representative for Invisible Children. "The chief financial officer is 23."

Last April 28, 80,000 of my peers attended staged protests for the Invisible Children Global Night Commute. Demonstrators slept overnight in the streets of 130 cities worldwide to protest the lack of international attention for the children forced to commute to the camps at night to avoid capture during the day.

"And these are all kids," Brennan said. "There aren't adults, like some 40-year-old wiser man who took over dictating what they do."

Eighty thousand people. That's almost the number of friends I have on MySpace. Kidding.

However, it isn't just individuals who draw attention on MySpace. Ideas and issues do, too. The One Campaign and Amnesty International are two of more than 20,000 MySpace groups listed as "Non-profit and Philanthropic" organizations.

"MySpace has been huge," Zwakenberg said. The "Invisible Children" documentary—it clearly not a narcissistic endeavor—was one of the most popular videos on MySpace last year.

Could MySpace actually be evidence of our potential? William Strauss, the coauthor of "Millennials Rising: The Next Great Generation,"says my peers, the "Millennials," aren't creating profiles, videos, and audio files on sites like MySpace and YouTube for purely narcissistic reasons.

"It's for sharing, and sharing is not narcissism," Strauss said. "As in any generation you will find examples of self-oriented behavior but we should not let youthful ambition be mischaracterized as narcissism."

Strauss and his colleague Neil Howe have been studying the Millennial generation since 1986. Their book "Generations" describes the patterns of four generation types and the mindsets and behaviors associated with them.

Strauss points to the decline in behaviors commonly associated with reckless and self-involved youth over the last 15 years, such as crime and sexual risk-taking, as evidence of the Millennials' sense of responsibility. "Like GIs, Millennials are a generation of improving trends, rising institutional trust, and greater teamwork," Strauss said.

Howe said Millennials possess an attitude toward civic duty he described as: "Let's go. Let's do it."

"I do feel your generation looks at boomers and how boomers are running government, and you feel you can run a more capable, less corrupt [government] with less cronies," Howe said.

Something is driving the demand for more options for alternative spring break at colleges. Boston College's alternative spring break program, for instance, offers students the opportunity to spend their week doing Habitat for Humanity-type projects in such places as Jamaica and the Appalachian Mountains.

"These programs have developed and become much more a part of the BC culture," said John McDargh, an associate professor of theology there. He said there are almost always more people applying for positions on the Appalachia and Nicaragua trips than positions available.

We might never know why someone chooses something selfless over something self-gratifying. I only know that my generation cannot be explained with one study. I know this because Brennan and Robertson-Forrest discuss poverty so passionately. I have seen Brennan joking about how tired she is one minute and almost jumping out of her chair with energy while talking about Africa the next.

"I really do feel blessed to know this," Brennan said about the situation documented by Invisible Children. "I feel so honored that I know what's going on somewhere all the way across the world that I want to share it with everyone. It blows your mind."

My problem with the study is it labels an entire generation with a blanket term. There are people doing good work who deserve better than that. Judging a demographic's perspectives and potential based purely on a narcissism index is like determining its intellect based purely on the average SAT score.

Yes, we love our Internet, but there are some who use it as a resource to positive ends because they see the world outside their posted photos and online diaries. Yes, we might even think we're special individuals sometimes. If we didn't, would we be able to accomplish much?

———

Daniel T. Swann wrote this piece for the April 23, 2007, edition of *The Boston Globe* <www.bostonglobe.com>.

Matters of Faith Find a New Prominence on Campus
BY ALAN FINDER (2007)

Peter J. Gomes has been at Harvard University for 37 years, and says he remembers when religious people on campus felt under siege. To be seen as religious often meant being dismissed as not very bright, he said.

No longer. At Harvard these days, said Professor Gomes, the university preacher, "There is probably more active religious life now than there has been in 100 years."

Across the country, on secular campuses as varied as Colgate University, the University of Wisconsin and the University of California, Berkeley, chaplains, professors and administrators say students are drawn to religion and spirituality with more fervor than at any time they can remember.

More students are enrolling in religion courses, even majoring in religion; more are living in dormitories or houses where matters of faith and spirituality are a part of daily conversation; and discussion groups are being created for students to grapple with questions like what happens after death, dozens of university officials said in interviews.

A survey on the spiritual lives of college students, the first of its kind, showed in 2004 that more than two-thirds of 112,000 freshmen surveyed said they prayed, and that almost 80 percent believed in God. Nearly half of the freshmen said they were seeking opportunities to grow spiritually, according to the survey by the Higher Education Research Institute at the University of California, Los Angeles.

Compared with 10 or 15 years ago, "there is a greater interest in religion on campus, both intellectually and spiritually," said Charles L. Cohen, a professor of history and religious studies at the University of Wisconsin, Madison, who for a number of years ran an interdisciplinary major in religious studies. The program was created seven years ago and has 70 to 75 majors each year.

University officials explained the surge of interest in religion as partly a result of the rise of the religious right in politics, which they said has made questions of faith more talked about generally. In addition, they said, the attacks of Sept. 11 underscored for many the influence of religion on world affairs. And an influx of evangelical students at secular universities, along with an increasing number of international students, means students arrive with a broader array of religious experiences.

Professor Gomes (pronounced like "homes") said a more diverse student body at Harvard had meant that "the place is more representative of mainstream America."

"That provides a group of people who don't leave their religion at home," he said.

At Berkeley, a vast number of undergraduates are Asian-American, with many coming from observant Christian homes, said the Rev. Randy Bare, the Presbyterian campus pastor. "That's new, and it's a remarkable shift," Mr. Bare said.

There are 50 to 60 Christian groups on campus, and student attendance at Catholic and Presbyterian churches near campus has picked up significantly, he said. On many other campuses, though, the renewed interest in faith and spirituality has not necessarily translated into increased attendance at religious services.

The Rev. Lloyd Steffen, the chaplain at Lehigh University, is among those who think the war in Iraq has contributed to the interest in religion among students. "I suspect a lot of that has to do with uncertainty over the war," Mr. Steffen said.

"My theory is that the baby boomers decided they weren't going to impose their religious life on their children the way their parents imposed it on them," Mr. Steffen continued. "The idea was to let them come to it themselves. And then they get to campus and things happen; someone dies, a suicide occurs. Real issues arise for them, and they sometimes feel that they don't have resources to deal with them. And sometimes they turn to religion and courses in religion."

Increased participation in community service may also reflect spiritual yearning of students. "We don't use that kind of spiritual language anymore," said Rebecca S. Chopp, the Colgate president. "But if you look at the students, they do."

Some sociologists who study religion are skeptical that students' attitudes have changed significantly, citing a lack of data to compare current students with those of previous generations. But even some of those concerned about the data say something has shifted.

"All I hear from everybody is yes, there is growing interest in religion and spirituality and an openness on college campuses," said Christian Smith, a professor of sociology at the University of Notre Dame. "Everybody who is talking about it says something seems to be going on."

David D. Burhans, who retired after 33 years as chaplain at the University of Richmond, said many students "are really exploring, they are really interested in trying things out, in attending one another's services."

Lesleigh Cushing, an assistant professor of religion and Jewish studies at Colgate, said: "I can fill basically any class on the Bible. I wasn't expecting that."

When Benjamin Wright, chairman of the department of religion studies at Lehigh, arrived 17 years ago, two students chose to major in religion. This year there are 18 religion majors, and there were 30 two and three years ago.

At Harvard, more students are enrolling in religion courses and regularly attending religious services, Professor Gomes said. Presbyterian ministries at Berkeley and Wisconsin have built dormitories to offer spiritual services to students and encourage discussion among different faiths. The seven-story building on the Wisconsin campus, which will house 280 students, is to open in August.

At Colgate, five Buddhist and Hindu students received permission to live in a new apartment complex on the edge of campus this year. They call their apartment Asian Spirituality House and they use it for meetings and occasional religious events.

The number of student religious organizations at Colgate has grown to 11 from 5 in recent years. The university's Catholic, Protestant and Jewish chaplains oversee an array of programs and events. Many involve providing food to students, a phenomenon that the university chaplain, Mark Shiner, jokingly calls "gastro-evangelism."

Among the new clubs is one created last year to encourage students to hold wide-ranging dialogues about spirituality and faith. Meeting over lunch on Thursdays in the chapel's basement, the students talk about what happens when you die or the nature of Catholic spirituality.

Called the Heretics Club (the chaplains were looking to grab students' attention), the group listened to John Gattuso talk about his book, "Talking to God: Portrait of a World at Prayer" (Stone Creek Publications, 2006), a collection of essays and photos about prayer in world religions.

"Do you need to believe in God in order to pray?" Mr. Gattuso asked.

The discussion was off and running, with one student saying one needed only to believe in "something outside yourself" and another saying that "sometimes 'Thank you' can be a prayer."

Afterward, several students talked about what attracted them to the sessions, besides the sandwiches, chips and fruit. Gabe Conant, a junior, said he wanted to contemplate personal questions about his own faith. He described them this way: "What are these things I was raised in and do I want to keep them?"

Alan Finder wrote this piece for the May 2, 2007, edition *of The New York Times* <www.nytimes.com>.

Schools of Thought: The Liberal-Conservative Divide on College Campuses
BY RICHARD JUST (2005)

During her first two years at the University of Pennsylvania, Stephanie Steward became convinced that she was being treated unfairly because of her political views. In her class on diversity and the law, a professor seemed obsessed with the evils of slavery. Another professor's defense of the estate tax struck her as excessively one-sided. *The Daily Pennsylvanian*, where she worked, seemed to exhibit subtle political bias. Eventually Steward decided that she had taken enough abuse. So last year the junior launched a newspaper of her own, *The Pennsylvania Independent*, and this year she will take the publication biweekly. Starting a newspaper costs money (her budget for this school year will run about $15,000). Fortunately for Steward, a portion of that money will come from the Intercollegiate Studies Institute (ISI), a conservative organization that funds college publications.

Steward's story will sound familiar to anyone who has talked to college conservatives. "It takes a little oppression to really get engaged and involved," says Evan Baehr, a junior at Princeton University, where he is editor in chief of the conservative *Princeton Tory* and president of the College Republicans. Like Steward, Baehr sees himself as an oppressed minority on his campus—and he, too, has turned to national conservative organizations for remedy. *The Tory* received tens of thousands of dollars last year from groups such as the Leadership Institute, the Young America Foundation and the ISI to fund its printing costs and to host speakers such as Jonah Goldberg, George Will and Daniel Flynn, author of *Why the Left Hates America*. Baehr says such speakers are necessary to counterbalance the influence of an overwhelmingly liberal faculty, many of whom he believes exhibit left-wing tendencies in their course materials. Don't conservative college professors also indulge their biases in the classroom? "I'm sure there are equally absurd cases on the other side," Baehr says, mentioning the faculty at Bob Jones University.

Although conservatives currently run the national government and are enjoying an upswing in media influence, conservative activists on campus still draw energy from feeling like a beleaguered minority—and they're not entirely wrong. In last year's American Freshman Survey, conducted annually by the University of California, Los Angeles, 27.8 percent of college freshmen nationwide identified themselves as liberal or far left while 21.3 percent identified themselves as conservative or far right. It was the first time since 1996 that the percentage of students identifying themselves as liberal or left in the survey decreased; the year before, 29.9 percent had identified themselves as liberal or far left, the most since 1975.

Liberal dominance is more pronounced at elite schools. Dartmouth is widely considered to be the most conservative school in the Ivy League. And yet, according to a voluntary e-mail poll by *The Dartmouth*, the school's student newspaper, 62 percent of students voted for Al Gore in 2000 compared with 23 percent for George W. Bush. At Princeton, generally considered the second-most conservative Ivy, 55 percent voted for Gore compared with 26 percent for Bush, according to a 2000 poll by *The Daily Princetonian* (of which I was then editor in chief). At the University of Pennsylvania, probably the third-most conservative Ivy, 67 percent chose Gore while 20 percent chose Bush, according to *The Daily Pennsylvanian*.

If these broad measurements—liberal vs. conservative, Gore voter versus Bush voter—were the only campus trends that mattered to the future health of progressive politics, liberals would be in reasonably strong shape. But unfortunately for progressives, college politics are more complex. I recently spoke to about 30 student leaders at universities throughout the country. Their perspectives on campus activism varied from school to school, but most agreed that though the right is still a minority on many campuses, it is undoubtedly an energized one. Like Steward and Baehr, conservatives are often fueled by two forces: their own sense of righteous indignation at professors, administrators and peers whom they believe have made college campuses inhospitable territory for conservative ideas; and the availability of funding from outside organizations, which allows them to channel this indignation into publications, speaker series—and, they hope, converts.

The siege mentality of campus conservatives and the substantial financial support they receive from outside groups have not escaped media notice. In May, *The New York Times Magazine* published a story about the rise of "hip" conservatives at Bucknell University. *The Economist* followed with a shorter piece in July on the growth of College Republicans, which has tripled its national membership in the last three years. "The leftists who seized control of the universities in the 1960s have imposed their world-view on the young with awesome enthusiasm, bowdlerizing textbooks of anything that might be considered sexist or racist, imposing draconian speech codes and inventing pseudo-subjects such as women's studies," *The Economist* wrote, offering a concise illustration of the current conservative mind-set on many campuses. As a student from Pennsylvania State University told the *Pittsburgh Post-Gazette* while attending a Young America Foundation conference in Washington this summer, "Our group is much smaller than the college Democrats, but at least we are making our voices known."

Campus conservatives have made the most of their self-conception as an oppressed minority. Their insurgency is just a natural "reaction against the professors and the administration, which tend to be liberal," says Dan Gomez chairman of Penn's College Republicans. Alicia Washington, president of Yale University's College Democrats agrees. Yale conservatives, she says, "knock a lot louder because there are so few of them." And if conservatives find that knocking louder helps them generate publicity, well, that's part of the point.

By contrast, campus progressives, though still more numerous, have two big problems: funding and fragmentation. Yoni Applebaum, who led the Columbia University organization that dispenses funding to student groups and worked with the nonpartisan Columbia Political Union (CPU), said the disparity was noticeable. "It was far easier for us at the Gee to locate external sources of funding to bring conservative speakers to campus than it was to locate sources of funding to bring Democratic speakers to campus," he says. The funding gap manifests itself in more subtle ways, too. "The liberal magazines don't look anywhere near as nice as the conservative magazines," says Emily Regan Wills, a senior at Yale and a leader of the school's Women's Center. Zac Frank, president of Columbia's College Democrats, marvels at the outside support available to conservative groups. "The national network they have is just astounding," he says. That national network serves as a pipeline for young conservatives, and it has churned out its share of success stories: Ralph Reed, Grover Norquist and, most famously, Karl Rove all held national positions in the College Republicans organization.

The number of progressive campus groups often dwarfs the number of conservative organizations, but that is both a strength and a weakness. Harvard's Web site, for instance, displays numerous student groups running the gamut from liberal to radical: the Environmental Action Committee; AIDS Education and Outreach; the Bisexual, Gay, Lesbian and Transgendered Supporters Alliance; the Black Students Association; the Black Men's Forum; the Coalition Against Sexual Violence; the Coalition for Drug Policy Reform; the Harvard-Radcliffe Women's Leadership Project; Youth at Harvard Against Handgun Violence; Students for Choice; Amnesty International; the Initiative for Peace and Justice and so on. The conservative counterparts are much fewer in number. This phenomenon exists at many schools, and on some campuses, student leaders say, the proliferation of liberal groups can lead to divisions in the progressive community.

It's not simply the number of organizations that matters—the ideological range of progressive groups tends to be much wider than those on the right. That fragmentation can be healthy, of course—what is college about, if not debating ideas?—but it can also create bitter and disabling divisions, particularly at schools with strong cultures of radicalism. Ethan Ris, president of Brown University's College Democrats, says that this past spring the Young Communist League took over efforts to organize protests against the war in Iraq. "We would show up to these meetings and be shouted down and called idiots. . . . My members would show up and have such a terrible time, they'd never want to go again." Yale's Wills who is herself no centrist—she voted for Gore only because she lived in the swing state of Pennsylvania and would have voted for Ralph Nader elsewhere—says the progressive community often ends up being dominated by its most extreme voices. "I am shocked often by what I am called moderate for saying," she says. "And 'moderate' in the activist community is a dirty word." Describing some activists as "hard-line" and "off-putting," she adds, "People who get committed to Yale activism often end up being very far to the left."

At Columbia, a school with a long tradition of radicalism, liberal students say that the vocal student chapter of the International Socialist Organization (ISO) has a chilling effect on more mainstream progressive activism. "I've met freshmen who've been wary of joining a political group because what they see on campus are these far-left groups who are not their cup of tea," says Samir Arora, who just graduated from Columbia and

was president of the CPU. Frank, of the College Democrats, says, "People see any identification with progressive issues as being, 'Oh, that's the ISO again.'"

Progressive students engaged in narrowly focused organizations may ignore liberal
electoral politics. "Sometimes it's difficult to work with single-issue groups," says Gerard
McGeary, president of Harvard's College Democrats. Alicia Washington of Yale agrees
that the strength of identity groups "in some ways does kind of detract." But other campus liberal leaders see identity groups as valuable gateways to political awareness for students who might otherwise remain on the sidelines. "It's a big group of people to get
our message out to," says Rich Eisenberg, president of Penn's College Democrats.

Another problem for the liberal side is durability. Single issue liberal organizations
often ride on the energy of a handful of students and may not outlive their graduations.
Changes in world events may also make narrowly defined groups obsolete, scattering to
the wind the political energy they briefly harnessed. Groups that sprang up to oppose
the Iraq War this past spring are a prime example. "Things form as news forms, and
then they die as news dies," Lucretia Fernandez, press secretary of Indiana University's
College Republicans, says of some progressive groups on her campus.

Still, campus conservatives say that the sheer number of liberal groups gives progressives more opportunities to lure students to campus activism. "Any sort of liberal issue
has a group at Penn, as opposed to the conservatives, who, as of now, have us," says
Gomez of Penn's College Republicans. With more groups, he says, "you can mobilize
so many more people, even though they may not be united by a common leadership."
As a result, conservatives at Penn and Princeton say they are trying to emulate the left by
encouraging the formation of new right-of-center political groups more narrowly tailored
around specific issues.

A bigger nemesis for both groups is a familiar one: apathy. Getting the message out
about political issues is a particular challenge when great swaths of the student body aren't
listening. To have a conversation with current college students about political activism, it's
practically a precondition to acknowledge that many students simply don't care about the
great debates of our time, or don't think that political engagement is worth the trouble.
There is, of course, some sample bias at work here: It makes sense that the average activist
would view his or her peers as politically apathetic, just as the typical cellist would probably view other students as insufficiently interested in attending orchestra concerts. And yet
it is impossible to avoid the fact that conversations about politics at colleges big and small,
liberal and conservative, urban and rural, private and public invariably turn toward the

fact that "the majority of students are apathetic," as Josh Fisher of the Bucknell Caucus for Economic Justice put it in speaking about his campus. Asked whether students at Bucknell are generally left or right of center, he says he doesn't know. "I couldn't say definitively because most people avoid topics of conversation like that," he says. "It's sort of an anti-intellectual environment." Katerina Seligmann of Columbia's Amnesty International chapter acknowledges that most of her peers are politically left of center. But, she adds, "There's a difference between people being liberals and people being activists."

Cutting through this apathy is the greatest challenge faced by campus activists, left and right—and possibly the one idea that unites the two sides. "When we're registering people by ourselves, we get 10 people per hour," says Eisenberg of Penn's College Democrats. "When we're registering with the College Republicans, we get 50 people an hour." Gomez, his Penn counterpart on the right, says that debates between the two groups—which take place once or twice a year—draw "the most participation of any one event that either of us do."

Humor is another way to coax students out of apathy, and a little effort goes a long way. Conservatives have been out in front on this one, probably because it's easier to poke fun at the establishment when you perceive yourself as being outside it. *The New York Times Magazine* documented how Bucknell conservatives have made a rite of annually penning something called "Penis Monologues," a response to the feminist play *The Vagina Monologues,* popular on many campuses. The stunt generates outrage and publicity, which is exactly what conservative students want.

Liberals may be watching and learning. Shortly after this year's State of the Union address, Peter Hackeman, opinions editor of *The Bucknellian,* the student newspaper, wrote a satirical draft of Bush's speech that wasn't bad. "Our intelligence sources tell us that Saddam has attempted to purchase high-strength aluminum tubes suitable for nuclear weapons production," he wrote, "but they were actually to be used for those low-tech phones with string connecting two aluminum cans. . . . Saddam Hussein has not credibly explained these activities. He clearly has much to hide. Just what are these string-and-can phones to be used for? If this is not evil, then evil has no meaning." Not as outrageous as the "Penis Monologues," to be sure, but give Bucknell's liberals points for effort.

The Iraq War was fertile ground for campus activism on both sides of the political spectrum. But most students agree that national politics in the last two years has moved into territory where campus conservatives feel more comfortable than their liberal peers. "It became a lot easier to be a conservative at college after September 11," says Angel

Rivera, president of Indiana University's College Republicans. Following the terrorist attacks, groups with names such as the Princeton Committee Against Terrorism and Columbia's Students United for America sprang up. Though many of these groups had bipartisan memberships, they clearly leaned right.

Many see this trend not as evidence that undergraduates have converted to neoconservatism en masse but rather as a manifestation of how contemporary college students feel about institutions—such as the military—that were largely opposed by their parents. In the most recent nationwide UCLA survey, 45 percent of students agreed "strongly" or "somewhat" with the idea of increasing military spending. In 1993, that number was 21.4 percent. Supporters of the Iraq War understood this situation. At Columbia, for instance, the College Republicans chapter was careful to advertise its rally as a "pro-troops" event rather than a "pro-war" one, explained Dennis Schmelzer, the organization's executive director. "The war in Iraq has been a great issue for us," says the group's president, Ganesh Betanabhatla.

A debate raged at the school over whether to bring the ROTC back to campus. And some liberals—revealing, perhaps, the inclinations of their generation—have found it difficult to dismiss the arguments of their more conservative peers. Dina Schorr, a founder of Toward Reconciliation, a Columbia group that advocates peaceful resolutions to international conflicts, struggled with the question of whether to sign a petition advocating the ROTC's return.

"If all of these liberal campuses don't have ROTC," she explained, "then how can you expect the military to change?" In the end, she signed.

On social issues, however, college students remain generally liberal. "Social issues [are] really our best shot among young, educated kids," says Owen Conroy, president of Princeton's College Democrats. Whatever else characterizes today's college students, this is surely the Tolerant Generation. The percentage of students supporting gay rights has consistently grown in UCLA's survey in recent years. Last year a record high of 59.3 percent supported gay marriage while a record low of 24.8 percent favored laws limiting homosexual rights. It is well documented that students are growing more ambivalent about ever having an abortion or personally approving of one, yet recently a majority still favored abortion rights. And 39.7 percent support legalizing marijuana, up from 16.7 percent in 1989. "It's definitely harder to sell them on socially conservative ideas," says Gomez of Republican efforts to enlist Penn students.

Whatever frustrations Gomez has experienced haven't sapped his sense of mission. Last year, to spark interest in their group, Republicans put up signs around campus that asked, "What Would Reagan Do?" When many were torn down—as campus posters often are—Gomez took it as a sign of anti-conservative bias. "If there were posters saying, 'What Would Carter Do?' they wouldn't have gotten torn down," he says. The deeply held belief that they are being persecuted on college campuses may make some conservatives seem a little paranoid. But it may also be strengthening their resolve.

College liberals confront a paradox: Their parents won many aspects of the battle for campuses some decades ago—freer sexuality, affirmative action, greater curricular and cultural diversity. Liberals of that generation came to dominate faculties, notably in the liberal arts. Today it's conservatives who feel like the opposition, and it's a lot easier to be outraged, dogmatic and zealously energized if you're not in charge.

But it's not clear that liberals are completely in charge. It's true that professors in departments like English, sociology and women's studies are disproportionately left of center, but in the parts of universities that lead directly to real power—business schools, law faculties, economics departments—the opposite is often true. Diversity of ideological views is, of course, healthy. When conservatives complain that their sociology professors teach from a liberal vantage point, liberals can retort that it's good for conservatives to challenge themselves by studying with liberal sociologists—just as it's good for liberals to challenge themselves by taking economics courses with market fundamentalists.

To spur activism, liberals have no shortage of topics to tap. The anti-sweatshop movement, which crested on campuses about four years ago, placed progressive activists in direct confrontation with their school administrations and also garnered sympathy from large portions of normally apathetic student bodies. Campaigns for higher wages for the lowest-paid workers at colleges have achieved similar results.

There are any number of other issues—from the death grip of commercialized athletic departments on university decision making to the outrageous use of federal work-study money to fund menial campus jobs rather than meaningful service opportunities—that are ripe for exploration by thoughtful, progressive undergrads. When campus liberals have enjoyed success and garnered publicity in recent years, they have carved out creative positions on issues that have allowed them to challenge both the institutions where they study and the larger society. Their victories have suggested that beneath the apathy, idealism is still the natural condition of youth.

———

Richard Just is the online editor of *The American Prospect* <www.prospect.org>, which published this piece in October 2003.

Laptops vs. Learning

BY DAVID COLE (2007)

"Could you repeat the question?"

In recent years, that has become the most common response to questions I pose to my law students at Georgetown University. It is usually asked while the student glances up from the laptop screen that otherwise occupies his or her field of vision. After I repeat the question, the student's gaze as often as not returns to the computer screen, as if the answer might magically appear there. Who knows, with instant messaging, maybe it will.

Some years back, our law school, like many around the country, wired its classrooms with Internet hookups. It's the way of the future, I was told. Now we are a wireless campus, and incoming students are required to have laptops. So my first-year students were a bit surprised when I announced at the first class this year that laptops were banned from my classroom.

I did this for two reasons, I explained. Note-taking on a laptop encourages verbatim transcription. The note-taker tends to go into stenographic mode and no longer processes information in a way that is conducive to the give and take of classroom discussion. Because taking notes the old-fashioned way, by hand, is so much slower, one actually has to listen, think and prioritize the most important themes.

In addition, laptops create temptation to surf the Web, check e-mail, shop for shoes or instant-message friends. That's not only distracting to the student who is checking Red Sox statistics but for all those who see him, and many others, doing something besides being involved in class. Together, the stenographic mode and Web surfing make for a much less engaged classroom, and that affects all students (not to mention me).

I agreed to permit two volunteers to use laptops to take notes that would be made available to all students. And that first day I allowed everyone to use the laptops they had with them. I posed a question, and a student volunteered an answer. I answered her with a follow-up question. As if on cue, as soon as I started to respond, the student went back to typing—and then asked, "Could you repeat the question?"

When I have raised with my colleagues the idea of cutting off laptop access, some accuse me of being paternalistic, authoritarian or worse. We daydreamed and did crosswords when we were students, they argue, so how can we prohibit our students, who are adults after all, from using their time in class as they deem fit?

A crossword hidden under a book is one thing. With the aid of Microsoft and Google, we have effectively put at every seat a library of magazines, a television and the opportunity for real-time side conversations and invited our students to check out whenever they find their attention wandering.

I feel especially strongly about this issue because I'm addicted to the Internet myself. I checked my e-mail at least a dozen times while writing this op-ed. I've often resolved, after a rare and liberating weekend away from e-mail, that I will wait till the end of the day to read e-mail at the office. Yet, almost as if it is beyond my control, e-mail is the first thing I check when I log on each morning. As for multitasking, I don't buy it. Attention diverted is attention diverted.

But this is all theory. How does banning laptops work in practice? My own sense has been that my class is much more engaged than recent past classes. I'm biased, I know. So I conducted an anonymous survey of my students after about six weeks—by computer, of course.

The results were striking. About 80 percent reported that they are more engaged in class discussion when they are laptop-free. Seventy percent said that, on balance, they liked the no-laptop policy. And perhaps most surprising, 95 percent admitted that they use their laptops in class for "purposes other than taking notes, such as surfing the Web, checking e-mail, instant messaging and the like." Ninety-eight percent reported seeing fellow students do the same.

I am sure that the Internet can be a useful pedagogical tool in some settings and for some subjects. But for most classes, it is little more than an attractive nuisance. Technology has outstripped us on this one, and we need to reassess its appropriate and inappropriate role in teaching. The personal computer has revolutionized our lives, in many ways for the better. But it also threatens to take over our lives. At least for some purposes, unplugging may still be the best response.

———

David Cole is a professor at Georgetown University Law Center. He wrote this piece for the April 7, 2007, edition of *The Washington Post* <www.washingtonpost.com>.

Disappearing Act: Where Have the Men Gone? No Place Good

BY MICHAEL GURIAN (2005)

In the 1990s, I taught for six years at a small liberal arts college in Spokane, Wash. In my third year, I started noticing something that was happening right in front of me. There were more young women in my classes than young men, and on average, they were getting better grades than the guys. Many of the young men stared blankly at me as I lectured. They didn't take notes as well as the young women. They didn't seem to care as much about what I taught—literature, writing and psychology. They were bright kids, but many of their faces said, "Sitting here, listening, staring at these words—this is not really who I am."

That was a decade ago, but just last month, I spoke with an administrator at Howard University in the District. He told me that what I observed a decade ago has become one of the "biggest agenda items" at Howard. "We are having trouble recruiting and retaining male students," he said. "We are at about a 2-to-1 ratio, women to men."

Howard is not alone. Colleges and universities across the country are grappling with the case of the mysteriously vanishing male. Where men once dominated, they now make up no more than 43 percent of students at American institutions of higher learning, according to 2003 statistics, and this downward trend shows every sign of continuing unabated. If we don't reverse it soon, we will gradually diminish the male identity, and thus the productivity and the mission, of the next generation of young men, and all the ones that follow.

The trend of females overtaking males in college was initially measured in 1978. Yet despite the well-documented disappearance of ever more young men from college campuses, we have yet to fully react to what has become a significant crisis. Largely, that is because of cultural perceptions about males and their societal role. Many times a week, a reporter or other media person will ask me: "Why should we care so much about boys when men still run everything?"

It's a fair and logical question, but what it really reflects is that our culture is still caught up in old industrial images. We still see thousands of men who succeed quite well in the professional world and in industry—men who get elected president, who own software companies, who make six figures selling cars. We see the Bill Gateses and John Robertses and George Bushes—and so we're not as concerned as we ought to be about the millions of young men who are floundering or lost.

But they're there: The young men who are working in the lowest-level (and most dangerous) jobs instead of going to college. Who are sitting in prison instead of going to college. Who are staying out of the long-term marriage pool because they have little to offer to young women. Who are remaining adolescents, wasting years of their lives playing video games for hours a day, until they're in their thirties, by which time the world has passed many of them by.

The old industrial promise—"That guy will get a decent job no matter what"—is just that, an old promise. So is the old promise that a man will be able to feed his family and find personal meaning by "following in his father's footsteps," which has vanished for millions of males who are not raised with fathers or substantial role models. The old promise that an old boys' network will always come through for "the guys" is likewise gone for many young men who have never seen and will never see such a network (though they may see a dangerous gang). Most frightening, the old promise that schools will take care of boys and educate them to succeed is also breaking down, as boys dominate the failure statistics in our schools, starting at the elementary level and continuing through high school.

Of course, not every male has to go to college to succeed, to be a good husband, to be a good and productive man. But a dismal future lies ahead for large numbers of boys in this generation who will not go to college. Statistics show that a young man who doesn't finish school or go to college in 2005 will likely earn less than half what a college graduate earns. He'll be three times more likely to be unemployed and more likely to be homeless. He'll be more likely to get divorced, more likely to engage in violence against women and more likely to engage in crime. He'll be more likely to develop substance abuse problems and to be a greater burden on the economy, statistically, since men who don't attend college pay less in Social Security and other taxes, depend more on government welfare, are more likely to father children out of wedlock and are more likely not to pay child support.

When I worked as a counselor at a federal prison, I saw these statistics up close. The young men and adult males I worked with were mainly uneducated, had been raised in families that didn't promote education, and had found little of relevance in the schools they had attended. They were passionate people, capable of great love and even possible future success. Many of them told me how much they wanted to get an education. At an intuitive level, they knew how important it was.

Whether in the prison system, in my university classes or in the schools where I help train teachers, I have noticed a systemic problem with how we teach and mentor boys that I call "industrial schooling," and that I believe is a primary root of our sons' falling behind in school, and quite often in life.

Two hundred years ago, realizing the necessity of schooling millions of kids, we took them off the farms and out of the marketplace and put them in large industrial-size classrooms (one teacher, 25 to 30 kids). For many kids, this system worked—and still works. But from the beginning, there were some for whom it wasn't working very well. Initially, it was girls. It took more than 150 years to get parity for them.

Now we're seeing what's wrong with the system for millions of boys. Beginning in very early grades, the sit-still, read-your-book, raise-your-hand-quietly, don't-learn-by-doing-but-by-taking-notes classroom is a worse fit for more boys than it is for most girls. This was always the case, but we couldn't see it 100 years ago. We didn't have the comparative element of girls at par in classrooms. We taught a lot of our boys and girls separately. We educated children with greater emphasis on certain basic educational principles that kept a lot of boys "in line"—competitive learning was one. And our families were deeply involved in a child's education.

Now, however, the boys who don't fit the classrooms are glaringly clear. Many families are barely involved in their children's education. Girls outperform boys in nearly every academic area. Many of the old principles of education are diminished. In a classroom of 30 kids, about five boys will begin to fail in the first few years of pre-school and elementary school. By fifth grade, they will be diagnosed as learning disabled, ADD/ADHD, behaviorally disordered or "unmotivated." They will no longer do their homework (though they may say they are doing it), they will disrupt class or withdraw from it, they will find a few islands of competence (like video games or computers) and overemphasize those.

Boys have a lot of Huck Finn in them—they don't, on average, learn as well as girls by sitting still, concentrating, multitasking, listening to words. For 20 years, I have been taking brain research into homes and classrooms to show teachers, parents and others how differently boys and girls learn. Once a person sees a PET or SPECT scan of a boy's brain and a girl's brain, showing the different ways these brains learn, they understand. As one teacher put it to me, "Wow, no wonder we're having so many problems with boys."

Yet every decade the industrial classroom becomes more and more protective of the female learning style and harsher on the male, yielding statistics such as these:

- The majority of National Merit scholarships, as well as college academic scholarships, go to girls and young women.
- Boys and young men comprise the majority of high school dropouts, as high as 80 percent in many cities.
- Boys and young men are 1½ years behind girls and young women in reading ability (this gap does not even out in high school, as some have argued; a male reading/writing gap continues into college and the workplace).

The industrial classroom is one that some boys do fine in, many boys just "hang on" in, many boys fall behind in, many boys fail in, and many boys drop out of. The boys who do fine would probably do fine in any environment, and the boys who are hanging on and getting by will probably re-emerge later with some modicum of success, but the millions who fall behind and fail will generally become the statistics we saw earlier.

Grasping the mismatch between the minds of boys and the industrial classroom is only the first step in understanding the needs of our sons. Lack of fathering and male role models take a heavy toll on boys, as does lack of attachment to many family members (whether grandparents, extended families, moms or dads). Our sons are becoming very lonely. And even more politically difficult to deal with: The boys-are-privileged-but-the-girls-are-shortchanged emphasis of the last 20 years (an emphasis that I, as a father of two daughters and an advocate of girls, have seen firsthand), has muddied the water for child development in general, pitting funding for girls against funding for boys.

We still barely see the burdens our sons are carrying as we change from an industrial culture to a post-industrial one. We want them to shut up, calm down and become perfect intimate partners. It doesn't matter too much who boys and men are—what matters is who we think they should be. When I think back to the kind of classroom I created for my college students, I feel regret for the males who dropped out. When I think back to my time working in the prison system, I feel a deep sadness for the present and future generations of boys whom we still have time to save.

And I do think we can save them. I get hundreds of e-mails and letters every week, from parents, teachers and others who are beginning to realize that we must do for our sons what we did for our daughters in the industrialized schooling system—realize that boys are struggling and need help. These teachers and parents are part of a social movement—a boys' movement that started, I think, about 10 years ago. It's a movement that gets noticed for brief moments by the media (when Columbine happened, when Laura Bush talked about boys) and then goes underground again. It's a movement very much powered by individual women—mainly mothers of sons—who say things to me like the e-mailers who wrote, "I don't know anyone who doesn't have a son struggling in school," or, "I thought having a boy would be like having a girl, but when my son was born, I had to rethink things."

We all need to rethink things. We need to stop blaming, suspecting and overly medicating our boys, as if we can change this guy into the learner we want. When we decide—as we did with our daughters—that there isn't anything inherently wrong with our sons, when we look closely at the system that boys learn in, we will discover these boys again, for all that they are. And maybe we'll see more of them in college again.

Michael Gurian, a family therapist and founder of the Gurian Institute <www.gurianinstitute.com>, an educational training organization, wrote this column for the December 4, 2005, edition of *The Washington Post* <www.washingtonpost.com>. His most recent book, written with Kathy Stevens, is *The Minds of Boys: Saving Our Sons From Falling Behind in School and Life.*

Too Many Women in College?
BY PHYLLIS ROSSER (2005)

Although American women still struggle for parity in many arenas, we have outpaced men in at least one: undergraduate college education. Currently, 57.4 percent of bachelor's degrees in the United States are earned by women, 42.6 percent by men. This is an almost exact reversal from 1970, when 56.9 percent of college graduates were males and 43.1 percent females.

We should be celebrated for this landmark achievement, but instead it has engendered fear. Read the headlines: "Falling Male College Matriculation an Alarming Trend," or "Admissions Officers Weigh a Heretical Idea: Affirmative Action for Men." Notice, too, that a major focus of first lady Laura Bush's new anti-gang task force is education for boys. As she's been quoted, "The statistics are pretty alarming. Girls are going to college much more than boys."

Few worried when college students were two-thirds men. But as early as February 1999, *U.S. News & World Report* predicted that the rising tide of women college grads could close the salary gap and move women into positions of power as heads of corporations, presidents of universities and political leaders. At the other extreme, the article suggested, college education might become devalued—considered "a foolhardy economic decision"—as has happened in other fields after women begin to predominate.

STILL RARE AT THE TOP

What *U.S. News* failed to mention was that women are still a rare presence at the top ranks of the corporate and professional world despite earning more college degrees than men for 23 years. Women undertake stronger academic programs than men in high school, and receive higher average grades than men in both high school and college, but haven't been able to translate that success into equitable money and power. Consider these disparities as well:

- Women currently earn nearly 59 percent of master's degrees, but men outstrip women in advanced degrees for business, engineering and computer-science— fields which lead to much higher-paying jobs than education, health and psychology, the areas where women predominate.
- Despite women's larger numbers as undergrads and in master's programs, men outnumber women in earning doctorates (54 percent) and professional degrees (53 percent).
- This year, the number of women applying to medical school outpaced men for the second time, but they are only predicted to be 33 percent of doctors by 2010.
- Women comprise nearly half of the students entering law schools, but they're miles from parity as law partners, professors and judges.

TESTS DON'T TELL THE WHOLE TALE

Women may lose a step on the career ladder even before they enter college. That's because, despite their greater number of bachelor's and master's degrees, women remain at a disadvantage in college admissions testing—which affects their acceptance at elite schools. The main purpose of the SAT—on which women averaged 44 points lower than men last year—is to predict first-year grades. However, it consistently underpredicts the college performance of women, who earn higher college grades than men.

Women's lower scores on the SAT have been shown to arise from several factors biased toward male performance, including the fact that it's a timed test and rewards guessing—and men tend to be more confident and risk-taking than women in such test situations. Also, the SAT puts many of the questions in a male context (such as sports), which can further lower female confidence about knowing the material.

In an attempt to even the gender playing field, a writing section that includes language questions and an essay was added to the SAT this year, after the University of California insisted that the test be more attuned to the skills necessary for college success. This may raise women's SAT scores somewhat, since writing tests are an area in which they have traditionally outperformed males.

Lower SAT scores keep qualified women from both attending the most competitive schools and from receiving National Merit Scholarships and other awards based on PSAT and SAT scores. The test biases against women then continue in graduate education, with such instruments as the Graduate Record Exam (GRE), Graduate Management Admissions Test (GMAT) and Law School Admissions Test (LSAT).

Thus, women have yet to predominate at the most prestigious colleges and universities, where graduates are tracked toward top leadership positions in society. With enormous numbers of both sexes applying to these schools, the admissions offices can choose their gender ratio. In 2005, men outnumbered women at all the Ivy League schools except Brown and Columbia. Women are also significantly outnumbered at universities specializing in engineering and physical science, such as Massachusetts Institute of Technology in Cambridge and California Institute of Technology in Pasadena.

AFFIRMATIVE ACTION—FOR MEN?

The greater percentage of women earning bachelor's degrees has given rise to some reactionary theories explaining why. Conservative analyst Christina Hoff Sommers insists the gap takes root in the more "girl-friendly" elementary school environment where boys are turned off to learning.

In *The War Against Boys: How Misguided Feminism Is Harming Our Young Men* (Simon & Schuster, 2000), Hoff Sommers claims that schoolboys are "routinely regarded as protosexists, potential harassers and perpetuators of gender inequity" who "live under a cloud of censure."

Even higher-education policy analyst Tom Mortensen, who has a special concern with underrepresented populations in higher education, also sees the college gender gap as part of a larger societal problem for men and boys. Mortensen says K–12 teachers, 75 percent of whom are women, are not providing the role models and learning styles boys need. Of course, this was never an issue during the decades when college graduates were mainly men, and hasn't drawn much notice since the end of the Civil War—the time when women began their continuing predominance as elementary school teachers.

If these theories seem to spring from a blame-the-women viewpoint, there is a legitimate concern about the decline in male graduates at private colleges, where the gap has been greatest (although public universities have also been affected). Admissions officers worry that their colleges' value will be lowered by an imbalance of female students: The larger the female majority, some say, the less likely either males or females will want to apply.

Speaking at a College Board conference several years ago, admissions officers agreed that a 60–40 female-to-male gender ratio was their upper limit. After that, said former Macalester College president Michael McPherson, "students will take notice." Small private colleges are now using what can only be called "male affirmative action" to increase male enrollment: actively recruiting men by emphasizing their science, math and engineering courses, adding sports programs (in violation of Title IX), sending extra mailings designed to attract men and even calling men to remind them of the admissions deadline.

"Probably no one will admit it, but I know lots of places try to get some gender balance by having easier admissions standards for boys than for girls," said Columbia University Teachers College president Arthur Levine to *The New York Times* national correspondent Tamar Lewin. Robert Massa, vice president of Dickinson College in Carlisle, Penn., has said that the school now evaluates prospective male students less on grades and more on measures where they typically do better, such as SAT scores. Adds Goucher College admissions vice president Barbara Fritze, "Men are being admitted to schools they never got into before, and offered financial aid they hadn't gotten before."

Massa reported that the number of first-year males at Dickinson rose from 36 percent to 43 percent in 2001 after they took affirmative action toward men, who were admitted with lower grades but comparable SAT scores. Women, meanwhile, had to be much better than men to make the cut: Nearly 62 percent of the women accepted to the school ranked in the top 10 percent of their high school class, compared to 42 percent of the men.

This new form of affirmative action, even if begun with all good intentions, could lead to bad college-admissions policy. What if a university decides it doesn't just want more men in attendance, but more white men? The whole notion of affirmative action as a way to help disadvantaged populations succeed could be turned on its head.

THE INCOME GAP

The real reason behind the undergrad gender gap may have much less to do with one's sex and more to do with income, race and class.

Jacqueline King, director of the Center for Policy Analysis at the American Council on Education in Washington, D.C., decided that media stories about the decline of white male enrollment didn't intuitively jibe with what she saw happening, so she took a closer look at college student data, analyzing it by sex, age, race/ethnicity and socioeconomic status. She found the gender gap in college enrollment for students 18 to 24 years of age in 1995–96 occurred among low-income students of all racial/ethnic groups except Asian Americans.

In fact, since 1995, many more women than men from households making less than $30,000 attend college. The latest available data, from 2003–04, shows there is an even smaller percentage of low-income males attending college than there were in 1995, and they are from every racial/ethnic group. African American and Native American students have the largest gender gaps—males comprise just 37 percent of all low-income African American students and 36 percent of low-income Native Americans. Low-income Hispanic men reach a slightly higher 39 percent, and low-income white males 41 percent (a drop from 46 percent in 1995). Asian Americans have the smallest gender gap, with 47 percent of that group's low-income college students being male.

Middle-income ($30,000–$70,000) male students maintained gender parity with females 10 years ago, but since then the numbers have dropped somewhat. This may mean that fewer men from the lower end of this income bracket are attending college, says Eugene Anderson, senior research associate at the American Council on Education.

At the highest income level ($70,000 or more), though, men and women in all ethnic groups attend college in nearly equal numbers.

No studies have been done to determine why more low-income women than men attend college, but there are theories. Economist Lester Thurow suggests that low-income men have been lured to the comfortable salaries of mechanical maintenance jobs. Low-income women, on the other hand, don't have such opportunities, and without a college degree, see themselves getting trapped in low-pay sales or service jobs, says King. Also, more men than women work in computer support or high-tech factories—jobs that don't require bachelor's degrees.

Overall, an increasing number of poor and working-class people are dropping out of college because of such reasons as escalating tuition and the attraction of high-paying factory work, according to a May piece in *The New York Times* ("The College Dropout Boom: Diploma's Absence Strands Many in the Working Class"). Harvard president Lawrence H. Summers goes so far as to call this widening of the education gap between rich and poor our "most serious domestic problem"—and recent changes in federal grant formulas may exacerbate it even further.

UPRISING: MINORITIES AND OLDER WOMEN

On the bright side, ethnic minorities have made impressive gains as college students since 1976, increasing their percentage in the total student body from 10 percent to 23 percent. Minority men's share of all bachelor's degrees has gone from 5 percent to 9 percent. But, again, minority women have outstripped them, more than doubling their share of bachelor's degrees, from 5 percent to 14 percent of the total degrees awarded.

Not only is that statistic a contributing factor to the overall gender gap, but another contributing factor is that women are the majority of older (25+) students—and that demographic has been returning to college in record numbers. The "oldsters" now make up 27 percent of the undergraduate student body, and 61 percent of older students are women. King found that many of these students were African American or Latina, attending community colleges to improve future earnings in health-related fields.

"This story is not one of male failure, or even lack of opportunity," says King, "but rather one of increased academic opportunity and success among females and minorities." Indeed, there has been no decline in bachelor's degrees awarded to men; the numbers awarded to women have simply increased.

Feminists should continue to be concerned about encouraging low-income and minority students to attend college, using the current momentum to give these problems the attention they deserve. But in the meantime, we must remain vigilant about attempts to roll back our educational gains. The fact is, we're a long way from threatening corporate America, so don't put the onus on women. Maybe it's just time to let men try to catch up to us, for a change.

Phyllis Rosser wrote this piece for the Fall 2005 edition of *Ms.* magazine <www.msmagazine.com>.

The College Dropout Boom
BY DAVID LEONHARDT (2005)

One of the biggest decisions Andy Blevins has ever made, and one of the few he now regrets, never seemed like much of a decision at all. It just felt like the natural thing to do.

In the summer of 1995, he was moving boxes of soup cans, paper towels and dog food across the floor of a supermarket warehouse, one of the biggest buildings in Chilhowie, in southwest Virginia. The heat was brutal. The job had sounded impossible when he arrived fresh off his first year of college, looking to make some summer money, still a skinny teenager with sandy blond hair and a narrow, freckled face.

But hard work done well was something he understood, even if he was the first college boy in his family. Soon he was making bonuses on top of his $6.75 an hour, more money than either of his parents made. His girlfriend was around, and so were his hometown buddies. Andy acted more outgoing with them, more relaxed. People in Chilhowie noticed that.

It was just about the perfect summer. So the thought crossed his mind: maybe it did not have to end. Maybe he would take a break from college and keep working. He had been getting C's and D's, and college never felt like home, anyway.

"I enjoyed working hard, getting the job done, getting a paycheck," Mr. Blevins recalled. "I just knew I didn't want to quit."

So he quit college instead, and with that, Andy Blevins joined one of the largest and fastest-growing groups of young adults in America. He became a college dropout, though nongraduate may be the more precise term.

Many people like him plan to return to get their degrees, even if few actually do. Almost one in three Americans in their mid-20's now fall into this group, up from one in five in the late 1960's, when the Census Bureau began keeping such data. Most come from poor and working-class families.

The phenomenon has been largely overlooked in the glare of positive news about the country's gains in education. Going to college has become the norm throughout most of the United States, even in many places where college was once considered an exotic destination—places like Chilhowie (pronounced chill-HOW-ee), an Appalachian hamlet with a simple brick downtown. At elite universities, classrooms are filled with women, blacks, Jews and Latinos, groups largely excluded two generations ago. The American system of higher learning seems to have become a great equalizer.

In fact, though, colleges have come to reinforce many of the advantages of birth. On campuses that enroll poorer students, graduation rates are often low. And at institutions where nearly everyone graduates—small colleges like Colgate, major state institutions like the University of Colorado and elite private universities like Stanford—more students today come from the top of the nation's income ladder than they did two decades ago.

Only 41 percent of low-income students entering a four-year college managed to graduate within five years, the Department of Education found in a study last year, but 66 percent of high-income students did. That gap had grown over recent years. "We need to recognize that the most serious domestic problem in the United States today is the widening gap between the children of the rich and the children of the poor," Lawrence H. Summers, the president of Harvard, said last year when announcing that Harvard would give full scholarships to all its lowest-income students. "And education is the most powerful weapon we have to address that problem."

There is certainly much to celebrate about higher education today. Many more students from all classes are getting four-year degrees and reaping their benefits. But those broad gains mask the fact that poor and working-class students have nevertheless been falling behind; for them, not having a degree remains the norm.

That loss of ground is all the more significant because a college education matters much more now than it once did. A bachelor's degree, not a year or two of courses, tends to determine a person's place in today's globalized, computerized economy.

College graduates have received steady pay increases over the past two decades, while the pay of everyone else has risen little more than the rate of inflation.

As a result, despite one of the great education explosions in modern history, economic mobility—moving from one income group to another over the course of a lifetime—has stopped rising, researchers say. Some recent studies suggest that it has declined over the last generation.

Put another way, children seem to be following the paths of their parents more than they once did. Grades and test scores, rather than privilege, determine success today, but that success is largely being passed down from one generation to the next. A nation that believes that everyone should have a fair shake finds itself with a kind of inherited meritocracy.

In this system, the students at the best colleges may be diverse—male and female and of various colors, religions and hometowns—but they tend to share an upper-middle-class upbringing. An old joke that Harvard's idea of diversity is putting a rich kid from California in the same room as a rich kid from New York is truer today than ever; Harvard has more students from California than it did in years past and just as big a share of upper-income students.

Students like these remain in college because they can hardly imagine doing otherwise. Their parents, understanding the importance of a bachelor's degree, spent hours reading to them, researching school districts and making it clear to them that they simply must graduate from college.

Andy Blevins says that he too knows the importance of a degree, but that he did not while growing up, and not even in his year at Radford University, 66 miles up the Interstate from Chilhowie. Ten years after trading college for the warehouse, Mr. Blevins, 29, spends his days at the same supermarket company. He has worked his way up to produce buyer, earning $35,000 a year with health benefits and a 401(k) plan. He is on a path typical for someone who attended college without getting a four-year degree. Men in their early 40's in this category made an average of $42,000 in 2000. Those with a four-year degree made $65,000.

Still boyish-looking but no longer rail thin, Mr. Blevins says he has many reasons to be happy. He lives with his wife, Karla, and their year-old son, Lucas, in a small blue-and-yellow house at the end of a cul-de-sac in the middle of a stunningly picturesque Appalachian valley. He plays golf with some of the same friends who made him want to stay around Chilhowie.

But he does think about what might have been, about what he could be doing if he had the degree. As it is, he always feels as if he is on thin ice. Were he to lose his job, he says, everything could slip away with it. What kind of job could a guy without a college degree get? One night, while talking to his wife about his life, he used the word "trapped."

"Looking back, I wish I had gotten that degree," Mr. Blevins said in his soft-spoken lilt. "Four years seemed like a thousand years then. But I wish I would have just put in my four years."

THE BARRIERS

Why so many low-income students fall from the college ranks is a question without a simple answer. Many high schools do a poor job of preparing teenagers for college. Many of the colleges where lower-income students tend to enroll have limited resources and offer a narrow range of majors, leaving some students disenchanted and unwilling to continue.

Then there is the cost. Tuition bills scare some students from even applying and leave others with years of debt. To Mr. Blevins, like many other students of limited means, every week of going to classes seemed like another week of losing money—money that might have been made at a job.

"The system makes a false promise to students," said John T. Casteen III, the president of the University of Virginia, himself the son of a Virginia shipyard worker.

Colleges, Mr. Casteen said, present themselves as meritocracies in which academic ability and hard work are always rewarded. In fact, he said, many working-class students face obstacles they cannot overcome on their own.

For much of his 15 years as Virginia's president, Mr. Casteen has focused on raising money and expanding the university, the most prestigious in the state. In the meantime, students with backgrounds like his have become ever scarcer on campus. The university's genteel nickname, the Cavaliers, and its aristocratic sword-crossed coat of arms seem appropriate today. No flagship state university has a smaller proportion of low-income students than Virginia. Just 8 percent of undergraduates last year came from families in the bottom half of the income distribution, down from 11 percent a decade ago.

That change sneaked up on him, Mr. Casteen said, and he has spent a good part of the last year trying to prevent it from becoming part of his legacy. Starting with next fall's freshman class, the university will charge no tuition and require no loans for students whose parents make less than twice the poverty level, or about $37,700 a year for a family of four. The university has also increased financial aid to middle-income students.

To Mr. Casteen, these are steps to remove what he describes as "artificial barriers" to a college education placed in the way of otherwise deserving students. Doing so "is a fundamental obligation of a free culture," he said.

But the deterrents to a degree can also be homegrown. Many low-income teenagers know few people who have made it through college. A majority of the nongraduates are young men, and some come from towns where the factory work ethic, to get working as soon as possible, remains strong, even if the factories themselves are vanishing. Whatever the reasons, college just does not feel normal.

"You get there and you start to struggle," said Leanna Blevins, Andy's older sister, who did get a bachelor's degree and then went on to earn a Ph.D at Virginia studying the college experiences of poor students. "And at home your parents are trying to be supportive and say, 'Well, if you're not happy, if it's not right for you, come back home. It's O.K.' And they think they're doing the right thing. But they don't know that maybe what the student needs is to hear them say, 'Stick it out just one semester. You can do it. Just stay there. Come home on the weekend, but stick it out.' "

Today, Ms. Blevins, petite and high-energy, is helping to start a new college a few hours' drive from Chilhowie for low-income students. Her brother said he had daydreamed about attending it and had talked to her about how he might return to college.

For her part, Ms. Blevins says, she has daydreamed about having a life that would seem as natural as her brother's, a life in which she would not feel like an outsider in her hometown. Once, when a high-school teacher asked students to list their goals for the next decade, Ms. Blevins wrote, "having a college degree" and "not being married."

"I think my family probably thinks I'm liberal," Ms. Blevins, who is now married, said with a laugh, "that I've just been educated too much and I'm gettin' above my raisin'."

Her brother said that he just wanted more control over his life, not a new one. At a time when many people complain of scattered lives, Mr. Blevins can stand in one spot—his church parking lot, next to a graveyard—and take in much of his world. "That's my parents' house," he said one day, pointing to a sliver of roof visible over a hill. "That's my uncle's trailer. My grandfather is buried here. I'll probably be buried here."

TAKING CLASS INTO ACCOUNT

Opening up colleges to new kinds of students has generally meant one thing over the last generation: affirmative action. Intended to right the wrongs of years of exclusion, the programs have swelled the number of women, blacks and Latinos on campuses. But affirmative action was never supposed to address broad economic inequities, just the ones that stem from specific kinds of discrimination.

That is now beginning to change. Like Virginia, a handful of other colleges are not only increasing financial aid but also promising to give weight to economic class in granting admissions. They say they want to make an effort to admit more low-income students, just as they now do for minorities and children of alumni.

"The great colleges and universities were designed to provide for mobility, to seek out talent," said Anthony W. Marx, president of Amherst College. "If we are blind to the educational disadvantages associated with need, we will simply replicate these disadvantages while appearing to make decisions based on merit."

With several populous states having already banned race-based preferences and the United States Supreme Court suggesting that it may outlaw such programs in a couple of decades, the future of affirmative action may well revolve around economics. Polls consistently show that programs based on class backgrounds have wider support than those based on race.

The explosion in the number of nongraduates has also begun to get the attention of policy makers. This year, New York became one of a small group of states to tie college financing more closely to graduation rates, rewarding colleges more for moving students along than for simply admitting them. Nowhere is the stratification of education more vivid than here in Virginia, where Thomas Jefferson once tried, and failed, to set up the nation's first public high schools. At a modest high school in the Tidewater city of Portsmouth, not far from Mr. Casteen's boyhood home, a guidance office wall filled with college pennants does not include one from rarefied Virginia. The colleges whose pennants are up—Old Dominion University and others that seem in the realm of the possible—have far lower graduation rates.

Across the country, the upper middle class so dominates elite universities that high-income students, on average, actually get slightly more financial aid from colleges than low-income students do. These elite colleges are so expensive that even many high-income students receive large grants. In the early 1990's, by contrast, poorer students got 50 percent more aid on average than the wealthier ones, according to the College Board, the organization that runs the SAT entrance exams.

At the other end of the spectrum are community colleges, the two-year institutions that are intended to be feeders for four-year colleges. In nearly every one are tales of academic success against tremendous odds: a battered wife or a combat veteran or a laid-off worker on the way to a better life. But over all, community colleges tend to be places where dreams are put on hold.

Most people who enroll say they plan to get a four-year degree eventually; few actually do. Full-time jobs, commutes and children or parents who need care often get in the way. One recent national survey found that about 75 percent of students enrolling in community colleges said they hoped to transfer to a four-year institution. But only 17 percent of those who had entered in the mid-1990's made the switch within five years, according to a separate study. The rest were out working or still studying toward the two-year degree.

"We here in Virginia do a good job of getting them in," said Glenn Dubois, chancellor of the Virginia Community College System and himself a community college graduate. "We have to get better in getting them out."

'I WEAR A TIE EVERY DAY'

College degree or not, Mr. Blevins has the kind of life that many Americans say they aspire to. He fills it with family, friends, church and a five-handicap golf game. He does not sit in traffic commuting to an office park. He does not talk wistfully of a relocated brother or best friend he sees only twice a year. He does not worry about who will care for his son while he works and his wife attends community college to become a physical therapist. His grandparents down the street watch Lucas, just as they took care of Andy and his two sisters when they were children. When Mr. Blevins comes home from work, it is his turn to play with Lucas, tossing him into the air and rolling around on the floor with him and a stuffed elephant.

Mr. Blevins also sings in a quartet called the Gospel Gentlemen. One member is his brother-in-law; another lives on Mr. Blevins's street. In the long white van the group owns, they wend their way along mountain roads on their way to singing dates at local church functions, sometimes harmonizing, sometimes ribbing one another or talking about where to buy golf equipment.

Inside the churches, the other singers often talk to the audience between songs, about God or a grandmother or what a song means to them. Mr. Blevins rarely does, but his shyness fades once he is back in the van with his friends.

At the warehouse, he is usually the first to arrive, around 6:30 in the morning. The grandson of a coal miner, he takes pride, he says, in having moved up to become a supermarket buyer. He decides which bananas, grapes, onions and potatoes the company will sell and makes sure that there are always enough. Most people with his job have graduated from college.

"I'm pretty fortunate to not have a degree but have a job where I wear a tie every day," he said.

He worries about how long it will last, though, mindful of what happened to his father, Dwight, a decade ago. A high school graduate, Dwight Blevins was laid off from his own warehouse job and ended up with another one that paid less and offered a smaller pension.

"A lot of places, they're not looking that you're trained in something," Andy Blevins said one evening, sitting on his back porch. "They just want you to have a degree."

Figuring out how to get one is the core quandary facing the nation's college non-graduates. Many seem to want one. In a *New York Times* poll, 43 percent of them called it essential to success, while 42 percent of college graduates and 32 percent of high-school dropouts did. This in itself is a change from the days when "college boy" was an insult in many working-class neighborhoods. But once students take a break—the phrase that many use instead of drop out—the ideal can quickly give way to reality. Family and work can make a return to school seem even harder than finishing it in the first place.

After dropping out of Radford, Andy Blevins enrolled part-time in a community college, trying to juggle work and studies. He lasted a year. From time to time in the decade since, he has thought about giving it another try. But then he has wondered if that would be crazy. He works every third Saturday, and his phone rings on Sundays when there is a problem with the supply of potatoes or apples. "It never ends," he said. "There's a never a lull."

To spend more time with Lucas, Mr. Blevins has already cut back on his singing. If he took night classes, he said, when would he ever see his little boy? Anyway, he said, it would take years to get a degree part-time. To him, it is a tug of war between living in the present and sacrificing for the future.

FEW BREAKS FOR THE NEEDY

The college admissions system often seems ruthlessly meritocratic. Yes, children of alumni still have an advantage. But many other pillars of the old system—the polite rejections of women or blacks, the spots reserved for graduates of Choate and Exeter—have crumbled.

This was the meritocracy Mr. Casteen described when he greeted the parents of freshman in a University of Virginia lecture hall late last summer. Hailing from all 50 states and 52 foreign countries, the students were more intelligent and better prepared than he and his classmates had been, he told the parents in his quiet, deep voice. The class included 17 students with a perfect SAT score.

If anything, children of privilege think that the system has moved so far from its old-boy history that they are now at a disadvantage when they apply, because colleges are trying to diversify their student rolls. To get into a good college, the sons and daughters of the upper middle class often talk of needing a higher SAT score than, say, an applicant who grew up on a farm, in a ghetto or in a factory town. Some state legislators from Northern Virginia's affluent suburbs have argued that this is a form of geographic discrimination and have quixotically proposed bills to outlaw it.

But the conventional wisdom is not quite right. The elite colleges have not been giving much of a break to the low-income students who apply. When William G. Bowen, a former president of Princeton, looked at admissions records recently, he found that if test scores were equal a low-income student had no better chance than a high-income one of getting into a group of 19 colleges, including Harvard, Yale, Princeton, Williams and Virginia. Athletes, legacy applicants and minority students all got in with lower scores on average. Poorer students did not.

The findings befuddled many administrators, who insist that admissions officers have tried to give poorer applicants a leg up. To emphasize the point, Virginia announced this spring that it was changing its admissions policy from "need blind"—a term long used to assure applicants that they would not be punished for seeking financial aid—to "need conscious." Administrators at Amherst and Harvard have also recently said that they would redouble their efforts to take into account the obstacles students have overcome.

"The same score reflects more ability when you come from a less fortunate background," Mr. Summers, the president of Harvard, said. "You haven't had a chance to take the test-prep course. You went to a school that didn't do as good a job coaching you for the test. You came from a home without the same opportunities for learning."

But it is probably not a coincidence that elite colleges have not yet turned this sentiment into action. Admitting large numbers of low-income students could bring clear complications. Too many in a freshman class would probably lower the college's average SAT score, thereby damaging its ranking by *U.S. News & World Report,* a leading arbiter of academic prestige. Some colleges, like Emory University in Atlanta, have climbed fast in the rankings over precisely the same period in which their percentage of low-income students has tumbled. The math is simple: when a college goes looking for applicants with high SAT scores, it is far more likely to find them among well-off teenagers.

More spots for low-income applicants might also mean fewer for the children of alumni, who make up the fund-raising base for universities. More generous financial aid policies will probably lead to higher tuition for those students who can afford the list price. Higher tuition, lower ranking, tougher admission requirements: they do not make for an easy marketing pitch to alumni clubs around the country. But Mr. Casteen and his colleagues are going ahead, saying the pendulum has swung too far in one direction.

That was the mission of John Blackburn, Virginia's easy-going admissions dean, when he rented a car and took to the road recently. Mr. Blackburn thought of the trip as a reprise of the drives Mr. Casteen took 25 years earlier, when he was the admissions dean, traveling to churches and community centers to persuade black parents that the university was finally interested in their children.

One Monday night, Mr. Blackburn came to Big Stone Gap, in a mostly poor corner of the state not far from Andy Blevins's town. A community college there was holding a college fair, and Mr. Blackburn set up a table in a hallway, draping it with the University of Virginia's blue and orange flag.

As students came by, Mr. Blackburn would explain Virginia's new admissions and financial aid policies. But he soon realized that the Virginia name might have been scaring off the very people his pitch was intended for. Most of the students who did approach the table showed little interest in the financial aid and expressed little need for it. One man walked up to Mr. Blackburn and introduced his son as an aspiring doctor. The father was an ophthalmologist. Other doctors came by, too. So did some lawyers.

"You can't just raise the UVa flag," Mr. Blackburn said, packing up his materials at the end of the night, "and expect a lot of low-income kids to come out."

When the applications started arriving in his office this spring, there seemed to be no increase in those from low-income students. So Mr. Blackburn extended the deadline two weeks for everybody, and his colleagues also helped some applicants with the maze of financial aid forms. Of 3,100 incoming freshmen, it now seems that about 180 will qualify for the new financial aid program, up from 130 who would have done so last year. It is not a huge number, but Virginia administrators call it a start.

A BIG DECISION

On a still-dark February morning, with the winter's heaviest snowfall on the ground, Andy Blevins scraped off his Jeep and began his daily drive to the supermarket warehouse. As he passed the home of Mike Nash, his neighbor and fellow gospel singer, he noticed that the car was still in the driveway. For Mr. Nash, a school counselor and the only college graduate in the singing group, this was a snow day.

Mr. Blevins later sat down with his calendar and counted to 280: the number of days he had worked last year. Two hundred and eighty days—six days a week most of the time—without ever really knowing what the future would hold.

"I just realized I'm going to have to do something about this," he said, "because it's never going to end."

In the weeks afterward, his daydreaming about college and his conversations about it with his sister Leanna turned into serious research. He requested his transcripts from Radford and from Virginia Highlands Community College and figured out that he had about a year's worth of credits. He also talked to Leanna about how he could become an elementary school teacher. He always felt that he could relate to children, he said. The job would take up 180 days, not 280. Teachers do not usually get laid off or lose their pensions or have to take a big pay cut to find new work.

So the decision was made. On May 31, Andy Blevins says, he will return to Virginia Highlands, taking classes at night; the Gospel Gentlemen are no longer booking performances. After a year, he plans to take classes by video and on the Web that are offered at the community college but run by Old Dominion, a Norfolk, Va., university with a big group of working-class students.

"I don't like classes, but I've gotten so motivated to go back to school," Mr. Blevins said. "I don't want to, but, then again, I do."

He thinks he can get his bachelor's degree in three years. If he gets it at all, he will have defied the odds.

———

David Leonhardt writes for *The New York Times* <www.nytimes.com>, where this article was published on May 24, 2005.

FROM READING TO WRITING

1. Michiko Kakutani and Alex Williams paint completely different pictures of Millennials' civic engagement. How do you think these authors would respond to each other? Taking into account each author's claims and counterclaims, write a hypothetical dialogue between Kakutani and Williams. What might their debate sound like? Whose argument do you find more convincing? Why?

2. The following articles each marshal Jean Twenge's research using the Narcissistic Personality Inventory. How does each writer evaluate and use this evidence?
   a. "Gen Y's Ego Trip Takes a Bad Turn"
   b. "LOOK@ME: Generation Next is Living Out Loud and Online"
   c. "Generation Me Does Plenty for Others"

3. Many of the authors in this chapter identify technology—be it MySpace, Facebook, or just laptops in general—as a central characteristic of college life. How do the following authors evaluate technology? What criteria do they use? Do you agree with their positions?
   a. David Cole
   b. Melissa Ludwig
   c. Daniel T. Swann

4. Compare the arguments presented in Michael Gurian's "Disappearing Act: Where Have the Men Gone? No Place Good" and Phyllis Rosser's "Too Many Women in College?" What claims do the authors make? How do they go about supporting those claims? What kinds of evidence do they use? Who is the audience for each piece? Which argument do you find more convincing? Why?

5. Writers in this chapter posit shifts in college populations in matters of faith (Alan Finder's "Matters of Faith Find a New Prominence on Campus"), political orientation (Richard Just's "Schools of Thought: the Liberal-Conservative Divide on College Campuses"), and class (David Leonhardt's "The College Dropout Boom"). Identify the causal argument in each of these articles. What do the authors see as the reasons for these changes?

Three

AFTER VIRGINIA TECH

Virginia Tech and Our Impoverished Language for Evil

BY GREGG EASTERBROOK (2007)

Katie Couric: "Just who was the shooter?" Charles Gibson: "Tonight—the survivors, their stories; the shooter, his background." Matt Lauer: "We've now got an identity of the shooter." Wolf Blitzer: "That is the shooter, Cho Seung-Hui."

Learning that there had been a mass killing at Virginia Tech, many in the press began to speak of the "shooter" who had brought horror to the campus: A shooter was loose, a shooter did this, a shooter did that. On ABC, CBS, and NBC news broadcasts in the 72 hours after the tragedy, the word "shooter" was heard roughly three times as often as "killer" or "murderer."

The fact that murder had happened at Virginia Tech was clear within hours, if not minutes, of initial reports. Yet plenty of media figures could not bring themselves to say that the killer was a killer, that the murderer was a murderer. Instead, they used "shooter," a weirdly neutral term that practically sounds like a skilled trade. To call someone a "shooter" is to say he was holding a firearm that discharged, but to imply nothing about any moral choice involved or the fact that it's bad to aim a pistol at a helpless person and pull the trigger. Same goes for the word "gunman," also used frequently by journalists and pundits.

There are times when neutral words like "shooter" and "gunman" are justified. In police investigations and legal proceedings that involve the determination of guilt or innocence, dispassionate terms should be used. In news reports about accusations that have not yet gone to trial, cautious phrasing is wise. But there was no possibility that the Virginia Tech deaths were caused by legitimate use of force, mistaken identity, self-defense, or some dreadful accident; the only possible explanation was mass homicide. To call Cho a "murderer" would have been a simple statement of fact. Yet, according to a Nexis search of major U.S. newspapers and wire stories, in the three days following the massacre, 2,516 stories contained the terms "shooter" or "gunman," while just 746 used "murderer" or "killer." And, a full week after the calamity, many news outlets—including CNN, MSNBC, and Fox News—were still referring to Cho as a "shooter."

Similarly odd was the frequent use of the phrase "shooting spree" to describe the Blacksburg horror. A spree is a gay, carefree outing. Those who say "shooting spree" make it sound as if killing at random is therapeutic, even recreational: He felt depressed, so he went on a shooting spree. The only term that fits what Cho did is "rampage," and a few reports used this word. But a disturbing number opted for "spree."

Commentators even tiptoed away from using the term "madman" to describe Cho. We don't need to be psychiatrists or even be aware of the demented materials he mailed to NBC News to determine that the Virginia Tech murderer was mentally ill. There simply are no circumstances under which a person of sound mind would slaughter 32 unarmed innocents. (Whether he was legally insane—unable to distinguish right from wrong—is a separate question. Most who suffer mental illness remain sane. Cho's suicide suggests he was sane; presumably, he killed himself to escape punishment for his crimes.) Yet, even as Cho's crazed messages and psychological-health profile have been revealed, news reports have treated the murderer's history gently. In one story, the worst *The New York Times* could bring itself to say was that the killer suffered a "troubled mental state" and "imbalance." Had the *Times* called Cho a "madman," the paper would have been criticized—for using a judgmental term about a mass murderer!

But we *should* be judgmental about murderers and others who commit moral horrors. Of course, one explanation for the popularity of terms like "shooter" may simply be that, with the proliferation of TV crime dramas, cop slang like "shooter" and "perp" has seeped into everyday language and hence into public discourse. But the larger, more troubling explanation has to do with morality. The Western press and intellectual realms were scoffing at the concept of evil long before George W. Bush cheapened the word through constant bandying. Media and thought leaders don't want to say that the man who chained the exit doors of Norris Hall before he started killing had a mind taken over by evil; they want to dismiss him as no more than a confused gunman, because they don't want to contemplate his demonstration that evil is entirely real. And so they use words like "shooter" that remove the moral dimension, making it seem like terrible events just happen—not that human wickedness causes terrible events. Many news reports spoke of the slaughter as if it had been a bad, bad car crash with no one really at fault.

That Cho became evil is distinct from whether society failed him at earlier points; you can sympathize with his earlier self and agree that someone suffering his condition deserved better care. But set aside whether evil results from psychosis—or from supernatural temptation, genetic flaws, free-will choice, trauma, poverty, wealth, or ideology: Evil exists and must be spoken of *as evil*, not in euphemism. On a windy Monday morning in Virginia, evil armed itself and performed the most despicable of acts: pleasure in the taking of innocent life. Evil will arm itself again. As George Orwell showed, unless we call a thing what it is, we can neither think about it clearly nor oppose it.

———

Gregg Easterbrook is a contributing editor at *The New Republic* and a visiting fellow at the Brookings Institution. He wrote this piece for the the May 5, 2007, edition of *The New Republic* <www.tnr.com>.

What Went Wrong?

BY NANCY SHUTE (2007)

A troubled loner who rarely spoke, hiding behind dark glasses. An English major whose creative writing was filled with violence and obscenity so disturbing that professors repeatedly urged him to get counseling. A kid who was bullied in high school for being painfully shy. An awkward young man whose text messages to female students annoyed them to the point that they reported him as a stalker. A college student who kept his grades up, but who appeared so depressed that an acquaintance told authorities he seemed suicidal.

Those are the stark clues that came forth about Seung Hui Cho's mental condition in the past two years. Plenty of people noticed he was struggling. In fact, quite a few tried to get him help. Cho was even briefly hospitalized as a suicide risk in 2005, then released when he told a judge he wasn't going to kill himself. The final, awful revelation came last week, when Cho fatally shot 32 students and faculty at Virginia Tech before turning a gun on himself.

Now, university administrators and campus mental health counselors across the country are re-examining their decades-long struggle to identify and treat mentally ill students. Many are also pondering whether they would have intervened in time if Cho had been one of their students. This painful second-guessing, though more anguished than ever, isn't new. But in recent years, the task has become more challenging, as an increasing number of students arrive on campus with serious mental illnesses such as schizophrenia. At the same time, university officials are told that mental health and privacy laws prohibit them from contacting parents unless the child is clearly a threat to himself or others. Universities have been sued for kicking out students who said they were suicidal—and also sued for not preventing suicides.

"The legal system and the medical system conspire to leave these kids more alone than they should be," says Edward Shapiro, a psychiatrist in Stockbridge, Mass., who often advises college counselors and administrators on these dilemmas. "If the kid isn't failing courses, if they're not hassling people, and they're doing their work, there's not much the colleges can do."

Chris Flynn, who directs Tech's counseling center, has declined to discuss Cho's case. But counselors around the country say they often see students with symptoms as serious as Cho's and struggle to identify which ones are at risk of harming themselves or others, and with how to get them to seek help.

Lucinda Roy, former chairman of Tech's English department, says she told campus police and administrators of her worries about Cho's antisocial behavior and disturbingly violent writing. She says Cho repeatedly rebuffed her suggestions that he get counseling. In December 2005, Cho was detained by campus police after a second female student complained that he had been stalking her via text message and an acquaintance reported to campus officials that Cho seemed suicidal. He was judged "an imminent danger to self or others as a result of mental illness" and was taken to Carilion St. Albans Behavioral Health, a private mental hospital near Radford, Va. A court-ordered medical examination found that Cho "denies suicidal ideations. He does not acknowledge symptoms of a thought disorder. His insight and judgment are normal." A magistrate ruled that Cho was free to go but told him to get outpatient counseling.

Involuntary commitments are exceedingly rare and are ordered only if the person appears in imminent danger, a point of frustration for counselors and family members worried about the safety of someone who is seriously ill. People whose mental problems make them suspicious and paranoid, as Cho appeared to be, often don't recognize that others could help, Shapiro says. "If they're not in sufficient trouble where they're compelled to talk to someone, they get isolated."

It seems clear now that Cho had been isolated, and deeply troubled, for years. Classmates at Westfield High School in Chantilly, Va., say he was bullied for being shy and having an accent. An uncle back in South Korea says that Cho was so quiet as a young boy that some people thought he was mute. But the profile that has emerged of a socially awkward, morose young adult could easily fit a good chunk of the 17 million students on American college campuses. Almost 10 percent of college students say they've seriously considered committing suicide. Thirty-seven percent say they've been so depressed it was difficult to function. More than 30 percent of freshmen say they're feeling overwhelmed a great deal of the time.

"You're supposed to be happy," says Eric Heiligenstein, a psychiatrist who is clinical director for mental health services at the University of Wisconsin-Madison. "College is supposed to be a great time." But that's not the reality for many young adults. In any given year, 14.8 percent of college students say they have been diagnosed with depression. It's also the age when people have the most trouble with drug and alcohol abuse. And it's when serious mental illnesses like schizophrenia and bipolar disorder start manifesting themselves, as the long process of brain development that began in the womb nears completion. Add to that the fact that students feel far more pressured by the high cost of college and the need to excel than in generations past, and it's no wonder that for many, the stresses of college are just too much.

In the past 10 years, much scientific effort has gone into trying to figure out a way to "profile" school shooters and other students who pose a threat so that they can be stopped before they act. A 2000 study of school shooters by the Secret Service found that there is no one profile: The shooters came from many different racial and ethnic backgrounds; were rich and poor, excellent students and D-minus types, socially isolated and popular.

Attempts to identify those who will commit suicide have been equally fruitless. One reason is that not many people kill themselves. Although about 6 percent of people think about committing suicide in a given year, less than 1 percent try, and of those, less than 1 in 70 succeeds. People who are intent on suicide often hide the fact. Suicide risk assessment protocols used by psychotherapists fail miserably at predicting who's most at risk; rather, they're intended to help pinpoint the patient's concerns. "You can't prevent these things," says Gregory Eells, director of student counseling at Cornell University in Ithaca, N.Y. "You can do some things to reduce risk."

Cornell, like many universities, has in recent years intensified its work to detect troubled students and lure them in for treatment. Four years ago, the school started training faculty and staff in how to recognize mental health problems and convince students that going for counseling is "smart" and "strong." Two psychologists are detailed full time to talk with professors and other community members who are worried about students. A phone triage service offers students instant telephone counseling, and informal "let's talk" hours station psychologists and social workers in campus buildings where people live and work.

Last fall, Cornell started screening all students who come to the health service for depression, even if they're just there to get a sprained ankle checked out. And like other schools, Cornell has created a multidisciplinary SWAT team comprising therapists, police, the dean of students, and dorm staffers who meet to discuss troubled students and create a coordinated response. All told, Eells says, students have many more opportunities for free, professional mental health care than young adults who aren't in school. That, he says, along with the lack of firearms on campus, helps account for the fact that suicide rates on American campuses are just half of those among young adults in general.

Campuses are also rethinking how—and whether—to get problem kids off the campus. Expelling students who are mentally ill is a hugely controversial act. Just weeks before the Tech shootings, Virginia became the first state in the nation to pass a law prohibiting schools from ousting students just because they have mental problems or are considered a suicide risk. The law was prompted by several widely publicized lawsuits, including two last year. In one, the City University of New York paid $65,000 to a student who sued because she was barred from her dorm after being hospitalized for a suicide attempt. And in the other, George Washington University reached a private settlement with a student who sued after it suspended him when he sought hospitalization for depression. "Everybody's looking at this in a liability context," says Karen Bower, an attorney for the Bazelon Center for Mental Health Law, who represented Jordan Nott, the GWU student. "It's really not about liability. It's about stereotypes about mental illness." Nott sued under the Americans With Disabilities Act, saying the university had discriminated against him because he was depressed.

In the wake of the slayings, more university administrators will turn to mandatory medical withdrawal as the solution, predicts Gary Pavela, retired director of judicial programs for the University of Maryland. That would be a mistake, he says. Even though the law presumes that young people on campus are adults and should be treated that way, parents feel that many a 20-year-old is just starting on the path to independence.

Still, campus mental health experts say that offering a student an honorable way to take a mental health break is often the best solution, particularly for students who are struggling with isolation and loneliness. "Families can be very helpful and supportive, even though students often feel that they don't want to add pressure or stress to their families, who have often made big sacrifices to support them," says Richard Kadison, director of Harvard's mental health service and author of College of the Overwhelmed. In some cases, Kadison says, parents might want to consider if a child would do better living at home and attending a school nearby.

One question is whether Cho's culture played a role in his apparent refusal to accept help. In general, experts say, members of minority groups in the United States are less likely to use mental health services. "In Korea, mental diseases carry significant stigma," says Young Shin Kim, an assistant professor of child and adolescent psychiatry at Yale University Medical School, who is Korean. "If you have a person in the family with a mental disorder, then your whole family is damned."

Cho's family emigrated from South Korea when he was 8 years old. His mother and father put in long hours in a dry cleaning shop near the family home in Centreville, Va. Cho's older sister, Sun-Kyung Cho, graduated from Princeton University and works for a contractor at the State Department. Cho, too, was poised for success, slated to graduate. "My brother was quiet and reserved, yet struggled to fit in," Sun-Kyung said in a statement. "We never could have envisioned that he was capable of so much violence."

Occasionally, Korean-American kids "have that sense of being of two worlds, not 100 percent Asian or American, and that as much as they are accepted they will never be fully accepted," says Daniel So, a youth pastor at the Korean United Presbyterian Church of San Diego. "It makes it that much harder when you're a teenager."

Of course, many native-born students share the same fears and frustrations. The most striking passages in a 2003 National Research Council report, "Deadly Lessons:

Understanding Lethal School Violence," talk about how all the young people in the afflicted communities lived lives almost wholly separate from their parents and other adults. "Parents and teachers were mostly unaware" of the shooters' frustrations "and of their universal belief that there was nowhere to turn."

College campuses are eerily similar, with few opportunities for mentoring and coaching, leaving many students living in a "youth ghetto." Pavela praises Roy, the English professor, for making multiple efforts to connect with Cho. "There has to be more intervention," Pavela says. "There has to be more from teachers and administrators. They have to be more involved in the lives of the students."

—With Avery Comarow

Nancy Shute wrote this article for the April 30, 2007 edition of *U.S. News & World Report* <www.usnews.com>.

Was Cho Seung-Hui Really Like the Columbine Killers?

BY DAVE CULLEN (2007)

Today is the eighth anniversary of the Columbine massacre, and it is a particularly disturbing one. With his sadistic creative writing, contempt for snotty rich kids, militaristic posing, and heavily plotted revenge fantasy, Virginia Tech killer Cho Seung-Hui has eerily reminded many Americans of Columbine murderers Eric Harris and Dylan Klebold. Cho apparently saw Klebold and Harris as kindred martyrs, giving the boys two separate shout-outs in his suicide manifesto. But how deep do the similarities run? And what can the multiyear effort to understand Klebold and Harris teach us about Cho?

Like Cho, the Columbine killers left a mountain of writings and videotapes, which seemed confusing when doled out in little sound bites. But in time, and in the context of all the evidence, investigators found Klebold's and Harris' ideas diabolically coherent and cohesive, fitting into highly recognizable patterns. Cho may prove tougher to comprehend, because he wasn't just confusing, but inarticulate. In person, he barely spoke. And the two plays that have surfaced are infantile.

Yet television analysts have Cho deconstructed already: He's a madman, he's a psychopath, a schizophrenic, a psychotic—or maybe just an angry depressive. Experts have rendered definitive diagnoses on every network—and they are wildly contradictory. The *Today* show alone has made a grand tour through the diagnostic manual. Thursday morning Matt Lauer proclaimed Cho "*clearly* a psychotic individual." Lauer described psychosis as an evolution from his previous diagnosis of depression. "We should make the differentiation there," Dr. Lauer advised.

A few hours after Cho's videos were aired on NBC *Nightly News*, CNN's Larry King hosted a panel on what drove the killer. A distinguished psychiatrist and psychotherapist who works with the mentally ill saw mental illness. "There are a lot of red flags here for some schizophrenialike or psychotic disorders," said Dr. Gail Saltz, psychiatrist at New York Presbyterian Hospital. Criminal profiler Pat Brown, who works with law enforcement, saw a sane, rational actor in control of his faculties. "He's a vicious psychopath," she said. "He wanted lots of power and control." And neurosurgeon Dr. Sanjay Gupta broached the possibility of physical damage to Cho's brain.

Aside from its brevity, King's discussion turned out to be one of the better examinations of Cho this week, because it pulled together the major theories onto one TV set. Experts from the various disciplines have been coalescing around three possibilities for Cho's underlying condition: depression, psychopathy, or psychosis. Those conditions, often conflated, are extremely different and would offer very different explanations for why Cho killed and what made him snap. (Cho's great-aunt added a fresh wrinkle Thursday, suggesting he might have been diagnosed autistic as a child. It remains to be seen whether this diagnosis was accurate or potentially evidence of another developing malady.)

The predominant initial theory, which still retains support, is that Cho suffered from anger fused with depression. With school shooters, the anger almost always begins with a loss. The definitive Secret Service study on school shooters found the killers varied in every trait except two: every shooter was male, and 98 percent had experienced a significant loss, grievance, or sense of failure. Two-thirds felt some sort of failure, and half had lost a loved one—typically meaning they'd been dumped. Everyone gets dumped and gets dumped on. "Most of us get angry, kick a trash can, drink a beer or two, and get over it," said Dr. Dwayne Fuselier, an expert on gunman psychology who headed the FBI's Columbine investigation. But for a few, the anger festers. "Anger turned inward results in depression," Fuselier said, "withdrawing from friends, relatives, etc."

Most get help or get over it; some get worse and kill themselves. But for a tiny percentage, suicide is not enough. The next step up is a "vengeful suicide," like shooting yourself in front of the wedding photo to splatter it with blood and brains. Some men—nearly always men—take it a step further and shoot the offending boss or girlfriend before himself. For a rare few, that still won't satisfy their rage. They blame everyone for their misfortune, and they want to make sure we feel it and that word travels. Life is hell, they insist, and it's not their fault. If they're going to die, you people will, too.

Columbine killer Dylan Klebold was a classic example of the angry depressive. He told us all about it in his journal and videos. Superficially, Klebold seems a lot like Cho: painfully shy, apparently depressive and suicidal. Both resorted to imaginary girlfriends. Klebold had an actual girl in mind—it was the love he imagined; he had never managed to speak to her. According to a roommate, Cho confided that he dreamed up a supermodel girlfriend named Jelly. She called him Spanky. In real life, Cho stalked a series of women, who spurned his advances and called the police. He rarely expressed emotion, but he was bottling up anger at perceived sleights and abuses. It all spilled out in monotone on his suicide videos: "You have vandalized my heart, raped my soul, and torched my conscience. . . . You have never felt a single ounce of pain your whole life. And you want to inject as much misery in our lives because you can, just because you can."

A smaller but significant number of experts see psychopathic traits in Cho. Klebold's partner, Eric Harris, was a textbook psychopath. Most psychopaths are nonviolent, but when they do turn to murder, the path is much simpler than for the depressive. They are convinced of their superiority and blame the rest of us for their predicament from the start. Cho demonstrated characteristic psychopathic contempt for his peers: "Your Mercedes wasn't enough, you brats," he complained. "Your golden necklaces weren't enough, you snobs." Vodka, Cognac, debaucheries—"you had everything." Psychopaths are cold, calculating, and ruthless, with no empathy for others, so our suffering bears no weight in their calculations. They are perfectly sane and suffer no mental illness—they just don't care. But Cho exhibited none of the social charm characteristic of most psychopaths. And their trademark manipulation and lying for pleasure remain to be seen in Cho.

And then there is the possibility that Cho was psychotic. Dr. Frank Ochberg, an expert on violence and psychiatry, began to wonder about psychoses when he read Cho's plays. Psychosis is a broad term covering a spectrum of severe mental illnesses, including paranoia and schizophrenia. Psychotics can grow deeply disoriented and delusional, hearing voices and hallucinating. In severe cases, they lose all contact with reality and literally don't know what they are doing. They sometimes act out of imaginary yet terrifying fear for their own safety, or instructions from imaginary beings. Anger management doesn't calm them: They truly cannot help themselves.

Several clues to psychosis jumped out at Ochberg in Cho's plays. The endings particularly interested him: "The bad guy wins," he said. Harris and Klebold wrote and illustrated innumerable fantasies, and whether they were portraying heroic Marines battling aliens or vicious killers knocking off students, their protagonist always triumphed. But Cho's protagonists were crushed. That's a common way for schizophrenics to depict their dark sides triumphing, Ochberg said.

The most striking difference between Cho and the Columbine killers is blood lust. Witnesses described Cho emptying his clips robotically Monday—barely a word or a facial expression. Harris and Klebold relished their rampage. They laughed and howled and taunted their victims mercilessly. And their anticipation was equally arousing. "I can taste the blood now," Harris wrote a year earlier. Dylan depicted the slaughter of fictional "preps" in graphic detail, capturing the wail of police sirens and blood splatters in the moonlight. Victims wet their pants and hyperventilated in fear. The huge, hulking murderer emanated "power, complacence, closure, and godliness."

Cho's videos described only *himself* raped, crucified, impaled, and slashed ear to ear. He resorted to pronouns like "it" or "this" to avoid even mentioning his murders, much less depicting them: "I didn't have to do this. . . . It's for my children. . . . I did it for them." In other monologues, he distanced himself even further, implying what he'd begun but refusing to name it: "You forced me into a corner and gave me only one option. The decision was yours. Now you have blood on your hands that will never wash off."

Arrogant, cocky killers do not behave this way.

Ochberg observed Cho's inability to relate to others, a blank affect, disordered thoughts, and perceptions wildly out of sync with reality. "I'm beginning to think he's not responding to abuse and neglect, he's responding to all the fantasies and delusions in his head," Ochberg said Wednesday afternoon. "He could be struggling to fight these things. I'm beginning to think we have a mentally ill guy." Ochberg was hesitant to express those views publicly, but as evidence accumulated and he continued discussions with colleagues, he leaned further in the direction of psychosis. Other leaders in the field tend to be drifting that way as well.

But the best of them are reserving final judgment. "It's hard to diagnose the dead," Ochberg said. "We're going to need more information."

———

Dave Cullen is completing a book on the Columbine killers. He also maintains The Columbine Navigator <www.davecullen.com/columbine>, a Web site about the massacre's numerous myths. Cullen wrote this piece for the April 20, 2007, edition of Slate <www.slate.com>.

Shootings

BY ADAM GOPNIK (2007)

The cell phones in the pockets of the dead students were still ringing when we were told that it was wrong to ask why. As the police cleared the bodies from the Virginia Tech engineering building, the cell phones rang, in the eccentric varieties of ring tones, as parents kept trying to see if their children were O.K. To imagine the feelings of the police as they carried the bodies and heard the ringing is heartrending; to imagine the feelings of the parents who were calling—dread, desperate hope for a sudden answer and the bliss of reassurance, dawning grief—is unbearable. But the parents, and the rest of us, were told that it was not the right moment to ask how the shooting had happened—specifically, why an obviously disturbed student, with a history of mental illness, was able to buy guns whose essential purpose is to kill people—and why it happens over and over again in America. At a press conference, Virginia's governor, Tim Kaine, said, "People who want to . . . make it their political hobby horse to ride, I've got nothing but loathing for them. . . . At this point, what it's about is comforting family members . . . and helping this community heal. And so to those who want to try to make this into some little crusade, I say take that elsewhere."

If the facts weren't so horrible, there might be something touching in the Governor's deeply American belief that "healing" can take place magically, without the intervening practice called "treating." The logic is unusual but striking: the aftermath of a terrorist attack is the wrong time to talk about security, the aftermath of a death from lung cancer is the wrong time to talk about smoking and the tobacco industry, and the aftermath of a car crash is the wrong time to talk about seat belts. People talked about the shooting, of course, but much of the conversation was devoted to musings on the treatment of mental illness in universities, the problem of "narcissism," violence in the media and in popular culture, copycat killings, the alienation of immigrant students, and the question of Evil.

Some people, however—especially people outside America—were eager to talk about it in another way, and even to embark on a little crusade. The whole world saw that the United States has more gun violence than other countries because we have more guns and are willing to sell them to madmen who want to kill people. Every nation has violent loners, and they tend to have remarkably similar profiles from one country and culture to the next. And every country has known the horror of having a lunatic get his hands on a gun and kill innocent people. But on a recent list of the fourteen worst mass shootings in Western democracies since the nineteen-sixties the United States claimed seven, and, just as important, no other country on the list has had a repeat performance as severe as the first.

In Dunblane, Scotland, in 1996, a gunman killed sixteen children and a teacher at their school. Afterward, the British gun laws, already restrictive, were tightened—it's now against the law for any private citizen in the United Kingdom to own the kinds of guns that Cho Seung-Hui used at Virginia Tech—and nothing like Dunblane has occurred there since. In Quebec, after a school shooting took the lives of fourteen women in 1989, the survivors helped begin a gun-control movement that resulted in legislation bringing stronger, though far from sufficient, gun laws to Canada. (There have been a couple of subsequent shooting sprees, but on a smaller scale, and with far fewer dead.) In the Paris suburb of Nanterre, in 2002, a man killed eight people at a municipal meeting. Gun control became a key issue in the Presidential election that year, and there has been no repeat incident.

So there is no American particularity about loners, disenfranchised immigrants, narcissism, alienated youth, complex moral agency, or Evil. There is an American particularity about guns. The arc is apparent. Forty years ago, a man killed fourteen people on a college campus in Austin, Texas; this year, a man killed thirty-two in Blacksburg, Virginia. Not enough was done between those two massacres to make weapons of mass killing harder to obtain. In fact, while campus killings continued—Columbine being the most notorious, the shooting in the one-room Amish schoolhouse among the most recent—weapons have got more lethal, and, in states like Virginia, where the N.R.A. is powerful, no harder to buy.

Reducing the number of guns available to crazy people will neither relieve them of their insanity nor stop them from killing. Making it more difficult to buy guns that kill people is, however, a rational way to reduce the number of people killed by guns. Nations with tight gun laws have, on the whole, less gun violence; countries with somewhat restrictive gun laws have some gun violence; countries with essentially no gun laws have a lot of gun violence. (If you work hard, you can find a statistical exception hiding in a corner, but exceptions are just that. Some people who smoke their whole lives don't get lung cancer, while some people who never smoke do; still, the best way not to get lung cancer is not to smoke.)

It's true that in renewing the expired ban on assault weapons we can't guarantee that someone won't shoot people with a semi-automatic pistol, and that by controlling semi-automatic pistols we can't reduce the chances of someone killing people with a rifle. But the point of lawmaking is not to act as precisely as possible, in order to punish the latest crime; it is to act as comprehensively as possible, in order to prevent the next one. Semi-automatic Glocks and Walthers, Cho's weapons, are for killing people. They are not made for hunting, and it's not easy to protect yourself with them. (If having a loaded semi-automatic on hand kept you safe, cops would not be shot as often as they are.)

Rural America is hunting country, and hunters need rifles and shotguns—with proper licensing, we'll live with the risk. There is no reason that any private citizen in a democracy should own a handgun. At some point, that simple truth will register. Until it does, phones will ring for dead children, and parents will be told not to ask why.

———

Adam Gopnik wrote this piece for the April 30, 2007, edition of *The New Yorker* <www.newyorker.com>.

We're Scaring Our Children to Death

BY PEGGY NOONAN (2007)

This week saw a small and telling controversy involving a mural on the walls of Roosevelt High School in Los Angeles. The mural is big—400 feet long, 18 feet high at its peak—and eye-catching, as would be anything that "presents a colorful depiction of the rape, slaughter and enslavement of North America's indigenous people by genocidal Europeans." Those are the words of the Los Angeles Times's Bob Sipchen, who noted "the churning stream of skulls in the wake of Columbus's Nina, Pinta and Santa Maria."

What is telling is not that some are asking if the mural portrays the Conquistadors as bloodthirsty monsters, or if it is sufficiently respectful to the indigenous Indians of Mexico. What is telling is that those questions completely miss the point and ignore the obvious. Here is the obvious: The mural is on the wall of a public school. It is on a public street. Children walk by.

We are scaring our children to death. Have you noticed this? And we're doing it more and more.

Last week of course it was Cho Seung-hui, the mass murderer of Virginia Tech. The dead-faced man with the famous dead-shark eyes pointed his pistols and wielded his hammer on front pages and TV screens all over America.

What does it do to children to see that?

For 50 years in America, whenever the subject has turned to what our culture presents, the bright response has been, "You don't like it? Change the channel." But there is no other channel to change to, no safe place to click to. Our culture is national. The terrorizing of children is all over.

Click. Smug and menacing rappers.

Click. "This is Bauer. He's got a nuke and he's going to take out Los Angeles."

Click. Rosie grabs her crotch. "Eat this."

Click. "Every day 2,000 children are reported missing . . ."

Click. Don Imus's face.

Click. "Eyewitnesses say the shooter then lined the students up . . ."

Click. An antismoking campaign on local New York television. A man growls out how he felt when they found his cancer. He removes a bib and shows us the rough red hole in his throat. He holds a microphone to it to deliver his message.

Don't smoke, he says.

This is what TV will be like in Purgatory.

It's not only roughness and frightening things in our mass media, it's politics too. Daily alarms on global warming with constant videotape of glaciers melting and crashing into the sea. Anchors constantly asking, "Is there still time to save the Earth? Scientists warn we must move now." And international terrorism. "Is the Port of Newark safe, or a potential landing point for deadly biological weapons?"

I would hate to be a child now.

. . .

Very few people in America don't remember being scared by history at least to some degree when they were kids. After Pearl Harbor, they thought the Japanese were about to invade California. If you are a boomer, you remember duck-and-cover drills. The Soviets had the bomb, and might have used it. I remember a little girl bursting into tears during the Cuban Missile Crisis when I was in grade school.

But apart from that, apart from that one huge thing, life didn't seem menacing and full of dread. It was the boring 1950s and '60s, and the nice thing about a boring era is it's never boring. Life is interesting enough. There's always enough to scare a child.

But now it's a million duck-and-cover drills, a thousand alarms, a steady drumbeat of things to fear.

Adults have earnest discussions about how more and more of our children are being prescribed antidepressants and anti-anxiety drugs. What do you think—could there be a connection here?

Why are we frightening our kids like this, with such insensitivity? Part of it is self-indulgence, part of it is profit, but not all of it is malevolent. Some of it is just mindless. Adults forget to think about kids. They forget what it's like to be a kid.

ABC's John Stossel is a person in media who knows. He did a piece recently on the public-service announcements warning about child abduction. He asked some children if the warnings worried them. Yes, they said. One little boy told him he worries every night "because I'm asleep and I don't know what's gonna happen."

. . .

Children are both brave and fearful. They'll walk up to a stranger and say something true that a grown-up would fear to say. But they are also subject to terrors, some of them irrational, and to anxieties. They need a stable platform on which to stand. From it they will be likely to step forward into steady adulthood. Without it, they will struggle; they will be less daring in their lives because life, they know, is frightful and discouraging.

We are not giving the children of our country a stable platform. We are instead giving them a soul-shaking sense that life is unsafe, incoherent, full of random dread. And we are doing this, I think, for three reasons.

One is politics—our political views, our cultural views, so need to be expressed and are, God knows, so much more important than the peace of a child. Another is money—there's money in the sickness that is sold to us. Everyone who works at a TV network knew ratings would go up when the Cho tapes broke.

But another reason is that, for all our protestations about how sensitive we are, how interested in justice, how interested in the children, we are not. We are interested in politics. We are interested in money. We are interested in ourselves.

We are frightening our children to death, and I'll tell you what makes me angriest. I am not sure the makers of our culture fully notice what they are doing, what impact their work is having, because the makers of our culture are affluent. Affluence buys protection. You can afford to make your children safe. You can afford the constant vigilance needed to protect your children from the culture you produce, from the magazine and the TV and the CD and the radio. You can afford the doctors and tutors and nannies and mannies and therapists, the people who put off the TV and the Internet and offer conversation.

If you have money in America, you can hire people who compose the human chrysalis that protects the butterflies of the upper classes as they grow. The lacking, the poor, the working and middle class—they have no protection. Their kids are on their own. And they're scared.

Too bad no one cares in this big sensitive country of ours.

———

Peggy Noonan is a contributing editor of *The Wall Street Journal* and author of "John Paul the Great: Remembering a Spiritual Father" (Penguin, 2005), which you can order from the Opinion-Journal bookstore. Her column appears Fridays on OpinionJournal.com, where this piece was published on April 27, 2007.

Making a Killing

BY MIKE WHITE (2007)

The first movie I ever made was called "Death Creek Camp." It told the age-old story of a group of teenage guys who set out on a fun-filled wilderness excursion only to be stalked and murdered by a psychopath disguised in a hockey mask and a blue kimono. It was no masterpiece of cinema.

Most of the scenes played out the same way—one of the fresh-faced hikers would get separated from the group. He would hear a noise in the bushes. "Bob? Jerry, is that you? Charlie?" Suddenly, from behind a tree, the stalker would pounce and blood would fly.

Why the killer wore a blue kimono was never explained nor why he wanted these nice campers dead. He was a deranged monster and that's what monsters do. As the filmmaker, I was more interested in how the ketchup would drip off the victim's cheek and where to plunge the retractable knife. I was 12.

The inspirations for this home movie (and the centerpieces of many Saturday night sleepovers) were slasher films like "Friday the 13th," "Halloween" and "Terror Train." My friends and I would eat junk food, drink soda and watch these cinematic bloodbaths until we dozed off, visions of gore and mayhem dancing in our heads.

Even though we all came from religious families—my father was a minister—it was rarely questioned whether our adolescent minds should be exposed to this kind of gruesome material. And clearly, we were the intended audience. My parents never sat and watched, nor did my sister, for that matter. The movies were titillating, shocking and dumb—and we teenage boys thought they were so cool. We devoured them and they, in turn, juiced us up.

After the horrific events at Virginia Tech, the relationship between violence in our movies and violence in our realities is being examined once again. Was Seung-Hui Cho inspired by a movie (the South Korean revenge flick "Oldboy") when he murdered 32 of his classmates and teachers? Was Mr. Cho a deranged predator in a horror film, or was he a lost kid who could have been reached?

Hollywood and defenders of violent films dismiss Virginia Tech as a "unique" event, arguing that Mr. Cho was profoundly alienated from our culture, not at all a product of it. They assert that there are law-abiding, sane American moviegoers who love the thrill of a visual bloodletting, and then there are mentally disturbed people like Mr. Cho, constitutionally wired to do damage—and never the twain shall meet.

These commentators insist there's no point debating which came first, the violent chicken or her violent representational egg, since no causal link has ever been proven between egg and chicken anyway. Besides, violent images can be found everywhere— on the news, in great art and literature, even Shakespeare!

For those who believe that violence in cinema consists of either harmless action spectacles or Martin Scorsese masterpieces, I might suggest heading down to the local multiplex and taking a look at some of the grotesque, morbid creations being projected on the walls. To defend mindless exercises in sadism like "The Hills Have Eyes II" by citing "Macbeth" is almost like using "Romeo and Juliet" to justify child pornography.

The notion that "movies don't kill people, lunatics kill people" is liberating to us screenwriters because it permits us to give life to our most demented fantasies and put them up on the big screen without any anxious hand-wringing. We all know there's a lot of money to be made trafficking in blood and guts. Young males—the golden demographic movie-makers ceaselessly pursue—eat that gore up. What a relief to be told that how we earn that money may be in poor taste, but it's not irresponsible. The average American teenage boy knows the difference between right and wrong and no twisted, sadistic movie is going to influence him.

My own experience as a teenager tells me otherwise. For my friends and me, movies were a big influence on our clothes and our slang, and on how we thought about and spoke to authority figures, our girlfriends and one another. Movies permeated our fantasy lives and our real lives in subtle and profound ways.

It's true nobody ever got shot in the face in my backyard, but there were acts of male bravado performed in emulation of our movie anti-heroes that ranged from stupid to cruel. And there were plenty of places where guys my age were shooting one another all the time. There still are. Can we really in good conscience conclude that the violence saturating our popular culture has no impact on our neighborhoods and schools?

The calamity at Virginia Tech is unfortunately not as unique an event as we'd like to think, but the sheer number of victims has grabbed our attention and inspired some collective soul-searching. As responsible Americans put their heads down on their desks and reflect, should the scribes of popular entertainment be excused to the playground? We screenwriters may be overgrown teenagers who still want to be cool, but we aren't 12 years old anymore. Maybe we're not responsible for Mr. Cho's awful actions, but does that abrogate our responsibility to the world around us?

Most of us who chose careers in this field were seduced by cinema's spell at an early age. We know better than anyone the power films have to capture our imaginations, shape our thinking and inform our choices, for better and for worse. At the risk of being labeled a scold—the ultimate in uncool—I have to ask: before cashing those big checks, shouldn't we at least pause to consider what we are saying with our movies about the value of life and the pleasures of mayhem?

———

Mike White is the screenwriter of "School of Rock" and, most recently, "Year of the Dog." He wrote this piece for the May 2, 2007, edition of *The New York Times* <www.nytimes.com>.

FROM READING TO WRITING

1. Gregg Easterbrook argues that the language we use to talk about Cho Seung-Hui has decidedly moral implications. Using the word "shooter" or "gunman" instead of "killer" or "murder," Easterbrook posits, "remove[s] the moral dimension, making it seem like terrible events just happen—not that human wickedness causes terrible events." Do you agree with this position? Why or why not?

2. Nancy Shute, in "What Went Wrong?" raises questions about campus security. What points does she see as potential sites of intervention for mentally-ill students? Write a letter to an appropriate USC administrator advocating one of her positions.

3. Taking into consideration Dave Cullen's article, how do the ways we categorize Cho Seung-Hui's condition affect our ideas on what needs to be done in order to prevent a similar incident from occurring?

4. How does Adam Gopnik suggest that we heal the nation after the Virginia Tech shootings? What are his reasons for this proposal? Is his evidence persuasive?

5. Both Peggy Noonan and Mike White make significant claims about the impact of violence in the media, but they get to these conclusions in different ways. Trace both Noonan and White's lines of reasoning. Where do their arguments overlap? Where do they diverge? Which do you find more effective? Why?

Four

NATIONALITY, RACE, AND IDENTITY

The Terrible, Horrible, Urgent National Disaster That Immigration Isn't

BY LAWRENCE DOWNES (2006)

Part 1: What's Wrong With 'Getting Tough on Immigration'

I. IMMIGRATION, OVERSIMPLIFIED

The arguments made by hard-line critics of immigration reform are depressingly simple, which makes them simply depressing.

They boil down to this: the immigration problems we have today, and a vast array of other problems, begin and end with immigrants themselves, the people who have committed the offense of being here illegally—or just being here, period, in undesirable numbers, with undesirable habits and undesirable effects on the health of the nation.

Their presence here is seen as overwhelmingly if not entirely bad, an unpardonable offense for which American citizens are made to suffer.

In this view, the problem is not going to be solved by repairing a complex system of immigration laws and regulations, by tinkering with the economic machinery to find a better fit between labor demand and supply, or by being more diligent about enforcing existing rules about workplaces and hiring. And it certainly won't be solved by being creative or more welcoming and humane toward immigrants in a way that rewards their hard work and desire to participate in the system more fully.

It will be solved by keeping people out, and kicking people out. Do that, the restrictionists insist, and you will help resolve a host of other problems—the invasion of neighborhoods and street corners by Latino men; the upsurge of gangs and drugs; urban congestion and suburban sprawl; human trafficking; the demise of white European culture and values; the strain on jails, hospitals and schools, and the threat to the very stability of the United States.

It's no wonder some people compare immigrant workers to locusts, bacteria or an occupying army. If you could find a 250-year-old American to discuss this, he or she would tell you how familiar this all sounds. Identical arguments were once made about Chinese laborers, Japanese-Americans, Roman Catholics, the Irish, Italians, and the original unloved—though fully documented—outsiders, African-Americans. Let's not even talk about American Indians.

II. THE DISTURBING ROLE PLAYED BY FEAR

Many of those who favor a get-tough approach to immigration do not like having their arguments mocked and their tolerance questioned. They hate being dumped into the loony bin with Colonel Custer, the Know-Nothings and the Ku Klux Klan.

That is understandable. But xenophobia is not restricted to a fringe element within the anti-immigration movement. Panicky arguments about the dangers of immigration have been made by supposedly responsible people—including members of the United States House and Senate, and state, county and local officials around the country. United States Representative Tom Tancredo of Colorado may be the best-known xenophobe in Congress. He created an immigration caucus to further his firebrand views. It now has about 100 members and a Web site that is a one-stop shop for fear-stricken anti-immigration arguments.

One member of Mr. Tancredo's caucus is John Culberson of Houston, who issued a "Border Security Alert" last October warning that "Al Qaeda terrorists and Chinese nationals are infiltrating our country virtually anywhere they choose from Brownsville to San Diego." Besides that, he said, "a large number of Islamic individuals have moved into homes in Nuevo Laredo and are being taught Spanish to assimilate with the local culture."

Because of that, Mr. Culberson said, "Full scale war is underway on our southern border, and our entire way of life is at risk if we do not win the battle for Laredo."

The view of America as a nation under siege led the United States House last December to pass an immigration bill, sponsored by James Sensenbrenner of Wisconsin, that sees the problem as entirely an issue of enforcement. It would make it a federal crime to live in the United States illegally, which would turn millions of immigrants into felons, ineligible to win any legal status. It would also make it a crime for churches and social service agencies to shield or offer support to illegal immigrants. The debate in the Senate over immigration reform had its own low moments, including the successful passage of a non-sequitur amendment by Senator James Inhofe of Oklahoma to declare English the country's national language—an undisguised swipe at Latino immigrants and their supposed reluctance to assimilate. A guest-worker program in the Senate bill was sharply scaled back after the Heritage Foundation, a conservative think tank, issued a report warning that if the bill as written passed, the country could end up swamped with up to 193 million new legal immigrants within 20 years. That number, greater than the populations of Mexico and Central America combined, was hysterically off the charts. The bill was hastily amended and the estimates revised downward to a still unrealistic 66 million, or 47 million if you count only net new arrivals, not people already here who would be legalized.(The Congressional Budget Office, by contrast, projects 8 million net new migrants over the next 10 years under the Senate bill. The National Foundation for American Policy, counting newcomers and immigrants already here, studied the Senate bill and came up with a figure of 28.48 million over 20 years, or 1.42 million a year. That's a lot, but far less than the anti-immigration number masseurs would have you believe.)

If you dig into the widely discussed arguments connecting immigrants to things like rampant overpopulation or the demise the English language, you will discern the influence of any number of hard-line restrictionist immigration organizations. Scratch those groups, and underneath you will usually find a kook. There are usually not many degrees of separation from ostensibly rational, often-quoted organizations like the Federation for American Immigration Reform, which calls itself a nonprofit, nonpartisan organization dedicated to research and policy study, and people like its co-founder John Tanton. The Southern Poverty Law Center, which tracks hate groups, says that Mr. Tanton, a retired Michigan eye doctor, "is widely recognized as the leading figure in the anti-immigration and 'official English' movements in the United States."

A profile on the law center's Web site says: "In addition to FAIR, where he still is a board member, Tanton has been a central player in an array of anti-immigrant, nationalist groups and institutes, including Pro English, U.S. Inc., Center for Immigration Studies (CIS), U.S. English, and Numbers USA."

Who is this Mr. Tanton? He is someone who has depicted Latino immigrants as a horde of alarmingly procreative Roman Catholics of questionable "educability," and who runs a publishing company, Social Contract Press, that sells titles on immigration topics like "The Camp of the Saints," that have been denounced as racist and vile.

The Anti-Defamation League, in a 2000 report on FAIR, traced its nativist roots and offered what it called "a glimpse into how advocacy can cross the line into a divisive and troubling tendency toward scapegoating of the foreign born." It's worth reading.

FAIR and its allies are is hardly the only hard-core immigration foes out there, and their more unprintable opinions would be rejected passionately by great numbers of people in the enforcement-only immigration camp. But their influence is still significant: their arguments mirror the immigration talking points of many leading conservatives. And it shows just how much of the current panic has its source not in people's gray matter, but in their viscera.

III. AN ARRAY OF TOO-COSTLY SOLUTIONS

The restrictionists have a variety of clear-cut solutions. But the reassurance they offer those who worry about immigration is a false one, for a simple reason: their price tags are simply too costly for them to be seriously considered. Anyone who seriously proposes them is engaging in little more than demagoguery.

Take the restrictionists' favorite solution: deporting 'em all. It is a straw man in the debate, because only the most rabid talk-show callers would be willing to pay that price— $200 billion or more, at least double the Department of Homeland Security budget. And that cost does not even count the psychic toll it would take on our nation to rip immigrants out of homes and workplaces and schools and eject them. As unlikely as we would be to pay this cost once, it is even less likely we would be willing to pay it again and again, as we would no doubt have to as new immigrants arrived to replace the ones who were sent home.

Then there is the hard-liners' other favorite solution—fortifying the border, which any restrictionist will tell you is the most urgent priority of immigration reform. Billions have already been lavished at the southern border—California, Arizona, New Mexico and Texas—in walls, patrols and technology. Since 1986, the border patrol budget has been raised 10 times, and the number of border patrol agents has gone up eightfold. The House of Representatives, in its disturbingly get-tough immigration bill, wants to erect a

700-mile wall, which will fatten a few powerful contractors' bottom lines by untold millions, and President Bush has already sent in the National Guard.

These price tags will only seem higher when measured against results.

We have already spent a lot on enforcement, and have precious little to show for it. A Wall Street Journal editorial titled "The Border Brigades" noted that "U.S. immigration policy at least since the passage of the Simpson-Mazzoli law in 1986 and certainly since the 1990's has emphasized 'security' above all else." But this has not slowed illegal immigration in the least. The Pew Hispanic Center reports that the population of illegal immigrants has shown "steady growth" in recent years, which is putting it mildly. In 1986, the last time the country was consumed with a debate about immigration reform, the illegal population was estimated at 3 million. Today it's 11 million to 12 million.

Those who are wedded to the iron-fisted approach oppose any immigration reform that would ease pressure at the border by including a temporary-worker program or granting visas to legalize people already here and their relatives waiting to enter. They will not admit, or do not understand, that they are simply insisting on throwing good money after bad.

IV. LOCAL FEAR AND LOATHING

America's approach to immigration has to be worthy of a nation built on immigration, and dedicated to the ideal of equality. Unfortunately, the measures that are being implemented at the local level—where most of the action is occurring—look a whole lot like bullying and bigotry.

Cities and counties in California, Arizona, New York and elsewhere have enacted ordinances cracking down on day laborers, the most visible and vilified members of the immigrant population. That does not mean that illegal immigrants are not being hired. It simply means the government is making their harsh lives harsher. Day laborers have been subject to police harassment and illegal evictions. And that does not include the freelance hostility and abuse directed at them by abusive contractors, regular citizens, protesters and vigilante groups like the Minuteman Civil Defense Corps.

Other places are focusing on ripping immigrants out of the social fabric—passing rules that bar them from being helped by the society they are contributing to. In April, Gov. Sonny Perdue of Georgia signed one of the harshest anti-immigration laws in the country, a package of restrictions that, among other things, requires adults seeking state benefits to prove they are here legally, and state agencies to check every employee's immigration status. Never mind that much of Georgia's economic vitality stems from the immigrants operating its textile mills, picking its peaches, preparing its meals and building and tidying its expansive suburbs.

Some of these outbursts are merely silly. In Danbury, Conn., the mayor has cracked down on volleyball, a favorite pastime of Ecuadoran immigrants. Nashville tried to ban taco trucks but not, tellingly, hot dog stands. Silly, but mean-spirited.

V. SENDING IN THE POLICE

Others local measures are more serious. The most wrongheaded of the local crackdown impulses may be the one to enlist state and local police to enforce immigration laws. Law-enforcement officials themselves hate it. City councils and police departments around the country are resisting efforts to make them shoulder what is and should remain a federal responsibility.

For example, Minneapolis and St. Paul's mayors and police chiefs have spoken out against a proposal by the Minnesota governor to enlist local police officers in immigration enforcement—and they are speaking for many other mayors and police chiefs who feel the same way. Chief John Harrington of the St. Paul Police Department told the St. Paul Pioneer Press that local cops were already buried in other work—like fighting violent crime—that was more urgent than checking people's immigration papers.

"The City of St. Paul doesn't have enough cops to handle the load of things we already have on the books, the basic city ordinances and statutes and those egregious federal crimes—drug trafficking, kidnapping, bank robbery—that we have now," Chief Harrington said. Checking up on immigrants, he insisted, would take his officers away from tracking down serious criminals, including sex offenders. He also argued that the cost of sending 550 officers for the six months of training that Immigrations and Customs Enforcement officials recommend could better be used fighting crime at home.

There is another way cracking down on immigrants hurts, rather than helps, in the fight against crime. As Chief Harrington and many others have pointed out, local police officers—unlike their federal counterparts—need the help of the community to do their jobs. Illegal immigrants are already a hidden population. Turning local cops against them will drive them further into the shadows. This will hinder investigations—witnesses will vanish, and criminals, uncaught and unpunished, will flourish.

Part 2: The Harder but Better Way

I. A 796-PAGE ATTEMPT TO DO BETTER

If the hard-liners trying to kill comprehensive immigration reform are a disciplined chorus singing one note, pure and bell-clear, the other side is more like a crowd struggling to pull together the "Messiah" in a stadium sing-along. They are an alliance of the dirt-poor and powerful, of plainspoken Republicans like Senators John McCain and Lindsey Graham and a lion-in-winter liberal, Edward Kennedy. They include business interests, some labor unions, editorial pages like this one and editorial pages not at all like this one. A diffident President Bush has been trying to fit in somewhere.

What unites these motley allies and distinguishes them from the hard-liners is their understanding that bountiful immigration is a blessing—a mixed blessing, but a blessing all the same. Their efforts to solve the problem lack clarity. They grapple with contradictions. Their approach, embodied in a 796-page brick of a Senate immigration bill, is at once punitive and forgiving. It throws money at the border but also includes a path to citizenship for many, though not all, of the illegal immigrants already here. It paves the way for millions more whose hopes of entering the country have been stymied, sometimes for decades, by bureaucratic backlogs.

Critics of the bill have called it unworkable and incomprehensible. They have a point. But flawed as it is, the Senate bill is the only one that acknowledges and seeks to enhance the contributions that immigrants make to this country's economy and culture. It's the only one that tries to enlist immigrants present and future, illegal and otherwise, in the job of making this country better. And therefore it is the only one with any hope of making the excruciatingly difficult and complicated cost-benefit equation of immigration end up in the black.

II. HOW BADLY WE NEED THEM

As a conduit for workers into this country, the existing immigration system is greatly out of balance with demand. The legal path for an unskilled worker to enter the United States is through one of about 5,000 visas issued for such workers each year, which means it is no path at all. The United States economy has adjusted, of course, by hiring temporary workers and illegal workers by the millions. The invisible hand doesn't ask for ID for the roughly 500,000 people who enter illegally each year.

Immigrants—legal and illegal—fill a vital niche in the American economy. They make up 12 percent of the United States population but 14 percent of its workers, according to the Congressional Budget Office. From 1994 to 2004, the agency said in a report last December, the number of foreign-born workers grew to 21 million from 13 million, a rise that accounted for more than half of the growth of the U.S. labor force. According to the American Immigration Lawyers Association, immigrants hold 40 percent of farming, fishing and forestry jobs in the United States, 33 percent of jobs in building and grounds maintenance, 22 percent of food preparation jobs and 22 percent of construction jobs. Tearing the approximately one third of those workers who are illegal away from their livelihoods and families would be ruinous to the economy, particularly the agricultural and tourism industries in states like California.

Throw away the arguments that immigrants are tax leeches. On the contrary. They pay more in taxes than they consume in services. They all pay sales taxes. Illegal immigrants who use fake Social Security numbers to get hired pay income and payroll taxes— but don't collect Social Security and are ineligible for Medicaid. The amount of unclaimed Social Security tax has more than doubled since the 1980's, to roughly $189 billion. Because immigrants tend to be younger and healthier than native born workers, they use government services more sparingly. A comprehensive study of immigration and its economic effects—"The New Americans: Economic, Demographic, and Fiscal Effects of Immigration," by James Smith and Barry Edmonston for the National Research Council in 1997—summed up its conclusions this way: Because immigrants on average have less education than the native-born, they earn less and pay lower taxes. But immigrants also consume far fewer services. As a result: the average immigrant pays nearly $1,800 more in taxes than he or she costs in benefits, even when you factor in the cost of public education for his or her children.

The report emphasizes that the proper way to understand these expenditures is as an investment in America's future. In a country that absorbs about one million newcomers per year, each yearly cohort of immigrants pays $80 billion more in taxes over the course of a lifetime than it consumes in services. In other words, there is no economic crisis being caused by immigration—but there could be one if it came to a halt.

An open letter to President Bush and Congress made the rounds of the Internet last week. Signed by more than 500 economists in varied fields, including five Nobel Prize winners, it argues that immigration is a net economic gain for America and its citizens and "the greatest anti-poverty program ever devised."

III. ACKNOWLEDGING THE COSTS

It would be wrong to argue that tighter enforcement has no place in sensible immigration reform, or that immigration does not bring with it an array of problems. There are all sorts of things that supporters of immigrants should—and do—own up to. It is not only good-hearted immigrant workers with sore feet, blisters and hungry families, for example, who pour across America's borders. Drugs, counterfeit goods and weapons do, too. No terrorists have been known to have entered from Mexico, but it could happen. If there were a realistic way of sealing the borders against all drug dealers, felons, and terrorists, we would certainly want to consider it. But there is not. Law enforcement should focus vigilantly on all of these, but the border is not where those battles will be won.

There is one conundrum of illegal immigration that is very real: the cost it imposes on people who would compete for jobs with undocumented low-skilled immigrants. It stands to reason—how could a job market absorb so many new people and not see wages fall? An often-cited study by two Harvard economists, George J. Borjas and Lawrence F. Katz, found that from 1980 to 2000, a wave of illegal immigration from Mexico had reduced the wages of high school dropouts in the United States by 8.2 percent.

But that study gave only a partial picture. It failed to account for the economic growth that immigrants cause—the many jobs that cheap immigrant labor creates, and the gaping demographic niche it fills. As Eduardo Porter pointed out in The Times in April, "Over the last quarter-century, the number of people without any college education, including high school dropouts, has fallen sharply. This has reduced the pool of workers who are most vulnerable to competition from illegal immigrants."

This is no consolation to the janitor in Los Angeles who has seen his job disappear, or the by-the-book contractor who can't compete with the fly-by-night operation that hires—and underpays and exploits—illegal day laborers by the truckload. Any serious attempt at immigration reform has to grapple with the fact that many Americans—young black men, among others—who have been overlooked and shunned in the job market for generations will likely continue to be overlooked. That is especially true as the economy hums along through the energy of immigrants, many of them illegal. If immigration decreases costs and increases the national prosperity, we need to find a way to make sure that those gains are shared with those on the low rungs of the economic ladder.

IV. ANGER ON THE GROUND

Farmingville, a working-class community on Long Island that has been utterly transformed by Latino immigration, is a prime example of the challenges that burgeoning immigration poses and the resentment it inspires. Longtime residents became acutely aware of the presence of dozens of Latino men on street corners and piling up in illegally subdivided rooming houses. This was a clear example of globalization at the local level, and to many in Farmingville the costs were obvious and unacceptable. Young men crowding the 7-Eleven parking lot, intimidating women and girls with sexually aggressive catcalls. Men urinating in the street, loitering and generally creating a nuisance of themselves. You couldn't talk to these people, and you couldn't make them go away.

They were the visible manifestation of broken borders, and some aggrieved people took it on themselves to solve the problem. They beat up workers and firebombed their homes. They held signs and marched. They harassed and heckled day laborers, they wrote letters and had meetings.

The Farmingville conflict is being repeated, in different forms, in communities across the United States. But the anti-immigrant activists in Farmingville accomplished nothing, unless you consider waging a successful battle against the creation of a day-labor hiring site a success. Five years after the furor erupted and became the subject of a well-regarded documentary, Farmingville has as many day laborers as ever. It doesn't have a hiring site.

V. THE COST ABROAD

There are many books that document the hardship for Latinos migrating to El Norte. The book "Coyotes" by Ted Conover, a white journalist with a fondness for living his stories, is a good one. In villages where most of the young men go abroad, the result is a a reliable stream of remittances to their hometowns—$25.5 billion in 2003, according to the Congressional Budget Office—which is a vital source of revenue for poor countries.

But it also means that communities, particularly small ones in the south of Mexico and Central America, lose their brightest, best and strongest men and women for months or years at a time. The energy that could be expended in making a community grow or a local business prosper is spent in another country, and while cash is welcome, it is often a poor substitute for having children and spouses at home, as the toll in broken families attests.

VI. UNCERTAIN POSSIBILITIES

The current immigration "system," if you can call it that, is broken. It's rich in perversities. So is the effort to fix it.

The House bill is simply noxious. The Senate alternative has some serious flaws. It attempts to divide the population of illegal immigrants into three groups, being relatively gentle on some immigrants and tough on others, depending on how many years they have been here. Millions of newer arrivals will have to volunteer to leave the country—to report to be deported. It's hard to imagine that a significant majority of them will ever do so. But in any case, it seems highly unlikely the full Congress could, in the current climate, pass anything as good as the Senate bill.

A significant number of pro-immigrant groups have already concluded that doing nothing—passing no immigration bill this year—would be better than passing some awkward hybrid of the existing Senate and House bills.

They may be right. With elections looming in November, the get-tough argument may have the upper hand. It is an approach supported by a majority of the House, backed up by thousands of constituents who have been making phone calls and mailing bricks (yes, actual bricks) to their elected representatives to drive the point home. But it's foolish to think that walling off America and reforming immigration through enforcement alone is anything but self-defeating.

It's not only because the costs of security are so high, or because the contributions that legal and illegal immigrants make to this country are so positive. Those who have been working as hard as the hard-liners have been to close this country off to people who came here to seek work and a future have a radically astringent vision of what this country should be. To militarize the border, to turn illegal immigrants into felons, means trying to reverse the polarity on the American magnet, to repel the people who have struggled, dreamed and died to get here.

It means turning this singular country into just another industrial power with a declining birthrate and a self-defeating antagonism to the foreign born. It means defining down what America stands for, no matter what the cost to the American economy, its traditions and values and moral standing.

It's dangerous. It's not rational. But the argument on the restrictionist side isn't about being rational. It's about being afraid.

—Lela Moore contributed research for this article.

———

Lawrence Downes wrote this piece, part of the Talking Points series, for the June 20, 2006, edition of *The New York Times* <www.nytimes.com>.

Honesty in Immigration
BY NEWT GINGRICH (2006)

The thousands of people we have seen marching in the streets of our cities and the planned May 1 boycott to protest U.S. immigration policy are the product of two decades of a fundamentally dishonest immigration system.

For more than 20 years, the United States has failed to control the borders or enforce immigration laws while many U.S. businesses have profited by breaking the law. In turn, the U.S. government failure to enforce the immigration laws has encouraged outright defiance of federal authority by certain state and local jurisdictions. Adding insult to this deplorable state of affairs is an immigration bureaucracy that has been slow, cumbersome, rude, heartless, and incompetent in the discharge of its duties.

This dishonest system has lured millions to enter our country illegally and obtain work here illegally.

WHERE ARE WE AND HOW SHOULD WE PROCEED?

A detailed set of policy recommendations can be found in a working paper that I released today at the American Enterprise Institute (www.aei.org). I have also recently recorded several radio commentaries on aspects of the immigration challenge. But let me provide here an overview.

First, it is essential to understand how big and how serious this problem is.

Second, it is equally essential to understand how big the changes will have to be to really solve the problem.

Third, it is important to follow a logical set of sequential, sustainable solutions that build a momentum that over time will result in a rational and orderly immigration policy acceptable to a majority of the American people.

Getting there is a matter of national survival both in immediate and in the long-term.

First, we must deal with the immediate. Open borders are a grave national-security threat. Why have a multibillion-dollar ballistic-missile-defense system when a terrorist can rent a truck and drive a weapon of mass destruction across the border? Gaining control of our borders is therefore an immediate and pressing national-security requirement. The secondary effect is that it would dramatically stem the flow of illegal immigration, illegal drugs, and the human trafficking of slaves (mostly female and mostly for sexual exploitation).

The longer-term threats of illegal immigration are economic and cultural.

Economically, in a world of vast income differences, instantaneous communications, and cheap travel (even when illegal), we cannot continue to allow a wide-open illegal employment system. The current flood of illegal migration if left unchecked for a period of decades will decisively undermine the economy in both economic and legal terms.

Culturally we have shifted from an integrating, English-speaking American citizenship focused model of immigration to an acceptance of foreign habits (which are going to include corruption), foreign loyalties (illustrated by the waving of foreign flags by many of the marchers, some with attitudes of contempt) and the insistence (not necessarily by immigrants) on creating non-English speaking legal and educational structures.

Instinctively, most Americans understand the corrosive effects of lawlessness on the economy and the culture. A USA Today poll two weeks ago recorded that 85 percent believe that to earn citizenship, immigrants should be required to learn English.

Note that in the same poll 84 percent would punish businesses that employ anyone not here legally, 81 percent would increase the number of officers patrolling the border, 60 percent would block them from using hospitals and schools, 61 percent say illegal immigration should be a crime and 52 percent would make it a crime to assist someone known to be here illegally.

Most Americans are open to people who want to become American, who will work hard, obey the law, and who are willing to learn English and American history. Within this framework of patriotic integration it is possible to be both pro-conservative and pro-immigrant.

LAW FIRST

But this framework cannot stand unless it is built upon the solid foundation of the rule of law.

For example, cities which receive hundreds of millions of dollars in aid from Washington block their police force from asking about an individual's legal status (88 percent of the country favors cutting such cities off from federal money). In 2004, there were zero (0) federal enforcement fines imposed on American employers who were breaking the law by hiring people illegally.

No one believes the border is anywhere close to being controlled. Few have confidence that the government will ever seriously do something about it. In the same regard, the idea that the federal government could actually run an effective identification program for worker visas is not credible either which is why every audience applauds when I suggest outsourcing it to Visa, MasterCard, or American Express.

The radical difference between this business as usual paper-tiger effort and the seriousness of the required metrics-based solution is startling.

Lawmakers in Washington are trapped because they keep trying to appease lawbreakers while their fellow Americans watch with disgust. On the other hand, if lawmakers boldly outline a real sequential and systematic set of solutions they could win the argument in the country and move towards a workable policy that honors our values. If they fail to do this, American voters will eventually impose their will on Washington with painful political consequences for some incumbents.

Why is it so hard for some Republicans to understand the center-right view that it is far better to have Left-liberal Senators filibustering against controlled borders and effective legality than it is to appease them while enraging conservatives? If the issues are defined and communicated correctly, center-right support would grow into the 80-percent range (look again at the USA Today poll numbers).

It is possible to describe the situation in terms which are for both legality and immigration, for both controlling the border and having a worker visa program, for being sympathetic to newcomers and determined to sustain American civilization and for respecting other languages while embracing English as the language necessary for success in America. It is possible to do this in terms which will be acceptable to most immigrants and to most Americans.

It is partially a question of what we are opposed to.

If the Left-liberal choice is this map of Texas and Mexico combined with the rest of the U.S. missing, and the Mexican flag flying above an upside down American flag at an American pubic school in Arizona and the people who not only break the law but refuse to learn English while saying publicly they want to reunite the Southwest with Mexico, then you can safely assume that more than 80% of Americans will oppose you.

Left-liberals understanding that they cannot defend the above, which is why they would like us instead to believe that they are fighting against racists who want to close the border, behave harshly against innocent people, break up families, exploit migrants, and live in a xenophobic world.

An intelligent center-Right coalition would be for both security and immigration, for accuracy in identity (including a voter card with id and a biometric worker visa card) and patriotic integration of those who want to become American.

An intelligent center-Right coalition would define the opposition in terms that would lead most honest migrants to feel comfortable with defining clearly the underlying anti-security, anti-accuracy, anti-American civilization patterns of the hard Left-liberals.

Most Republicans could be convinced to articulate and follow an intelligent center-Right coalition if they understood it and understood the power of the language and the power of the definitions.

SEQUENCING

Charles Krauthammer has it right. There has to be a sequence of reestablishing trust.

First, control the borders with decisive legislation aggressively implemented with tight deadlines. Once we have stopped the illegal flow of people we will have demonstrated the seriousness necessary to gain both the credibility and the leverage needed to implement the next steps. Fortunately, a bipartisan consensus has emerged that securing the borders is indeed priority number one. Three national leaders have it right in their shared view that border control is the first step. Senator Frist is exactly right when he wrote recently that "to build confidence among Americans and Congress that the government takes border security seriously, we have to act to help get the border under control right now." Senator Clinton is also right when she recently recognized the need for a "smart fence" along the border to enhance security. And Democratic National Committee Chairman Howard Dean is also correct when he said last week that "the first thing we want is tough border control."

Accordingly, the Congress should pass a border-control bill immediately. There is no reason the Congress cannot immediately pass such a bill, and then concentrate on additional immigration reform measures later. The Congress should immediately act on this one aspect of immigration reform around which there is widespread agreement. America needs real border control immediately.

Second, establish patriotic integration and the primacy of English (English first, not English only) combined with a requirement that Americans can only vote in American elections and applicants for citizenship have to select where their loyalty is.

Third, establish real enforcement against unlawful employment by employers and especially against employers who are breaking both immigration and taxation laws. Make clear that the dishonest hiring and tax evasion of the last two decades are over and there will be expensive penalties for people who break American immigration law. Insist that cities enforce the law or lose their federal funding. All this can be done with the right incentives and without rounding up anyone.

Fourth, establish an outsourced worker visa program with a biometric identity card, a background check, and a 24/7 computerized real time verification capability so no business can claim ignorance. Permit businesses to send workers home to apply for their worker visa as a deductible business expense. Eliminate the fly-by-night subcontractor shams that are clearly set up to evade the law. Maximize the opportunity and the incentives for people who are here to return home and become legal.

Note that none of the above requires direct action against people who are here illegally. None of these steps will break up families or cause undue hardship. The focus of all these initial efforts is to stop the attraction of new people and to dry up the illegal jobs. If illegal jobs cannot be found, people will have no choice but to pursue legal means to employment.

Implemented correctly, these steps would convince people about the seriousness of the new policy and its enforcement creating a much more rational environment to discuss the emotional and complex situations affecting families and long time workers and residents.

As we transform our immigration system from a dishonest to an honest one, it is understandable that those living and working here illegally—especially those who have lived and worked here illegally for a long period of time—would be anxious and fearful about the future. While our two-decade-long failure does not mean that we are required to maintain a dishonest system, it does mean that must have a humanitarian period of transition as we replace an illegal channel of immigration with a legal one.

There is a huge difference between a cautious limited policy of integrating the people attracted by a dishonest and shameful policy (the deliberate cultivation of illegality over the last 20 years) and amnesty which will only reinforce the message of the dishonest past and create a wave of people who will continue to pour in expecting the continuation of the yesterday's failed policies.

If lawmakers can agree to the first four steps we have plenty of time to think through and work out the details of a humane, compassionate, and legitimate process of patriotic integration for people who were lured to America by an incompetent government and lawbreaking businesses and who do not deserve to bear the full brunt of popular anger at such dishonest and hypocritical policies.

If the American people see that their leaders are serious and determined to control the border then create an effective worker-visa program along with a comprehensive program of patriotic integration into American civilization they will be much more supportive of a program for helping those with deep connections to America find their legal place in American society.

———

Former House Speaker Newt Gingrich is a senior fellow at the American Enterprise Institute and author of *Winning the Future: A 21st Century Contract with America*. He wrote this piece for the April 26, 2006, edition of the *National Review Online* <www.nationalreview.com>.

Ugly, the American

BY JAMES PONIEWOZIK (2006)

Few prime-time TV characters are more American than Betty Suarez. On ABC's hit comedy-soap Ugly Betty, she's a fashion-magazine assistant who is distinctly unfashionable—chunky sweaters, frizzy hair, bear-trap braces—but succeeds through good old Yankee values like perseverance, optimism and hard work. Smart and sweet-hearted, she embodies the Puritan-Shaker-Quaker principle of valuing inner good over outer appearance. She's as Norman Rockwell as a chestnut-stuffed turkey. The actress who plays her is even named America Ferrera.

And yet—if you listen to some politicians and pundits—she should have been booted out of the country years ago. Betty's father is an illegal immigrant from Mexico. To hear Lou Dobbs and Pat Buchanan tell it, our fellow citizens are boiling with resentment against people like Betty. Taking our kids' spots in college! Helping themselves to our orthodontia! Stealing low-paid magazine jobs that rightfully belong to American trust-fund babies!

So why do some 14 million people a week watch and root for her? Because it's easier to hate a straw man—or a straw Mexican—than a person, even a fictional one. And because, as our pop culture shows, Americans' attitude toward foreigners is more complex than the build-a-fencers would make it.

On its face, the political debate is about illegal immigration—law, security and fairness. But this immigration panic, like past ones, taps into fears not limited to illegals. Who gets to say what American culture is? Is there enough room—and prosperity—to go around? Ugly Betty's overarching story is metaphorically about the same battle. Betty is an outsider at Mode magazine not just because she dresses badly but also because of things that have to do directly with her ethnicity. She grosses out her skinny, preening, (mostly) Anglo co-workers by bringing empanadas for lunch. Her features are broad and unmistakably Mesoamerican. (Ferrera is strikingly pretty in real life.) On her first day at work, she wears a hideous poncho with GUADALAJARA emblazoned on it.

Betty's scheming co-workers resent her in the same way immigration demagogues do: she's an interloper. Yet she succeeds—and even wins over some of her Mode enemies— for exactly that reason. Like generations of immigrants, legal or not, she brings fresh eyes, a tireless work ethic and a different perspective to revitalize a tired institution. (Like Borat, she's in the tradition of the outsider who helps America see itself.) Ironic, amid the effete fashionistas, that she's the one the audience identifies with as an everyday American.

It's no coincidence that Ugly Betty the series is itself an immigrant, a remake of a worldwide-sensation telenovela franchise. That's what makes our pop culture so vital: from TV to music to fashion, it is constantly transfused by foreigners who are able to out-American Americans.

Take reality TV. It embodies everything there is to love and despise about this country— ambition and greed, free-spiritedness and vulgarity, boldness and shamelessness. But it is an American staple that was pioneered overseas, much like pizza and gunpowder. American Idol is British. Big Brother, Dutch. Survivor, Swedish and imported by Mark Burnett, a Brit. And every week on reality shows, Americans embrace foreigners with Emma Lazarene openness—Heidi Klum and Simon Cowell, East European and Latin hoofers on Dancing with the Stars, Mexican boxers on The Contender and a Siberian drag queen on America's Got Talent.

Reality TV may be so hospitable to immigrants because it's a fun house mirror of the immigrant experience. You leave your comfort zone and prove your worth with little more than gumption and (maybe) talent. Wherever you come from, you embrace a new, anything-goes culture that values chutzpah over tradition and propriety. Emigré Burnett's shows, like The Apprentice, are full of Horatio Algerisms about industry and opportunity— not unlike Ugly Betty.

Political observers suggest that immigration law will be one of the areas where a Democratic Congress and a Republican White House may be able to reach consensus. Before they do, they should flick on a TV. They would see that you can pass laws and put up walls but it is much harder to erect a fence around your culture. (Just ask the French.) That while borders need to be protected, new blood is what makes this country the maddening, fantastic free-for-all that it is. And that what makes Betty ugly is, in the long run, what makes us America the beautiful.

———

Media and television critic James Poniewozik wrote this column for the November 27, 2006, edition of Time magazine <www.time.com>.

As American as Vartan, Luis and Na

BY CINDY CHANG (2006)

To the people who suggest it might be easier if he calls himself Victor, Vartan Zhamkochyan has a simple answer: no way. And though his last name is more of a tongue twister than his first name, that, too, is nonnegotiable.

Mr. Zhamkochyan and his wife, Naira Mnatsakanyan, shunned the time-honored immigrant tradition of anglicizing their names when they became United States citizens last month. Both are determined to keep using their full Armenian names, despite the obvious inconveniences.

"They can't say my first name or my last name," said Ms. Mnatsakanyan (whose full name is pronounced NIGH-rah meh-naht-sah-KHAN-yahn), 35, an accounting student from Burbank, outside Los Angeles. "It's really hard for them. But I love for them to try and say it, since it's my name, it's my father's name."

Hayedeh or Heidi? Estuardo or Steve? Simhe Kohnovalsky or Sam Cohn? From the ragtag Polish farmer at Ellis Island to the wealthy businessman who arrives on a first-class flight from Tehran, immigrants with names likely to trip up the average American have to confront questions about one of the most defining pieces of a person's identity.

Plenty of immigrants still change their names to something easier for their new compatriots to pronounce. But unlike their Ellis Island predecessors, modern immigrants live in a multicultural society where assimilation no longer means having to sever all ties to where they are from.

Today's anglicizations are less likely to be forced by bosses or teachers and more likely to be the product of careful consideration about the tradeoff between fitting in and giving up a part of one's heritage, immigrants and cultural experts say.

Increasing acceptance of non-mainstream names seems an inevitable next step, as immigrant pride finds a prominent place on the national stage—witness the millions of Spanish speakers chanting "Si, se puede" ("Yes, we can") in the streets last spring—and new Americans maintain a firm grip on their native languages, foods and customs.

Only 16 percent of the nearly 700,000 people who became naturalized citizens in the last year requested a name change, according to statistics from the United States Citizenship and Immigration Services. The rest decided to stick with given names like Quirino, Takero, Wenyi and Erendira.

"Obviously, early in the 20th century, with the whole Americanization movement, people were encouraging the immigrant community to be more American," said Marian Smith, the immigration services historian. "If you fast forward 50 years, you find an America where people say that's something you really have to think about, how much of your identity is your name. To even suggest to someone that they change their name is to suggest there's something wrong with their name as it is."

While many choose American first names for their offspring, that is also changing. Angel was the most popular name for Hispanic boys born in New York City in 2005, according to its Health and Mental Hygiene Department, with Jose and Luis also among the top 20. There were 162 Carloses, 95 Giovannis, 41 Guadalupes, 25 Anjalis and 17 Yukis born to New Yorkers last year.

In a country where falafel and pad thai are now nearly as commonplace as Chinese takeout, some children of immigrants are even reclaiming their ethnic names, suddenly announcing that they will no longer use the American first names their parents gave them but will henceforth be known as Aiko or Ying-hui.

"We feel much more accepted into American society now," said Hongxia Liu, who came to the United States from Beijing in 1986 and has kept her Chinese name, which means rainbow. "Why not keep our own identity, our cultural heritage, including the name, especially the name coming from your parents?"

Ms. Liu, the director of an international legal assistance center in Washington, says that friends puzzle over how to pronounce her name, especially the "x." She tells them to think of it like the "sh" sound.

She and her husband, Jianye Wang, named their daughter and son Lumay and Jayon — derivatives of the Chinese names Lumei and Jiyang. The Wang children, now teenagers, love their names.

"We wanted to keep the Chinese identity but in the meantime make them easy to pronounce and remember," Ms. Liu said.

Tina Cordova, who owns a construction company in Albuquerque, grew up in an era when many Hispanic parents avoided speaking Spanish at home in the hope that their children would grow up to be wholly American. Her father, Anastasio Antonio

Cordova, always went by Tony, and he named his four children Tina, Tammy, Matthew and William.

Now, all of Ms. Cordova's immigrant employees go by names like Santiago and Alejandro. Her grandchildren, Marcus Philimon and Demetrius Anthony, have names that, if not traditionally Mexican, are a departure from the "Leave It to Beaver" names of her generation.

"Everyone was trying back then to fit in, hence me and my brothers and sister have very American names," said Ms. Cordova, 47. "Now there's a tendency toward not feeling so uncomfortable naming your children something that sounds ethnic."

Based on data compiled from birth certificates, Stanley Lieberson, a Harvard sociology professor, concluded that until the 1980's, immigrants quickly conformed to prevailing norms in naming their children. But he also noticed that African-American names diverged increasingly from the mainstream in a pattern that correlated with growing social status and racial pride. A similar trend may be developing among immigrants today.

"Declaring I am whatever it is I am is cool now, where it might not have been earlier, partly because of a greater tolerance to nonassimilation," Professor Lieberson said. "There is a shift over time toward ethnic assertiveness."

Frank and Na Hong, like many other Asian immigrants, gave their two children American first names and Korean middle names. Their son, Timothy Seung-Ho Hong, often fended off ethnic slurs while growing up in Seattle and New Orleans.

But in college, Mr. Hong took ethnic studies classes and joined Asian-American advocacy groups. When he moved back to New Orleans six years ago, Mr. Hong started going by Seung-Ho, later shortening it to Seung after people had trouble pronouncing the full name.

The transition has mostly gone smoothly, though his father still slips up and addresses him as Timmy. People routinely butcher the name, calling him Shawn or Sang—it is pronounced "Sung"—and are more likely to assume that he is a foreigner. But for Mr. Hong the inconvenience is worth it.

"I wanted to more strongly connect with my history, my culture and having my name be kind of like a reminder of who I am," said Mr. Hong, 30, who is the legislative director for a New Orleans city councilwoman.

Some Asian-Americans who started out using their ethnic first names switched to more traditional American names, only to reclaim their original names as adults. After moving to Indiana from Southern California, Fumiko Chino's parents decided she would have a tough enough time being half Japanese in the Midwest without having a foreign-sounding name. From then on, she was known by her middle name, Catherine.

Ms. Chino is now using her Japanese name again, and three of her four siblings have also reverted.

"I love the fact that it's an old Japanese name," said Ms. Chino, 29, who until recently worked in the art department of an anime film company in Houston. "People who are Fumikos are in their 70's. It's unique, and I like that. It also helps clarify who I am. I hate getting the question, 'What are you?'"

In Hollywood, too, where name changes are as common as nose jobs, the tide may be turning, as Asian actresses like Zhang Ziyi and Gong Li star in big-budget productions.

The actress Ming-Na tried going by Maggie and Doris as a teenager, an attempt to fit in better at a school in the Pittsburgh area, where she was the only Asian student. But she said none of those names felt right, and she stuck with her given name as she tried to forge a career in Hollywood, even rejecting advice from Wayne Wang, the director of "The Joy Luck Club," that she anglicize it.

She went on to become one of Hollywood's best-known Asian-American actresses. At her suggestion, the Chinese-American doctor she played on "ER" underwent a name change from Deb to Jing-Mei.

"What's great is that as you grow up, you have a stronger idea of who you are and pride about your heritage," she said. "It becomes more of, 'No, no, you guys have got to come around to learn how to pronounce our names.'"

———

Cindy Chang wrote this piece for the October 12, 2006, edition of *The New York Times* <www.nytimes.com>.

Welcome Candy, Sam, & George: Immigrants Change Countries, and Their Names

BY YVONNE ABRAHAM (2007)

They entered ornate, flag-filled halls, ready to swear their first oaths of allegiance: Jiong Ping Huang from China; Mohammad Hussam Sawar from Syria; Dung Thanh Ho from Vietnam; and Gjergji Cani from Albania.

They emerged after moving ceremonies, bearing proof of their new US citizenship, smiles, and something else. Jiong Ping was now Candy. Mohammad became Sam. Dung was now Brandy. Gjergji became George.

"I adjusted to my new environment," said Cani, a Medford accounts coordinator who immigrated to the United States with his family five years ago. "Here, diversity is the norm, but you have to adapt yourself in this new culture."

The roiling national debate over immigration has been largely driven by questions of how waves of new arrivals are remaking American society.

But the urge to assimilate in the most conspicuous way—changing one's name—remains surprisingly strong in this era of cultural diversity.

A Globe review of 1,000 recent name changes filed at the US District Court in Boston found the desire to adopt American names was especially common among Asians, whose given names have pronunciations that can confound Americans. Arab and Muslim immigrants, whose names have brought them closer scrutiny in recent years, were also disproportionately represented.

Until the 1960s, immigration historians say, most immigrants took new names to ease their transition to American life. But in that decade, the rise of the civil rights movement triggered a new pride in ethnicity. At the same time, the number of countries sending people to the United States greatly expanded, making foreigners—even those with unfamiliar names—more a part of the fabric here.

Still, nationally, about 16 percent of immigrants who become citizens change their names, according to the most recent statistics available from the US Citizenship and Immigration Services.

And while no comprehensive tally is kept by Massachusetts, the Globe found that during a three-month period that ended in January, 20 percent of those who became naturalized citizens selected new names. Of those, approximately 1 in 3 chose to Americanize their names.

While the Globe review is not scientific, patterns emerged: Vietnamese immigrants were most likely to choose common American names to replace their original ones, followed by immigrants from China. In part, that reflects a greater desire to blend in, specialists said.

The Vietnamese, many of whom came here as refugees, are eager to move on, said Muzaffar Chishti, director of the Migration Policy Institute office at the New York University School of Law.

"For people who didn't come from that level of insecurity, the psychological need is not that powerful," Chishti said.

Hiep Chu, executive director of VietAID, a community organization in Dorchester, said another force is at work among the Vietnamese: an intense desire to succeed in the mainstream.

"Changing their name is one of the things they think will help them advance into American society," Chu said.

Jenny Streeling, 26, a Vietnamese immigrant and student at Worcester Polytechnic Institute, changed her name from Dinh Tieu Dang when she became a citizen in December. She said she did so because, "my name is so hard to pronounce; I didn't feel comfortable in class."

Streeling's parents were not pleased.

"They'd like me to be comfortable with the name I have," she said.

Chu said, however, that more Vietnamese parents want their children to have American names, like most of the youngsters in his Vietnamese language program do.

Two of Chu's siblings changed their names, to Henry and Elizabeth, when they became citizens. He kept his given name and chose Vietnamese names for his two children, who were born in America.

"I don't think we have to sacrifice anything to be American, not even my name," he said. "I absolutely feel that would be a loss, culturally, identity-wise."

His children have sometimes found their names a challenge. Chu said he once saw his daughter, DanThuy, argue with another girl who would not try to say her Vietnamese name. He sat his daughter down when she was 6 and offered her the chance to change it to something easier to pronounce. She refused.

"She's 16 now, and she's really proud of her name," Chu said.

The workplace exerts its own pressure, especially if immigrants have names co-workers struggle to pronounce.

"The workplace is where practicality collides with political correctness," said Shawn Saucier, spokesman for Citizenship and Immigration Services. "'How much time do I spend trying to learn his name?' 'How much time does he spend trying to teach me his name?'"

Sze Lun Wong, a student at Bunker Hill Community College, changed her first name to April when she was naturalized last fall, fearing her Chinese name would hurt her chances of landing a job. Wong, who arrived from Hong Kong in 2001, said her teachers have trouble saying her name. She worries that employers will look down on her.

"You write down your Chinese name, they think, maybe you just came here, maybe you can't handle the job," she said. "They want to hire people from here. Now, people will think I am born here, maybe my English is good, maybe I'm able to handle the job and be in America."

Wong said her parents were unhappy she would no longer be known as Sze Lun, which means "family support."

"In China, your name has meaning, and they wish it will be good for you for your whole life," Wong said.

Each of the immigrants interviewed by the Globe said they had to weigh competing questions when deciding whether to change their name: How difficult would their lives here be if they kept their given names? And how much would they be giving up if they abandoned them?

For George Cani, it wasn't much of a struggle: After emigrating with his family from Albania five years ago, he simply switched to the English version of his given name, Gjergji.

It has made navigating life in the United States much simpler, he said. "The root of the name is same," said Cani. "But it's easier for communicating."

Like others, Cani said he feels more confident with a more common name: "If you spell a foreign name for people, I don't think you are very welcomed," he said.

Vanitha Kumar's former name, Vanitha Vijaykumar, was "a mouthful," she said, creating all manner of e-mail mix-ups at the high-tech company where she worked. She wasn't particularly attached to her old name, she said, since last names are not commonly used in India. So she lopped off the beginning of her surname when she became a citizen.

"It was mostly to make it easier on others, and us, I guess," said the Fitchburg resident.

For Mary Elizabeth Gray, the calculation was far more difficult. The 43-year-old social worker, who was born in Turkey, changed her first name, from Muhubet, which is pronounced "MOO-hoo-bet."

"Nobody could pronounce it," said Gray, a resident of Randolph. "And it was a disadvantage for me, in advancing my career, and everything else."

She said that since Sept. 11, 2001, her given name has held her up, especially at airports, and subjected her to unwanted scrutiny. She said she was often called upon to defend Islam, even though she is not practicing.

"It is very amazing," she said. "They see my name, and no matter what passport I have, they ask where I come from, do I know about the Shia and the Sunni. It was really becoming uncomfortable for me. You feel like you're defending yourself every single day."

But since she changed her name, Gray hasn't felt quite right: Perhaps she gave up too much to fit in more easily, she said.

"I do regret it," she said, explaining that she chose Mary Elizabeth because it came closest to her old name. "I feel like that's not really me. I really want to continue the name my grandmother gave me."

She is now considering changing her name back.

"I should deal with it in a different way; I should ignore people," she said. "I should not just give up who I am."

Yvonne Abraham wrote this piece for the February 4, 2007, edition of *The Boston Globe* <www.bostonglobe.com>.

Fade to Blonde

As an experiment in ethnic identity, a proud, political Latina reaches for the bleach
BY BELÉN ARANDA ALVARADO (2007)

When I think of the space where Latinas and blondness meet, I always remember Iris, a Puerto Rican classmate from my days at Columbia University. Iris was one of those women whom men generally like and women generally don't. She was more comfortable with playful banter than serious exchanges, and it was rumored she liked flirting with other women's boyfriends. But to many of the other Latinas in our class—at least those newly politicized and hyper ethnically aware, like me—she was guilty of larger crimes. Iris once infamously represented the Puerto Rican student group by offering free salsa lessons while wearing a white ruffled peasant blouse, hoop earrings and bright red lipstick. She never disguised her love of traditional, totally un-PC frat parties, the kind where they played AC/DC's "You Shook Me All Night Long" to pack the dance floor. And she dyed her hair blond. An orange-y, brassy blond.

At the time, my biggest desire was to make my light-skinned Chilean self look as identifiably Latina as possible. Saddled with a hair texture that was, at best, ethnically ambiguous and, at worst, simply wavy, I coveted Iris's naturally tight, corkscrew curls. It was the kind of mane I would've described as "Jewish hair" when I was still going to high school in Rockville, but now it seemed to be Caribbean-beauty perfection. Iris's decision to color it was unfathomable, a sure sign of succumbing to mainstream "white is right; blond is better" beauty standards. It couldn't have puzzled me more if she'd slapped on some blue contact lenses and asked us to call her Madison. Didn't she love her brown self?

I solved my own hair dilemma by visiting the JC Penney salon while on a trip home and getting the chunky white girl behind the counter to give me a spiral perm. She botched it enough that I got my money returned, but, to my elation, people back at school let me know that they thought this—my botched perm—was my true hair. They assumed I'd been blowing it straight until then. Joy! My ethnic identity unmistakably announced.

After our 1995 graduation, more than 10 years would pass until I would see Iris again. It would be at a reception hosted by Columbia's Latino alumni group, and, in the weeks before, I would think of Iris frequently. She would show up brunette. But there would be another blonde in attendance — me.

A few weeks before the reception, I was asked to go blond for this article. The editor was looking for someone politically aware and proud of her Latina looks. I literally wrote the book on Latina beauty. (Really. It's on Amazon.com.) What's more, I just happened to have already marked on my calendar a perfect testing ground for this change-of-tresses: the reunion, where friends would be receiving awards for going on hunger strikes and taking over buildings to persuade the university to add a Latino studies major. Imagine the escandalo when I walked in blond.

My former classmates, I imagined, would think I'd done it for the usual reason: to snag a little of the love our society ladles on blondes. Consider a study cited in the Chronicle of Philanthropy last year: When the researchers sent a bunch of undergrads out collecting donations door-to-door, pretty girls unsurprisingly brought in the most money — but blondes far out-raised equally fly-looking brunettes. Yet another study related that, given a choice of hair color, most men making more than $75,000 a year would pick blond partners. A scientific article by a McGill University anthropologist posited that the reason there are so many flaxen-haired Europeans may be that during the Ice Age, when successful male hunters were in short supply, women with eye-catching blond hair had a mating-game advantage over their darker peers.

Latinos come in all colors, but our standard mix of European, African and indigenous heritage means that naturally golden hair, while it does occur, is rare. So any bonus blondness brings is beyond pretty much the whole ethnic group — which, on some level, feels unfair and infuriating. No wonder so many of us turn to chemicals: Across the board, Latinas buy more hair care products — including dyes and the attendant deep-conditioning treatments — than women in any other ethnic group. And no wonder the Latinas who equate going blond with changing your name from María to Mary disdain their frosting cap-, highlighting brush-wielding sisters.

I'm aware of all this. And I love being Latina: I'm convinced that, at some point or another, everyone who isn't part of our cool cultural hybrid secretly wishes they could be. But 10 years past college, I craved another sort of privilege: that of unburdened whimsy. If white women can change their hair color the way they change their lipstick — with complete impunity and no worries over "correctly" representing their community —

why couldn't I? Even women's studies majors now march on Washington in tight pink baby-tees that scream, "This is what a feminist looks like!" So had enough time gone by that I could be a righteous, fierce, representin' Latina, and yet go blond?

I told the editor I'd do it.

As soon as I got off the phone, I went out and bought the beauty bible for Latinas on the lightening path: Us Weekly, the supermarket rag that regularly features photo after photo of dyed and highlighted Latina celebs. Jessica Alba, Jennifer Lopez, Shakira, Eva Mendes—they're all there, having gotten lighter-haired as their stars rose. (Cameron Diaz is claiming she's going to stick to her new brown locks, but I suspect it's a post-breakup dye job—meant to shock, not to stay.) In the issue I bought, practically the only Latina celeb missing was beautiful, intelligent, raven-tressed Salma Hayek. I love Salma. I bet she'd kill in a big-budget superhero flick (like Jessica) or as the girlfriend to corrupt cop Denzel Washington (like Eva). But instead she seems—to me at least—to be one of the most under-appreciated Latina actresses out there. Why don't we see her more? I wasn't even sure what new movie Jessica Alba was in, but there she was full-page in another tabloid, getting her nails done at a charity event. Maybe if Salma got highlights . . .

I called various salons in town and started getting an education in the economics of blondness. While the women's magazines I read as a teen promised easy blond streaks via lemon juice, the truth is that taking hair from jet black (that's me) to something approximating blond requires many chemicals, many salon hours and many dollars. The cheapie drugstore, do-it-yourself route isn't available, as the chemicals needed to strip dark hair of its pigment aren't legally sold to anyone without a beautician's license. (And with good reason. The smell alone is enough to cause tears.) Salons around town gave me preliminary estimates starting from $250 to $500—emphasizing that the bill was liable to grow once the stylists actually got a look at my hair. And that was without the expensive conditioning shampoos and weekly deep-conditioning treatments I'd need afterward, to prevent my ends from splitting, frizzing and breaking off completely.

I decided that I'd go to a Dominican-owned salon I'd seen close to my home in Wheaton. A Latina hairdresser, I reasoned, would have experience taking a client with chemically relaxed hair like mine from one end of the color spectrum to the other. And the salon would do it for the bargain-basement $250—all The Washington Post was willing to spend.

It took not one, but two days of six-hour sessions to get to a passably blond hair color. At the end of the first, I left thinking I looked strawberry blond. At home, my neighbor set me straight: My hair was actually Irish-jig red. I could have auditioned for "The Lord of the Dance." After much on-the-phone complaining—and then begging—with my stylist ("You were happy with it when you left," she kept saying, impatiently, in Spanish), she took me in for another session, gratis, to add blond highlights. And that, she told me, was as blond as I was going to get. My hair certainly didn't look God-given, but at least it could reasonably be described as blond.

When I got home, my sister, her boyfriend, my neighbor and my boyfriend gathered around. The unanimous verdict: a thumbs-up. Only one person registered disapproval: my 5-year-old daughter, Natalia. "Mami, you painted your hair," she said, running her hands over my tresses. "Your hair is dark like mine."

I've always been the culturally conscious parent, making sure she had plenty of "Dora the Explorer" DVDs to offset the glossy, blond perfection of Cinderella, Sleeping Beauty, Barbie and countless other mermaids and fairies. But in my rush to seize my blond moment, it hadn't occurred to me that my daughter might connect my change to her own stunning, raven hair. I'd be going back to my real hair color soon, I told myself.

In her book *Blonde Like Me*, author Natalia Ilyin describes the blond effect as "a gentle rise in the tidewaters of public friendliness." In her brightest moments, the blond Ilyin reports, she was the recipient of impulsive marriage proposals and the cause of minor traffic accidents; at times she felt like "power and sex personified"—exactly as I'd always thought blond life would be.

My expectations for myself were more modest. A compliment—or a drink?—from a stranger. Salesclerks with suddenly improved attitudes. A heightened interest in what I had to say.

In the first few days, my new hair color definitely gave me a little buzz. At brunch, my family suggested that it flattered my skin tone, maybe even more than my natural color did. And my boyfriend's growled comment, "You look gooood," had me feelin' frisky. We were both getting a nice boost from my frosted tresses.

But there were unexpected bumps along the way. The day after my initial salon visit, my reflection caught me by surprise as I came out of a bathroom stall. What I saw in that unself-conscious moment: bland, blah, like-everybody-else-ness. I'm light-skinned, with what can be described as Caucasian features. To many people—Latinos and Anglos alike—I don't "look Latina." Until that moment, I'd had no idea that I wielded my black hair in the same way that I use the accent in my first name and my long, vowel-ending hyper-ethnic last name: as a banner, letting people know in no uncertain terms "Sí, soy Latina!" Without it, I felt erased.

Entire books have been written about blondness. Ilyin's made the biggest impression, because there I found a perfect description of my motivations: I was what Ilyin calls an "ironic blond," someone making a statement with an overt appropriation of a style not originally intended for her. Think Madonna, Li'l Kim or RuPaul, who, when questioned about the politics of his wigs, said, "I'm not going to pass as white, and I'm not trying to . . . [but] I want to create outrageous sensation, and blond hair against brown skin is a gorgeous, outrageous combination."

Gorgeous outrageousness was also what I was after, especially as I prepared to attend the Latino alumni reception at my alma mater. Imagining gasps and looks of horror, I planned ahead, getting a spray tan and even considering (briefly) wearing the blue contact lenses that would create a perfect fake hair/fake eyes/fake tan triumvirate of wildly inappropriate personal grooming choices for a politically correct college-educated Latina. Oh, the whispers, the stares, the scandal!

But when I arrived at the dinner and met friends I hadn't seen in years, they embraced me and said . . . "Hi." I felt the need to explain my experiment, but if the women said anything about my hair, it was that they really liked it. That threw me off. They weren't supposed to actually like me as a blonde, much less tell me I looked better. I waited expectantly for the reaction from one friend in particular, Jenny. An architect of the hunger-strike-building-takeover-sparking-massive-national-media-attention endeavor, she was Puerto Rican, worked for a nonprofit and lived in a predominantly Latino section of town. In other words, homegirl was down. When she saw me she, said, "Oh, you changed your hair." I complimented her on her 'do, and I'm pretty sure that after that we went and got a drink from the open bar. Nothing else. Nada.

There was only one friend, a black woman, who told me she thought I looked "less Latina." On a black or darker-skinned Latina woman, she said, blond was okay; they'd never be mistaken for either being white or wanting to look as if they were. But on me, with my fair skin and straight hair, it was too close to "passing" for her comfort. The closest I can get to blond-on-brown outrageousness is to get a fake tan. But no one would think I was embarking on a subversive beauty experiment. They'd just assume I was trying to get a job at Hooters.

Iris was now a brunette working for the Cleveland port authority. She'd attended this Latino alumni event every year since its inception, she said, flying in from Ohio for the weekend. She seemed amused that I remembered her as a blonde.

"It was such a short time in my life," she told me later. She said there'd been a price to pay for the color change at the time. From Latinos of both genders, she said, "the reaction was, 'You're too whitewashed.'" But it had been worth it. The change had allowed her to step out of the stereotyped role of the submissive Latina. "It was like Mariah with Mimi, like Madonna with Dita," she said. "I felt like I was a different character, more free, more daring."

Who knew? Iris had been an ironic blonde, too.

According to Iris, Latino men had been particularly disapproving of her change. I'd had a different experience. About a week before, on a weekday afternoon, a guy probably 10 years younger than I had sidled up as I was waiting to cross a street and said: "Hey, ma, you look good! You got a man?" At the time, I was pushing my sleeping daughter in her stroller—a scenario that, in my experience, deters most men. But not this guy. He even worked her into his whole approach: "She yours?" he asked. "Aw, she beautiful just like you." Either he was really, really hard up, I'd thought, or the blond hair really was working a mojo of some kind.

But the men at the Latino reunion—the same Ivy Leaguers who had known Iris years before—ignored my blondness completely. Forget any ramped-up flirtatiousness, it was hard getting them to talk to me at all. When I finally approached one and asked point-blank, "Do you notice anything different about me?" he got such a panicked look on his face that I thought maybe, by accident, I'd asked him if I looked fat. "You changed your hair. It's what women do," he practically wailed.

A few weeks later, Jenny and I had brunch, and I broached the topic of blondness again. "I only heard from someone else later that you were doing it for an article, and I have to say I was relieved," she told me. A-ha! Here it was: the "What were you think-ing?" discussion, the outrage at a hegemonic white-dominant concept of beauty that left all non-blondes to feel marginalized. Heated debate! Emotional exchanges!

"I think it was the wrong tone of blond, and I think that is a mistake a lot of Latina women make," she explained. "I've been thinking about going blond, too, and I wanted to figure out how to get the right blond, instead of that orangy blond so many of us get that I just think looks so tacky."

Afterward, I e-mailed around to see how many of the women I'd seen or talked to since changing my hair color shared Jenny's caveat. A number of them e-mailed back in the affirmative. Going blond was fine, but the wrong shade? Eeewww. So we can be upper-crusty Bergdorf blondes, but not drugstore blondes?

Apparently so.

There had been a time, in the early, giddy days of my blondness, when I'd considered keeping the new color, at least for a while. The Post had promised to take me back to my natural black, but maybe, I'd thought, it could be persuaded to pay for a touch-up instead? In the name of research? Now, despite tons of conditioner, my hair looked dried, frizzy and beat. I'd tried re-dyeing my eyebrows myself, to match my tresses, and that looked terrible, too. It's not that I didn't want the kind of hair my friends were saying was "the right kind" of blond. I just didn't have the money. And it wasn't worth it to spend any of my own funds on coloring.

If the experiment had ended there, it might have left me with the impression that all you need for politically liberated, whimsy-inspired blondness is fistfuls of cash. But then came the wedding.

A Latina friend was getting married. The reception was held in a funky loft space, and I was full of the pleasure of attending—until I found my table. There, accompanied by her preternaturally tan, distractingly handsome Latino boyfriend and sporting both a short aqua mini-dress and a head of perfect, white-gold hair, sat my doppelganger, another dyed Latina. She was talking—no joke—about vacationing in St. Barth's. Far from the only rubia at the party—there's a saying that Latinas don't go gray, we go blond, and the older generation at this shindig bore that out—she was the only one who rankled me.

With astonishing quickness, I made a series of decisions about who she was. I decided that if I settled down next to her and asked her how she kept her double-processed ends from splitting or what conditioner she used, she'd probably whip out a much-handled photo of a blond baby, swear it was her and insist that she was "simply going back to nature." She probably tries to live her life as a real blonde, I thought. And gets away with it, too. Because she probably has the money and time that can give anyone a swinging, shiny Pantene ad head of hair. She wasn't an ironic blonde like me.

I ended up leaving the wedding early. On the way home, though, a thought struck me. About a week before, I'd been on the phone with one of my Latino friends from business school, and told him I'd gone blond. "Then you can get a job at Sin City," he joked, referring to a local strip club frequented by young, working-class Latinos. We had both laughed. Being compared to a stripper hadn't bothered me—there's something so unapologetic and edgy about the stereotypical stripper look. But the idea of being confused with a blonde who might be trying to pass was horrifying. The problematic blonde, for me, was the woman at my table, who, despite my own complicated feelings about being blond, I immediately assumed was trying to hide her ethnicity. But then, where did that leave the bleached-blond Latina? If your hair is "not the right tone," then you're tacky, cheap, orange. And irony, as Iris's experience showed, is no protection. But if your privilege—both of skin color and of wallet—allows you to execute the transformation too well, you're trying to pass?

Damned if you do; damned if you don't.

After the wedding incident, it was all work and no fun, as my poor locks strained under too many chemical processes. I wasn't sure I'd really gotten to the bottom of the blond conundrum, but I knew I'd had enough. A second wedding gave me just the push I needed to go back to brunette. My roots had long been showing, as my boyfriend himself had pointed out. The blond hair had to go.

I did what many a Latina has done in moments like this: I called my cousin. As a real-life hairdresser, she's subjected herself to various hair color incarnations. When she came to save me with a color rinse and shag haircut, she herself was sporting a tongue-in-cheek platinum mullet with deep purple on the sides. "You'd better really be ready to go back to being brunette," she scolded me. She said she'd had too many clients come in claiming to want some change, only to end up crying in her stylist's chair. "These women," she sighed, shaking her head. "In the end, they just can't handle it."

And there it was. I, in fact, do have a deep connection with her customers, Latina and non-Latina alike. I didn't like this change. The change in status from being more Obviously Hispanic to Ethnically Ambiguous, at best. The misinterpreted intentions. It was all too stressful.

I'll stay brown and proud, *muchas gracias*.

Though I'd still love to try those blue contact lenses . . .

———

Belén Aranda-Alvarado is a brunette marketing manager in New York City, where she lives with her daughter, Natalia—also a brunette. She wrote this piece for the March 11, 2007, edition of *The Washington Post* <www.washingtonpost.com>.

Typecasting Muslims as a Race
MATTHAI CHAKKO KURUVILA (2006)

As the war on terror heads into its sixth year, a new racial stereotype is emerging in America. Brown-skinned men with beards and women with head scarves are seen as "Muslims"—regardless of their actual faith or nationality.

Law enforcement measures, politicians, religious leaders and the media have contributed to stereotyping Muslims as a race—echoing the painful history of another faith.

"Muslims are the new Jews," said Paul Silverstein, an anthropology professor at Reed College in Oregon who studies the intersection of race, immigration and Islam. "They're the object of a series of stereotypes, caricatures and fears which are not based in a reality and are independent of a person's experience with Muslims."

The Muslim caricature has ensnared Hindus, Mexicans and others across the country with violence, suspicion and slurs. And it has given new form to this country's age-old dance around racial identity.

With fair skin, green eyes and brown hair, Dailyah Patt is white. But when she puts on a head scarf, Patt has discovered, people see her as something altogether different.

The Modesto, California-born convert to Islam has had people categorize her as Palestinian, and she's been told: "Go back to your own country." So Patt removes the hijab, as the head scarf is commonly referred to, when she goes to job interviews or has to fly.

"I can pass as Christian," said Patt, 27, a Palo Alto, California, resident, who was frustrated by repeated airport security interrogations until she stopped wearing a scarf. She feels "oppressed" for feeling forced into shedding a required article of the faith.

Nida Khalil, on the other hand, is Palestinian, spent many of her teenage years in the West Bank city of Ramallah, and deeply identifies with Palestinian politics. A nonpracticing Muslim, she doesn't wear a head scarf. People tell her they think she is Latino.

She can't think of a single instance in the past five years when she's felt harassed for looking like someone from the Middle East.

"I feel really badly for women who have to live in the U.S. that do wear hijab," said Khalil, 26, a San Mateo, California, resident. "I can't even imagine all the snickers or stares . . . or the disrespect they get from Western fanatics."

Patt and Khalil's experiences show how race works, say scholars who study the phenomenon: People often project their assumptions onto others based on physical characteristics, even ignoring their own experiences.

Caricaturing a faith as a race poses particular problems because there is no set of shared physical characteristics. For example:

- Most Arabs in the United States, such as Ralph Nader, are not Muslims.
- Many Palestinians are Christian. Indonesia is the world's most populous Muslim country, but its residents don't resemble the stereotype.
- African Americans make up more than a quarter of the U.S. Muslim population, more than any other ethnicity. Complicating matters, Muslims who are black often are confused with Black Muslims, Nation of Islam followers, who abide different beliefs.

"You can't define what a Muslim looks like," said Saifulloh Amath, 23, a San Jose, California, resident who is Cham, an ethnic group native to Vietnam and Cambodia. His family has been Muslim as long as it can trace. But he is taken for a "devout Buddhist." "You can't stereotype all of humanity under one dress code," Amath said. "In the middle of the Vietnamese jungle, you have people who speak Arabic," the language of the Quran.

For women, the stereotype revolves around wearing a scarf, which complies with a religious requirement to cover their hair.

For men, the caricature has almost nothing to do with faith because there's no physical attribute unique to Muslim men. The male stereotype involves beards and skin, eye and hair color, and names.

"Sam" Hachem usually doesn't introduce himself by his real first name. With sandy-brown hair and gray-green eyes, the clean-shaven Hachem said people often guess after hearing his accent that he is "Eastern European."

But once he gets comfortable with someone, Hachem usually tells them his first name is Hussein and that he's a Lebanese immigrant.

At that point, people react. They immediately move to subjects around terrorism.

Once when he revealed his name at a bar, someone joked and asked him if he was going to blow up the place. Hachem retorted, laughing, "No, there's not enough people."

"When they hear the name, I'm a totally different person," said Hachem, 29, a non-practicing Muslim. "They automatically think of trouble."

The Oakland resident believes he could easily use his real name full time in the Bay Area, which he thinks is accepting of difference. It's just easier to start off with Sam.

The idea of mass violence in the name of religion is a millennia-old theme in many faiths. But the Sept. 11, 2001, attacks gave Americans their most dramatic and direct experience with violence under the banner of Islam. The act of 19 hijackers has been assumed to represent the beliefs of the estimated 6 million Muslims in America, regardless that few share their beliefs.

That narrow prism has been exaggerated by many factors, such as antagonism toward Islam among some evangelical Christians, who have described Islam as "evil" and have viewed the war in Iraq as an opportunity for conversions.

But beliefs are hard to spot on the street, said Professor Howard Winant, a sociologist of race at UC Santa Barbara and co-author of "Racial Formation in the United States." And stigma demands a physical image.

"We have to get racial, because it's got to work through appearance in some way," Winant said.

Intensified law enforcement scrutiny, especially at airports, has played a large part in creating this new racial identity, say Winant and other academics who have studied the "racialization" of Muslims.

Immediately after Sept. 11, across the United States more than 1,000 men from Muslim countries were detained, mostly on immigration charges. The majority were deported.

The U.S. Department of Justice acknowledged that many of the accusations of terrorism that resulted in immigration arrests have been generated solely by race-based perceptions. In one instance—out of many cases revealed in 2003 by the department's inspector general—a tipster called the FBI about a grocery store that he said was run by "Middle Eastern men" and seemed to have "too many people to run a small store." One man was arrested.

Then, in 2002 and again in 2003, men and boys living in the United States from roughly 20 Muslim countries who didn't have permanent residency were required to register with immigration officials or face deportation.

Politicians and military leaders have characterized Islam as evil. Army Lt. Gen. William Boykin, an evangelical Christian, has told church groups that the U.S. war on terrorism has a religious foundation. "Satan wants to destroy this nation, he wants to destroy us as a nation, and he wants to destroy us as a Christian army," he said in 2003.

And President Bush has been inconsistent in his characterizations of Islam. In 2003, making good on a campaign promise, he issued guidelines that banned racial profiling by federal law enforcement. But there was one exception: national security, including immigration.

Days after the Sept. 11 terrorist attacks, he denounced bigotry toward Muslims and declared from a Washington, D.C., mosque that "Islam is peace." But this summer, after an alleged plan to blow up planes headed from London to the United States was thwarted, Bush said Aug. 10 that the United States "is at war with Islamic fascists."

"The United States has always had this tendency to racialize its international conflicts domestically, to view international conflicts as domestic threats," said Winant, the UC Santa Barbara professor. "As a nation of immigrants, it's the easiest place in the world to internalize its external conflicts."

During World War II, Germans, Italians and, in particular, Japanese were viewed as suspicious on national security grounds. Similarly, the rise of communism in the Soviet Union was paralleled by Red Scares at home in the 1920s and again in the 1950s.

Winant said the Arab-Israeli conflict has helped frame stereotypes of Arabs and Muslims.

"The U.S. is so heavily allied with Israel that the kind of day-in, day-out demonization of Arabs that is associated with that conflict comes home with a vengeance to the United States," he said.

. . .

News and entertainment media also play a role in cultivating this new racial image, consciously or not.

The image of Muslims is closely associated with conflict—the wars in Iraq, Afghanistan and Israel, or the Emmy Award-winning Fox show "24," which has dramatized terrorism.

The news cycle's barrage of images, from Guantanamo and Abu Ghraib to Iraq and Afghanistan, "gets transformed into an archetypal image of a terrorist," said Professor Jess Ghannam, chief of medical psychology at UCSF. "That gets internalized very quickly into the 'Muslim/Arab' stereotype."

This happens regardless of whether people know or meet individual Muslims, said Ghannam, affirming assertions made by several other scholars.

The media image has had a particularly devastating effect on men who are Sikh, a 500-year-old monotheistic faith indigenous to India.

Sikhs don't cut their hair, so Sikh men have beards. They also wear turbans in public, which is very rare for an American Muslim man, particularly outside of a religious context. But Taliban members and al Qaeda leaders, whom few Americans have encountered, wear them. Sikhs have been repeatedly attacked and several killed as a result.

On July 30, a Santa Clara man stabbed a Sikh grandfather because, as a prosecutor said upon filing charges, the assailant "wanted to seek revenge for Sept. 11 and attack a member of the Taliban."

. . .

Stereotyping Muslims has had other profound effects, with 60 percent of respondents to a national poll released Aug. 29 telling researchers with the Quinnipiac University Polling Institute in Connecticut that authorities should single out people who look "Middle Eastern" for security screening at locations such as airports and train stations.

Another national study released last month, by economics researchers at the University of Illinois, found that the earnings of Muslim and ethnically Arab men working in the United States dropped about 10 percent in the years after the Sept. 11, 2001, terrorist attacks.

Ghannam, the UCSF professor, said it has also resulted in an increased number of Muslims suffering from anxiety, depression and traumatic stress.

"It's a psychological assault on one's identity," he said.

Nonetheless, for many, the racialization of Muslims has become something to embrace.

Omair Ali was stunned by the perception that the religion of Islam would have anything to do with the terrorist attacks. Mirroring the story of many others in the Bay Area, the San Jose resident became more religious after the attacks. He started wearing a skullcap and grew a beard, only the latter of which is required by stricter observers of the faith.

Ali wants people to see his good acts in daily life as a testament to the faith. The physical image helps remind him to be righteous, he said.

"When you become a visible Muslim, people are watching you," said Ali, 29. "If you do anything bad—if you cuss, or spit or cut someone off on the road—it goes directly back to the faith. It makes you more conscious."

. . .

Racial stereotyping is also present within the Muslim community. Muslims were among the slaves imported from Africa at least as early as the 1600s. And African Americans later established mosques around the nation. Yet, African American Muslims have long complained that Arab Muslims don't treat them as full members of the faith.

"When you're an African American Muslim, you're dealing with two kinds of bigotry: the bigotry of white America and also with Arab bigotry," said Adisa Banjoko, 36, of Fremont, California.

Banjoko said that he's had days where he's been followed in a department store by security, believing his blackness gives him a propensity toward crime. Later, he'll go to a store run by an Arab Muslim and greet the owner with the Arabic "Salaam alaikum," a Muslim greeting that means "Peace be upon you," but the store owner won't return "the salaams."

"Immigrants very quickly understand how racial categories in the U.S. work, the pecking order and the desire to whiten oneself," said Michigan State Professor Salah Hassan, who has written about the post-Sept. 11 racialization of Muslims. "You definitely have that kind of bigotry."

Silverstein, the Reed College anthropology professor, believes there is a potentially dangerous endgame to the racialization of Muslims, just as in France, where French-born Muslim youths reject French identity and conflicted with authorities last year.

By contrast, American Muslims have long been vigorously campaigning that there's little dissonance between being Muslim and American.

But if through law enforcement and political measures "people are signaled long enough that they're not American," Silverstein said, "then America is going to stand in Muslim American minds as a bad thing, as something they would resist."

———

Matthai Chakko Kuruvila wrote this piece for the September 3, 2006, edition of *The San Francisco Chronicle* <www.sfchronicle.com>.

What's Wrong with This Picture?

Race isn't a factor when my generation chooses friends
BY JUSTIN BRITT-GIBSON (2007)

"It's no big deal," I tell myself. I'm sitting on the subway in Manhattan with Caroline, a woman I'm seeing. Her head rests on my shoulder, her auburn hair tangled in my scarf. Though it should be the last thing on my mind, I can't help but wonder what inspires the elderly African American woman across from us to shake her head disapprovingly: the Detroit Tigers cap I'm wearing or the company I'm keeping. After all, my beloved Tigers had recently defeated the New York Yankees in the American League playoffs. Then again, I'm also a young black man sharing an affectionate arm with a white woman.

As a 25-year-old member of the post-Gen X generation dubbed the "Millennials," I'm used to displays of warmth between interracial couples being ignored or barely noticed. They're hardly on our minds at all.

A similar carefree attitude toward racial mixing reigned at Springbrook High School in Silver Spring, Maryland, where I shared cafeteria tables and Nintendo controls with friends whose parents hailed from Pakistan, Haiti, Ethiopia, Colombia—and Pittsburgh. To my parents' generation, our devil-may-care attitude toward diversity is striking, a symbol of racial progress. Ninety-five percent of 18-to-29 year olds have friends from different racial backgrounds, according to a Washington Post-Kaiser-Harvard poll. Many Millennials take it further: To us, differences in skin color are largely irrelevant. That's not to say that young minorities never experience racial inequality. Prejudices still exist, and serious economic gaps still yawn between racial and cultural groups. But I feel fortunate to live in an era when, in choosing friends or dates, race can be among the least of my concerns. Essentially, it's no big deal.

But it felt like a big deal on that subway—much as it did two years ago in Rome when Federico, a new Italian acquaintance, casually inquired, "Do you listen to black music?" I was a Temple University senior studying art and film in Italy's eternal city. It was my first night out with fellow students. We ended up at a small, smoke-filled dive where we met five 20-something men who spoke in stilted English and didn't hide their attraction to the women in our pack. Eager to ingratiate ourselves with the locals, we accepted their invitation to join them.

I had been told by a black student previously with the program that many Italians don't take kindly to people of color, so Federico's question set off an alarm. Lowering my beer, I calmly asked what "black music" was. When Federico admiringly cited artists such as Tupac, Notorious B.I.G. and Snoop Dogg, I realized this was his way of describing hip-hop, that his intention was no different from my own clumsy attempts to describe my adoration of Italian cinema. Federico just hoped to make a new hip-hop-appreciating friend—and he did.

In Rome, I learned that whatever I was told to expect, it was best to assume nothing. My five months there also taught me that the indifference to skin color stretches way beyond American soil. Federico and his crew treated me like a brother—they even referred to me as "brother." Not once during my stay did anyone ever treat me as unequal; my skin color was never a subject of discussion—at least not to my face.

Weeks after that first meeting, Federico's posse took us to an underground club in the city's college district. Throngs of dreadlocked Italians were smoking joints, drinking beer, grooving to the rhythms of Bob Marley, Steel Pulse and other reggae icons. Most striking was how comfortable these Italians seemed in their appropriated shoes, adopting a foreign culture and somehow making it theirs. The scene reinforced my sense of how far we've come since the days when people dressed, talked and celebrated only that which sprang from their own background. For the first time in my life, I was fully aware of the spiritual concept that we're all simply one.

That sense hasn't left me. Everywhere I look, I see young people—such as my two younger brothers, a Japanese-anime-obsessed 11-year-old and a pastel-Polo-sporting 21-year-old—adopting styles, hobbies and attitudes from outside the culture in which they were raised. Last month in a Los Angeles barbershop, I was waiting to get my trademark Afro cut when I noticed a brother in his late teens sitting, eyes closed, as the barber clipped his hair into a "'frohawk," the punk-inspired African American adaptation of the mohawk. Asked why he chose the look, the guy, without looking up, shrugged, "Something different." Immediately, I understood. Minutes later, his "different" cut became my new look.

Sporting a 'frohawk doesn't mean I'll be pulling kickflips in a pair of Vans at the local skate park anytime soon—I favor Gap jeans, European-cut shirts, British Wallabees and street-smart hoodies. Increasingly, fashion is a mix of everything. My generation's embrace of various subcultures makes once-autonomous racial groups difficult to categorize. Friends who live in different parts of the country all report seeing blacks, whites, Latinos and Asians adopting facets of one another's cultures without taking flak from members of their own group.

Just a decade ago, Matthew Hencke, a biracial independent filmmaker who grew up in Washington, was called "Uncle Tom" by black students at schools he attended, he said, "because of the music I listened to or the clothes I wore." Hencke, who now lives in Manhattan, was scorned for wearing Rolling Stones and Lynyrd Skynyrd T-shirts—even though he adored the Fugees and Scarface. "My problem was, why couldn't I like everything?" said Hencke, who believes that hip-hop artists such as Kanye West, Pharrell and Lupe Fiasco have made diverse choices acceptable by saying, "Yeah I'm black, but I love rock music, skateboarding and wearing preppy clothes—and that's okay."

Millennials' cross-cultural tastes don't just affect how we dress or wear our hair; they influence our romantic choices. In my case, it isn't about seeking the most exotic woman. It's about liking whom I like—black, brown, white or yellow. Dating outside the bounds of our own ethnicity is fairly common among people my age, as indicated by a 2005 Gallup poll finding that about 60 percent of 18- to 29-year-olds say they have dated outside their race. The general consensus among my diverse body of friends is: Who cares?

For the record, I've dated black women and expect to date more of them. My high school sweetheart happened to be Korean; I don't recall ever being criticized for our relationship, perhaps because so many other kids had similar ones. Reactions were equally blas? to cross-cultural relationships I had in college and beyond. In fact, the only disapproval I've noted when I'm with a woman who isn't black has been from black women.

Last fall, I was in a shoe store with Caroline when I noticed a beautiful sister staring at us. As we passed her, she muttered "Too bad" to her girlfriend. "It's sad," said Hencke, whose wife of six years is white. "I come from a family where my mother's black and my father's white . . . my own upbringing was colorblind. Race was never an issue in my family." I can relate. Having been raised by progressive, racially tolerant parents, I never feared incurring their wrath for bringing home a girl who didn't have a matching tan. Lately at movies, bars and restaurants in New York, Los Angeles and the Washington area, friends and I have seen an increase in black women dating men of other races. Still, considering black men's high rates of unemployment and incarceration, I understand black women's concerns about "losing" eligible brothers to women of other ethnicities.

So does my friend Majeedah Johnson, a 25-year-old African American writer living in the District of Columbia. "If you meet someone you're compatible with who's outside your ethnic background, that's great," she said. "But if [the attraction] is based on self-hatred or prejudice, I have a problem with it." No kidding. A former college roommate of mine dated white women exclusively. His rationale: Because of the stereotype that black women are too strong, difficult and self-righteous, he perceived white women as an easier option. His skewed perception is very un-Millennial. Brothers who reject black women—or any group of women—are as foolish and repugnant as the white racists whom they despise. As Majeedah put it, "They're the ones missing out."

Of course, having been raised in a diverse middle-class neighborhood in Silver Spring and having attended a large, urban university probably has everything to do with my viewpoint. Barry Canty, 33, is a black Los Angeles filmmaker whose upcoming indie-comedy "L.A. Proper" features a racially diverse cast of 20- and 30-somethings. Canty said that although many in our generation live or were raised in comparatively color-blind settings, those in more segregated communities probably see things differently. "What separates many minorities from embracing diversity is their socioeconomic background," he said.

In Mecklenburg County, N.C., where Canty grew up in a diverse middle-class neighborhood, the lower you were on the economic totem pole, the more segregated your neighborhood was. "In high school, many of the poorer blacks were shocked at how easy it was for me to interact with people of other races," he said. "I think their point of view was affected by their economic status."

Perhaps it seems that Millennials like me are deaf, dumb and blind to the continuing injustices that people of color face. Racism isn't extinct; its effects are ongoing. Earlier this month in East Texas, Chris Wright, a 26-year-old African American, was hospitalized in critical condition after being dragged by a truck driven by a 24-year-old white man who turned himself in and faces assault charges. Wright's girlfriend is white, and according to his family, the incident marked the brutal conclusion of racial taunts the couple has endured for months. The NAACP is pushing to have the assault classified as a hate crime.

As horrific as that incident was, it's important to acknowledge progress and to keep fighting for an even more tolerant society. Although popular, multiethnic TV shows such as "Grey's Anatomy," "Heroes" and "Lost" reflect our nation's and world's ever-increasing diversity, the most powerful force for bringing diversity into American homes is the Internet. Web sites such as MySpace, Friendster and Facebook have created multicultural and ethnic social networks that have made it possible to connect with and befriend people from a universe of cultures just a click away.

The recent uproar over journalist Kenneth Eng's infamous article "Why I Hate Blacks" in AsianWeek showed that some Millennials—Eng is 23—aren't there yet. Eng's abusive grocery list of reasons why people should continue to "discriminate against blacks" was outrageous—and instructive. My initial reaction wasn't anger but pity for the author, who probably constructed his hateful assumptions based on his negative encounters with African Americans. His article, however wrongheaded, was like this one—observations drawn from scenes of his own unique experiences.

As strongly as I disagree with his statements, I have no problem with him freely speaking his mind. Everyone in this country has a right to be heard. It's his opinion. Considering how many real advances Americans have made when it comes to tolerance, I have to say:

No big deal.

Justin Britt-Gibson is a Los Angeles freelance journalist and screenwriter. He wrote this piece for the March 18, 2007, edition of *The Washington Post* <www.washingtonpost.com>.

Race Wasn't an Issue to Him, Which Was an Issue to Me

BY KIM MCLARIN (2006)

His name was Jerry. A nice man, late 40's, funny and smart, divorced with two grown children, a social worker who had dedicated his professional life to working with troubled kids.

He was also—let's be honest—the first to come around. He was the first man after my own divorce to raise an eyebrow, to take an interest after my ex not only moved out but moved on. Funny and smart and dedicated to troubled kids is all admirable, but in truth I would have said yes to a drink with a four-foot gaptoothed troll had one smiled my direction. The self-confidence of a 40-year-old divorced mother of two is a shaggy thing.

So the fact that Jerry was also white I noted but decided to file away for now. Why worry about it right out of the gate? Yes, race had been an issue in my marriage—not the issue perhaps, but an issue nonetheless. What I did not know was whether race arose as a problem because I am black and my ex is white or because I am a person who grapples with race and he is not.

That my ex does not grapple with race he would not dispute; he does not care to read, think or talk about it, and he wondered why I did. My ex believed I always went looking for race, but I didn't; race came looking for me.

And when it did, I would stand and call its name: when officials in our inner-ring suburb talked about closing our "borders" against a wave of nonresident students sneaking into our schools; when a white woman at my gym reached up, uninvited, and petted my locks like she was petting a dog; when my sick mother received one level of medical care and my ex's sick sister received another. At such times he tried to understand my feelings, but he did not share them, and even talking about it made him uncomfortable.

It's a dividing line as real as any in America—those who grapple with race and those who do not. But like most dividing lines, it's impossible to tell on which side a person stands by looking at them, or at least that's what I thought at the time. So why get ahead of myself with Jerry? Why dig for land mines when I may not make it past the way he slurps his beer?

We met for drinks. Sparkwise, I felt little, but we ended up talking and laughing easily for more than an hour. I told him I was a writer; he told me his five favorite books and how they had shaped his life. He told me he had gone to a seminary as a boy but eventually left the Catholic church; I told him I'd been raised a Pentecostal but mellowed into Methodism as an adult. We talked about our children, travels, mutual love of the blues and mutual dislike of the cold, and then he said he would like to read my books; he thought he would like them. I said he well might not.

"How do you deal with it when people you know don't like your work?" he asked.

I quoted a playwright whose name I could not remember who admitted in an interview that he told his friends if there was a choice between being honest and being kind in talking about his work, they should choose to be kind. "Don't value your opinion over my feelings," the playwright said.

Jerry nodded. "Some people use honesty like a weapon."

"Like a switchblade," I said. "Like a bayonet. They slice up your heart with all these ugly, hurtful words and then, while you're bleeding on the floor, they hand you a Band-Aid: 'I was only being honest.'"

"Honesty is overrated," Jerry agreed.

So the following day, when he e-mailed his attraction, I tried to be both honest and kind. No spark, I wrote, but he was great, good company. If he was looking for "the one," I was probably not going to be her. But if he simply sought intelligent dinner companionship some Friday evening, I'd be more than game.

Not a bayonet, I thought, but a butter knife. And still it hurt.

"Ouch," he replied, and disappeared.

By the time he resurfaced a few months later, I had suffered through two terrible blind dates, joined an online dating service, carried on several e-mail conversations that died, actually talked on the phone with a few men, met three for drinks, backed away carefully from each, then canceled the service.

A few of these men were black, the others white, and in no case did I find anything remotely resembling chemistry. In fact, so utterly lacking in connection were these encounters that it made me appreciate anew how rare is connection. In the face of human isolation, race seemed to retreat a little.

So when Jerry called again, I decided to let the spark thing coast, because at least he and I could talk. "My wounds are licked," Jerry said. "Have dinner with me."

"Why not," I said. Maybe, in time, the spark would come.

We talked and laughed for four hours, then necked like teenagers in the parking lot in the rain. The next day we e-mailed and text-messaged each other. It was all so much fun, such a heady relief after the months of loneliness.

But then, on our third date, things changed. First, he was late and I was irritable. Earlier, I'd had a frustrating discussion with several white undergraduates in my Literature of Slavery class. All semester I had struggled to teach them to think critically about race and slavery and history, to have them challenge their assumptions. They insisted, for example, that racial divisions were as old as time and that the myth of African inferiority preceded slavery, not, as I suggested, the other way around. And they argued that racial genetics were more than skin deep, whether I wanted to believe it or not. How else to account for the way black athletes dominate some professional sports?

That evening, when I shared my frustrations with Jerry, he wondered if the students didn't have a point. "What about all those Kenyan marathon runners?" he asked. "Isn't it possible there's some genetic reason for that? Isn't it possible blacks are just better athletes than whites?"

A perfectly innocent question. Yet something small and painful flickered inside my chest. Logically, if one accepts a genetic physical superiority of blacks, one must also accept the possibility of intellectual superiority in whites. Did he not consider that notion? Did he reject it out of hand, or subconsciously believe it? And if I wondered these things aloud would he, like my ex, judge me bitter or oversensitive?

I mentioned an essay I'd given my students in which the anti-racism advocate Tim Wise suggests that no one brought up in America can claim to be free of racist indoctrination, that doing so only perpetuates the crime. "What Wise says is that we all must recognize and confront the legacy of the past," I explained.

"I don't think everyone is racist," Jerry said. "Maybe racialized. But that's not a bad thing."

By now my hands were trembling, so I did not ask what he meant by that. I had the feeling that even if he tried to explain I would not understand. James Baldwin said being black in America is like walking around with a pebble in your shoe. Sometimes it scarcely registers and sometimes it shifts and becomes uncomfortable and sometimes it can even serve as a kind of Buddhist mindfulness bell, keeping you present, making you pay attention.

This is why, among other reasons, I engage with race, but not all black people do. I know several interracial couples in which both people swear race is never an issue, almost never comes up at all. I believe them, but it amazes me. And I know one thing: I can never join that pack.

My ex did not grapple with race, at first because he did not have to, being a white man in America, and later because it frightened him. This difference was a small but steady river that ran between us, and the more he tried to ignore it the more I clawed at the banks, and the more I clawed at the banks the larger the river swelled until, at last, we were engulfed. A black person who grapples with race cannot be with a white person who doesn't. Whether a black person who grapples with race can be with a black person who doesn't is a different and unresolved question for me, but on the first point I'm solid.

So when Jerry called and asked if I would meet him for a drink, I agreed, but this time I went only to tell him. We met a bar with billiard tables. He wanted to teach me to play but I said we wouldn't have time.

"I can't see you again," I said.

He blinked with surprise. "Why?" he said, finally.

I used my bayonet: "Because you're white, and it costs too much for me to date a white man. It cost me to be married to a white man for 13 years. I can't do it again."

"That's ridiculous," he said, after a minute. "That's the most ridiculous thing I've ever heard."

"Which proves my point," I said. "It's not ridiculous."

"You can't be with any white man?"

"No, I don't think I can."

I may as well face it. Because, after all, Jerry was a good man who worked with troubled kids and lived his life open to relationships with people of different races. And yet I couldn't be with him, even though, unlike my ex, he did seem willing to grapple with race.

But he was nearly 50 and his grappling apparently was just beginning, whereas mine started at 5. For nearly 50 years he'd lived in America and yet it surprised him that race might even be an issue for us. There was an innocence in this, an innocence born of being white. An innocence I could neither share nor abide.

"It costs me too much," I repeated.

We were silent for a minute. Behind us balls clicked and people laughed.

"And now," Jerry said, "it's costing me."

Kim McLarin's latest novel is *Jump at the Sun* (William Morrow). She lives near Boston, and she wrote this piece for the September 3, 2006, edition of *The New York Times* <www.nytimes.com>.

Shades of Black

LOUIS CHUDE-SOKEI (2007)

Although not quite able to pass for white, Sen. Barack Obama (D-Ill.) has been able to pass for African American. He is biracial, but not white; black, but not African American; American but not African. What has entranced the country more than his somewhat vague policies is Obama's challenge to conventional racial and cultural categories.

Among African Americans, discussions about his racial identity typically vacillate between the ideologically charged options of "black" versus "not black enough" or between "black" and "black, but not like us."

But there is a third side to Obama—and also to the politics of racial passing in America.

The population of African immigrants in the United States is rapidly growing. Since 1990, about 50,000 Africans have come to the United States annually, more than in any of the peak years of the international slave trade, which was abolished in 1807. They add to the steady influx of black immigrants from other continents and the Caribbean, and those who have been in the United States for generations but who don't racially and culturally define themselves as African American.

These blacks feel cramped by the narrowness of American racial politics, in which "blackness" has not just defined one's skin color but has served as a code word for African American. To be heard and to be counted, these black immigrants must often pass as African American, sometimes against their will.

Obama is not the first prominent black to defy conventional American racial and cultural categories. People identified former Secretary of State Colin L. Powell's Jamaican ancestry as the quality that made his blackness different. When in the mid-1990s it seemed possible that he would run for president, the pride of the Caribbean immigrant community was nearly palpable. He emboldened Caribbean immigrants to resist African American pressures to erase their own cultural and historical distinctiveness.

In such distinctions between black immigrants and African Americans lay buried a history of competitive intra-racial tensions and cultural differences that have never been resolved.

In addition to black immigrants' need to hold onto their own identities, many whites have historically tended to regard black immigrants as a model minority within a troublesome native-born black population. A good proportion of immigrants tend to be better educated than African Americans, don't have the "chip" of racial resentment on their shoulder and exhibit the classic immigrant optimism about assimilation into the mainstream culture. Many whites, however, exploit these differences to magnify the problems of African Americans while avoiding charges of racism. And because these differences often result in greater employment and more educational opportunities for immigrants and their descendants, they also feed tensions between native and immigrant blacks.

The complex history of black immigrant and African American interaction and distinction has been masked by a tendency in American politics to treat "black" and African American as interchangeable categories. It is further masked by an African American cultural politics that arrogates to itself the official word on racial matters. For black immigrants, African American culture can be as alien and as hostile as mainstream America.

Because Powell didn't run for president, the intra-racial differences and historical tensions between immigrant and native-born blacks that his candidacy might have brought to national attention remain largely unknown. "Black" effectively continued to mean African American.

But, from a black immigrant perspective, Obama's run for the presidency carries the promise of spotlighting this "category crisis" at long last. There is the possibility of a conversation in which Africans in the U.S., along with other black immigrant groups, may emerge distinctly from the all-consuming category of "black."

These issues have been present in scholarship and education for some time. Tensions between native and foreign-born blacks are rising in higher education because universities are reputedly using black immigrants, at the expense of the native-born, to diversify their student bodies. In this case, black immigrants are the primary beneficiaries of the blanket category of "black."

Add to this a shifting academic terrain in which traditional black studies are threatened by increasingly popular courses and programs that have a diaspora or Africana slant and do not put African American history or experiences center stage. It's now not uncommon to hear African American scholars and students complaining about the increasing presence of Caribbean and African blacks in black studies departments. Indeed, these kinds of tensions erupted at UC Berkeley two years ago and reflect the continuing struggle over the redefining of "black" in American life and thought.

As the numbers of black immigrants and their progeny grow to challenge the numerical supremacy of the native black minority, can a challenge to African Americans' cultural dominance, racial assumptions and politics be far behind? Especially because black immigrants generally and increasingly differ from native-born African Americans in their views on race, racism and political affiliations. They also are less responsive to American racial traumas, which helps explain why some civil rights leaders are unsure of Obama's loyalties to African American causes. Because his political "blackness" is independent of their sanction and emerges from outside their histories, it threatens their cultural and political authority.

So Obama does not transcend race, as some might dream. Instead, he represents a set of tensions that go beyond black and white. On one hand, there is America's complex and still unresolved relationship with African Americans and, on the other, an emergent black immigrant presence that is less willing to politically or socially pass for "black" and that has unresolved and unspoken issues of its own.

In Obama, we witness how one set of tensions works with and against the other. Immigrant status is deployed not against race but against the messy and unresolved tensions of domestic American racial relationships. And in this, whether he wins or loses, Obama is definitely a sign of the country's future.

––––––––

Louis Chude-Sokei, an associate professor of literature at the University of California-Santa Cruz, is the author of *The Last 'Darky': Bert Williams, Black-on-Black Minstrelsy and the African Diaspora*. He wrote this piece for the February 18, 2007, edition of the *Los Angeles Times* <www.latime.com>.

FROM READING TO WRITING

1. If a stranger asked you to describe your ancestry, what would you say? In what ways are you tied to the heritage of your ancestors? How does this heritage affect your life?

2. List the identities that you feel are part of your life. Where do their identities have their roots? How do these identities work together or cause conflict in your life?

3. What does it mean to be an American? Discuss at least three of the articles and essays in this chapter in your answer.

4. Do you think the United States has an immigration problem? Explain.

5. How do the founding ideals of the country play into the debates (past or present) about immigration?

6. What role do the media play in breaking down or perpetuating stereotypes based on collective identities? Think of an example.

7. Cindy Chang and Yvonne Abraham each wrote an article using the same basic data on the number of immigrants who change their names. Compare how they use this information. Do the articles say the same thing?

8. Justin Britt-Gibson and Kim McLarin have some very different things to say about how and why race matters in their personal relationships. Explain the position each writer takes and how each presents his or her position to the audience. Which writer do you think is most effective in conveying his or her argument to the reader? Why? Which position is closer to your own? Explain.

9. In her essay "Fade to Blonde," Belén Aranda Alvarado writes, "If white women can change their hair color the way they change their lipstick—with complete impunity and no worries over 'correctly' representing their community—why couldn't I?" Based on your reading of the essay, what is Alvarado's point here? How does she reconcile her desires?

10. Explain this quote from Louis Chude-Sokei's essay "Shades of Black": "So Obama does not transcend race, as some might dream. Instead, he represents a set of tensions that go beyond black and white."

Five

MODERN LOVE

Love in the Digital Age
BY ALICE MATHIAS (2007)

This winter I was in a class called Romantic Comedy. Shakespeare, you might ask? Umm . . . no. We're talking "You've Got Mail." I figured this had to be the Rocks for Jocks of the film department, but as it turned out, Rom-Com was no sunset stroll down the beach. We dragged our feet through Freudian readings of "Bringing Up Baby" and analyzed the shift from modernism to postmodernism by contrasting "The Apartment" with "Annie Hall." All I wanted to do was kick back with some popcorn and take a vacation from my not-so-"Moonstruck" freezing-cold Dartmouth winter, but unfortunately there would be an exam.

For this exam, we had to bust out our crystal balls and write an essay predicting the future of the romantic comedy genre. Our professor raised several issues to consider. Among them was the fact that zero Renaissance Dartmouth men had signed up for this pretty-big class. Our professor was a guy. He liked sappy movies. Was this a generational thing?

One of my classmates suggested a revealing answer. Perhaps a heterosexual Romeo might be paranoid about listing Romantic Comedy as one of his courses in his Facebook profile. He might imagine that Juliet was out there somewhere, stalking through cyberspace looking for the One. What if she were to check out his course load, see that he was in Chick Flicks 101, and assume he was therefore "interested in: men"? This stereotype-fueled miscommunication could be the dagger that might murder their chances of ever meeting face-to-face! Talk about tragedy.

My classmate's hypothesis demonstrates how young people today think about relationships and identity—that is, in terms of Facebook.com. Men (and women!) of my generation are undergoing an unprecedented emotional crisis that has little to do with gender roles. We are trapped in the Age of the Emoticon :(

Young people today are more inclined than ever to drool over love stories in the flickering privacy of the movie theater, because in our own realities, the classic process of romance is as endangered as—well, the movie theater. We have entered a post-butterflies era. Romantic comedy's nerve-wracking meet cutes, blind dates, love letters and eye contact have been kicked out of our love lives by MySpace, Match.com, AOL Instant Messenger and e-mail. The mystery man has been expelled from our virtual paradise. His identity has been unveiled by Google, and guess what? He's no Cary Grant.

My first (and arguably most notable) faux-mance started in seventh grade when a boy in my class asked me to be his girlfriend on AOL. That relationship came to an abrupt end days later when we accidentally bumped into each other in the cafeteria and failed to overcome the challenge of improvising un-spell-checked conversation. (I had just had my braces tightened, so I got away with pretending my teeth were too sore for me to talk.)

Communication has been streamlined by the Internet, and something essential to the process of falling in love has been lost. We can type up carefully crafted statements rather than go face-to-face and improvise from the heart, thereby risking embarrassment, vulnerability or Oscar-worthy dialogue. We can Google our way into the museums of each other's identities—and fall in love there.

If we get up the nerve to e-mail or IM our love interests, we can correspond at a comfortable pace (i.e., however long it takes us to come up with witty, well-crafted messages). They will assume we're taking our time to respond because we're busy fighting off that parade of knights in shining armor who are begging to be listed with us in a Facebook relationship. They don't know we're staring longingly at that one picture that pops up when we Google them, and we don't have to worry about whether or not they're staring longingly back! (Bonus: No one has to deal with that awkward "who's paying?" question.)

Flirting has been transformed into a digital process. We don't even have to touch each other to "hook up." We can just hook up to the Internet.

The difficulty of negotiating what happens in each arena of reality probably explains why the word "awkward" has shot to the top of my generation's lexicon. My classmates and I charade our way through first dates, trying to keep track of what's been said versus what's been read on the Internet ahead of time. We have to fake it through "Where are you from?" conversation, and if we let something slip that reveals we've done our research, it's awkward.

It gets even more complicated than that.

That real-life Archibald Leach was probably no Cary Grant (the pseudonym under which Archie was advertised to adoring audiences). But today, we are all walking, breathing Cary/Archie complexes—part public, part (we hope) private.

We are all so submerged in one another's gazes that it's almost natural to act as though we're always in a movie. (Thanks to all those security cameras out there, we pretty much are!) Like movie stars, we are sensitive to the fact that everything we do and say (every mistake we make and every triumph at which we "boo-yah") could be witnessed and speculated about in public forums by just about anyone in the world.

Granted, many of us have not yet established much of a reputation on the Internet; as we get older we will undoubtedly accumulate more and more hits on our Google resumes. But we cannot separate ourselves from our Internet alter egos. Both are relevant players in our job searches, friendships and love lives.

Our children may even Google us someday. We're never going to be able to ground them for doing anything without being exposed as hypocrites. Whoops.

The truth is, my greatest concern is not with how the Internet will influence romance. Romance is a privilege. One can get through life without it. I'm concerned about emotion in general.

I'm worried that we are becoming desensitized to the fact that there are actual human beings whose lives and feelings are being shaped by things that are so easy to mindlessly type into e-mails, chat rooms, Facebook wall posts and blogs.

Maybe I'm just skeptical about emotional relationships because I haven't met the right person, i.e. "Entourage" star Adrian Grenier. (Cut to: me swooning.) Who knows, Adrian might be hypnotized by fate to read this online declaration of my love for him and consider e-mailing me, thereby unleashing a flood of digital interactions that might culminate in a (mind-bogglingly awkward) real-life encounter. Of course, this is never going to happen because just before he e-mails me, he'll Google my name (just to make sure I'm not a freak), and find out that I am, indeed, apparently quite appalling, according to recent comments on blogs in response to my April 1st post on this site. Everyone's ability to "get to know Alice Mathias" online may very well be the beginning and end of my social life and my chances at scoring that M.R.S. I'm purportedly looking for. (From Mr. Grenier or any other Internet-savvy, earth-dwelling guy for that matter.)

All joking aside, I am willingly putting myself out there for criticism in a public forum. That said, it is important to understand that similar attempts at identity destruction are happening to innocent people in every corner of cyberspace—to people who aren't asking for it.

For example, Dartmouth students have recently had to deal with the construction of the Web site boredatbaker.com (which has cousins at the other Ivies, the Massachusetts Institute of Technology, New York University and Stanford). Intended as a community tool, this Web site has mutated into a forum for the anonymous publication of very personal attacks on students who must try their best not to be emotionally affected when people publicly question their sexuality, comment on their physical appearance and speculate about their value as humans.

In anonymous Internet attacks, people can say things they would never mention aloud while looking their target in the eye. No one need take any personal responsibility. The victims of these unfortunate manifestations of free speech must suspend their emotions and try to trust that people around them (including love interests) aren't the ones who are writing or consuming this stuff. The safest thing to do in our boredatbaker-shadowed community is to be emotionally isolated from everyone until graduation brings escape.

So I guess the question remains: what does all this mean for the future of romantic comedy?

———

Alice Mathias was a columnist for The Dartmouth at Dartmouth College, in Hanover, N.H., when she wrote this piece for a *New York Times* online series called "The Graduates: Eight College Seniors Face the Future" <http://thegraduates.blogs.nytimes.com> on April 17, 2007. In June, she graduated with a degree in creative writing and film and television.

This Is Emo
BY CHUCK KLOSTERMAN (2003)

No woman will ever satisfy me. I know that now, and I would never try to deny it. But this is actually okay, because I will never satisfy a woman, either.

Should I be writing such thoughts? Perhaps not. Perhaps it's a bad idea. I can definitely foresee a scenario where that first paragraph could come back to haunt me, especially if I somehow became marginally famous. If I become marginally famous, I will undoubtedly be interviewed by someone in the media,[1] and the interviewer will inevitably ask, "Fifteen years ago, you wrote that no woman could ever satisfy you. Now that you've been married for almost five years, are those words still true?" And I will have to say, "Oh, God no. Those were the words of an entirely different person—a person whom I can't even relate to anymore. Honestly, I can't image an existence without ___. She satisfies me in ways that I never even considered. She saved my life, really."

Now, I will be lying. I won't really feel that way. But I'll certainly say those words, and I'll deliver them with the utmost sincerity, even though those sentiments will not be there. So then the interviewer will undoubtedly quote lines from *this* particular paragraph, thereby reminding me that I swore I would publicly deny my true feelings, and I'll chuckle and say, "Come on, Mr. Rose. That was a literary device. You know I never really believed that."

But here's the thing: I *do* believe that. It's the truth now, and it will be in the future. And while I'm not exactly happy about that truth, it doesn't make me sad, either. I know it's not my fault.

It's no one's fault, really. Or maybe it's everyone's fault. It should be everyone's fault, because it's everyone's problem. Well, okay . . . not *everyone*. Not boring people, and not the profoundly retarded. But whenever I meet dynamic, nonretarded Americans, I notice that they all seem to share a single unifying characteristic: the inability to experience the kind of mind-blowing, transcendent romantic relationship they perceive to be

---

1. Hopefully Charlie Rose, if he's still alive.

a normal part of living. And someone needs to take the fall for this. So instead of blaming no one for this (which is kind of cowardly) or blaming everyone (which is kind of meaningless), I'm going to blame John Cusack.

I once loved a girl who almost loved me, but not as much as she loved John Cusack. Under certain circumstances, this would have been fine; Cusack is relatively good-looking, he seems like a pretty cool guy (he likes the Clash and the Who, at least), and he undoubtedly has millions of bones in the bank. If Cusack and I were competing for the same woman, I could easily accept losing. However, I don't really feel like John and I were "competing" for the girl I'm referring to, inasmuch as her relationship to Cusack was confined to watching him as a two-dimensional projection, pretending to be characters who don't actually exist. Now, there was a time when I would have thought that detachment would have given me a huge advantage over Johnny C., inasmuch as *my* relationship with this woman included things like "talking on the phone" and "nuzzling under umbrellas" and "eating pancakes." However, I have come to realize that I perceived this competition completely backward; it was definitely an unfair battle, but not in my favor. It was unfair in Cusack's favor. I never had a chance.

It appears that countless women born between the years of 1965 and 1978 are in love with John Cusack. I cannot fathom how he isn't the number-one box-office star in America, because every straight girl I know would sell her soul to share a milkshake with that motherfucker. For upwardly mobile women in their twenties and thirties, John Cusack is the neo-Elvis. But here's what none of these upwardly mobile women seem to realize: They don't love John Cusack. They love Lloyd Dobler. When they see Mr. Cusack, they are still seeing the optimistic, charmingly loquacious teenager he played in *Say Anything*, a movie that came out more than a decade ago. That's the guy they think he is; when Cusack played Eddie Thomas in *America's Sweethearts* or the sensitive hit man in *Grosse Pointe Blank*, all his female fans knew he was only acting . . . but they assume when the camera stopped rolling, he went back to his genuine self . . . which was someone like Lloyd Dobler . . . which was, in fact, someone who *is* Lloyd Dobler, and someone who continues to have a storybook romance with Diane Court (or with Ione Skye, depending on how you look at it). And these upwardly mobile women are not alone. We all convince ourselves of things like this—not necessarily about *Say Anything*, but about any fictionalized portrayals of romance that happen to hit us in the right place, at the right time. This is why I will never be completely satisfied by a woman, and this is why the kind of woman I tend to find attractive will never be satisfied by me. We will both measure our relationship against the prospect of fake love.

Fake love is a very powerful thing. That girl who adored John Cusack once had the opportunity to spend a weekend with me in New York at the Waldorf-Astoria, but she elected to fly to Portland instead to see the first U.S. appearance by Coldplay, a British pop group whose success derives from their ability to write melodramatic alt-rock songs about fake love. It does not matter that Coldplay is absolutely the shiftiest fucking band I've ever heard in my entire fucking life, or that they sound like a mediocre photocopy of Travis (who sound like a mediocre photocopy of Radiohead), or that their greatest fucking artistic achievement is a video where their blandly attractive frontman walks on a beach on a cloudy fucking afternoon. None of that matters. What matters is that Coldplay manufactures fake love as frenetically as the Ford fucking Motor Company manufactures Mustangs, and that's all this woman heard. "For you I bleed myself dry," sang their block-head vocalist, brilliantly informing us that stars in the sky are, in fact, yellow. How am I going to compete with that shit? That sleepy-eyed bozo isn't even making sense. He's just pouring fabricated emotions over four guitar chords, and it ends up sounding like love. And what does that mean? It means she flies to fucking Portland to hear two hours of amateurish U.K. hyperslop, and I sleep alone in a $270 hotel in Manhattan, and I hope Coldplay gets fucking dropped by fucking EMI and ends up like the Stone fucking Roses, who were actually a better fucking band, all things considered.

Not that I'm bitter about this. Oh, I concede that I may be taking this particular example somewhat personally—but I do think it's a perfect illustration of why almost everyone I know is either overtly or covertly unhappy. Coldplay songs deliver an amorphous, irrefutable interpretation of how being in love is supposed to feel, and people find themselves wanting that feeling for real. They want men to adore them like Lloyd Dobler would, and they want women to think like Aimee Mann, and they expect all their arguments to sound like Sam Malone and Diane Chambers. They think everything will work out perfectly in the end (just like it did for Helen Fielding's Bridget Jones and Nick Hornby's Rob Fleming), and they don't stop believing, because Journey's Steve Perry insists we should never do that. In the nineteenth century, teenagers merely aspired to have a marriage that would be better than that of their parents; personally, I would never be satisfied unless my marriage was as good as Cliff and Clair Huxtable's (or at least as enigmatic as Jack and Meg White's).

Pundits are always blaming TV for making people stupid, movies for desensitizing the world to violence, and rock music for making kids take drugs and kill themselves. These things should be the least of our worries. The main problem with mass media is that it makes it impossible to fall in love with any acumen of normalcy. There is no "normal," because everybody is being twisted by the same sources simultaneously. You can't compare your relationship with the playful couple who lives next door, because they're probably modeling themselves after Chandler Bing and Monica Geller. Real people are actively trying to live like fake people, so real people are no less fake. Every comparison becomes impractical. This is why the impractical has become totally acceptable; impracticality almost seems cool. The best relationship I ever had was with a journalist who was as crazy as me, and some of our coworkers liked to compare us to Sid Vicious and Nancy Spungen. At the time, I used to think, "Yeah, that's completely valid: We fight all the time, our love is self-destructive, and—if she was mysteriously killed—I'm sure I'd be wrongly arrested for second-degree murder before dying from an overdose." We even watched *Sid & Nancy* in her parents' basement and giggled the whole time. "That's us," we said gleefully. And like I said—this was the *best* relationship I ever had. And I suspect it was the best one she ever had, too.

Of course, this media transference is not all bad. It has certainly worked to my advantage, just as it has for all modern men who look and talk and act like me. We all owe our lives to Woody Allen. If Woody Allen had never been born, I'm sure I would be doomed to a life of celibacy. Remember the aforementioned woman who loved Cusack and Coldplay? There is absolutely no way I could have dated this person if Woody Allen didn't exist. In tangible terms, she was light-years out of my league, along with most of the other women I've slept with. But Woody Allen changed everything. Woody Allen made it acceptable for beautiful women to sleep with nerdy, bespectacled goofballs; all we need to do is fabricate the illusion of intellectual humor, and we somehow have a chance. The irony is that many of the women most susceptible to this scam haven't even *seen* any of Woody's movies, nor would they want to touch the actual Woody Allen if they ever had the chance (especially since he's proven to be an *über*-pervy clarinet freak). If asked, most of these foxy ladies wouldn't classify Woody Allen as sexy, or handsome, or even likable. But this is how media devolution works: It creates an archetype that eventually dwarfs its origin. By now, the "Woody Allen Personality Type" has far greater cultural importance than the man himself.

Now, the argument could be made that all this is good for the sexual bloodstream of Americana, and that all these Women Who Want Woody are being unconsciously conditioned to be less shallow than their sociobiology dictates. Self-deprecating cleverness has become a virtue. At least on the surface, movies and television actively promote dating the nonbeautiful: If we have learned anything from the mass media, it's that the only people who can make us happy are those who don't strike us as being particularly desirable. Whether it's *Jerry Maguire* or *Sixteen Candles* or *Who's the Boss* or *Some Kind of Wonderful* or *Speed Racer,* we are constantly reminded that the unattainable icons of perfection we lust after can never fulfill us like the platonic allies who have been there all along.[2] If we all took media messages at their absolute face value, we'd all be sleeping with our best friends. And that does happen, sometimes.[3] But herein lies the trap: We've also been trained to think this will *always* work out over the long term, which dooms us to disappointment. Because when push comes to shove, we really *don't* want to have sex with our friends . . . unless they're sexy. And sometimes we *do* want to have sex with our blackhearted, soul-sucking enemies . . . assuming *they're* sexy. Because that's all it ever comes down to in real life, regardless of what happened to Michael J. Fox in *Teen Wolf.*

The mass media causes sexual misdirection: It prompts us to *need* something deeper than what we *want.* This is why Woody Allen has made nebbish guys cool; he makes people assume there is something profound about having a relationship based on witty conversation and intellectual discourse. There isn't. It's just another gimmick, and it's no different than wanting to be with someone because they're thin or rich or the former lead singer of Whiskeytown. And it actually might be worse, because an intellectual relationship isn't real *at all.* My witty banter and cerebral discourse is always completely contrived. Right now, I have three and a half dates worth of material, all of which I pretend

2. The notable exceptions being *Vertigo* (where the softhearted Barbara Bel Geddes gets jammed by sexpot Kim Novak) and *My So-called Life* (where poor Brian Krakow never got any play, even though Jordan Catalano couldn't fucking read).
3. "Sometimes" meaning "during college."

to deliver spontaneously.[4] This is my strategy: If I can just coerce women into the last half of that fourth date, it's anyone's ball game. I've beaten the system; I've broken the code; I've slain the Minotaur. If we part ways on that fourth evening without some kind of conversational disaster, she probably digs me. Or at least she thinks she digs me, because who she digs is not really me. Sadly, our relationship will not last ninety-three minutes (like *Annie Hall*) or ninety-six minutes (like *Manhattan*). It will go on for days or weeks or months or years, and I've already used everything in my vault. Very soon, I will have nothing more to say, and we will be sitting across from each other at breakfast, completely devoid of banter; she will feel betrayed and foolish, and I will suddenly find myself actively trying to avoid spending time with a woman I didn't deserve to be with in the first place.

Perhaps this sounds depressing. That is not my intention. This is all normal. There's not a lot to say during breakfast. I mean, you just woke up, you know? Nothing has happened. If neither person had an especially weird dream and nobody burned the toast, breakfast is just the time for chewing Cocoa Puffs and/or wishing you were still asleep. But we've been convinced not to think like that. Silence is only supposed to happen as a manifestation of supreme actualization, where both parties are so at peace with their emotional connection that it cannot be expressed through the rudimentary tools of the lexicon; otherwise, silence is that the magic is gone and the relationship is over (hence the phrase "We just don't talk anymore"). For those of us who grew up in the media age, the only good silence is the kind described by the hair metal band Extreme. "More than words is all I ever needed you to show," explained Gary Cherone on the *Pornograffiti* album. "Then you wouldn't have to say that you love me, cause I'd already know." This is the difference between art and life: In art, not talking is never an extension of having

---

4. Here's one example I tend to deploy on second dates, and it's rewarded with an endearing guffaw at least 90 percent of the time: I ask the woman what religion she is. Inevitably, she will say something like, "Oh, I'm sort of Catholic, but I'm pretty lapsed in my participation," or "Oh, I'm kind of Jewish, but I don't really practice anymore." Virtually everyone under the age of thirty will answer that question in this manner. I then respond by saying, "Yeah, it seems like everybody I meet describes themselves as 'sort of Catholic' or 'sort of Jewish' or 'sort of Methodist.' Do you think all religions have this problem? I mean, do you think there are twenty-five-year-old Amish people who say, 'Well, I'm *sort of* Amish. I currently work as a computer programmer, but I still believe pants with metal zippers are the work of Satan.'"

nothing to say; not talking always means something. And now that art and life have become completely interchangeable, we're forced to live inside the acoustic power chords of Nuno Bettencourt, even if most of us don't necessarily know who the fuck Nuno Bettencourt is.

When Harry Met Sally hit theaters in 1989. I didn't see it until 1997, but it turns out I could have skipped it entirely. The movie itself isn't bad (which is pretty amazing, since it stars Meg Ryan and Billy Crystal), and there are funny parts and sweet parts and smart dialogue, and—all things considered—it's a well-executed example of a certain kind of entertainment.[5] Yet watching this film in 1997 was like watching the 1978 one-game playoff between the Yankees and the Red Sox on *ESPN Classic*: Though I've never sat through the pitch sequence that leads to Bucky Dent's three-run homer, I know exactly what happened. I feel like I remember it, even though I don't. And—more important—*I know what it all means*. Knowing about sports means knowing that Bucky Dent is the living, breathing, metaphorical incarnation of the Bo Sox's undying futility; I didn't have to see that game to understand the fabric of its existence. I didn't need to see *When Harry Met Sally*, either. Within three years of its initial release, classifying any intense friendship as "totally a *Harry-Met-Sally* situation" had a recognizable meaning to everyone, regardless of whether or not they'd actually seen the movie. And that meaning remains clear and remarkably consistent: It implies that two platonic acquaintances are refusing to admit that they're deeply in love with each other. *When Harry Met Sally* cemented the plausibility of that notion, and it gave a lot of desperate people hope. It made it realistic to suspect your best friend may be your soul mate, and it made wanting such a scenario comfortably conventional. The problem is that the *Harry-Met-Sally* situation is almost always tragically unbalanced. Most of the time, the two involved parties are not really "best friends." Inevitably, one of the people has been in love with the other from the first day they met, while the other person is either (a) wracked with guilt and pressure, or (b) completely oblivious to the espoused attraction. Every relationship is fundamentally a power struggle, and the individual in power is whoever likes the other person less. But *When Harry Met Sally* gives the powerless, unrequited lover a reason to live. When this person gets drunk and tells his friends that he's in love with a woman who only sees him as a buddy, they will say, "You're

---

5. "A certain kind" meaning "bad."

wrong. You're perfect for each other. This is just like *When Harry Met Sally*! I'm sure she loves you—she just doesn't realize it yet." Nora Ephron accidentally ruined a lot of lives.

I remember taking a course in college called "Communication and Society," and my professor was obsessed by the belief that fairy tales like "Hansel and Gretel" and "Little Red Riding Hood" were evil. She said they were part of a latent social code that hoped to suppress women and minorities. At the time, I was mildly outraged that my tuition money was supporting this kind of crap; years later, I have come to recall those pseudo-savvy lectures as what I *loved* about college. But I still think they were probably wasteful, and here's why: Even if those theories are true, they're barely significant. "The Three Little Pigs" is not the story that is fucking people up. Stories like *Say Anything* are fucking people up. We don't need to worry about people unconsciously "absorbing" archaic secret messages when they're six years old; we need to worry about all the entertaining messages people are consciously accepting when they're twenty-six. They're the ones that get us, because they're the ones we try to turn into life. I mean, Christ: I wish I could believe that bozo in Coldplay when he tells me that stars are yellow. I miss that girl. I wish I was Lloyd Dobler. I don't want anybody to step on a piece of broken glass, I want fake love. But that's all I want, and that's why I can't have it.

The Secret Love Lives of Teenage Boys

Social scientists who study young love are discovering that,
contrary to popular belief, male adolescents don't just want to have fun
BY LEV GROSSMAN (2006)

In 1995 Peggy Giordano did a study of high school yearbooks. She was leafing through one when something caught her eye about the notes people had written there, something about their rawness and their honesty. "I was amazed at some of the messages that the boys were writing to girls," Giordano says. "They seemed to be so emotional and so heartfelt. It didn't seem to jibe with the picture of boys' only wanting one thing and objectifying young women."

Giordano is not the typical target audience for a mash note written in a yearbook. She's a professor of sociology at Bowling Green State University in Ohio, and the object of her most recent investigations is not the kind of thing you would think social scientists spend their time on. Her quarry, sociologically speaking, is the elusive, zealously guarded heart of the modern-day teenage boy. Giordano—an author of such articles as "A Conceptual Portrait of Adolescent Romantic Relationships" and "Hooking Up: The Relationship Contexts of 'Nonrelationship' Sex"—believes something most people don't: not only do adolescent boys have hearts, but they're also the biggest romantics around.

It's a theory that runs counter to the story our culture usually tells us about teenage boys—that they have abandoned dating and monogamy for hooking up and "friends with benefits." But Giordano believed the prevailing wisdom was wrong, and in 2001, with the help of two colleagues, professors Wendy Manning and Monica Longmore, she set out to test it.

But how? The existing sociological literature wasn't much help. "There really hasn't been much on romantic relationships" among adolescents, Giordano says with a sigh. "And what there has been is really much more focused on sex itself." Moreover, the earlier work all seemed to be missing a crucial element: past sociologists had compiled reams of data about behavior—what teens do—but not much about what that behavior meant to them—what teens actually feel. Giordano didn't just want to know if a boy told his girlfriend he loved her. She also wanted to know if he really meant it.

But she was aware that not all stereotypes about teenage boys are wrong: they scare easily; they're reluctant to talk about their emotions, and when they do, they're not particularly good at it. So when Giordano and her colleagues decided to undertake a large-scale study of the secret love life of teenagers, they approached their subjects the way you would treat warriors of the Yanomamo: with scientific objectivity and extreme caution.

For a staging ground, the researchers chose nearby Lucas County, a largely urban county in Ohio that contains Toledo. Using school records, they assembled a finely calibrated random sample of 1,316 boys and girls drawn from the seventh, ninth and 11th grades. Finding their subjects was one thing; getting the kids to talk openly was another. A certain amount of tact would be essential. "It's sort of creepy to be talking to a woman interviewer about your sex life," admits Giordano, who is 58. Each interview was started by one of Giordano's staff, who after a few minutes would hand the interviewee a laptop computer preloaded with questions. "I was really not in favor of the laptop administration because I'm coming out of a tradition where you really want to look the person in the eye," Giordano says. But teenagers today are used to reading on a monitor and pouring their hearts out onto a keyboard. "Basically the kids really like it," says Giordano. "They're from that generation, so they just roll with it."

For the interview questions, Giordano and her colleagues could draw on the wisdom of generations of sociologists, whose calling in life is to take messy, intimate personal experiences and social attitudes and turn them into discreet, orderly, crunchable numbers. A question designed to gauge how attached a teen is to his or her partner might offer choices such as "I would rather be with X than anyone else," "I am very attracted to X," "X always seems to be on my mind" and so on. The researchers then used the responses to analyze each subject's feelings about his or her love life. Each teenager was assigned scores in categories like "communications awkwardness," "confidence in navigating romantic relationships," "heightened emotionality," "influence" and "power." Having translated the interpersonal dynamics of puppy love into cold, hard numbers, Giordano could then add them up, read the results and draw her conclusions.

One thing she learned was that she was right. On the love scale, boys scored equally with girls. They were at least as emotionally invested in their romantic relationships as their partners. About 100 of the boys and girls were randomly chosen for additional, in-depth, face-to-face interviews that were taped. The responses were revelatory in their passionate forthrightness. "You think of it as this way: [Would] you give up your whole life, you know . . . to save Jenny's life?" one boy said, trying to explain his feelings about his girlfriend. "I'm like a little girl in a relationship," another boy confided. "[At first it] just seemed like every time I was around her I couldn't talk. I was getting butterflies in my stomach, I was just, like, discombobulated or something." Such sentiments were echoed across race and ethnic lines.

And here's something that surprised even Giordano: both boys and girls agreed that girls have the power in heterosexual relationships, including when it comes to sex. "She wanted to do it more than I did," said an 18-year-old male. "She said that I wasn't mature enough and, you know, all that stuff . . . I was too young, I was scared, I didn't know what I was doing, I wasn't ready for it . . . [But] she was my girlfriend, and that's what she wanted." The picture of young love that was developing was so different from society's perceptions that Giordano went over the data with extra care. "I would have to think every once in a while, am I just wrong here?" she says. "And then I would think, O.K., let me think about all the different men and boys that I know. They're really nice. I would have to add it up, just think about all the people, you know? It's really a question of numbers."

There were exceptions, of course. Take "Donny," a boy who filled the classic role of the player. At 17, he estimated that he'd had 35 sexual partners, some of whose names he couldn't recall. He had cheated on his girlfriends. He confessed to some physical abuse of them. But the really notable thing about Donny was how few Donnys there were. Fewer than a quarter of the boys surveyed felt that other kids thought of them as players. "That number of [Donny types] is in fact smaller than everybody believes," Giordano says.

It seems as if popular culture is waking up to the reality of the emotionally responsive male. Willowy, sensitive actors like Tobey Maguire and Topher Grace are looming larger on marquees. For every Charlie Sheen, there's a Jon Cryer. The irony is that boys seem to be the last ones to get the news. "It's like a shared misunderstanding," Giordano says. "One of the boys said that he'd never talk to his friends this way, the way that he talked to the interviewer, because those boys don't have the feelings that he has."

Lev Grossman wrote this piece for the September 4, 2006, issue of *Time* magazine <www. time.com>.

Do Smart Girls Finish Last in Love?

BY LAURA VANDERKAM (2006)

Back in my single days, my friends and I used to joke about a dating dilemma we called "dropping the P-bomb."

"Where did you go to school?" a gentleman would inquire at a party.

"Oh, in New Jersey." We'd smile and try to change the subject. No luck.

"Where in New Jersey?"

"Um, Princeton?"

We'd grip our drinks and wait. Would he scurry away? That's what we expected—especially as we began collecting graduate degrees and serious paychecks.

Growing up as a smart, ambitious girl in America, you can't miss the assumption that neither of those attributes wins you points in the love game.

In 2002, Sylvia Ann Hewlett's book, *Creating a Life: Professional Women and the Quest for Children,* claimed that only 60% of high-achieving women in their 40s and early 50s were married vs. 76% of men and 83% of extremely high-earning men. Pulitzer Prize-winning columnist Maureen Dowd subsequently rued that despite succeeding beyond the dreams of her Irish maid ancestors, her odds of landing a husband might have jumped if she, too, never aspired to anything beyond keeping house.

Dumb it down, we learned. Men don't make passes at girls who wear glasses.

There's just one problem. It's not true—not anymore. A growing body of research finds that the success penalty—the lower marriage rates among high-achieving women vs. their lower-achieving sisters—has nearly disappeared.

"VOLLEY WITH AN EQUAL"

"While there are certainly some men who want a woman to play fetch for them, the majority of men, and certainly the ones we would want to date, are definitely looking to volley with an equal," says Christine Whelan, author of the new book *Why Smart Men Marry Smart Women.* As children of egalitarian baby boomer moms and dads hit their 20s and 30s, high-achieving women now marry at the same rate as others, they just do so a few years later. The first part of that sentence is reason to celebrate. The latter is more worrisome. Later marriages tend to mean later and fewer births, and this country needs the bright kids bright moms raise. Though given how quickly society has changed on the first count, there's every reason to hope that soon young women will succeed in changing the second part, too.

Whelan, herself a Princeton grad who's getting married next summer, combed through years of Census data, studies and a Harris poll that she commissioned. The finding? Hewlett and Dowd missed a big shift that's just showing up on the radar among high achievers, whom Whelan defines as women with graduate degrees and/or incomes in the top 10% for their age.

In the bad old days— alas, as recently as the 1980s— a woman with a graduate degree was 16% less likely to be married by age 44 than a woman with a high school diploma. Now, while 55% of women with graduate degrees marry by age 29 vs. 61% of other women, after 30, the odds reverse. A single, 30-year-old woman with a graduate degree has about a 75% chance of getting married. A single 30-year-old woman with less education has about a 66% chance.

The Center for Economic and Policy Research reports that women ages 28 to 35 who earn more than $55,000 a year (roughly the top 10%) are just as likely to be married as other women who work full-time. Indeed, Whelan's survey found that 90% of high-achieving men want a spouse who is as smart as they are, and 71% say a woman's success makes her more desirable as a wife. Maybe it's because these men do want to marry Mommy—72% of moms of high-achieving men worked outside the home as they raised their sons.

So why does the myth persist? Blame the higher age of first marriage for women with graduate degrees or high paychecks—fueled by a belief that starting a family during grad school, or during the early years of a "big" job, is impossible. These women marry, on average, around age 30; women overall first marry at about 25. From ages 25 to 30, Whelan notes, "you'll go to many weddings on your own," believing bad news after bad bouquet tosses.

REASON TO WORRY

But though it's reassuring to know the odds of marrying are good, the older age of first marriage for high-achieving women is not so reassuring. Despite headlines about professional women becoming single moms by choice, most won't have children out of wedlock, so later marriages mean later births. Indeed, America's brightest people—men and women—tend to delay childbearing.

This may be a choice, though it's too bad for society that successful people aren't so successful in the Darwinian sense.

But even this, I believe, will change. New York's sidewalks these days are clogged with $700 double strollers pushed by the nannies of high-achieving parents who can afford such wheels. Trendsetting Manhattan's preschool age population soared 26% from 2000–04; from Britney Spears to Angelina Jolie, young moms are becoming hip.

When women decide that they want to get married, they tend to make it happen. They approach dates with open minds. They ask to be set up. They seal the deal.

Until now, young women haven't adopted that mindset in graduate school or in the early years of their big careers because they believe the myth that it's impossible to have it all.

If the marriage penalty can disappear in a generation, though, there's no reason that young women can't demand that suitors, schools and employers work on a different timetable when it comes to families, too.

That will take guts, but so does being honest during party chitchat. In time, we can learn to do both.

———

Laura Vanderkam, author of the forthcoming *Grindhopping: Build a Rewarding Career Without Paying Your Dues*, is a member of the board of contributors for *USA Today* <www.usatoday.com>, where this piece was published on October 17, 2006.

Long-Term Love
BY JULIE HANUS (2006)

"Divorce," I remember repeating dully, after my mother told me my uncle was separating from the woman I always had known as aunt. Silence separated us as I stumbled toward a meaning. "You mean they're not going to live together anymore?"

I should have known better. I am, after all, the child of a second marriage. My older half brother should have been proof that not all relationships last forever. But my uncle and aunt were a ritual presence in my childhood. My birthday meant a trip with them to the city; holidays, a picturesque meal piled on their dining room table. Each summer brought a picnic on their rural Wisconsin farm. (Even a visit to their bathroom was a ceremonial occasion, when I inspected the circle of shaving soap, a curiosity to a kid accustomed to the hum of electric razors.) These undisturbed and familiar patterns left little space to imagine anything would ever change.

The easy explanation for my surprise is to say I was a kid. I could have elaborated naively on "love," or "getting married," but was oblivious to the guts of a long-term relationship. (Mattel makes neither a Golden Anniversary Ken, nor a Trial Separation Barbie.) My uncle's divorce was the first I had ever known, and I had years to live before I would begin to understand the complex, everyday arrangements of friends and family (to say nothing of my own) as they got together, stayed together, and sometimes split apart.

But even as we age, and complexities become commonplace, the language of happy-ever-after seems to linger. Last time I checked a popular website, where users declare their goals, more than 4,000 Net-savvy souls have signed up "to fall in love." More than 3,000 want "to get married." Only 32 aim "to have a long-term relationship." And only a few exacting users have vowed "to fall in love with someone who will always love me back."

The distinction is surely semantic; the terms love and marriage imply, even assume, a long-term relationship. Yet "true love always" clearly beats "long term" in the cachet department, and these trends in diction also reflect our broader cultural conversations.

To prove the point, spend a couple weeks in *Utne*'s library of more than 1,200 magazine titles. Try to find a how-to, or a why-at-all, story on what makes a long-term relationship work—an honest description of the struggles, the joys, the petty betrayals, the everyday triumphs of making a relationship last. I tried, and I came up nearly empty-handed.

Instead, there are commentaries on the government's involvement in legal recognition of relationships, treatises suggesting monogamy is passé, endless stories about falling in and out of love. These all are important conversations, and they serve as a sounding board for the political and cultural obsessions of the day. And yet . . . the implied long-term relationship underlies it all, in every hope-for and loss-of.

The long-term relationship requires the marathon treatment—training, commitment, and strategy—but fascination hovers with the beginning and the end. (Imagine if we clamored to ask "Who ran well in the middle, up that mild grade, and around the city hall?" and not "Who won, and who sprang quickly from the gate?")

Maybe some couples share a fated, seamless union and coast with grace from one stage of partnership to the next. But most of us struggle, triumph, and struggle again. We make mistakes and corrections, require constant revision. And it seems, as a whole, we are silent participants; our hard work remains unspoken. What would it mean to speak honestly about the difficulties of the long haul? It might drain the romance from our stories, but it could also expand our abilities to imagine, negotiate, and tend our relationships as they truly are.

Shared wisdom could make us happier in our relationships, too. One recent study of long-term relationships, reported in *Science and Theology News* (Dec. 2005), suggests that knowledge is bliss: Couples who reported taking time to negotiate, plan, and execute actions to better their relationships also reported the highest levels of satisfaction.

Who are these highly developed people, I wonder, and why am I so often flying by the seat of my pants? After his divorce, my uncle gave me one scrap of insight, which I have repeated as I blundered through my own somewhat-sacred unions and messy-if-happy arrangements. What he said was this: We are capable of loving more than one person in a lifetime.

Several years ago, I sat alone in a bathtub, all pruned up in long-gone-lukewarm water, and found that I had forgiven a lover for cheating. If it had been a decision, I might have chosen differently. Instead, it was the cold, boring truth, the only thing left when my grudge circled the drain. I don't regret my actions: choosing to stay, to keep trying. I do regret feeling so terrifically alone, and oddly guilty. I was convinced no one would understand, no one would respect the way I felt.

Perhaps I was unreasonable in my embarrassment, conceited to imagine no one would understand. The fact is that all of us who are involved in long-term relationships, whether we're at the beginning, midway, or end, have something in common. Keeping quiet about our failures and successes ensures that we'll repeat each other's mistakes. And celebrate our victories alone.

What prevents us from making these conversations an everyday part of our lives? Cultural taboo? Linguistic difficulties? Ancient Sanskrit and Persian languages, writes Daniel Pinchbeck in *Arthur* magazine (Sept. 2005), have more than 80 words that we translate in English only as "love." We may be strangled by verbal paucity. We might lack an easy way to explain a person who is our sometime-partner, sometime-friend, sometime-lover, but there must be ways to talk about such an improbable yet unfailingly attractive venture.

A little over a year ago, I sat once again at my uncle's dining room table. Every inch of it was crowded with traditional Thanksgiving fare, and around it were gathered people who were more or less family. Stepchildren passed plates to grandchildren; ex-wives sat alongside new partners. Not everyone was there, but no one would have been unwelcome. It was a scene I could not have imagined as a child nor predicted as an adult. But the memory buoys me.

I don't know much more now about what it takes to make a long-term relationship hum and purr—or if a smoothly functioning machine should even be a goal. But I am committed to trying to find out. I figure talking about it is a decent first step.

———

Julie Hanus wrote this piece for the March/April 2006 issue of Utne magazine <www.utne.com>.

A Prince Charming for the Prom
(Not Ever After, Though)

BY FRANK PAIVA (2005)

Lately I've become wary of the question "Frank, what are you doing next Saturday night?" In the month of May it can only mean one thing: I'm going to yet another prom. And no, I'm not doing a favor for a cousin. Cousins are out. I'm this century's new answer to the last-minute prom date: the gay best friend.

By the end of June I'll have worn the tuxedo I swiped from the school drama department three or four times. While most 18-year-old guys are preparing for their one big night, I'm whipping up more magical evenings than Lance Burton or David Copperfield.

I am also swimming in corsages. I went to the florist today for the second time this week, and she gave me a suspicious look. Does she know what I'm up to? After all, I can't be the only one who understands that gay is the new cousin.

Until recently this wasn't really possible, because most gay men postponed coming out until college or later, if they came out at all. But now more and more young men are coming out in high school. I knew I was gay in sixth grade and came out in eighth. Originally I didn't plan to tell anyone until ninth grade, when I would enroll in a new school, but I decided I needed to let people know who I really was.

My decision had a traumatic aftermath. How is a school supposed to handle the coming out of an eighth grader? My middle school also contained an elementary school, and alarmed parents feared for their little children, worried, I suppose, that I might convert them or something.

I endured a set of excruciating meetings with school administrators during which parameters for my behavior were discussed. That and the cruelty of my classmates left me feeling isolated and scared, and I found myself turning mostly to girls for support and friendship.

Although things improved in high school, I still found myself relying primarily on friendships with girls, some of whom I met at summer drama camps and who attended different schools.

As I see it, these girls saved me, and now it's my turn to save them. Dancing a few steps in a beautified gymnasium is the least I could do to thank the girls who helped me become who I am.

I don't even have to go broke doing this. Any girl who's progressive enough to go to her prom with a gay guy understands that it's no longer the 1950's and that I shouldn't have to pay for everything.

They also understand I won't turn into a drunken, groping creep in the middle of the evening, so I figure it's an even trade.

And unlike the goofy cousin who might arrive in a ruffled, powder-blue tux and tell embarrassing stories about computer camp, I'm a safe, chic choice. Neither of us will blush with sexual tension when it comes time to attach corsage to bosom. I won't make a fool of my date or myself with awkward straight-boy dancing. And I'll help her figure out the details of her dress and hairstyle. After all, we wouldn't want anyone committing social suicide on the biggest night of our tender young lives.

As the gay date, I also make one of the evening's most unpleasant moments a breeze. I have no problem meeting the girl's parents, a typical sticking point for most guys, because I know that wise and open-minded parents are smart enough to realize that a gay guy is their daughter's best and safest prom bet.

If I were a worried mother of a dateless daughter, I would scour the hip coffee shops of my town waving a rainbow flag in search of recruits. It might cause my daughter to die of embarrassment, but at least she would have a fabulous night out and wouldn't make me a grandmother anytime soon.

At the proms themselves, though, I'm supposed to be straight, so I do my best. Am I ever worried about being found out? Not really. My friend Katie goes to a Catholic high school, and at her prom I even passed rigid nun interrogation.

On our way through the lineup of nun inspectors, they shook my hand and eyed me up and down before pronouncing me a fit suitor. So what do I have to worry about? Then again, maybe nuns aren't known for their finely tuned gay-dar.

One thing I've discovered in my brief barrage of proms is that they're all pretty much the same. There's that sense of finality, of going out with a bang.

Gay or not, there's still that stomach-churning feeling of anticipation as you and your date see each other in your formal dress for the first time. There's the poor couple wearing the absolute wrong ensemble. There's that burned-out feeling in the early morning from so much fun packed into so little time. Rest assured that the onset of horror from wondering what the pictures will look like decades from now is there every time as well.

But sometimes our expectations get the better of us, and the prom's real purpose is lost. It's one of the last times to be together and have fun as a class before everyone scatters and comes back to the reunion 10 years later balding, divorced, wildly successful or exactly, pathetically the same.

Whether you loved your own prom, hated it, missed it, only made it to the parking lot or were too drunk to remember, there's no denying it's a milestone that happens only once. Or, in my case, several times.

The one thing I can't understand is why many of my female friends, who are charming, attractive and fun to be with, don't have straight male suitors to accompany them. Surely the school halls aren't filled with date-snatching floozies offering the one thing no teenage guy, except the gay best friend, can say no to. So I've got to believe I see things in these girls that straight guys can't because with me the element of sexual attraction was never there to begin with.

Many young gay men make friends with the cool girls who fly under the radar because they don't possess conventional good looks and they don't put out. We get to know these girls for the things about them that matter.

Sometimes I want to hold up a sign that says: "Here! Date this girl, you idiot!" Of course if they aren't smart enough to figure out a girl is worth dating, they probably aren't worthy of the girl in the first place.

Perhaps this is why certain girls and certain gay guys become such good friends in high school. They're waiting for an environment that isn't based on popularity or games, an atmosphere where they can thrive.

While I've had an excellent time in high school these past four years, I have to believe there is something better out there for me in years to come. I know many of my friends feel the same way.

We've all heard famous women talk about how they were ostracized in high school or unpopular with the boys, only later to become gorgeous and desired. Even though they ended up successful, they never had that high school experience of the prom, that one magical time that can never be taken away. I'm here to provide this to many future famous women, even if I don't get it for myself.

As much as I'd like to, I will not be attending my own school's prom with a guy. My florist must know this because each time I walk in, she always flips past the boutonniere section of her prom accessories book.

I wish this weren't the case. I wish I could take someone with me, because I've got prom dreams of my own. They involve buying expensive ingredients at the gourmet food store and spending the entire day making dinner with my date. We would enjoy the food even more knowing we put all the effort into making it ourselves.

When we walked into the dance, the two of us would initially stun people, not because we were two guys but just because we looked great. I wouldn't care if I had to learn to make clothes myself if it meant avoiding that awkward "I rented this, and it doesn't quite fit" look. I would be able to hold his hand all night without feeling weird or attracting attention. By the time it was over, we would be so tired we wouldn't even care.

Right now, however, my prom dream is just that. My school is a great place, but out of about 500 students, there are only a few other openly gay kids. (There are also a handful of openly bisexual girls, but that's considered trendy, so they don't count.)

I'm pretty brave, but sorry, I just don't feel ready to take a boy to prom. I once tried to take a boy to a school dance, and it was just too weird. It felt like every eye was focused on us for all the wrong reasons.

Maybe things will be better for younger guys. I hope so.

At my school, attending the prom in groups of friends is normal and acceptable, so that's what I'm doing. Time to drag out that tuxedo again. But I'm looking forward to it. I will thank my friends for the great times and try not to focus on the thing I cannot yet have. I'll walk in feeling sad and knowing that, for better or worse, I'll be leaving these people in the fall. We'll all go off to our own lives. Who knows what'll happen in mine?

All proms have their cheesy themes, and ours is no exception. "Let the Dreams Begin!" cries out from invitations and prom updates throughout our school.

My dream began a long time ago. I'm just waiting for it to come true.

———

Frank Paiva graduated from the Lakeside School in Seattle in 2005. This essay appeared in the May 29, 2005, edition of *The New York Times* <www.nytimes.com>.

The Lonely American Just Got a Bit Lonelier
BY HENRY FOUNTAIN (2006)

For as long as humans have gathered in groups, it seems, some people have been left on the outside looking in. In postwar America in particular, the idea that loneliness pervades a portion of society has been a near-constant. Only the descriptions have changed: the "lonely crowd" alienation of the 1950's; the grim career-driven angst of the 70's and 80's; the "Bowling Alone" collapse of social connections of the 90's.

There is a new installment in the annals of loneliness. Americans are not only lacking in bowling partners, now they're lacking in people to tell their deepest, darkest secrets. They've hunkered down even more, their inner circle often contracting until it includes only family, only a spouse or, at worst, no one.

And that is something the Internet may help ease, but is unlikely to cure.

A recent study by sociologists at Duke and the University of Arizona found that, on average, most adults only have two people they can talk to about the most important subjects in their lives—serious health problems, for example, or issues like who will care for their children should they die. And about one-quarter have no close confidants at all.

"The kinds of connections we studied are the kinds of people you call on for social support, for real concrete help when you need it," said Lynn Smith-Lovin, a sociologist at Duke and an author of the study, which analyzed responses in interviews that mirrored a survey from 1985. "These are the tightest inner circle."

The study "should provide a wake-up call to our society," said Bill Maier, a vice president and psychologist in residence with Focus on the Family, the evangelical Christian group. "We're missing out on deep, meaningful interpersonal relationships."

Yet within the analysis there was at least a suggestion of hope.

"The one type of relationship that actually went up was talking over personally important things with your spouse," Dr. Smith-Lovin said.

Like "Bowling Alone," the essay and, later, book by Robert D. Putnam, a public policy professor a Harvard, the Duke study suggested that a weakening of community connections is in part responsible for increasing social isolation. More people are working and commuting longer hours and have little time for the kinds of external social activities that could lead to deeper relationships.

So the closest ties increasingly are limited to family members, in particular to spouses.

"That's probably a result of the fact that men's and women's lives are more structurally similar now than in 1985," Dr. Smith-Lovin said. It's more likely that both spouses are working at jobs that are important to them, and men are more involved around the house. "Spouses literally have more to talk about," she said.

Dr. Maier, for one, sees that as cause for at least some optimism in a society whose fast pace generally bodes badly for family life. "To hear that people are investing more in their nuclear family is a positive thing," he said.

The Internet is also cause for some optimism, because it has made it easier to maintain ties among family members who have become scattered. Those ties inevitably developed over long-term, face-to-face contact, but e-mail can help keep them strong.

"E-mail really does help maintain your social networks," said John Horrigan, associate director of the Pew Internet and American Life Project. Recent Pew surveys, he said, found that "when you contact family by e-mail, you share important and serious things."

Still, Dr. Smith-Lovin said, any optimism must be tempered. For one thing, having only one confidant, even if that confidant is a spouse, leaves a person extremely vulnerable if the spouse dies or the marriage disintegrates.

And in the end, she and others pointed out, e-mail or instant messaging is no substitute for face-to-face contact. "E-mailing somebody far way is not the same as them going to pick up your child at daycare or bringing you chicken soup," she said.

Dr. Putnam said the new study reinforced much of what he had reported in "Bowling Alone," which had been criticized by some academics as a faulty analysis that ignored other social and economic trends. And even if the new study points to a rise in spouses as confidants, that is not especially cause to rejoice, he said. "It's like with global warming, if we learn that temperatures are going to rise slightly less than we thought," he said. "It's still a problem."

"Sure, you might say, we've still got our wives or husbands or mothers," he said. "That's true. But gosh, the number of friends you have is a strong predictor of how long you live."

The impact goes beyond the individual, as well. "There are effects on my neighbors of my not knowing them," he said. For one thing, "If I don't know them well and they don't know me, that has a demonstrable effect on the crime rate."

Dr. Horrigan said there was anecdotal evidence that some members of a community use e-mail and the Internet "to keep up with people very close by." The Internet can help expand social networks, although the ties it creates are not as strong as those the Duke researchers are concerned with. Yet they can be useful.

His group's research has shown that the Internet is increasingly being used during life's "major moments"—to gather information or advice when making a big financial investment, deciding where to live, or choosing a college for a child. The research has shown that "people were more likely to get help through their social network" for those kinds of decisions.

Still, Dr. Putnam said, "The real interesting future is how can we use the Net to strengthen and deepen relationships that we have offline."

———

Henry Fountain wrote this piece for the July 2, 2006, edition of *The New York Times* <www.nytimes.com>.

FROM READING TO WRITING

1. As many of the authors in this chapter suggest, our expectations for love and romance are changing. Drawing on at least two pieces from this chapter in your discussion, explain why you think this might be (and, more specifically, what might be transforming these expectations). Do you think these changes are a good thing? Why or why not?

2. Even though the reality of "long-term love" may have changed, according to Julie Hanus, "the language of happy-ever-after seems to linger." Take a traditional fairy tale and re-tell it, taking into account the characteristics of modern love discussed in the chapter. (Hint: If you have a hard time getting started, think of *Shrek* or *Happily N'Ever After*.)

3. Define a successful romantic relationship. Be sure to provide specific criteria. Do you know a couple who fits this definition?

4. Lev Grossman, Laura Vanderkam, and Frank Paiva suggest that evolving gender roles have altered our ideas on modern love. According to these authors, how have gender roles changed? How do they evaluate these changes?

5. How has technology influenced modern love? Use evidence from "Love in the Digital Age," "The Lonely American Just Got a Bit Lonelier," and your personal experience to support your argument.

Six

OVERWEIGHT AMERICA

Why America Has to Be Fat

BY MICHAEL S. ROSENWALD (2006)

I am fat. Sixty pounds too hefty, in my doctor's opinion. Probably 80 pounds, in my fiancee's view.

Being fat makes me a lot of things—a top contender for type II diabetes, for instance, or a heart attack, or stroke, maybe even a replacement knee or hip. My girth also puts me in familiar company, with about two-thirds of the U.S. population now considered overweight.

But in many ways, my being fat also makes me pretty good for the economy.

You've read the headlines: America's problem with bulging waistlines has reached pandemic proportions, according to federal health officials, who warn that obesity is becoming society's No. 1 killer. But as doctors wrestle with the problem, economists have been pondering which corporations and industries benefit, and the role that changes in the overall economy have played in making us fat to begin with.

It turns out, economists say, that changes in food technology (producing tasty, easy-to-cook food, such as french fries) and changes in labor (we use to be paid to exercise at work, now we pay to exercise after work) combined with women's importance in the workforce, not the kitchen, have combined to produce industries able to cheaply and efficiently meet the demands of our busy lives. The cookie industry. The fast-food industry. Potato chips. Soda. The chain-restaurant industry, with its heaping portions of low-priced, high-calorie foods.

In some ways, we are better off in this Fat Economy. Many people work in easier, better-paying jobs, which help pay for their big homes in the suburbs. Women don't have to spend two hours preparing dinner every night; many have risen to unprecedented levels of corporate and political power. Flat-panel plasma TVs hang over fireplaces, which can be lit using the same remote control for flipping channels. But the unintended consequence of these economic changes is that many of us have become fat. An efficient economy produces sluggish, inefficient bodies.

"The obesity problem is really a side effect of things that are good for the economy," said Tomas J. Philipson, an economics professor who studies obesity at the University of Chicago, a city recently named the fattest in America. "But we would rather take improvements in technology and agriculture than go back to the way we lived in the 1950s when everyone was thin. Nobody wants to sweat at work for 10 hours a day and be poor. Yes, you're obese, but you have a life that is much more comfortable."

For many corporations, and even for physicians, Americans' obesity has also fattened the bottom line. William L. Weis, a management professor at Seattle University, says revenue from the "obesity industries" will likely top $315 billion this year, and perhaps far more. That includes $133.7 billion for fast-food restaurants, $124.7 billion for medical treatments related to obesity, and $1.8 billion just for diet books—all told, nearly 3 percent of the overall U.S. economy.

Did you know, according to consumer-research firm Mintel Group, that we guzzled $37 billion in carbonated beverages in 2004? The same year, we spent $3.9 billion on cookies—$244 million of which were Oreo cookies sold by Kraft Foods for about $3.69 a package. In 2003, we splurged $57.2 billion on meals at restaurants such as Denny's, Chili's and Outback Steakhouse (a personal favorite). Potato chip sales hit $6.2 billion in 2004.

"Put simply, there is a lot of money being made, and to be made, in feeding both oversized stomachs and feeding those enterprises selling fixes for oversized stomachs," Weis wrote in 2005 in the Academy of Health Care Management Journal. "And both industries—those selling junk food and those selling fat cures—depend for their future on a prevalence of obesity."

And the prevalence of obesity won't fade anytime soon. According to David M. Cutler, an economist at Harvard University, Americans' waistlines are caught in a simple accounting quagmire. In a 2003 paper titled "Why Have Americans Become More Obese?" Cutler wrote: "As an accounting statement, people gain weight if there is an increase in calories taken in or a decrease in calories expended."

On the calories-expended side of the Fat Economy, economists have noted that changes in the workplace have caused us to burn fewer calories. Prior to the 1950s, jobs often meant hard labor. We lifted heavy things. We worked outside. Our desks—if we had them—did not come equipped with computers. We lived in urban environments, walking most places.

Now many Americans work in offices in buildings with elevators. If we walk anywhere, it's to lunch—to TGI Friday's or the corner burrito shop. We live in the suburbs, we drive to and from work and—in my case—to and from the mailbox. We pay $60 a month for the privilege of lifting something heavy in a gym we have to drive to. (I belong to two gyms, in the hope that guilt will cause me to visit at least one.) And we also must pay to exercise by giving up our free time. Do we work out, or do we drive the kids to their soccer game, where we can sit and watch? Do we work out, or do we download new songs from iTunes?

"People are just not willing to give up their leisure time," Philipson said. "People don't want to pay to exercise with their leisure time."

Which brings us to the calories-consumed side of the ledger. If we don't expend calories, they add up and turn into pounds. Thirty-five hundred calories generally equals one pound. So behold, for argument's sake, the french fry. An order of large fries at McDonald's puts 520 calories into one's body. It is well known, at least by this consumer, that an order of large fries can generally be placed, filled and consumed in a matter of minutes.

But this was not always so, Cutler said.

Before World War II, if you wanted a french fry, you went to the store, bought potatoes, took them home, washed them, peeled them, sliced them and fried them. "Without expensive machinery, these activities take a lot of time," Cutler said. "In the postwar period, a number of innovations allowed the centralization of french fry production." Now fries are prepped in factories using sophisticated technologies, then frozen at sub-40-degree temperatures and shipped to a restaurant, where they are deep-fried, or to someone's home, where they are microwaved. Either way, they are served up in a matter of minutes.

French fries helped drive up U.S. potato consumption by 30 percent between 1977 and 1995, but they mean more than that—they symbolize the convergence of the economic and technological changes that have made us fat. Cutler and Philipson have noted that when women joined the workplace, they left behind some of the labor that traditionally went into cooking meals. This happened as technology increasingly allowed for mass production and preparation of food. Much of this type of food—be it french fries, potato chips, frozen dinners or quick meals at restaurants—contains more calories.

We expend fewer calories and take more in. The pounds add up. Hence, the Fat Economy.

"The structure of the economy has made us more obese," Cutler said. "That is clearly true. What businesses do is they cater to what we want, whether what we want is really in our long-term interests or not. So people are obese and they want to diet, but they also want things to be immediately there. Manufacturers and storeowners make that possible. The upside is nobody spends two hours a day cooking anymore."

So do Americans have to be fat for the economy to thrive? The economy would not exactly crash if people stopped spending money on french fries and meals at TGI Friday's. Economists think the money would just be spent differently or in different places. Specific industries would adapt—as many have already, offering more healthful choices—to meet changing demands. No business can survive by selling things people don't want.

In fact the overall long-term economic costs of obesity are many. The $10,000 of extra medical care that the overweight require over their lifetimes certainly makes a doctor's wallet fatter, but it could bankrupt the health insurance industry. Also, research shows that while more women have entered the workforce, their wages, particularly for white women, sink if they are overweight.

Much of the long-term financial burden for obesity will fall on the shoulders of U.S. corporations, which already fork out billions of dollars a year in sick time and insurance costs related to obesity illnesses, and on American taxpayers, through their contributions for programs such as Medicare and Medicaid. What's more, shorter lifespans will more quickly take millions of educated people out of the workforce.

For that last problem, the Fat Economy has already found ways to innovate and profit. In Lynn, Ind., there is a company called Goliath Casket that makes caskets up to 52 inches wide. The company's Web site, which can be found at <www.oversizecasket. com/>, notes that Goliath's founder quit his job as a welder in 1985, saying: "Boys, I'm gonna go home and build oversize caskets that you would be proud to put your mother in."

———

Michael S. Rosenwald wrote this piece for the January 22, 2006, edition of *The Washington Post* <www.washingtonpost.com>.

Eat This Now!

BY SUSAN BRINK AND ELIZABETH QUERNA (2005)

It's everywhere. Tank up your car, and you walk past soft pretzels with cheese sauce. Grab a cup of coffee, and you see doughnuts, danishes, and cookies the size of hubcaps. Stop at Staples for an ink cartridge, and you confront candy bars at the register.

Stroll past the receptionist's desk at the office, and find somebody's leftover Christmas cookies, Valentine's Day candy, Easter Peeps, birthday cake, or vacation saltwater taffy. "We're just surrounded. Food is available every time you turn around," says Marilyn Tanner, dietitian at Washington University School of Medicine in St. Louis.

Overeating and its lethal companion underexercising are the recognized culprits in this country's rise in obesity rates. Today, two thirds of American adults are obese or overweight. A national team of researchers reported in last week's *New England Journal of Medicine* that obesity already reduces the current life expectancy in the United States by four to nine months.

What's worse, they project that the rise in obesity rates among children and teens could knock off as many as five years from today's average of 77 years as overweight people in that generation grow up and die prematurely. Diseases associated with obesity, such as diabetes, heart disease, kidney disease, and some cancers, are likely to strike at younger ages. It would be the first time in 200 years that children would be statistically likely to live shorter lives than their grandparents.

It's a controversial prediction, called speculative and "excessively gloomy" by Samuel Preston, a demographer at the University of Pennsylvania.

And the outcome is far from inevitable. All it would take to change that dire prediction is to have millions of people change their habits. That means diet, exercise, and a strong will within every individual to pass up high-calorie temptations. Right?

It's not that easy, as every failed and yo-yo dieter knows. The playing field is heavily tilted—by advertising, fast-paced lives, convenience foods, and treats every time you turn around—away from healthful eating choices. Many experts in nutrition, public health, and law believe that the national obesity problem doesn't simply come down to millions of failures of individual will.

ATTITUDE SHIFT

A generation ago, it was considered rude to eat in front of others. Now, Americans eat everywhere, all day long—an average of five meals a day, counting snacks. Cars have cupholders, but they arguably need trays, too. Americans eat 30 meals a year in their vehicles. "That's the average. I'm sure it's higher when it comes to people driving to work," said Harry Balzer, vice president of the NPD Group, a consumer marketing research firm that tracks how Americans eat. "Look at our cars. They look like restaurants."

Riddled with anxiety, we take our meals with equal parts pleasure and guilt. We might say an internal no a dozen times a day, then give in to the Krispy Kreme near the bus stop on the way home. Or if we pass up the doughnut shop, we get home only to find that the latest issue of Cooking Light has arrived in the mail—with a cover photo of pecan pie. We have few common rituals around dining but a common hurried pace through eating. All of these triggers and gustatory seductions play into an obesity epidemic—even as the messages manipulate the national obsession with health.

Food is more than a way of staying alive, more than an edible commodity. "Food is never just the physical product itself," says Stephanie Hartman, who teaches a course at Catholic University of America in Washington, D.C., called Food and Media. "It's invested with national meanings, associated with comfort and nostalgia. There are class associations. Food can be elegant or cultured." Or it can carry a reverse snobbery. Where once the elite sampled truffles, today they might seek the best barbecued ribs or the richest macaroni and cheese.

Certainly, the descendants of immigrants may still prepare pasta or pirogi recipes handed down from the old country, but Americans as a whole don't have shared food values. We don't all cook with the same oil, have an attachment to a certain variety of plum, or dine with predictable ceremony. Such culinary eclecticism may make us uniquely vulnerable to fads. "We don't have a culture of eating, a national cuisine, a traditional way of eating that guides us," says Tanner. "So we fall prey to the latest fad or scientific pronouncement. The fact that we're more responsive to medical trends makes us more responsive to marketing." As soon as science tells us that oat bran is good for preventing heart disease, people start buying potato chips sprinkled with oat bran. "This is who we are. We're always looking for the newest way to attack this problem. We're going to try to figure out this health issue by eating," says Balzer.

Why, even when we know better, do we succumb to the lure of rich desserts and nutritionally empty snacks? Why is the look—even stronger, the smell—of the forbidden so compelling? "I've seen evidence that bakeries and supermarkets pipe faked aromas out in the store," says Doug Kysar, a professor at Cornell Law School who teaches consumer law and studies deceptive advertising. "Things like taste and smell and sight can overcome one's awareness. The classic example is the candy gantlet at the supermarket. We have a long-term desire to maintain a healthful life, but the short-term desire can trump the long-term."

Marketers know what works. They tell us we're worth it, that we deserve it. "Magnify that by 45,000 different products, add in the fake bakery smell, the mood music in supermarkets calculated to lower blink rates to a somnolent state, the way the aisles are set up to keep people in the store for a longer time—that's an enormous amount of situational forces to weaken the will," says Kysar.

FOOD TO SELL

America is truly a horn of plenty. In the early 1980s, food production came to an average of 3,300 calories a day available to every person. Then farm policy changed, and farmers no longer plowed food under or slaughtered animals to be entitled to subsidies. Today, America produces enough food to allow every man, woman, and child 3,900 calories a day. "That additional food production had to be sold," says Marion Nestle, professor in the department of nutrition at New York University and author of Food Politics. "One of the first things that happened was portion sizes started getting bigger."

Many Americans feel entitled to big servings or a top-of-the-line chocolate bar as a way to get some short-term happiness. "You walk past a doughnut shop, and you say, 'Yum. Doughnuts.' Part of you says, 'No, I'll get fat.' But another part is like Scarlett O'Hara saying, 'Tomorrow is another day.' This feels good now," says Gail Saltz of the New York Psychoanalytic Institute.

Almost all of us are prone to comfort ourselves with food when we feel deprived in other ways. Many families have forsaken the shared meal and the long time of food preparation, dining, and cleanup as a communal effort. Along with it, they've lost an important psychological support. "If we take a good hour and a half to talk about our day, go slowly through the meal, maybe have a glass of wine—we're much more psychologically filled at the end of that meal than if I decide to eat alone. Then, I'm going to grab a hamburger and some chips," says psychoanalyst Kathryn Zerbe, vice chair for psychotherapy at Oregon Health and Science University.

Of course, we can just say no. But it's a David and Goliath fight. We're battling an entire environment, massive societal change, government policy, and billions of dollars in advertising.

Susan Brink and Elizabeth Querna wrote this piece for the March 28, 2005, edition of *US News and World Report* <www.usnews.com>.

A Desired Epidemic: Obesity and the Food Industry
BY DEBORAH COHEN (2007)

In the Middle Ages, alchemists sought to turn common metals into gold. Today some doctors and scientists seeking to prevent and treat obesity in the United States are attempting an equally difficult transformation. They want to change people, their willpower, their lifestyles, their metabolism, even their DNA to make it harder to gain weight and easier to lose it.

However, transforming people with drugs, weight-loss surgery, genetic engineering, hypnosis and other extreme steps is not the answer to obesity, because people are not the problem.

The problem is the food industry, which provides us with the calories we consume but washes its hands of responsibility for causing the worldwide obesity epidemic. Food industry marketers say they are only offering people what they want and that individuals choose what they put in their mouths.

Is it plausible that two out of three Americans have an eating disorder? And if we really believe that people are choosing to eat foods that are making them fat, does that mean we think that two-thirds of Americans are foolish, stupid, and lazy? Or that overweight and obese people have weaker characters and are morally inferior to people who have a normal weight?

The food industry spends billions of dollars each year to develop products, packaging, advertising and marketing techniques that entice us to buy more food because selling more food means making more profits. And businesses exist to make profits.

Food marketers test whether the color, the font size of words and the images used to market food will grab our attention by studies of eye movement. They conduct focus groups to come up with catchy names and symbols that recall positive memories and thoughts to condition a response that may lead us to purchase their products. And food marketers work to increase the frequency with which we see their products and their presence in stores, wanting to make their products always available.

The food industry also alters the nutritional content of foods to make them longer lasting on store shelves by increasing fats, sugars, and salt, making it less healthy for the average person to consume them.

Much evidence shows that individuals are not the cause of America's obesity epidemic. A wealth of research on marketing and decision-making reveals that people are easily manipulated, biased and influenced to make decisions that are not in their own best interests by how choices are presented to them.

Daniel Kahneman and Amos Tversky won a Nobel Prize by proving that rational decision-making is limited. Another school of research indicates that people typically make decisions about what and how much to eat unconsciously and can be manipulated to eat excessively without their awareness, simply by altering factors such as portion size, variety, ambience and packaging.

Just as a bell became a cue for Pavlov's dog to salivate, the current environment has ubiquitous cues that condition people to eat, even when they know they shouldn't. It is very difficult for people to resist the largely reflexive and automatic nature of our response to available food.

We can throw up our hands and say that's the way it is, and let the marketing that is leading more Americans to become obese and ill go unchecked.

A wiser choice would be to demand that government bring more regulation to the food environment, making sure that what is available is healthy, and that the contents of foods are transparent and easily understandable, even to those who are illiterate. Such regulation could reduce the magnitude of flawed decision-making by individuals by presenting us with healthier choices. And such regulation is literally a matter of life and death.

Food marketing efforts are the modern Sirens, leading us inexorably to chronic diseases and sometimes to early deaths. Just as Ulysses was able to defeat the Sirens by having his men plug their ears and tie him to the mast, today we need active protection from an aggressive food industry that is luring us to obesity and illness.

People who are overweight and obese are unknowing victims of a food environment created for corporate profits rather than health. When people suffer from an unhealthy environment that is cutting years from their lives, they need help from government to assure healthy conditions through regulation and enforcement.

As a society, regulation has served us well. We regulate building construction as a means of assuring quality and value. If contractors use substandard materials or techniques, good inspectors will require the work to be done right before approval is granted.

We regulate the car industry. Seat belts and air bags have saved tens of thousands of lives. We regulate the alcohol industry, only allowing sales in licensed establishments to people 21 and over, and have found fewer alcohol-related traffic fatalities in localities with more controls. We regulate water quality, air quality and tobacco.

Today we view clean air and water as a right to which we are entitled. Regulation is an assertion of, and not an infringement to, our rights. Regulation of the food environment is the next right we need to claim.

An estimated 150 million Americans are overweight or obese. Too many will die before their time due to heart disease, diabetes and other ailments. While the nation remains focused on waging war on terrorism, which has claimed thousands of lives, millions are dying prematurely because they aren't getting the government protection they need from the Sirens of the food industry.

———

Deborah Cohen is a physician and a senior natural scientist at the RAND Corporation, a non-profit research organization. She is the co-author of the book *Prescription for a Healthy Nation, a New Approach to Improving Our Lives by Fixing Our Everyday World* (Beacon Press). This piece was published on February 20, 2007, at www.washingtonpost.com.

The Big, Fat American Kid Crisis . . .
And 10 Things We Should Do About It

BY ELEANOR RANDOLPH (2006)

The problem is all too obvious. At the mall, the movie theater or the airport, the evidence appears in the flesh—altogether too much of it. Americans are now officially supersized, overweight, obese even. This is true of almost two thirds of American adults, but what is more alarming, it is also true of millions of American children. The "little ones" aren't so little anymore.

Yes, they are gently labeled "chunky," "husky" or "plus-sized" by the clothes marketers who are adding larger and larger sizes to the children's racks. But these euphemisms can't cover up the unpleasant reality that too many of our kids are so dangerously overweight that they are spilling out of their childhood—too chubby for their car seats or too uncomfortable as they squeeze into their little desks at elementary school. But the real problem is not aesthetics or the need to save classroom space. Childhood obesity has become a national medical crisis.

Over the last 30 years, obesity rates have doubled among pre-schoolers and tripled for those age 6 to 11. For those added pounds, the young are starting to pay a terrible price. Adult diabetes has rapidly become a childhood disease. Pediatricians are seeing high cholesterol and high blood pressure and other grown-up problems in their patients. Teachers and school psychiatrists are coping with a plague of shame and distress among children whose size subjects them to hazing and other cruelties by their classmates.

Many overweight kids even suffer from sleep apnea, the snoring disease that usually afflicts middle-aged men and women with beer bellies. Adolescent apnea means that students are irritable, sleepy and ready to catch any cold germ that lands on their No. 2 pencil at school.

The National Institutes of Health estimates that Americans will take five years off our average lifespan in a few years if we don't curb obesity, especially among the young. The Centers for Disease Control and Prevention has estimated that the obesity epidemic is already costing our health care system about $79 billion a year. And that bill is expanding as fast as the national waistline.

America's culture of "personal responsibility" means that we are quick to blame fat people for their condition. Certainly, anyone overweight bears part of the responsibility for their condition, and each person whose body mass index is over 25 needs to be part of any solution to the obesity epidemic. The comedian Billy Connolly has a point when he suggests, "If you want to lose a bit of weight, don't eat anything that comes in a bucket."

But Americans are not getting fatter because of a sudden shortage of self-discipline. There are broader social forces at work that are conspiring to overload Americans—particularly American children—with calories while reducing the amount time and effort spent burning those calories away.

A good deal of the fault lies with Big Food, the name, echoing Big Tobacco, that critics have given to food companies that keep trying to foist dangerous food choices on the American public, including children. We should encourage young people—and particularly the nation's 9 million overweight children—to take responsibility for their weight and health. But we should also start to consider childhood obesity a social problem, and take action as a nation.

Here are 10 places to start:

1. STOP BOMBARDING CHILDREN WITH JUNK FOOD ADS

It's easy to blame young people for eating badly. But this generation has been confronted with something previous generations never faced: an unprecedented wave of sophisticated, multimedia advertising designed to hook them on unhealthy food before they are old enough understand what is happening.

Children's television has become an incredibly efficient way to sell soda, candy, salty snacks, and other junk foods. Although the industry pretends there's confusion, the evidence is clear. Children younger than 8-years-old cannot tell the difference between advertising and entertainment on television. Some in the food industry have exerted at least a modicum of restraint (Kraft has put limits on ads aimed at toddlers, for example, and Coca-Cola avoids programs for those under 12), but it's too hard for the corporations to police themselves.

In the 1970's, the Federal Trade Commission proposed a rule to ban or severely restrict all television advertising to children. But guess what? The food lobbyists didn't like it, so Congress passed something it called "The Federal Trade Commission Improvements Act of 1980." The "improvements" in this case include stripping the agency of the authority to restrict advertising—a clear improvement from the point of view of Big Food. Instead of banning children's ads, the Congress gave us a voluntary system that is funded by the industry and doesn't really work.

So, kid's television is a Pinocchio's Land of Toys—a sugary world where all the candy one can eat eventually turns children into junk-food donkeys. Extra-large donkeys. The Center for Science in the Public Interest recently announced plans to file a lawsuit in Massachusetts against the Kellogg Company and Viacom (which owns Nickelodeon) after determining that 88 percent of the ads on children's television were for cookies, pastries, sugary cereals, candy and other junk food. The center, allied with a Boston-based group called Campaign for a Commercial-Free Childhood, argues that the advertising aimed at toddlers as young as two years old is "creepy" and "predatory."

They're right. Those ads—including an ad for Apple Jacks cereal that made an apple look menacing and grumpy—can launch a lifetime of bad eating habits. Congress should give the F.T.C. back its authority to regulate children's television commercials, and the F.T.C. should start protecting children from junk food propaganda.

2. PROSELYTIZE FOR HEALTHY EATING

It's time for elected officials, and other prominent people, especially young people, to use their bully pulpits, and the powers of their office or their fame, to send a message to kids about how to eat right. One excellent model in this regard is Gov. Mike Huckabee of Arkansas, who has made healthy living a personal crusade.

Huckabee was diagnosed with Type 2 diabetes, and his doctors told him that if he didn't lose weight, he wasn't likely to live much longer. Huckabee, who used to joke that he weighed almost as much as a cement truck, dropped more than 100 pounds, and began such an intense exercise regime that he now runs marathons.

As a missionary for healthier living, the Arkansas governor speaks publicly, often, about the importance of healthy eating and exercise. And he has launched a program called "Healthy Arkansas," which encourages people to exercise and eat well. Among other things, the state allows workers a half hour off each day to exercise and free pedometers are available to help measure how many miles they cover per workday.

Since his heart surgery, Bill Clinton has also taken his turn speaking out against child-hood obesity. Earlier this year, he and the Robert Wood Johnson Foundation announced an $8 million initiative to encourage children to eat better and exercise more. He has also joined with the American Heart Association to start the Alliance for a Healthier Generation, which offers an obesity newsletter and tips for combating childhood obesity. The alliance has also entered into a partnership with Nickelodeon to foster healthier lifestyles for children.

These initiatives are great, but they are easily drowned out by the massive advertising campaigns of Big Food. More elected officials, celebrities and foundations need to speak out. Athletes and movie and television stars and the music crowd idealized by the young could be particularly influential. They could beam this message into every young head: eating junk food and staring at a computer or television screen all day is simply not cool. Dancing is cool. Carrots are cool. Fruit, which does not naturally come in loops, is cool.

3. BAN THE JUNK FOOD IN SCHOOLS

Another reason this generation is fatter than its predecessors is that junk food has never been as easily accessible as it is right now. Food in school used to be limited to the mystery meats and limp vegetables served up in the cafeteria. But the soda, fast food and junk food industries have fought hard to get a foothold in schools, and they have been extraordinarily successful.

Big food has been remarkably strategic about plotting its assault on the schools. It has promised woefully under-funded school systems a share of the take from vending machines, or outright cash gifts. Many school systems have caved.

According to a 2005 report by the Government Accountability Office, 83 percent of elementary schools, 97 percent of middle schools and 99 percent of high schools sell junk food from vending machines or school stores. Parents' groups, and other civically minded people, are beginning to fight back, trying to extricate junk food from the schools. But many states (including New York) seem to be circling the issue while they let the sweet, sugar and bad fat industry continue adding to the adolescent waistline.

A bipartisan amendment offered recently to the National School Lunch Act in Congress would prohibit the sale in schools of any foods that are too high in fat, sodium and sugar. The law currently permits the sale of many unhealthy foods in the cafeteria if they contain at least five percent of certain vitamins and minerals. That means candy bars (think peanuts) and ice cream (cream) and chips (corn). You don't have to be a registered dietician to know that a Snickers bar or a bag of Cheetos should not meet anyone's definition of healthy eating. The biggest benefit from this amendment would be to stop the sale of drinks and snacks from vending machines anywhere in a public school during school hours.

The U.S. Department of Agriculture should be able to regulate all food being served in schools, and states and local school districts should also uphold higher standards. Children are required by law to attend school, where they become a captive audience for whatever food and beverages are available. We should not allow the soft drink and junk food industries to push their products on children on school property.

Until the law changes, we're stuck with voluntary measures.

President Clinton recently brokered such a deal in which the nation's largest soda companies agreed to keep non-diet soda out of elementary and middle schools. It is an important step, though it does not go as far as it should. The ban does not cover sports drinks or diet sodas, both of which present health risks for young people. It also does not cover all of the many non-beverage products that continue to be dangled before children at school. And it does not cover high school, where the need for better nutrition is every bit as great as in the lower grades.

4. UPGRADE THE SCHOOL SNACK

It is not enough to keep unhealthy snacks away from children. We need to provide them with healthy alternatives.

Senator Tom Harkin, a Democrat from Iowa who has been active in the fight against childhood obesity, has a smart idea about snacking. He has started a pilot program that allows the government to give away fresh fruits and vegetables as snacks at over 100 schools and two Indian tribal organizations, mostly in the Midwest.

The "Harkin Snack," as we'd like to call it, should be offered at schools across the country. On an average day, less than half of American children (45 percent) eat any fruit at all, according to the Center for Science in the Public Interest. Part of giving away these fresh fruits and vegetables at school may be a way of introducing it to the many young people who think corn is a kind of Halloween candy.

5. TAX THE FATTENERS

America has a long tradition of "sin taxes" aimed at products like cigarettes and alcohol, partly to discourage their use, and partly to recoup some of the costs that these products impose on society. Junk food should be subject to such a tax. There should be an especially high tax on trans fats, a test-tube food product that is present in a lot of processed foods and is believed to be a leading contributor to heart disease.

Just as federal gas taxes are earmarked for highway construction, fat taxes could be earmarked for special programs that could help counter the problems caused by junk food—helping to pay for after-school athletic programs or the rising medical costs of fighting diabetes among the young. Another good use of the money would be an advertising campaign, modeled on the anti-smoking campaigns, that counteracts the messages Big Food is sending out about junk food.

Expect Big Food to fight back—and hard. As the movie "Thank You For Smoking" recently reminded us, corporations spend a lot of time and money getting out a positive message about their products—even if those products are tobacco, firearms and alcohol.

For a taste of what Big Food is already doing, check out The Center for Consumer Freedom, a collection of anti-public-service messages funded by the restaurant and junk food industries.

6. STOP SUBSIDIZING JUNK FOOD

Agricultural subsidies got their start during the Great Depression, to help starving farmers to survive. Today, they are largely a form of corporate welfare for large farmers. In addition to costing taxpayers dearly, these subsidies are creating some unhealthy incentives for big agriculture.

A prime example is the roughly $40 billion in corn subsidies government has handed out over the last decade. They've encouraged farmers, not surprisingly, to raise a lot of corn. Too much of this taxpayer-subsidized corn is being used to produce high-fructose corn syrup, which is now so cheap that it has practically replaced sugar in many processed foods.

Nutritionists suggest that high-fructose corn syrup, which is showing up in foods of all kinds, is a stealth reason why Americans are getting fat. An American Journal of Clinical Nutrition study shows how Type 2 diabetes and sweetener use have soared together over the last 25 years. There needs to be a broad-based attack on the overuse of high-fructose corn syrup, including better labeling requirements, and public education. But an obvious place to start is removing the taxpayer subsidy on corn converted to sweeteners.

Nobody wants to get rid of sweets altogether, but the American sweet tooth has been recklessly over-indulged in recent decades. Sweeteners should be a rare treat, not a staple of the Western diet.

7. START SUBSIDIZING HEALTHY FOOD FOR POOR PEOPLE

Another key reason children are eating badly is that junk food is cheap. It is often a lot cheaper than fresh fruits and vegetables. "If you tell a family, you really ought to be eating more salads and fresh fruit, and this is a low-income family, we're essentially encouraging them to spend more money," Adam Drenowski, professor of epidemiology at the University of Michigan, told the Associated Press last year. The most effective way to help poor people to eat better is to help them pay the bills. Governor Huckabee of Arkansas has been trying to change his state's food stamps program to give a bonus to people when they spend money on fruits and vegetables, and reducing the value of the food stamps when they are spent on junk food. It is a great idea, but sadly the federal government has been resisting granting permission—and it is hard to believe the political influence of Big Food isn't part of the reason.

Members of Congress should amend the food stamps law to build in an express reward for spending directed at healthy food, and a penalty for buying junk. Other states should also follow Governor Huckabee's lead and push for state-level changes.

8. LABEL FOOD IN CHAIN RESTAURANTS

Labeling of food in restaurants lags far behind labeling in supermarkets. Consumers who eat out but want to eat right are mostly dining in the dark. At one time, that didn't matter. But in today's hurried world, most Americans spend about half their food budget outside the home. Many products that are served in fast-food restaurants—like Chicken McNuggets—are not found in nature, and a consumer would have no way of knowing exactly what they are getting nutritionally without more data provided by the restaurant. (McDonald's does provide nutritional information, though not as prominently as it could.) At the very least, consumers at chain restaurants have a right to know the data—calories, fat, saturated fat, trans fat, salt, sugar and high-fructose corn syrup—in every dish.

The restaurant industry managed to win an exemption from the 1990 law that requires nutrition labeling on most foods and drinks we buy at the store. It's time to close that loophole for the chains that have standard fare and standard menus. So far, power brokers in Congress and the White House have been listening more to the restaurateurs than to the customers. If we want to hold people responsible for their food choices—a common refrain of Big Food—we have to give them the information they need to make informed choices.

9. EDUCATE PARENTS AND TEACHERS

Parents have a key role to play in combating childhood obesity. They have enormous influence (though certainly nowhere near as much as they would like) over what their children eat, and how much exercise they get. Unfortunately, many parents are themselves not very knowledgeable about obesity and healthy living.

With nearly half of New York City's elementary school students either overweight or obese, Dr. Thomas Frieden, New York City's health commissioner, launched an effort last fall to educate parents, make healthier food available and press schools for more physical fitness. Some other cities are energized as well. Philadelphia's Food Trust found little healthy food options in many inner-city stores (only one store offer individual-sized low-fat milk and none had fresh fruit). So they began pushing the stores, snack food distributors and even food companies to make better choices available.

California has been a pioneer, launching a rigorous anti-obesity program in schools two years ago. In Arkansas, for the past three years, the state has been weighing children in school, and sending home confidential notes to parents whose children are overweight. Since the program began, the state's childhood obesity rate has inched down slightly.

Other states should quickly follow the lead of California and Arkansas. Along with information about their children's weight, parents need educational materials that explain how to help their children eat right, the recommended intake for nutrition and calories for children of different ages and the amount of time they should be active every day.

10. EXERCISE FOR EVERYBODY

As any nutritionist can attest, controlling food intake is only half of the battle in keeping thin. The other half is exercise. It is no secret that too many children are not running, jumping or moving around enough. There are many reasons, from the rise of video games to the carpooling culture, which means that many children scarcely do more than walk across the parking lot on an average day.

An important part of the solution should be organized athletic activity in the schools. Unfortunately, too many physical education classes are mired in the distant past. They should be re-imagined to use their limited time in the most efficient way.

One experiment by researchers at the University of Wisconsin found that in old-fashioned gym classes, by the time clothing is changed and attendance taken, only about 25 minutes is left for actual exercise. The study showed that fitness classes that focused on simply keeping kids moving allowed children an average of 42 minutes of exercise per class, and did more to help them lose weight and keep fit.

In this age of high-consequence testing, schools are understandably focused on reading and math scores, and ultimately, on college placement rates. But physical fitness is important for its own sake as a means of keeping children healthy, relaxed and energetic enough to learn well. Schools should devote more of their self-improvement efforts toward making more energetic play time in the earlier years and more inventive physical education programs for adolescents.

No one favors childhood obesity. But too many companies and their stockholders are more concerned about profit than products. And too few adults, from elected officials to school principals, are giving the problem the attention it deserves. This is not an issue that can be solved with a few narrow fixes—by shifting to diet drinks and going for cookies that are labeled low-fat. With more than a majority of Americans overweight, obesity and near-obesity are now society's problems. And the oversized American now requires a change in the national culture, starting in the high chair.

—Lela Moore contributed research for this article.

Eleanor Randolph wrote this piece, part of the Talking Points series, for the May 10, 2006, edition of *The New York Times* <www.nytimes.com>.

from The Fat Girl's Guide to Life

BY WENDY SHANKER (2004)

INTRODUCTION

I went on a sixteen-year odyssey of self-loathing and self-doubt. Instead of a Cyclops, I faced off against Jenny Craig. Instead of Sirens, vast quantities of chocolate-chip banana muffins attempted to lure me from my true path. The odyssey's over now. The monsters, both the ones I discovered and the ones I created, have been vanquished. Now I know that there's nothing wrong with me mentally or physically. I'm just fat, that's all.

I didn't win by epiphany, or a life-changing conversation; nor was I shot by a magic bullet. This was a war of attrition; I simply decided I'd had enough. Enough of looking in the mirror and cursing myself out before I'd even brushed my teeth. Enough of punishing myself and my body by reading Danielle Steel in the shade while everyone else was swimming in the pool. Enough of looking up at mirrored ceilings in elevators to assure myself that I was pretty. Enough of squeezing into nylon undergarments that cut off my circulation and left red welts in my skin. Enough of giving away my hard-earned cash to undo a situation that steadily got less undoable.

Honestly, given the choice between being fat or putting myself through the drama of trying to be thin, I'd rather be fat.

It's not that I've "given up on myself" or "let myself go." I don't sit around in my jammies eating bonbons all day. I go to the gym four or five times a week. I count up my proteins and carbohydrates, and usually record what I eat in a little notebook at the end of the day. I follow the latest medical news and research new ideas. I go to the doctor to stay on top of my blood pressure, cholesterol, and triglycerides. I haven't stopped trying to finesse my body into a shape that would make life easier for me and simpler for society to accept.

But I've certainly changed my standards. And I've changed my attitude.

I encourage you to diet and exercise and liposuck and Ab-Roll if that's really what you want, and if you're convinced that you have to change your body to make yourself happy.

But if it's not . . .

If it's really what you think your husband wants . . .

If it's really what you think your mother wants . . .

If it's really what you think Cameron Diaz wants . . .

If it's what you think you've been doing for just about forever and it isn't working and some days you just hope a car will run you over but you're pretty sure that you're so fat that the speeding vehicle will simply bounce off of you . . . then it's time to stop and reevaluate.

It's time to change our attitudes about this whole body-image business. It *is* a business. It *is* an image. But it is *YOUR* body, which contains *YOUR* mind, which can be a whole lot easier to change than the width of your thighs or the shape of your ass.

We should be able to laugh at an issue as silly as cellulite, but we don't. Can we at least try to evaluate beauty on our own terms instead of the terms we've decided to accept from *Vogue* and Hollywood and your aunt Gertrude and the girl who won "Best Booty" in high school? Shouldn't we teach men to lust for something other than women with little-girl bodies and Playboy Bunny breasts? And can't we figure out a better way to spend our time and money while we're in the process?

I'm not a doctor. I'm not a therapist. I don't have a degree in health education. I'm just a professional ex-dieter with a chip on my shoulder and a mission on my mind. There are too many women just like me who know more information about fat grams than about foreign policy, who spend more time counting calories than communicating with friends. That ain't right.

I'm going to take a good hard look at the weight loss industry, the government, media and celebrities, family and friends, feelings, fashion, and feminism. All of these things affect the way I think about myself and my body and the strategies I've used to come to terms with the skin I'm in. It's been a long, uphill battle.

Now I champion anti-dieting with the best of 'em, but I have to admit I still have my good days and my bad days. I swear off calorie counting, but secretly hope that someday I'll come up with the resolve to ban bagels from my life. I've pretty much resolved that I'll never mold a bicep out of my bat wings, but I still lift weights at the gym. I'm not one hundred percent self-satisfied, but I'm trying; I'm closer. I'm not pushing for complete self-acceptance; self-tolerance is a perfectly reasonable place to begin. I'm not in touch with my Goddess Power, I don't think I have a fabulous body, and I'm certainly not about to chant some New Agey "just love yourself" mantra. I don't look in the mirror and see a beautiful, bountiful me with a sunset on the horizon and doves flitting around in the air. But I no longer apologize for who I am or how I look. I have more important things to do.

So do you. You have a career to pursue, you have creativity to develop, you have a family to raise, and you have friends to love. You live in a society in the midst of major transition that needs your attention and your help. In light of what's happening to women across the globe—rape, poverty, lack of health care, lack of legal rights, and civil war on a daily basis—our obsession with calorie counting seems ridiculous.

We are ready, willing, and able to change the way the world sees us. But to do that, we start by changing the way we see ourselves. Friends won't stop making helpful yet asinine suggestions about corn oil and couscous until you tell them that their suggestions are asinine, not helpful. Bullies won't stop making fun of you until you stand up to them. Magazines won't start putting fat girls in their pages until you start buying magazines that already feature fat girls in their pages. Manufacturers won't stop making fattening fat-free food until you stop eating it. And don't expect Brad Pitt to make out with Camryn Manheim in his next movie, or the captain of the football team to push aside the head cheerleader so he can get some face time with the chubby yet sweet yearbook editor until you are ready to accept those changes yourself.

The good news is that the wheels are already in motion. We have fat girls starring on Broadway and in prime-time TV shows. We are heroines in best-selling novels, and our faces (and bodies) are finally showing up in mainstream women's magazines. We are going to win this battle. After all, we are bigger than they are. There are more of Us than there are of Them (68 percent of the American female population wear a size 12 or larger). So why are we scared to fight back? Why do we shoulder the responsibility of failure ("I have no willpower"/"I'm not trying hard enough"/"I'm a loser"/"It's because of my period") instead of challenging the system? Has it occurred to you that if you can't reach your goal weight at Diet Center then maybe something is wrong with the goal weight and not wrong with you? If you suck down Slim-Fast shakes, feel hungry and irritable, do the plan to the letter, and still don't lose weight, have you considered that it's not the piece of cinnamon toast you ate last Tuesday that messed you up? If you work out like a triathlete and still have flab hanging from your arms, did you ever think that maybe those are just the arms you've got and even if you hired Jennifer Aniston's trainer to kick you into gear you still wouldn't feel comfy in a tube top?

The truth is, women who wear a size 2 often feel just crappy about themselves and think they look as big as houses. So go ahead and feel fat. Or, if the f-word doesn't apply to you, substitute "zitty." Or "curly-haired." Or "short." Whatever. If you have a physical attribute that's going to keep you from getting a $20 million paycheck from a Hollywood studio, then we have a lot in common.

Maybe you'll relate to body changes that are beyond your control (say, from illness or accident or pregnancy), or body changes that you regret to this day (like Cheetos overload, or sitting on your couch all day watching *Ricki Lake* reruns, or breaking the seal on Baskin-Robbins Jamoca Almond Fudge for the first time). You may be thinking about those five elusive pounds you want to lose, or the fifty-five, or the hundred and five.

I suggest that you take it a step further. Think about how much time you've spent thinking about that poundage, and the time you've spent punishing yourself about that poundage. Then I'd like you to imagine NOT doing that. Instead, imagine the relief you'd feel if you could walk past a plate-glass window without cursing your reflection. Imagine not sucking it in when your office crush object strolls by. Imagine walking around on a windy day without holding your shirt out in front of you so it doesn't brush your belly.

Now imagine if we all did it. The Fat Girls and the Skinny Chicks. The Beauty Queens and the Dowdy Spinsters, the Flaming Queens and the Butch Rodeo Riders. The Movie Stars and the PR Agents, the Senators and the Interns, the Personal Shoppers and the Supermarket Clerks. The Soccer Moms and the CEOs. Mmm . . . all that free time on our minds that we aren't using to rip ourselves to shreds. All that money in our wallets that we're not going to spend on fat-free, sugar-free, taste-free sorbet. That's a lot of minutes and a lot of money from a lot of women who have a lot of brain power.

This book is for you, whether you feel fat or look fat or act fat or none of the above. I hope that by the end of it you'll understand the difference between being fat and being FAT. You are going to take all the time and energy you've been wasting thinking about your body and work on the stuff that really matters to you as an individual. You just may find that the thing you thought you wanted—a thin body—isn't really what you need the most.

I figure: If we can't take it off, then we might as well just take it on.

CHAPTER 1: FROM 'FAT' TO 'FAT'

Wendy is a fat girl's name.
—*Monica (Courteney Cox Arquette) on* Friends

I start by telling the friend or coworker or acquaintance that I'm writing a book called *The Fat Girl's Guide to Life.* He or she usually looks me over from head to toe before choosing words carefully. "But Wendy, I don't think of you as—." This generally takes a second, because it's hard to say the word—"fat."

I know, sweetie, because you think fat is something really awful. You think fat means "loserish" and "lame" and "disgusting" and "hopeless." None of those words describe me. But I'm here to tell you that "fat" is a word. It's an adjective. Like "tall" or "brunette" or "female" or "Jewish" or "smart," which are other adjectives that describe me. By any standard you can find—societal norms, a doctor's chart, a clothing rack, my own personal ideals—I am most definitely fat. So go ahead and start thinking of me that way.

THE F-WORD

"Fat."

If you ever want to make people visibly uncomfortable, just say the f-word out loud.

You can refer to yourself as fat ("Hi, I'm fat!") or acknowledge that someone else is fat ("She's pretty, but she sure is fat!"), but either way, you're pretty much guaranteed to freak someone out.

"Fat" is the word I use to describe my physical stature. I use it without apology. The more I use it, the more comfortable I feel with it, and the less power it has to hurt me when someone else uses it as an insult. When I describe myself to someone else, I like to say I'm fat, but it usually scares the hell out of 'em. I don't know what they picture— maybe one of those people Richard Simmons has to suck out of a house with a forklift. By now I've said the word so many times that it really doesn't bother me anymore. I don't mind the word; it's the associations I can do without. What's the worst thing some- one can say to me? "You're fat!"? No duh. I just told you that.

"Fat" literally means "containing or full of fat; oily; greasy . . . said of meat." It also means "prosperous; profitable; lucrative; valuable." Screw the dictionary definitions; in our society, "fat" means bad. Unless you're on one of those high-fat, no-carb diets, that

is. In that case, set yourself up with a slab of bacon and some eggs Benedict on the side—
without the English muffin, of course.

"But Wendy," says my poor innocent friend/relative/victim, "since 'fat' is such a loaded
word, isn't there a different one you can use?"

Sure. I could use "overweight," or "plus size," or "curvaceous," or any of a million
others, and I do. But why not call it like I see it? The word that I like the most, and the
one that I think aptly describes my body, is "fat." The opposite of thin. I like it. It's short,
it's sweet, it's surprisingly compact.

But why do I call myself a fat girl instead of a fat woman? Personally, using the word
"girl" conjures up the energy of "girl power," aka the fun side of feminism. "Fat girl" is
also one of those phrases in our collective unconscious—like "the fat kid"—that's desperately in need of a mental makeover. One night—and this is recently—I was on a packed
subway train minding my own business. As the train pulled into my stop I said "Excuse
me," so I could start weaving my way through a knot of people. Right behind me, this
teenage girl who had been making out with her boyfriend the whole ride said in a really
loud voice, "FAT GIRL COMING THROUGH!" I can't begin to tell you how surprised
I was, how humiliated I felt. I didn't get my composure back until I was off the train and
it was too late to say something in response. I mean, I'm ME. Fantastic ME. I'm the
thirty-one-year-old you-go-girl, writing the book you are reading this very minute, but
that little phrase cut me to the quick. I don't know why she said it. I'm pretty sure that it
was about her and not me—maybe she wanted to impress her boyfriend, maybe she
needed to let him know that she would never get fat (like me), maybe I reminded her of
her mother or sister or friend or ex-friend or some girl at school she hates. Maybe she was
pissed that my big fat ass was taking up valuable subway seat space and I had been too
lost in my own thoughts to notice.

And what was I supposed to say to her? I know what I would have asked her if I had
the moment back again. I'd calmly ask her why. "Why say that? What are you trying to
accomplish? I'm not going to be mean to you, like you were to me, I just want to know
why." It's not my job to defend myself against this girl. It's her job not to attack me.

Still, it's hard to be called "fat" and just roll with it. I think of poor Fergie. You know,
Sarah Ferguson, flame-haired duchess and current spokesmodel for Weight Watchers.
British tabloids regularly referred to her as "the Duchess of Pork." Journalists printed a
story that said 82 percent of men would rather sleep with a goat than Fergie. But a recent
news story from Reuters revealed that Fergie "recently came face to face with the author

of the 'Duchess of Pork' headline that most haunted her, only to find that her enemy was a jovial, balding, middle-aged man who had no idea of the years of distress he had caused. Before long she was joking with him, realizing suddenly that the writer bore her no malice and never had. 'He was paid to be clever, end of story. It occurred to me that we survive our critics by knowing that their agendas, at heart, may have little to do with us,' she said." Kind of like my little lady on the subway. Props to Fergie for calling her tormentor out, but what a shame that she had to hurt for so many years. Can you relate?

Words are just a bunch of letters in a row. A word isn't negative, it's our connotation that is. The words can stay the same; it's our attitudes about them that have to change. You've seen this evolution happen in the gay community with the word "queer." Once reviled, the word "queer" now demands respect and pride. Only a few years ago, would you have thought that a show called *Queer Eye for the Straight Guy* would be a hit on network television? Could *The Fat Pick on the Skinny Chick* be far behind?

Like gay men have, we need to reappropriate "fat" and take back the power of the word, But just because I'm opening the floodgates on "fat" doesn't mean that someone outside the fold is allowed to take it too far. Yes, I am a Fat Girl. And I am coming through. But to the rest of you riding the train with me, I hope this is what will come through loud and clear: Keep your insults to yourself.

————

Writer and comedian Wendy Shanker, whose website can be found at <www.wendyshanker. com>, lives in New York City. Her book *The Fat Girl's Guide to Life* was published in 2004 by Bloomsbury USA.

Why We Hate Fat People

BY J. ERIC OLIVER (2005)

O besity! Ugh. Those people are so gross. It's sick. How could they let themselves get that way?"

It is remarkable how often I've heard comments like this one when I tell people about the book I am writing, *Fat Politics*. Most thin people I've met seem to have a pretty harsh view toward the obese. Over the past three years, I've heard scores of unsolicited invectives of disgust and contempt for fat people, particularly from educated, middle-class folks who otherwise pride themselves on being rational and fair-minded. Even more interesting is how they assume that I, as an affluent thin person, naturally share in their horror. Like a group of white folks surreptitiously sharing a racist joke, many thin middle-class people will easily convey their disdain for the obese if no fat people are around.

Although there is a logic to why thinness is valued, it does not sufficiently explain the vehemence against fat people. Clearly, the loathing of fatness comes from another source, and that source is fear. As with any type of prejudice, the animosity toward fat people originates in some much deeper anxieties over self and social status. For not only is thinness a convenient way for middle-class people to assert their moral superiority and boost their self-image, it also serves to rationalize the social inequalities that exist between various social groups.

Find this hard to believe? Listen closely to how Americans criticize fat people and you'll find rationalizations that are remarkably similar to those historically used to justify negative attitudes toward all marginalized groups in America. Fat people are thought to be gluttonous, lustful, greedy, lazy, weak-willed, and lacking any kind of self-control. If fat people are targets of our contempt, it is only because they have brought this on themselves with their unwillingness to take responsibility for their own actions.

The ideology that underscores this prejudice is an ethos of individualism and self-reliance. As with blacks and the poor, fat people are thought to violate some of the most fundamental tenets in American political culture: that all people are fundamentally responsible for their own welfare; that self-control and restraint are the hallmarks of virtue; and that all Americans are obliged to work at improving themselves. These views derive partly from our liberal political tradition that emphasizes the importance of individual freedom and rights and the restraint of government power. And, as we've seen, they also come from America's Anglo-Protestant heritage that emphasized individuals' unique responsibility for demonstrating their worth before God. This individualism has also been accentuated by two hallmarks of American economic development—laissez-faire capitalism and entrepreneurship—which both celebrate the good that individual initiative promotes in the free market. Whether it is the rugged frontiersman, the lonesome cowboy, or the Horatio Alger stories of the self-made man, American heroes are notable for their individual pluck, initiative, and isolation.

The importance of this individualistic ethos continues to be evident in contemporary American attitudes toward the poor. Most Americans dislike welfare programs, not because they are opposed to helping others, but because they think that relying on government aid betrays a lack of self-reliance and individual responsibility. In situations in which poverty is seen to be beyond the person's control (such as with children or the elderly), Americans are quite willing to embrace government spending. Programs including Head Start and Social Security enjoy wide support because they are seen to assist the "deserving" poor. Conversely, able-bodied adults are held responsible for their own condition and are thought not to be deserving of aid or government redistribution of wealth. This individualistic ethos thus serves as an important rationale for justifying the tremendous gulf between rich and poor in the United States: barring a few exceptions, if people are poor, they only have themselves to blame.

Nor does this individualistic ethos stop with the poor—it is also at the heart of many white Americans' racial attitudes. Most whites know that it is no longer publicly acceptable to express racist stereotypes and, unlike a generation ago, most whites no longer publicly voice negative stereotypes of blacks, support segregation or oppose interracial marriage. When surveyed, most white Americans strongly endorse the principle of racial equality. But this does not mean racial bias has disappeared. Instead, according to many race scholars, whites now couch their racial resentment in rhetoric of individual responsibility. Blacks are not denigrated because they are fundamentally less intelligent, lazy, or some other stereotype; rather, blacks are denigrated because they fail to embrace principles of individual self-reliance and self-control. Like the poor, blacks are held accountable for racial disparities in income, employment, and wealth because of their own moral failure. Policies that promote racial equality, such as affirmative action, are discredited because blacks are believed to be unable to live up to the individualistic norms of self-reliance.

WE BLAMED THE FAT PERSON

The same individualistic ethos that underscores Americans' attitudes toward race and class is also at the heart of their antipathy toward fat people. As with their views of poor people and blacks, most white Americans see fat people as violating the tenets of discipline and self-control. In two national surveys I conducted for this book, more than 64 percent of Americans believe overweight people are "fat because they lack self-control," and more than 70 percent ranked individual laziness as the most important cause of obesity. The University of Kansas psychologist Christian Crandall has shown that most Americans also believe that fat people are morally deviant, self-indulgent, and unwilling to correct their own behavior. Not surprisingly, people who express a prejudice against fat people also endorse a worldview that emphasizes traditional values, individual responsibility, and the notion that "people get what they deserve."

Conversely, if someone is believed to be fat for reasons beyond their control, then the contempt quickly changes to sympathy and compassion. Experiments have shown that anti-fat attitudes diminish when people think that obesity is glandular in origin. Americans dislike fatness because they think it indicates a person's unwillingness to be responsible and self-monitoring: as with the poor, if someone is fat, they only have themselves to blame. In fact, people who have strong anti-fat attitudes also tend to be more hostile toward minorities and the poor. In the national survey I conducted, more than 80 percent of people who believed that blacks are "welfare dependent" or that the poor are "irresponsible" also believed that overweight people are fat because they lack self-control, much higher rates than the general population.

Given the confluence of racial and class prejudice with anti-fat sentiments, it is not surprising that apprehension of body fat is strongest among middle-class whites. Whites are five times more likely to report feeling ashamed of their weight than blacks or Latinos, even though the latter two groups have much higher body weights on average. Nor are anti-fat attitudes about others nearly as strong or prevalent among minorities as they are among whites. The similarity between modern racism and anti-fat attitudes may also explain these racial differences. As blacks or Latinos experience racial stigmatization in the same terms as the moral condemnation that is applied to the obese, it is logical that body size as well skin color have become intertwined as a part of their cultural identity.

But perhaps the greatest reason why fat prejudice is so intertwined with class and racial prejudice is because America's poor and minorities are much fatter, on average, than its middle-class whites. Nearly one in three African Americans and one in four Latinos are obese, compared with only one in five non-Latino whites. Body sizes also vary consistently by education and income—27 percent of high school dropouts are obese compared to only 16 percent of college graduates; people below the poverty line are nearly 15 percent more likely to be obese than those not in poverty. Indeed, the very highest levels of obesity are among people in both categories—nearly 50 percent of poor black and Latino women are technically obese (that is, have a Body Mass Index of 30 or above).

With obesity so prevalent among minorities and the poor, condemning fatness is an effective way of highlighting their "moral failure" and justifying their continued marginalization. After all, if poor black people are unable to control their weight, the reasoning goes, then it is surely another indication of their inability to exercise self-control in general. Thereby, they deserve whatever low social conditions they live in and should be subject to greater restriction in terms of their moral behaviors. In truth, the higher body weights of minorities and the poor have little to do with their own "moral weakness." The logic of America's food industry almost predetermines that the poor will have higher body weights than the affluent. Meanwhile, genetic evidence suggests that people of non-European ancestry are more biologically predisposed toward weight retention. Yet, despite these facts, minorities and the poor are still blamed for weighing "too much" while thin, middle-class people can view their slenderness as a signal of their own superiority.

THE REAL PROBLEM OF OBESITY

America is a society gripped by fear. We are afraid of crime, terrorism, drugs, environmental collapse, economic decline, moral erosion, and numerous other threats. Much of this fear, however, is directed at the wrong things. For example, the economist Steven Levitt has shown that, despite all the hoopla over gun control, guns are much less dangerous, statistically speaking, for children than something far more benign: swimming pools. The average American child is one hundred times more likely to die by drowning in a pool than from a gun. Nevertheless, most parents would be much more concerned about their children playing at a house where they think a gun might be than they would be about them playing at a house with a swimming pool.

A similar type of misperception is happening with obesity. There is perhaps no greater fiction in the United States than the idea that we are worried about being fat because of its implications for our health. While the media and public health establishment may be sounding ever more hysterical alarms over the growing weight of the population, it is not because our obesity actually represents a verifiable health threat. Rather, it is because we are afraid of fat.

Compare how obesity is being handled as a public health issue versus another major killer, automobiles. Last year more than 43,000 Americans died in automobile wrecks, far more than the numbers estimated to have died from "weighing too much." Moreover, unlike the estimated figures with obesity, these are verifiable numbers. Yet, outside of a handful of environmentalists, few people are talking about an epidemic of driving in this country. We have no pejorative terms like "overdriven" in our language. Although we have numerous mechanisms for ensuring driver safety, we still allow increasingly dangerous vehicles including Hummers and SUVs to roam largely unrestricted despite the threats they pose to our collective health.

Given the general lack of concern about driving relative to its real impact on deaths, it seems highly implausible that we are worried about obesity because of its health consequences or its medical costs. In fact, in terms of our collective health or economic well-being, we shouldn't worry. Yet, it is obesity, not other, more demonstrable risks to health and mortality, such as driving, that are capturing the headlines.

This obsession with weight and obesity goes beyond the financial interests of the health-industrial complex and taps into something much more powerful: the racial and economic anxieties of America's middle class. One reason Americans so readily accept that obesity must be a major problem is because obesity is associated with those at the bottom end of America's social ladder. Thus, if obesity is growing, it surely must be a sign of American decline.

Indeed, it is precisely because it is such a powerful symbol that obesity has been adopted by so many different groups. Among conservatives, it is evidence of the growing moral degeneration of America: the fact that we are getting fatter only shows that we are getting lazier, and more lustful, and moving farther away from the Anglo-Protestant tradition that defined American greatness. Among liberals, obesity represents the increasing power of international corporations and food companies in making us heavy against our will. Among whites, it taps into latent racial fears that come with America's growing ethnic diversity—the growth of obesity parallels the increasing numbers of Latinos and African Americans relative to a shrinking white majority. And among the economic elite (the group in America most preoccupied with weight), obesity taps into a sense of social insecurity.

Ultimately, however, the reason that so many people think the rise of obesity is a cause for alarm is because of our own chronic feelings of helplessness. In an era of corporate downsizing, globalization, and mass marketing, Americans often report that more and more of their lives seem beyond their control. Our bodies remain one of the last areas where we feel that we should be able to exercise some autonomy—a view that is only stoked by the diet, fitness, and cosmetic industries. Yet the fact that we continue to gain weight despite all our dieting, nutrition advice, and working out belies just how little control we may actually have. It is our anxiety with our own powerlessness and status much more than any health issue that is driving the perception that our growing weight is an epidemic disease.

———

This essay, published on December 4, 2005, in the *Chicago Sun Times* <www.suntimes.com>, is an excerpt from *Fat Politics: The Real Story Behind America's Obesity Epidemic* by J. Eric Oliver, an associate professor of political science at the University of Chicago.

Your Appearance, Good or Bad, Can Affect the Size of Your Paycheck

BY STEPHANIE ARMOUR (2005)

When Jennifer Portnick wanted to be a Jazzercise franchisee, she says, she was denied. The reason: The company had a policy that required exercise instructors to appear fit. Portnick, who weighed 240 pounds, didn't pass.

So she filed a civil complaint under a San Francisco ordinance that bans discrimination based on weight and height. The company changed its policy, and she dropped her complaint.

Portnick's story is just one example of how physical appearance can affect employment. A growing body of research supports what many suspect: In the workplace, an employee's physical appearance is a powerful symbol that affects job success.

"The issue was my image. I never thought I'd be complaining about discrimination," says 41-year-old Portnick, who now is a personal trainer and teaches intermediate aerobics classes every other Saturday for people of all sizes at World Gym. "We talk so much in workplaces about diversity. Do we want everyone to fit into one mold? I don't think that helps any company."

Jazzercise officials say they don't believe they discriminated against Portnick.

The new research, as well as high-profile lawsuits alleging appearance-based discrimination, is raising new awareness about how looks hurt—or help—careers. It also has some organizations such as the International Size Acceptance Association calling for legal protections based on appearance.

In some cases, they're getting it. Michigan bans discrimination based on height and weight. Santa Cruz, Calif., bars discrimination based on height, weight or physical characteristics. Washington, D.C., outlaws employment discrimination based on personal appearance. In San Francisco, it's illegal to discriminate against employees because of their weight and height.

But, for the most part, employees have no protection from appearance-based discrimination unless policies also single out workers based on their race, gender or age. Some employers, such as the Borgata Hotel Casino & Spa in Atlantic City, say it's not discriminatory to require that employees conform to appearance standards.

"Employers are free to be unfair," says Bill O'Brien, a Minneapolis-based employment lawyer. "Other than some protected classes, there isn't a great deal employees can do about it. We saw it first on the playground, when the popular people who were the leaders chose other people like them as friends."

But what began on the playground can have a profound impact on paychecks. In a recent analysis, the Federal Reserve Bank of St. Louis reviewed various economic studies to find possible links between looks and wages. The study's conclusion: A worker with below-average looks tended to earn significantly less—on average 9% less—per hour than an above-average-looking employee. And those with above-average looks tended to earn 5% more than their average-looking colleagues.

"If someone looks like Brad Pitt or Julia Roberts, and society values that, that attribute is built into wages," says Michael Owyang, an economist who worked on the analysis.

AN INTANGIBLE ASSET

Looking good on the job is an intangible asset that can be important, just as sharp technology skills or the ability to be a team player can give certain workers an edge.

It's important enough that Patti Pao, 40, vice president of brand management at David's Bridal in Conshohocken, Pa., never goes to a meeting without putting on lipstick. Says Pao: "You're a personification of who you work for."

It's the reason Matt Kennedy, 24, a public relations account executive in Orlando, no longer wears his hair to work in a fashion that looks like a modified mohawk. Instead, he wears glasses and sweeps his hair to the side in a style he describes as a bit like Clark Kent.

"Before, I was struggling to get a job. Then I got three job offers in one week," Kennedy says. "On the weekends, I wear my trendy clothes and jeans that are bleached out."

It's the reason Brian Chernicky, 30, owner of the newly founded San Diego-based Real Online Marketing, wears a pair of fake glasses when wooing clients. He thinks it makes him look smarter. "Marketing is perception," he says.

Looking good on the job is one reason that mortgage broker Bill Schneider, 34, underwent hair transplant surgery.

"I manage 60 guys in my office, a lot of younger guys," says Schneider, of Boca Raton, Fla. "They used to look at me as different from them. I used to look 40. Now guys come up and talk to me more comfortably, as a friend."

Some employers also agree that looks matter. Intranet software firm Mindbridge Software in Norristown, Pa., requires formal business attire on the job. Men must wear ties, can't have beards and can't wear their hair past shoulder length. Also, employees can't have visible body piercings or tattoos. "Clients like to see a workforce that looks real conservative," says Scott Testa, chief operating officer. "We have people complain about it and people who like it."

The approach is different from that of other software firms, which generally have laid-back dress codes, because the firm wanted to differentiate itself and present a businesslike image to clients.

HEIGHT AND WEIGHT FACTORS

It's not just a pretty face that helps boost wages. An employee's height and weight also play a role. For the book *Blink* by Malcolm Gladwell, half of the companies on the Fortune 500 were polled about the height of their CEOs. On average, male CEOs were just under six feet tall, or three inches taller than the average man.

It's a bias that some struggle with. Dan Okenfuss, public relations vice president at Little People of America, a group that represents people of short stature, says employees who don't fit societal norms can feel singled out.

"People with dwarfism are capable of doing anything in the workplace," he says. "Some members feel they have been slighted, that they didn't get the promotion they wanted, and size may have been a factor. Companies need leaders to be tall and broad-shouldered."

Another area where employees feel an impact is their weight. A study done in part by New York University sociologist Dalton Conley found that an increase in a woman's body mass results in a decrease in her family income and her job prestige. Men, however, experience no such negative effect.

For women, a 1% increase in body mass as measured by the body mass index results in a 0.6 percentage point decrease in family income. The work, sponsored by the National Bureau of Economic Research, was based on 3,335 men and women.

As health care costs climb and national attention turns to the problem of obesity in the USA, overweight workers are feeling pressure to slim down. The latest data from the National Center for Health Statistics show that 30% of U.S. adults age 20 and older (more than 60 million people) are obese.

In a case that has attracted widespread attention, the Borgata Hotel Casino & Spa bans bartenders and cocktail waitresses (known as Borgata Babes) from gaining more than 7% of their body weight from the time they begin weigh-ins. That means a 125-pound woman couldn't gain more than 8.75 pounds.

Those who do gain more receive a 90-day unpaid suspension, and after that, may be fired. Some employees upset by the policy filed a lawsuit and civil-rights complaints, which are pending. Employees have claimed the policy amounts to discrimination based on sex and disability.

The question of whether weight is a disability under the federal Americans with Disabilities Act is still being decided in the courts, but in many cases courts have determined that being obese is not a disability protected by the law.

Richard Chaifetz, president of ComPsych, a Chicago-based employee assistance provider, says overweight employees may not be as productive.

More than 20% of very overweight employees have low morale, almost twice that of employees of healthy weights, according to a June survey by ComPsych. The survey was based on a poll of more than 1,000 client organizations.

Allen Steadham of the International Size Acceptance Association disagrees. He says he believes heavier employees are just as productive.

Overweight employees "are more likely to be as productive, or more productive," Steadham says. "People are standing up for themselves with lawsuits. High-profile cases are bringing attention to the issue, and that brings change."

When employees sue, they tend to argue that appearance standards or hiring based on looks have evolved into racism or other illegal discrimination.

Abercrombie & Fitch agreed last year to pay $50 million to settle a lawsuit with the government after a class-action lawsuit claimed employees were discriminated against. The lawsuit claimed the retailer hired white, attractive-looking men for sales and put minority workers in stockroom positions.

NO POWDER, NO BLUSH

In another case, Darlene Jespersen, a former casino bartender at Harrah's Entertainment, sued her Reno-based employer after she was fired for not wearing makeup. She had worked there for 20 years and had not regularly worn makeup.

The firm requires that women wear makeup, defined as powder or foundation, blush, lipstick and mascara. The 9th U.S. Circuit Court of Appeals heard arguments in the case last month after a lower court ruled in favor of Harrah's.

The company's policy has since been revised, says spokesman David Stow, and makeup is no longer mandatory. That change is not a result of the lawsuit but because of concerns from employees, Stow says. Stow also said Harrah's offered Jespersen her job back and agreed to waive their appearance standard for her.

"Our main goal is to ensure all our employees have a professional and well-groomed appearance when they come into contact with the public," Stow says.

Jennifer Pizer, Jespersen's lawyer, says the conditions of her re-employment were not suitable and that other women at work would resent her if she got special exemption not to wear makeup. She is not going back to work at this time.

"She felt it was a humiliation to have to wear the makeup," Pizer says. "There is a particular impact on women in our economy, especially in businesses catering to the public: 'All the women should be 16 and look like the girl next door.' Well, society isn't like that."

———

Stephanie Armour wrote this piece for the July 20, 2005, edition of *USA Today* <www.usatoday.com>.

FROM READING TO WRITING

1. Identify the ways in which the readings in this chapter present causal arguments. Then, use specific details from the readings to develop your own position on the cause of America's obesity.

2. Propose a national solution for dealing with the problem of overweight America.

3. Deborah Cohen, in "A Desired Epidemic: Obesity and the Food Industry," and Susan Brink and Elizabeth Querna, in "East This Now!" argue that America's weight problem is not about lack of individual will but an issue of deceptive advertising and marketing and fad dieting. Can you cite any examples of companies taking advantage of or deceiving consumers?

4. How is body-image culturally constructed?

5. Stereotypes about overweight people plague society. What other social issues are stereotyped in such sweeping ways throughout public consciousness? What are the sources of such images?

6. What is the effect of the ethos presented by Wendy Shanker in her excerpt from *The Fat Girl's Guide to Life*? Who do you think is her target audience? Why?

7. Comment on Eleanor Randolph's proposals in "The Big Fat American Kid Crisis . . . and 10 Things We Should Do about It." How does she present her argument? Is she effective in making her proposals seem feasible? Explain.

8. Eric Oliver says, "For not only is thinness a convenient way for middle-class people to assert their moral superiority and boost their self-image, it also served to rationalize the social inequalities that exist between various social groups." Analyze his argument. Do you agree or disagree? Examine his use of sources and statistics to bolster his position.

Seven

GLOBAL WARMING

The War of the Words

Whether it's climate 'chaos,' 'change' or 'crisis,' language comes first in the environment fight

BY JERRY ADLER (2007)

What is the most pressing environmental issue we face today? "Global warming"? The "greenhouse effect"? At the Oscar ceremonies, Al Gore referred to a "climate crisis," but in his State of the Union address President Bush chose the comparatively anodyne phrase "climate change." They all refer to the same thing, but the first rule of modern political discourse is that before addressing any empirical problem each side must "frame the debate" in the most favorable way. If you doubt it, just try to get a Republican to utter the phrase "estate tax" rather than "death tax." Behind the overt campaign to head off whatever it is—environmental heating? thermal catastrophe?—is a covert struggle over what we should even call it.

In recent years this has played out largely as a contest between "global warming" and "climate change." Bush's use of the latter was consistent with Republican practice, which calls for de-emphasizing the urgency of the situation, as recommended in a 2002 memo by strategist Frank Luntz. Unlike the "catastrophic" connotations of global warming, Luntz wrote, "climate change sounds a more controllable and less emotional challenge." So should activists favor "global warming"? Well, not necessarily. Richard C.J. Somerville, a leading researcher on—um, worldwide calorification?—at Scripps Institution of Oceanography, thinks "global warming" is problematic because it puts the focus on worldwide average temperature, rather than the more serious regional dangers of storms, floods and drought. More pointedly, a leading Democratic strategist, Celinda Lake, actually endorsed

"climate change" in 2004 on the grounds that "global warming" only works for half the
year. "Every time we'd use the term in the winter, people would say, 'It doesn't feel that
warm to me'," she said. (For the record, she now believes the issue has penetrated the
public's awareness to the point where it doesn't matter much what it's called.) Similarly,
it's been suggested that Americans have been slower than Europeans to grasp the magnitude of the impending disaster because they think of temperature in Fahrenheit, while
scientists—and most of the rest of the world—use the Celsius scale, on which the numbers are smaller. A predicted temperature rise of, say, 3 degrees Celsius sounds less alarming than the equivalent swing of 5.4 degrees in the units most Americans are familiar with.

In any case, "global warming" seems to have won out over its rivals, if one can judge
by *The New York Times*, where for each of the last three years "global warming" has outpaced references to "climate change" by almost exactly two to one—or an even bigger
margin if you throw out articles that are actually about changes in the economic or cultural climate. Both of these phrases have triumphed over "greenhouse effect," which
was the most common term in the early 1980s, when the phenomenon of—atmospheric
pyrogenesis?—first came to public attention. Arguably, if your goal is to affect public
attitudes and policies, "greenhouse effect," which refers to the buildup of heat-trapping
gases in the atmosphere, puts the emphasis in the wrong place, on the mechanism
rather than the outcome. George Lakoff, the Berkeley professor of linguistics and cognitive science, is a strong backer of the dark horse "climate crisis," which is also favored by
Gore (along with the rather more cumbersome term he used in his congressional testimony last month, "planetary emergency"). "'Climate change' doesn't suggest immediate action," says Lakoff. "'Climate crisis' says immediate action needed. The framing is
not just a matter of labels, it's modes of thought. In Europe they use 'climate chaos'."

So that ought to settle it, except, of course, that this is a kind of crisis for which neither human experience nor language has quite prepared us: a slow-motion crisis, requir-
ing heroic action now to head off disaster decades down the road. Somerville was on the
losing side of a public debate last month in New York, sponsored by Intelligence Squared
U.S., and he believes he lost in part because the proposition was framed as "Global Warming Is Not a Crisis." The other side, which included the novelist and, uh, meteorological-
calamity skeptic Michael Crichton, was able to convince a narrow majority of the audience
that "crisis" is the wrong term for whatever it is humanity is dealing with. "I don't like
words that leave me vulnerable to charges of being alarmist," says Somerville. "Using

crisis conveys the notion this is hopeless. But there's a lot that can be done about this. I'm still looking for the right words to describe what's happening, but it's not keeping me from trying to stop it."

––––––––

Jerry Adler wrote this piece for the April 16, 2007, issue of *Newsweek* magazine <www. newsweek.com>.

Yelling 'Fire' on a Hot Planet
BY ANDREW C. REVKIN (2006)

Global warming has the feel of breaking news these days.

Polar bears are drowning; an American city is underwater; ice sheets are crumbling. *Time* magazine proclaimed that readers should be worried. Very worried. There are new hot-selling books and a batch of documentaries, including one starring former Vice President Al Gore and his climate-evangelist slide show that is touted as "the most terrifying movie you will ever see."

Are humans like frogs in a simmering pot, unaware that temperatures have reached the boiling point? Or has global warming been spun into an "alarmist gale," as Richard S. Lindzen, a climatologist at M.I.T. wrote in a recent *Wall Street Journal* op-ed article?

There is enough static in the air to simultaneously confuse, alarm and paralyze the public. Is global warming now a reality? What do scientists know for sure and when are they just guessing?

And what can truly be accomplished by changing behavior? After all, there are still the traditional calls to limit heat-trapped greenhouse-gas emissions, but a growing number of experts are also saying what was once unthinkable: humans may have to adapt to a warmer globe.

Here, an attempt to shed a little light in all the heat.

WHAT WE KNOW

Between the poles of real-time catastrophe and nonevent lies the prevailing scientific view: without big changes in emissions rates, global warming from the buildup of green-house gases is likely to lead to substantial, and largely irreversible, transformations of climate, ecosystems and coastlines later this century.

The Earth's average surface temperature rose about 1 degree over the 20th century, to around 59 degrees, but the rate of warming from the 1970's until now has been three times the average rate of warming since 1900. Seas have risen about six to eight inches globally over the last century and the rate of rise has increased in the last decade.

In 2001, a large team of scientists issued the latest assessment of climate change and concluded that more than half of the recent warming was likely to have been caused by people, primarily because we're adding tens of billions of tons of carbon dioxide and other long-lived greenhouse gases to the atmosphere, mainly by burning coal and oil.

There is no serious debate any more about one thing: more of these gases will cause more warming. Dr. Lindzen, who contends any human climate influence is negligible and has long criticized those calling global warming a catastrophe, agreed on this basic fact in his article.

At the same time, few scientists agree with the idea that the recent spate of potent hurricanes, European heat waves, African drought and other weather extremes are, in essence, our fault. There is more than enough natural variability in nature to mask a direct connection, they say.

Even recent sightings of drowned polar bears cannot be firmly ascribed to human influence on climate given the big cyclical fluctuations of sea ice around the Arctic.

WHAT IS DEBATED

The unresolved questions concern the pace and extent of future warming and the impact on wildlife, agriculture, disease, local weather and the height of the world's oceans—in other words, all of the things that matter to people.

The latest estimates, including a study published last week in the journal *Nature*, foresee a probable warming of somewhere around 5 degrees should the concentration of carbon dioxide reach twice the 280-parts-per-million figure that had been the norm on earth for at least 400,000 years. This is far lower than some of the apocalyptic projections in recent years, but also far higher than mild warming rates focused on by skeptics and industry lobbyists.

As a result, by 2100 or so, sea levels could be several feet higher than they are now, and the new normal on the planet for centuries thereafter could be retreating shorelines as Antarctic and Greenland ice sheets relentlessly erode.

Rivers fed by mountain glaciers, including those nourishing much of south Asia, could shrivel. Grand plans to restore New Orleans and the Everglades would be rendered meaningless as seawater advances. Manhattan would become New Orleans—a semi-submerged city surrounded by levees. In summers, polar bears would be stuck on the few remaining ice-clotted shores around the largely blue Arctic Ocean.

Projections of how patterns of drought, deluges, heat and cold might change are among the most difficult, and will remain laden with huge uncertainties for a long time to come, said M. Granger Morgan, a physicist and policy expert at Carnegie Mellon University in Pittsburgh.

For example, while computer simulations of the climate consistently show that the centers of big continents are likely to grow drier, and winters and nights generally warmer, they cannot reliably predict conditions in Chicago or Shanghai.

WHAT'S THE RUSH?

By the clock of geology, this climate shift is unfolding at a dizzying, perhaps unprecedented pace, but by time scales relevant to people, it's happening in slow motion. If the bad stuff doesn't happen for 100 years or so, it's hard to persuade governments or voters to take action.

And there is the rub. Many scientists say that to avoid a doubling of carbon dioxide concentrations, energy efficiency must be increased drastically, and soon. And by mid-century, they add, there must be a complete transformation of energy technology. That may be why some environmentalists try to link today's weather to tomorrow's problem. While scientists say they lack firm evidence to connect recent weather to the human influence on climate, environmental campaigners still push the notion.

"The issue clearly has an urgency problem," said Billy Parish, a founder of Energy Action, a coalition of student groups. "Maybe I'm just a paranoid that sees global warming everywhere, but the here-and-now effects do seem to be mounting, and I think we need to connect the dots for people."

A Gallup survey last month shows that people are still not worried about climate change. When participants were asked to rank 10 environmental problems, global warming was near the bottom, far below water pollution and toxic waste (both now largely controlled).

Without a connection to current disasters, global warming is the kind of problem people, and democratic institutions, have proved singularly terrible at solving: a long-term threat that can only be limited by acting promptly, before the harm is clear.

Problems that get attention are "soon, salient and certain," said Helen Ingram, a professor of planning, policy and design at the University of California, Irvine.

Stressing the problem's urgency could well be counterproductive, according to *Americans and Climate Change*, a new book by the Yale School of Forestry and Environmental Studies.

The book notes that urgency does not appear to be something that can be imposed on people. Moreover, it says, "Urgency is especially prone to being discounted as unreasoned alarmism or even passion."

Among its recommendations, the Yale book suggests something radical: drop the reluctance to accept adaptation as a strategy. Adaptation to climate extremes has long been derided by many environmentalists as defeatism. But, the book says, adaptation may help people focus on the reality of what is coming—and that may motivate them to cut emissions to limit chances of bigger changes to come.

Actions could range from developing drought-resistant crops to eliminating federal insurance and other subsidies that have long encouraged coastal development.

Could stressing adaptation work? The Yale group calls global warming "the perfect problem"—meaning that a confluence of characteristics make it hard, if not impossible, to solve. Its impact remains clouded with scientific uncertainty, its effects will be felt over generations, and it is being amplified by everything from microwaving a frozen dinner to bringing electricity to an Indian village.

"I wish I were more optimistic of our ability to get a broad slice of the public to understand this and be motivated to act," said David G. Hawkins, who directs the climate program at the Natural Resources Defense Council, a private group.

In an e-mail message, he wrote: "We are sensory organisms; we understand diesel soot because we can smell it and see it. Getting global warming is too much of an intellectual process. Perhaps pictures of drowning polar bears (which we are trying to find) will move people but even there, people will need to believe that those drownings are due to our failure to build cleaner power plants and cars."

Andrew C. Revkin wrote this piece for the April 23, 2006, edition of *The New York Times* <www.nytimes.com>.

Be Worried, Be Very Worried

The climate is crashing, and global warming is to blame
BY JEFFREY KLUGER (2006)

No one can say exactly what it looks like when a planet takes ill, but it probably looks a lot like Earth. Never mind what you've heard about global warming as a slow-motion emergency that would take decades to play out. Suddenly and unexpectedly, the crisis is upon us.

It certainly looked that way last week as the atmospheric bomb that was Cyclone Larry—a Category 4 storm with wind bursts that reached 125 m.p.h.—exploded through northeastern Australia. It certainly looked that way last year as curtains of fire and dust turned the skies of Indonesia orange, thanks to drought-fueled blazes sweeping the island nation. It certainly looks that way as sections of ice the size of small states calve from the disintegrating Arctic and Antarctic. And it certainly looks that way as the sodden wreckage of New Orleans continues to molder, while the waters of the Atlantic gather themselves for a new hurricane season just two months away. Disasters have always been with us and surely always will be. But when they hit this hard and come this fast—when the emergency becomes commonplace—something has gone grievously wrong. That something is global warming.

The image of Earth as organism—famously dubbed Gaia by environmentalist James Lovelock—has probably been overworked, but that's not to say the planet can't behave like a living thing, and these days, it's a living thing fighting a fever. From heat waves to storms to floods to fires to massive glacial melts, the global climate seems to be crashing around us. Scientists have been calling this shot for decades. This is precisely what they have been warning would happen if we continued pumping greenhouse gases into the atmosphere, trapping the heat that flows in from the sun and raising global temperatures.

Environmentalists and lawmakers spent years shouting at one another about whether the grim forecasts were true, but in the past five years or so, the serious debate has quietly ended. Global warming, even most skeptics have concluded, is the real deal, and human activity has been causing it. If there was any consolation, it was that the glacial pace of nature would give us decades or even centuries to sort out the problem.

But glaciers, it turns out, can move with surprising speed, and so can nature. What few people reckoned on was that global climate systems are booby-trapped with tipping points and feedback loops, thresholds past which the slow creep of environmental decay gives way to sudden and self-perpetuating collapse. Pump enough CO_2 into the sky, and that last part per million of greenhouse gas behaves like the 212th degree Fahrenheit that turns a pot of hot water into a plume of billowing steam. Melt enough Greenland ice, and you reach the point at which you're not simply dripping meltwater into the sea but dumping whole glaciers. By one recent measure, several Greenland ice sheets have doubled their rate of slide, and just last week the journal *Science* published a study suggesting that by the end of the century, the world could be locked in to an eventual rise in sea levels of as much as 20 feet. Nature, it seems, has finally got a bellyful of us.

"Things are happening a lot faster than anyone predicted," says Bill Chameides, chief scientist for the advocacy group Environmental Defense and a former professor of atmospheric chemistry. "The last 12 months have been alarming." Adds Ruth Curry of the Woods Hole Oceanographic Institution in Massachusetts: "The ripple through the scientific community is palpable."

And it's not just scientists who are taking notice. Even as nature crosses its tipping points, the public seems to have reached its own. For years, popular skepticism about climatological science stood in the way of addressing the problem, but the naysayers—many of whom were on the payroll of energy companies—have become an increasingly marginalized breed. In a new TIME/ABC News/Stanford University poll, 85% of respondents agree that global warming probably is happening. Moreover, most respondents say they want some action taken. Of those polled, 87% believe the government should either encourage or require lowering of power-plant emissions, and 85% think something should be done to get cars to use less gasoline. Even Evangelical Christians, once one of the most reliable columns in the conservative base, are demanding action, most notably in

February, when 86 Christian leaders formed the Evangelical Climate Initiative, demanding that Congress regulate greenhouse gases.

A collection of new global-warming books is hitting the shelves in response to that awakening interest, followed closely by TV and theatrical documentaries. The most notable of them is *An Inconvenient Truth*, due out in May, a profile of former Vice President Al Gore and his climate-change work, which is generating a lot of prerelease buzz over an unlikely topic and an equally unlikely star. For all its lack of Hollywood flash, the film compensates by conveying both the hard science of global warming and Gore's particular passion.

Such public stirrings are at last getting the attention of politicians and business leaders, who may not always respond to science but have a keen nose for where votes and profits lie. State and local lawmakers have started taking action to curb emissions, and major corporations are doing the same. Wal-Mart has begun installing wind turbines on its stores to generate electricity and is talking about putting solar reflectors over its parking lots. HSBC, the world's second largest bank, has pledged to neutralize its carbon output by investing in wind farms and other green projects. Even President Bush, hardly a favorite of greens, now acknowledges climate change and boasts of the steps he is taking to fight it. Most of those steps, however, involve research and voluntary emissions controls, not exactly the laws with teeth scientists are calling for.

Is it too late to reverse the changes global warming has wrought? That's still not clear. Reducing our emissions output year to year is hard enough. Getting it low enough so that the atmosphere can heal is a multigenerational commitment. "Ecosystems are usually able to maintain themselves," says Terry Chapin, a biologist and professor of ecology at the University of Alaska, Fairbanks. "But eventually they get pushed to the limit of tolerance."

CO_2 AND THE POLES

As a tiny component of our atmosphere, carbon dioxide helped warm Earth to comfort levels we are all used to. But too much of it does an awful lot of damage. The gas represents just a few hundred parts per million (p.p.m.) in the overall air blanket, but they're powerful parts because they allow sunlight to stream in but prevent much of the heat from radiating back out. During the last ice age, the atmosphere's CO_2 concentration was just 180 p.p.m., putting Earth into a deep freeze. After the glaciers retreated but before the dawn of the modern era, the total had risen to a comfortable 280 p.p.m. In just the past century and a half, we have pushed the level to 381 p.p.m., and we're feeling the effects. Of the 20 hottest years on record, 19 occurred in the 1980s or later. According to NASA scientists, 2005 was one of the hottest years in more than a century.

It's at the North and South poles that those steambath conditions are felt particularly acutely, with glaciers and ice caps crumbling to slush. Once the thaw begins, a number of mechanisms kick in to keep it going. Greenland is a vivid example. Late last year, glaciologist Eric Rignot of the Jet Propulsion Laboratory in Pasadena, Calif., and Pannir Kanagaratnam, a research assistant professor at the University of Kansas, analyzed data from Canadian and European satellites and found that Greenland ice is not just melting but doing so more than twice as fast, with 53 cubic miles draining away into the sea last year alone, compared with 22 cubic miles in 1996. A cubic mile of water is about five times the amount Los Angeles uses in a year.

Dumping that much water into the ocean is a very dangerous thing. Icebergs don't raise sea levels when they melt because they're floating, which means they have displaced all the water they're ever going to. But ice on land, like Greenland's, is a different matter. Pour that into oceans that are already rising (because warm water expands), and you deluge shorelines. By some estimates, the entire Greenland ice sheet would be enough to raise global sea levels 23 feet, swallowing up large parts of coastal Florida and most of Bangladesh. The Antarctic holds enough ice to raise sea levels more than 215 feet.

FEEDBACK LOOPS

One of the reasons the loss of the planet's ice cover is accelerating is that as the poles' bright white surface shrinks, it changes the relationship of Earth and the sun. Polar ice is so reflective that 90% of the sunlight that strikes it simply bounces back into space, taking much of its energy with it. Ocean water does just the opposite, absorbing 90% of the energy it receives. The more energy it retains, the warmer it gets, with the result that each mile of ice that melts vanishes faster than the mile that preceded it.

That is what scientists call a feedback loop, and it's a nasty one, since once you uncap the Arctic Ocean, you unleash another beast: the comparatively warm layer of water about 600 feet deep that circulates in and out of the Atlantic. "Remove the ice," says Woods Hole's Curry, "and the water starts talking to the atmosphere, releasing its heat. This is not a good thing."

A similar feedback loop is melting permafrost, usually defined as land that has been continuously frozen for two years or more. There's a lot of earthly real estate that qualifies, and much of it has been frozen much longer than two years—since the end of the last ice age, or at least 8,000 years ago. Sealed inside that cryonic time capsule are layers of partially decayed organic matter, rich in carbon. In high-altitude regions of Alaska, Canada and Siberia, the soil is warming and decomposing, releasing gases that will turn into methane and CO_2. That, in turn, could lead to more warming and permafrost thaw, says research scientist David Lawrence of the National Center for Atmospheric Research (NCAR) in Boulder, Colo. And how much carbon is socked away in Arctic soils? Lawrence puts the figure at 200 gigatons to 800 gigatons. The total human carbon output is only 7 gigatons a year.

One result of all that is warmer oceans, and a result of warmer oceans can be, paradoxically, colder continents within a hotter globe. Ocean currents running between warm and cold regions serve as natural thermoregulators, distributing heat from the equator toward the poles. The Gulf Stream, carrying warmth up from the tropics, is what keeps Europe's climate relatively mild. Whenever Europe is cut off from the Gulf Stream, temperatures plummet. At the end of the last ice age, the warm current was temporarily blocked, and temperatures in Europe fell as much as 10°F, locking the continent in glaciers.

What usually keeps the Gulf Stream running is that warm water is lighter than cold water, so it floats on the surface. As it reaches Europe and releases its heat, the current grows denser and sinks, flowing back to the south and crossing under the northbound Gulf Stream until it reaches the tropics and starts to warm again. The cycle works splendidly, provided the water remains salty enough. But if it becomes diluted by freshwater, the salt concentration drops, and the water gets lighter, idling on top and stalling the current. Last December, researchers associated with Britain's National Oceanography Center reported that one component of the system that drives the Gulf Stream has slowed about 30% since 1957. It's the increased release of Arctic and Greenland meltwater that appears to be causing the problem, introducing a gush of freshwater that's overwhelming the natural cycle. In a global-warming world, it's unlikely that any amount of cooling that resulted from this would be sufficient to support glaciers, but it could make things awfully uncomfortable.

"The big worry is that the whole climate of Europe will change," says Adrian Luckman, senior lecturer in geography at the University of Wales, Swansea. "We in the U.K. are on the same latitude as Alaska. The reason we can live here is the Gulf Stream."

DROUGHT

As fast as global warming is transforming the oceans and the ice caps, it's having an even more immediate effect on land. People, animals and plants living in dry, mountainous regions like the western U.S. make it through summer thanks to snowpack that collects on peaks all winter and slowly melts off in warm months. Lately the early arrival of spring and the unusually blistering summers have caused the snowpack to melt too early, so that by the time it's needed, it's largely gone. Climatologist Philip Mote of the University of Washington has compared decades of snowpack levels in Washington, Oregon and California and found that they are a fraction of what they were in the 1940s, and some snowpacks have vanished entirely.

Global warming is tipping other regions of the world into drought in different ways. Higher temperatures bake moisture out of soil faster, causing dry regions that live at the margins to cross the line into full-blown crisis. Meanwhile, El Niño events—the warm pooling of Pacific waters that periodically drives worldwide climate patterns and has been occurring more frequently in global-warming years—further inhibit precipitation in dry areas of Africa and East Asia. According to a recent study by NCAR, the percentage of Earth's surface suffering drought has more than doubled since the 1970s.

FLORA AND FAUNA

Hot, dry land can be murder on flora and fauna, and both are taking a bad hit. Wildfires in such regions as Indonesia, the western U.S. and even inland Alaska have been increasing as timberlands and forest floors grow more parched. The blazes create a feedback loop of their own, pouring more carbon into the atmosphere and reducing the number of trees, which inhale CO_2 and release oxygen.

Those forests that don't succumb to fire die in other, slower ways. Connie Millar, a paleoecologist for the U.S. Forest Service, studies the history of vegetation in the Sierra Nevada. Over the past 100 years, she has found, the forests have shifted their tree lines as much as 100 feet upslope, trying to escape the heat and drought of the lowlands.

Such slow-motion evacuation may seem like a sensible strategy, but when you're on a mountain, you can go only so far before you run out of room. "Sometimes we say the trees are going to heaven because they're walking off the mountaintops," Millar says.

Across North America, warming-related changes are mowing down other flora too. Manzanita bushes in the West are dying back; some prickly pear cacti have lost their signature green and are instead a sickly pink; pine beetles in western Canada and the U.S. are chewing their way through tens of millions of acres of forest, thanks to warmer winters. The beetles may even breach the once insurmountable Rocky Mountain divide, opening up a path into the rich timbering lands of the American Southeast.

With habitats crashing, animals that live there are succumbing too. Environmental groups can tick off scores of species that have been determined to be at risk as a result of global warming. Last year, researchers in Costa Rica announced that two-thirds of 110 species of colorful harlequin frogs have vanished in the past 30 years, with the severity of each season's die-off following in lockstep with the severity of that year's warming.

In Alaska, salmon populations are at risk as melting permafrost pours mud into rivers, burying the gravel the fish need for spawning. Small animals such as bushy-tailed wood rats, alpine chipmunks and piñon mice are being chased upslope by rising temperatures, following the path of the fleeing trees. And with sea ice vanishing, polar bears—prodigious swimmers but not inexhaustible ones—are starting to turn up drowned. "There will be no polar ice by 2060," says Larry Schweiger, president of the National Wildlife Federation. "Somewhere along that path, the polar bear drops out."

WHAT ABOUT US?

It is fitting, perhaps, that as the species causing all the problems, we're suffering the destruction of our habitat too, and we have experienced that loss in terrible ways. Ocean waters have warmed by a full degree Fahrenheit since 1970, and warmer water is like rocket fuel for typhoons and hurricanes. Two studies last year found that in the past 35 years the number of Category 4 and 5 hurricanes worldwide has doubled while the wind speed and duration of all hurricanes has jumped 50%. Since atmospheric heat is not choosy about the water it warms, tropical storms could start turning up in some decidedly non-tropical places. "There's a school of thought that sea surface temperatures are warming up toward Canada," says Greg Holland, senior scientist for NCAR in Boulder. "If so, you're likely to get tropical cyclones there, but we honestly don't know."

WHAT WE CAN DO

So much for environmental collapse happening in so many places at once has at last awakened much of the world, particularly the 141 nations that have ratified the Kyoto treaty to reduce emissions—an imperfect accord, to be sure, but an accord all the same. The U.S., however, which is home to less than 5% of Earth's population but produces 25% of CO_2 emissions, remains intransigent. Many environmentalists declared the Bush Administration hopeless from the start, and while that may have been premature, it's undeniable that the White House's environmental record—from the abandonment of Kyoto to the President's broken campaign pledge to control carbon output to the relaxation of emission standards—has been dismal. George W. Bush's recent rhetorical nods to America's oil addiction and his praise of such alternative fuel sources as switchgrass have yet to be followed by real initiatives.

The anger surrounding all that exploded recently when NASA researcher Jim Hansen, director of the Goddard Institute for Space Studies and a longtime leader in climate-change research, complained that he had been harassed by White House appointees as he tried to sound the global-warming alarm. "The way democracy is supposed to work, the presumption is that the public is well informed," he told TIME. "They're trying to deny the science." Up against such resistance, many environmental groups have resolved simply to wait out this Administration and hope for something better in 2009.

The Republican-dominated Congress has not been much more encouraging. Senators John McCain and Joe Lieberman have twice been unable to get through the Senate even mild measures to limit carbon. Senators Pete Domenici and Jeff Bingaman, both of New Mexico and both ranking members of the chamber's Energy Committee, have made global warming a high-profile matter. A white paper issued in February will be the subject of an investigatory Senate conference next week. A House delegation recently traveled to Antarctica, Australia and New Zealand to visit researchers studying climate change. "Of the 10 of us, only three were believers," says Representative Sherwood Boehlert of New York. "Every one of the others said this opened their eyes."

Boehlert himself has long fought the environmental fight, but if the best that can be said for most lawmakers is that they are finally recognizing the global-warming problem, there's reason to wonder whether they will have the courage to reverse it. Increasingly, state and local governments are filling the void. The mayors of more than 200 cities have signed the U.S. Mayors Climate Protection Agreement, pledging, among other things, that they will meet the Kyoto goal of reducing greenhouse-gas emissions in their cities to 1990 levels by 2012. Nine eastern states have established the Regional Greenhouse Gas Initiative for the purpose of developing a cap-and-trade program that would set ceilings on industrial emissions and allow companies that overperform to sell pollution credits to those that underperform—the same smart, incentive-based strategy that got sulfur dioxide under control and reduced acid rain. And California passed the nation's toughest automobile-emissions law last summer.

"There are a whole series of things that demonstrate that people want to act and want their government to act," says Fred Krupp, president of Environmental Defense. Krupp and others believe that we should probably accept that it's too late to prevent CO_2 concentrations from climbing to 450 p.p.m. (or 70 p.p.m. higher than where they are now). From there, however, we should be able to stabilize them and start to dial them back down.

That goal should be attainable. Curbing global warming may be an order of magnitude harder than, say, eradicating smallpox or putting a man on the moon. But is it moral not to try? We did not so much march toward the environmental precipice as drunkenly reel there, snapping at the scientific scolds who told us we had a problem.

The scolds, however, knew what they were talking about. In a solar system crowded with sister worlds that either emerged stillborn like Mercury and Venus or died in infancy like Mars, we're finally coming to appreciate the knife-blade margins within which life can thrive. For more than a century we've been monkeying with those margins. It's long past time we set them right.

—With reporting by Greg Fulton/Atlanta, Dan Cray/Los Angeles, Rita Healy/Denver, Eric Roston/Washington, With reporting by David Bjerklie, Andrea Dorfman/New York, Andrea Gerlin/London

———

Jeffrey Kluger wrote this piece for the April 3, 2006, edition of *Time* magazine <www.time.com>.

Climate of Fear: Global-Warming Alarmists Intimidate Dissenting Scientists into Silence

BY RICHARD LINDZEN (2006)

There have been repeated claims that this past year's hurricane activity was another sign of human-induced climate change. Everything from the heat wave in Paris to heavy snows in Buffalo has been blamed on people burning gasoline to fuel their cars, and coal and natural gas to heat, cool and electrify their homes. Yet how can a barely discernible, one-degree increase in the recorded global mean temperature since the late 19th century possibly gain public acceptance as the source of recent weather catastrophes? And how can it translate into unlikely claims about future catastrophes?

The answer has much to do with misunderstanding the science of climate, plus a willingness to debase climate science into a triangle of alarmism. Ambiguous scientific statements about climate are hyped by those with a vested interest in alarm, thus raising the political stakes for policy makers who provide funds for more science research to feed more alarm to increase the political stakes. After all, who puts money into science—whether for AIDS, or space, or climate—where there is nothing really alarming? Indeed, the success of climate alarmism can be counted in the increased federal spending on climate research from a few hundred million dollars pre-1990 to $1.7 billion today. It can also be seen in heightened spending on solar, wind, hydrogen, ethanol and clean coal technologies, as well as on other energy-investment decisions.

But there is a more sinister side to this feeding frenzy. Scientists who dissent from the alarmism have seen their grant funds disappear, their work derided, and themselves libeled as industry stooges, scientific hacks or worse. Consequently, lies about climate change gain credence even when they fly in the face of the science that supposedly is their basis.

To understand the misconceptions perpetuated about climate science and the climate of intimidation, one needs to grasp some of the complex underlying scientific issues. First, let's start where there is agreement. The public, press and policy makers have been repeatedly told that three claims have widespread scientific support: Global temperature has risen about a degree since the late 19th century; levels of CO_2 in the atmosphere have increased by about 30% over the same period; and CO_2 should contribute to future warming. These claims are true. However, what the public fails to grasp is that the claims neither constitute support for alarm nor establish man's responsibility for the small amount of warming that has occurred. In fact, those who make the most outlandish claims of alarm are actually demonstrating skepticism of the very science they say supports them. It isn't just that the alarmists are trumpeting model results that we know must be wrong. It is that they are trumpeting catastrophes that couldn't happen even if the models were right as justifying costly policies to try to prevent global warming.

If the models are correct, global warming reduces the temperature differences between the poles and the equator. When you have less difference in temperature, you have less excitation of extratropical storms, not more. And, in fact, model runs support this conclusion. Alarmists have drawn some support for increased claims of tropical storminess from a casual claim by Sir John Houghton of the U.N.'s Intergovernmental Panel on Climate Change (IPCC) that a warmer world would have more evaporation, with latent heat providing more energy for disturbances. The problem with this is that the ability of evaporation to drive tropical storms relies not only on temperature but humidity as well, and calls for drier, less humid air. Claims for starkly higher temperatures are based upon there being more humidity, not less—hardly a case for more storminess with global warming.

So how is it that we don't have more scientists speaking up about this junk science? It's my belief that many scientists have been cowed not merely by money but by fear. An example: Earlier this year, Texas Rep. Joe Barton issued letters to paleoclimatologist Michael Mann and some of his co-authors seeking the details behind a taxpayer-funded analysis that claimed the 1990s were likely the warmest decade and 1998 the warmest year in the last millennium. Mr. Barton's concern was based on the fact that the IPCC had singled out Mr. Mann's work as a means to encourage policy makers to take action. And they did so before his work could be replicated and tested—a task made difficult because Mr. Mann, a key IPCC author, had refused to release the details for analysis. The scientific community's defense of Mr. Mann was, nonetheless, immediate and harsh. The president of the National Academy of Sciences—as well as the American Meteorological Society and the American Geophysical Union—formally protested, saying that Rep. Barton's singling out of a scientist's work smacked of intimidation.

All of which starkly contrasts to the silence of the scientific community when anti-alarmists were in the crosshairs of then-Sen. Al Gore. In 1992, he ran two congressional hearings during which he tried to bully dissenting scientists, including myself, into changing our views and supporting his climate alarmism. Nor did the scientific community complain when Mr. Gore, as vice president, tried to enlist Ted Koppel in a witch hunt to discredit anti-alarmist scientists—a request that Mr. Koppel deemed publicly inappropriate. And they were mum when subsequent articles and books by Ross Gelbspan libelously labeled scientists who differed with Mr. Gore as stooges of the fossil-fuel industry.

Sadly, this is only the tip of a non-melting iceberg. In Europe, Henk Tennekes was dismissed as research director of the Royal Dutch Meteorological Society after questioning the scientific underpinnings of global warming. Aksel Winn-Nielsen, former director of the U.N.'s World Meteorological Organization, was tarred by Bert Bolin, first head of the IPCC, as a tool of the coal industry for questioning climate alarmism. Respected Italian professors Alfonso Sutera and Antonio Speranza disappeared from the debate in 1991, apparently losing climate-research funding for raising questions.

And then there are the peculiar standards in place in scientific journals for articles submitted by those who raise questions about accepted climate wisdom. At *Science* and *Nature*, such papers are commonly refused without review as being without interest. However, even when such papers are published, standards shift. When I, with some colleagues at NASA, attempted to determine how clouds behave under varying temperatures, we discovered what we called an "Iris Effect," wherein upper-level cirrus clouds contracted with increased temperature, providing a very strong negative climate feedback sufficient to greatly reduce the response to increasing CO_2. Normally, criticism of papers appears in the form of letters to the journal to which the original authors can respond immediately. However, in this case (and others) a flurry of hastily prepared papers appeared, claiming errors in our study, with our responses delayed months and longer. The delay permitted our paper to be commonly referred to as "discredited." Indeed, there is a strange reluctance to actually find out how climate really behaves. In 2003, when the draft of the U.S. National Climate Plan urged a high priority for improving our knowledge of climate sensitivity, the National Research Council instead urged support to look at the impacts of the warming—not whether it would actually happen.

Alarm rather than genuine scientific curiosity, it appears, is essential to maintaining funding. And only the most senior scientists today can stand up against this alarmist gale, and defy the iron triangle of climate scientists, advocates and policymakers.

———

Richard Lindzen, the Alfred P. Sloan Professor of Atmospheric Science at MIT, wrote this essay for the April 12, 2006, edition of *The Wall Street Journal* <www.wsj.com>.

Global Warming: Who Loses—and Who Wins?

Climate change in the next century (and beyond) could be enormously disruptive, spreading disease and sparking wars. It could also be a windfall for some people, businesses, and nations. A guide to how we all might get along in a warming world.

BY GREGG EASTERBROOK (2007)

Coastal cities inundated, farming regions parched, ocean currents disrupted, tropical diseases spreading, glaciers melting—an artificial greenhouse effect could generate countless tribulations.

If Earth's climate changes meaningfully—and the National Academy of Sciences, previously skeptical, said in 2005 that signs of climate change have become significant—there could be broad-based disruption of the global economy unparalleled by any event other than World War II.

Economic change means winners as well as losers. Huge sums will be made and lost if the global climate changes. Everyone wonders what warming might do to the environment—but what might it do to the global distribution of money and power?

Whether mainly natural or mainly artificial, climate change could bring different regions of the world tremendous benefits as well as drastic problems. The world had been mostly warming for thousands of years before the industrial era began, and that warming has been indisputably favorable to the spread of civilization. The trouble is that the world's economic geography is today organized according to a climate that has largely prevailed since the Middle Ages—runaway climate change would force big changes in the physical ordering of society. In the past, small climate changes have had substantial impact on agriculture, trade routes, and the types of products and commodities that sell. Larger climate shifts have catalyzed the rise and fall of whole societies. The Mayan Empire, for instance, did not disappear "mysteriously"; it likely fell into decline owing to decades of drought that ruined its agricultural base and deprived its cities of drinking water. On the other side of the coin, Europe's Medieval Warm Period, which lasted from around 1000 to 1400, was essential to the rise of Spain, France, and England: Those clement centuries allowed the expansion of farm production, population, cities, and universities, which in turn set the stage for the Industrial Revolution. Unless greenhouse-effect theory is completely wrong—and science increasingly supports the idea that it is right—21st-century climate change means that sweeping social and economic changes are in the works.

To date the greenhouse-effect debate has been largely carried out in abstractions—arguments about the distant past (what *do* those 100,000-year-old ice cores in Greenland really tell us about ancient temperatures, anyway?) coupled to computer-model conjecture regarding the 22nd century, with the occasional Hollywood disaster movie thrown in. Soon, both abstraction and postapocalyptic fantasy could be pushed aside by the economic and political realities of a warming world. If the global climate continues changing, many people and nations will find themselves in possession of land and resources of rising value, while others will suffer dire losses—and these winners and losers could start appearing faster than you might imagine. Add artificially triggered climate change to the volatility already initiated by globalization, and the next few decades may see previously unthinkable levels of economic upheaval, in which fortunes are won and lost based as much on the physical climate as on the business climate.

It may sound odd to ask of global warming, What's in it for me? But the question is neither crass nor tongue-in-cheek. The ways in which climate change could skew the world's distribution of wealth should help us appreciate just how profoundly an artificial greenhouse effect might shake our lives. Moreover, some of the lasting effects of climate change are likely to come not so much from the warming itself but from how we react to it: If the world warms appreciably, men and women will not sit by idly, eating bonbons and reading weather reports; there will be instead what economists call "adaptive response," most likely a great deal of it. Some aspects of this response may inflame tensions between those who are winning and those who are losing. How people, the global economy, and the international power structure adapt to climate change may influence how we live for generations. If the world warms, who will win? Who will lose? And what's in it for you?

LAND

Real estate might be expected to appreciate steadily in value during the 21st century, given that both the global population and global prosperity are rising. The supply of land is fixed, and if there's a fixed supply of something but a growing demand, appreciation should be automatic. That's unless climate change increases the supply of land by warming currently frosty areas while throwing the amount of *desirable* land into tremendous flux. My hometown of Buffalo, New York, for example, is today so déclassé that some of its stately Beaux-Arts homes, built during the Gilded Age and overlooking a park designed by Frederick Law Olmsted, sell for about the price of one-bedroom condos in Boston or San Francisco. If a warming world makes the area less cold and snowy, Buffalo might become one of the country's desirable addresses.

At the same time, Arizona and Nevada, blazing growth markets today, might become unbearably hot and see their real-estate markets crash. If the oceans rise, Florida's rapid growth could be, well, swamped by an increase in its perilously high groundwater table. Houston could decline, made insufferable by worsened summertime humidity, while the splendid, rustic Laurentide Mountains region north of Montreal, if warmed up a bit, might transmogrify into the new Poconos.

These are just a few of many possible examples. Climate change could upset the applecarts of real-estate values all over the world, with low-latitude properties tanking while high latitudes become the Sun Belt of the mid-21st century.

Local changes in housing demand are only small beer. To consider the big picture, examine a Mercator projection of our planet, and observe how the Earth's landmasses spread from the equator to the poles. Assume global warming is reasonably uniform. (Some computer models suggest that warming will vary widely by region; for the purposes of this article, suffice it to say that all predictions regarding an artificial greenhouse effect are extremely uncertain.) The equatorial and low-latitude areas of the world presumably will become hotter and less desirable as places of habitation, plus less valuable in economic terms; with a few exceptions, these areas are home to developing nations where living standards are already low.

So where is the high-latitude landmass that might grow more valuable in a warming world? By accident of geography, except for Antarctica nearly all such land is in the Northern Hemisphere, whose continents are broad west-to-east. Only a relatively small portion of South America, which narrows as one travels south, is high latitude, and none of Africa or Australia is. (Cape Town is roughly the same distance from the equator as Cape Hatteras; Melbourne is about the same distance from the equator as Manhattan.) More specifically, nearly all the added land-value benefits of a warming world might accrue to Alaska, Canada, Greenland, Russia, and Scandinavia.

This raises the possibility that an artificial greenhouse effect could harm nations that are already hard pressed and benefit nations that are already affluent. If Alaska turned temperate, it would drive conservationists to distraction, but it would also open for development an area more than twice the size of Texas. Rising world temperatures might throw Indonesia, Mexico, Nigeria, and other low-latitude nations into generations of misery, while causing Canada, Greenland, and Scandinavia to experience a rip-roarin' economic boom. Many Greenlanders are already cheering the retreat of glaciers, since this melting stands to make their vast island far more valuable. Last July, *The Wall Street Journal* reported that the growing season in the portion of Greenland open to cultivation is already two weeks longer than it was in the 1970s.

And Russia! For generations poets have bemoaned this realm as cursed by enormous, foreboding, harsh Siberia. What if the region in question were instead enormous, temperate, inviting Siberia? Climate change could place Russia in possession of the largest new region of pristine, exploitable land since the sailing ships of Europe first spied the shores of what would be called North America. The snows of Siberia cover soils that have never been depleted by controlled agriculture. What's more, beneath Siberia's snow may lie geologic formations that hold vast deposits of fossil fuels, as well as mineral resources. When considering ratification of the Kyoto Protocol to regulate greenhouse gases, the Moscow government dragged its feet, though the treaty was worded to offer the Russians extensive favors. Why might this have happened? Perhaps because Russia might be much better off in a warming world: Warming's benefits to Russia could exceed those to all other nations combined.

Of course, it could be argued that politicians seldom give much thought—one way or the other—to actions whose value will become clear only after they leave office, so perhaps Moscow does not have a grand strategy to warm the world for its own good. But a warmer world may be much to Russia's liking, whether it comes by strategy or accident. And how long until high-latitude nations realize global warming might be in their interests? In recent years, Canada has increased its greenhouse-gas output more rapidly than most other rich countries. Maybe this is a result of prosperity and oil-field development—or maybe those wily Canadians have a master plan for their huge expanse of currently uninhabitable land.

Global warming might do more for the North, however, than just opening up new land. Temperatures are rising on average, but *when* are they rising? Daytime? Nighttime? Winter? Summer? One fear about artificially triggered climate change has been that global warming would lead to scorching summer-afternoon highs, which would kill crops and brown out the electric power grid. Instead, so far a good share of the warming—especially in North America—has come in the form of nighttime and winter lows that are less low. Higher lows reduce the harshness of winter in northern climes and moderate the demand for energy. And fewer freezes allow extended growing seasons, boosting farm production. In North America, spring comes ever earlier—in recent years, trees have flowered in Washington, D.C., almost a week earlier on average than a generation ago. People may find this creepy, but earlier springs and milder winters can have economic value to agriculture—and lest we forget, all modern societies, including the United States, are grounded in agriculture.

If a primary impact of an artificially warmed world is to make land in Canada, Greenland, Russia, Scandinavia, and the United States more valuable, this could have three powerful effects on the 21st-century global situation.

First, historically privileged northern societies might not decline geopolitically, as many commentators have predicted. Indeed, the great age of northern power may lie ahead, if Earth's very climate is on the verge of conferring boons to that part of the world. Should it turn out that headlong fossil-fuel combustion by northern nations has set in motion climate change that strengthens the relative world position of those same nations, future essayists will have a field day. But the prospect is serious. By the middle of the 21st century, a new global balance of power may emerge in which Russia and America are once again the world's paired superpowers—only this time during a Warming War instead of a Cold War.

Second, if northern societies find that climate change makes them more wealthy, the quest for world equity could be dealt a huge setback. Despite the popular misconception, globalized economics have been a positive force for increased equity. As the Indian economist Surjit Bhalla has shown, the developing world produced 29 percent of the globe's income in 1950; by 2000 that share had risen to 42 percent, while the developing world's share of population rose at a slower rate. All other things being equal, we might expect continued economic globalization to distribute wealth more widely. But if climate change increases the value of northern land and resources, while leaving nations near the equator hotter and wracked by storms or droughts, all other things would not be equal.

That brings us to the third great concern: If climate change causes developing nations to falter, and social conditions within them deteriorate, many millions of jobless or hungry refugees may come to the borders of the favored North, demanding to be let in. If the very Earth itself turns against poor nations, punishing them with heat and storms, how could the United States morally deny the refugees succor?

Shifts in the relative values of places and resources have often led to war, and it is all too imaginable that climate change will cause nations to envy each other's territory. This envy is likely to run both north-south and up-down. North-south? Suppose climate change made Brazil less habitable, while bringing an agreeable mild clime to the vast and fertile Argentinean pampas to Brazil's south. São Paulo is already one of the world's largest cities. Would a desperate, overheated Brazil of the year 2037—its population exploding—hesitate to attack Argentina for cool, inviting land? Now consider the up-down prospect: the desire to leave low-lying areas for altitude. Here's an example: Since its independence, in 1947, Pakistan has kept a hand in the internal affairs of Afghanistan. Today Americans view this issue through the lens of the Taliban and al-Qaeda, but from Islamabad's perspective, the goal has always been to keep Afghanistan available as a place for retreat, should Pakistan lose a war with India. What if the climate warms, rendering much of Pakistan unbearable to its citizens? (Temperatures of 100-plus degrees are already common in the Punjab.) Afghanistan's high plateaus, dry and rocky as they are, might start looking pleasingly temperate as Pakistan warms, and the Afghans might see yet another army headed their way.

A warming climate could cause other landgrabs on a national scale. Today Greenland is a largely self-governing territory of Denmark that the world leaves in peace because no nation covets its shivering expanse. Should the Earth warm, Copenhagen might assert greater jurisdiction over Greenland, or stronger governments might scheme to seize this dwarf continent, which is roughly three times the size of Texas. Today Antarctica is under international administration, and this arrangement is generally accepted because the continent has no value beyond scientific research. If the world warmed for a long time—and it would likely take centuries for the Antarctic ice sheet to melt completely—international jockeying to seize or conquer Antarctica might become intense. Some geologists believe large oil deposits are under the Antarctic crust: In earlier epochs, the austral pole was densely vegetated and had conditions suitable for the formation of fossil fuels.

And though I've said to this point that Canada would stand to become more valuable in a warming world, actually, Canada and Nunavut would. For centuries, Europeans drove the indigenous peoples of what is now Canada farther and farther north. In 1993, Canada agreed to grant a degree of independence to the primarily Inuit population of Nunavut, and this large, cold region in the country's northeast has been mainly self-governing since 1999. The Inuit believe they are ensconced in the one place in this hemisphere that the descendants of Europe will never, ever want. This could turn out to be wrong.

For investors, finding attractive land to buy and hold for a warming world is fraught with difficulties, particularly when looking abroad. If considering plots on the pampas, for example, should one negotiate with the current Argentinian owners or the future Brazilian ones? Perhaps a safer route would be the contrarian one, focused on the likelihood of falling land values in places people may leave. If strict carbon-dioxide regulations are enacted, corporations will shop for "offsets," including projects that absorb carbon dioxide from the sky. Growing trees is a potential greenhouse-gas offset, and can be done comparatively cheaply in parts of the developing world, even on land that people may stop wanting. If you jump into the greenhouse-offset business, what you might plant is leucaena, a rapidly growing tree species suited to the tropics that metabolizes carbon dioxide faster than most trees. But you'll want to own the land in order to control the sale of the credits. Consider a possible sequence of events: First, climate change makes parts of the developing world even less habitable than they are today; then, refugees flee these areas; finally, land can be snapped up at Filene's Basement prices—and used to grow leucaena trees.

WATER

If Al Gore's movie, *An Inconvenient Truth*, is to be believed, you should start selling coastal real estate now. Gore's film maintains that an artificial greenhouse effect could raise sea levels 20 feet in the near future, flooding Manhattan, San Francisco, and dozens of other cities; Micronesia would simply disappear below the waves. Gore's is the dooms-day number, but the scientific consensus is worrisome enough: In 2005, the National Academy of Sciences warned that oceans may rise between four inches and three feet by the year 2100. Four inches may not sound like a lot, but it would imperil parts of coastal Florida and the Carolinas, among other places. A three-foot sea-level rise would flood significant portions of Bangladesh, threaten the national survival of the Netherlands, and damage many coastal cities, while submerging pretty much all of the world's trendy beach destinations to boot. And the Asian Tigers? Shanghai and Hong Kong sit right on the water. Raise the deep a few feet, and these Tiger cities would be abandoned.

The global temperature increase of the last century—about one degree Fahrenheit—was modest and did not cause any dangerous sea-level rise. Sea-level worries turn on the possibility that there is some nonlinear aspect of the climate system, a "tipping point" that could cause the rate of global warming to accelerate markedly. One reason global warming has not happened as fast as expected appears to be that the oceans have absorbed much of the carbon dioxide emitted by human activity. Studies suggest, however, that the ability of the oceans to absorb carbon dioxide may be slowing; as the absorption rate declines, atmospheric buildup will happen faster, and climate change could speed up. At the first sign of an increase in the rate of global warming: Sell, sell, sell your coastal properties. Unload those London and Seattle waterfront holdings. Buy land and real property in Omaha or Ontario.

An artificial greenhouse effect may also alter ocean currents in unpredictable ways. Already there is some evidence that the arctic currents are changing, while the major North Atlantic current that moves warm water north from the equator may be losing energy. If the North Atlantic current falters, temperatures could fall in Europe even as the world overall warms. Most of Europe lies to the north of Maine yet is temperate because the North Atlantic current carries huge volumes of warm water to the seas off Scotland; that warm water is Europe's weathermaker. Geological studies show that the North Atlantic current has stopped in the past. If this current stops again because of artificial climate change, Europe might take on the climate of present-day Newfoundland. As a result, it might depopulate, while the economic value of everything within its icy expanse declines. The European Union makes approximately the same contribution to the global economy as the United States makes: Significantly falling temperatures in Europe could trigger a worldwide recession.

While staying ready to sell your holdings in Europe, look for purchase opportunities near the waters of the Arctic Circle. In 2005, a Russian research ship became the first surface vessel ever to reach the North Pole without the aid of an icebreaker. If arctic sea ice melts, shipping traffic will begin transiting the North Pole. Andrew Revkin's 2006 book, *The North Pole Was Here*, profiles Pat Broe, who in 1997 bought the isolated far-north port of Churchill, Manitoba, from the Canadian government for $7. Assuming arctic ice continues to melt, the world's cargo vessels may begin sailing due north to shave thousands of miles off their trips, and the port of Churchill may be bustling. If arctic polar ice disappears and container vessels course the North Pole seas, shipping costs may decline—to the benefit of consumers. Asian manufacturers, especially, should see their costs of shipping to the United States and the European Union fall. At the same time, heavily trafficked southern shipping routes linking East Asia to Europe and to America's East Coast could see less traffic, and port cities along that route—such as Singapore—might decline. Concurrently, good relations with Nunavut could become of interest to the world's corporations.

Oh, and there may be oil under the arctic waters. Who would own that oil? The United States, Russia, Canada, Norway, and Denmark already assert legally complex claims to parts of the North Pole seas—including portions that other nations consider open waters not subject to sovereign control. Today it seems absurd to imagine the governments of the world fighting over the North Pole seas, but in the past many causes of battle have seemed absurd before the artillery fire began. Canada is already conducting naval exercises in the arctic waters, and making no secret of this.

Then again, perhaps ownership of these waters will go in an entirely different direction. The 21st century is likely to see a movement to create private-property rights in the ocean (ocean property rights are the most promising solution to overfishing of the open seas). Private-property rights in the North Pole seas, should they come into existence, might generate a rush to rival the Sooners' settlement of Oklahoma in the late 1800s.

Whatever happens to our oceans, climate change might also cause economic turmoil by affecting freshwater supplies. Today nearly all primary commodities, including petroleum, appear in ample supply. Freshwater is an exception: China is depleting aquifers at an alarming rate in order to produce enough rice to feed itself, while freshwater is scarce in much of the Middle East and parts of Africa. Freshwater depletion is especially worrisome in Egypt, Libya, and several Persian Gulf states. Greenhouse-effect science is so uncertain that researchers have little idea whether a warming world would experience more or less precipitation. If it turns out that rain and snow decline as the world warms, dwindling supplies of drinking water and freshwater for agriculture may be the next resource emergency. For investors this would suggest a cautious view of the booms in China and Dubai, as both places may soon face freshwater-supply problems. (Cost-effective desalinization continues to elude engineers.) On the other hand, where water rights are available in these areas, grab them.

Much of the effect that global warming will have on our water is speculative, so water-related climate change will be a high-risk/high-reward matter for investors and societies alike. The biggest fear is that artificially triggered climate change will shift rainfall away from today's productive breadbasket areas and toward what are now deserts or, worse, toward the oceans. (From the human perspective, all ocean rain represents wasted freshwater.) The reason Malthusian catastrophes have not occurred as humanity has grown is that for most of the last half century, farm yields have increased faster than population. But the global agricultural system is perilously poised on the assumption that growing conditions will continue to be good in the breadbasket areas of the United States, India, China, and South America. If rainfall shifts away from those areas, there could be significant human suffering for many, many years, even if, say, Siberian agriculture eventually replaces lost production elsewhere. By reducing farm yield, rainfall changes could also cause skyrocketing prices for commodity crops, something the global economy has rarely observed in the last 30 years.

Recent studies show that in the last few decades, precipitation in North America is increasingly the result of a few downpours rather than lots of showers. Downpours cause flooding and property damage, while being of less use to agriculture than frequent soft rains. Because the relationship between artificially triggered climate change and rainfall is conjectural, investors presently have no way to avoid buying land in places that someday might be hit with frequent downpours. But this concern surely raises a red flag about investments in India, Bangladesh, and Indonesia, where monsoon rains are already a leading social problem.

Water-related investments might be attractive in another way: for hydropower. Zero-emission hydropower might become a premium energy form if greenhouse gases are strictly regulated. Quebec is the Saudi Arabia of roaring water. Already the hydropower complex around James Bay is one of the world's leading sources of water-generated electricity. For 30 years, environmentalists and some Cree activists opposed plans to construct a grand hydropower complex that essentially would dam all large rivers flowing into the James and Hudson bays. But it's not hard to imagine Canada completing the reengineering of northern Quebec for hydropower, if demand from New England and the Midwest becomes strong enough. Similarly, there is hydropower potential in the Chilean portions of Patagonia. This is a wild and beautiful region little touched by human activity—and an intriguing place to snap up land for hydropower reservoirs.

ADAPTATION

Last October, the treasury office of the United Kingdom estimated that unless we adapt, global warming could eventually subtract as much as 20 percent of the gross domestic product from the world economy. Needless to say, if that happens, not even the cleverest portfolio will help you. This estimate is worst-case, however, and has many economists skeptical. Optimists think dangerous global warming might be averted at surprisingly low cost (see "Some Convenient Truths," September 2006). Once regulations create a profit incentive for the invention of greenhouse-gas-reducing technology, an outpouring of innovation is likely. Some of those who formulate greenhouse- gas-control ideas will become rich; everyone will benefit from the environmental safeguards the ideas confer.

Enactment of some form of binding greenhouse-gas rules is now essential both to slow the rate of greenhouse-gas accumulation and to create an incentive for inventors, engineers, and businesspeople to devise the ideas that will push society beyond the fossil-fuel age. *The New York Times* recently groused that George W. Bush's fiscal 2007 budget includes only $4.2 billion for federal research that might cut greenhouse-gas emissions. This is the wrong concern: Progress would be faster if the federal government spent nothing at all on greenhouse-gas-reduction research—but enacted regulations that gave the private sector a significant profit motive to find solutions that work in actual use, as opposed to on paper in government studies. The market has caused the greenhouse-gas problem, and the market is the best hope of solving it. Offering market incentives for the development of greenhouse-gas controls—indeed, encouraging profit making in greenhouse-gas controls—is the most promising path to avoiding the harm that could befall the dispossessed of developing nations as the global climate changes.

Yet if global-warming theory is right, higher global temperatures are already inevitable. Even the most optimistic scenario for reform envisions decades of additional greenhouse-gas accumulation in the atmosphere, and that in turn means a warming world. The warming may be manageable, but it is probably unstoppable in the short term.

This suggests that a major investment sector of the near future will be climate-change adaptation. Crops that grow in high temperatures, homes and buildings designed to stay cool during heat waves, vehicles that run on far less fuel, waterfront structures that can resist stronger storms—the list of needed adaptations will be long, and all involve producing, buying, and selling. Environmentalists don't like talk of adaptation, as it implies making our peace with a warmer world. That peace, though, must be made—and the sooner businesses, investors, and entrepreneurs get to work, the better.

Why, ultimately, should nations act to control greenhouse gases, rather than just letting climate turmoil happen and seeing who profits? One reason is that the cost of controls is likely to be much lower than the cost of rebuilding the world. Coastal cities could be abandoned and rebuilt inland, for instance, but improving energy efficiency and reducing greenhouse-gas emissions in order to stave off rising sea levels should be far more cost-effective. Reforms that prevent major economic and social disruption from climate change are likely to be less expensive, across the board, than reacting to the change. The history of antipollution programs shows that it is always cheaper to prevent emissions than to reverse any damage they cause.

For the United States, there's another argument that is particularly keen. The present ordering of the world favors the United States in nearly every respect—political, economic, even natural, considering America's excellent balance of land and resources. Maybe a warming world would favor the United States more; this is certainly possible. But when the global order already places America at No. 1, why would we want to run the risk of climate change that alters that order? Keeping the world economic system and the global balance of power the way they are seems very strongly in the U.S. national interest—and keeping things the way they are requires prevention of significant climate change. That, in the end, is what's in it for us.

―――――

Gregg Easterbrook wrote this piece for the April 2007 issue of *The Atlantic Monthly* <www.theatlantic.com>.

Earth without Humans

Just how profound an impact have we had on our planet?
An intriguing thought experiment reveals all.
BY BOB HOLMES (2006)

Humans are undoubtedly the most dominant species the Earth has ever known. In just a few thousand years we have swallowed up more than a third of the planet's land for our cities, farmland and pastures. By some estimates, we now commandeer 40 per cent of all its productivity. And we're leaving quite a mess behind: ploughed-up prairies, razed forests, drained aquifers, nuclear waste, chemical pollution, invasive species, mass extinctions and now the looming spectre of climate change. If they could, the other species we share Earth with would surely vote us off the planet.

Now just suppose they got their wish. Imagine that all the people on Earth—all 6.5 billion of us and counting—could be spirited away tomorrow, transported to a re-education camp in a far-off galaxy. (Let's not invoke the mother of all plagues to wipe us out, if only to avoid complications from all the corpses). Left once more to its own devices, Nature would begin to reclaim the planet, as fields and pastures reverted to prairies and forest, the air and water cleansed themselves of pollutants, and roads and cities crumbled back to dust.

"The sad truth is, once the humans get out of the picture, the outlook starts to get a lot better," says John Orrock, a conservation biologist at the National Center for Ecological Analysis and Synthesis in Santa Barbara, California. But would the footprint of humanity ever fade away completely, or have we so altered the Earth that even a million years from now a visitor would know that an industrial society once ruled the planet?

If tomorrow dawns without humans, even from orbit the change will be evident almost immediately, as the blaze of artificial light that brightens the night begins to wink out. Indeed, there are few better ways to grasp just how utterly we dominate the surface of the Earth than to look at the distribution of artificial illumination. By some estimates, 85 per cent of the night sky above the European Union is light-polluted; in the US it is 62 per cent and in Japan 98.5 per cent. In some countries, including Germany, Austria, Belgium and the Netherlands, there is no longer any night sky untainted by light pollution.

"Pretty quickly—24, maybe 48 hours—you'd start to see blackouts because of the lack of fuel added to power stations," says Gordon Masterton, president of the UK's Institution of Civil Engineers in London. Renewable sources such as wind turbines and solar will keep a few automatic lights burning, but lack of maintenance of the distribution grid will scuttle these in weeks or months. The loss of electricity will also quickly silence water pumps, sewage treatment plants and all the other machinery of modern society.

The same lack of maintenance will spell an early demise for buildings, roads, bridges and other structures. Though modern buildings are typically engineered to last 60 years, bridges 120 years and dams 250, these lifespans assume someone will keep them clean, fix minor leaks and correct problems with foundations. Without people to do these seemingly minor chores, things go downhill quickly.

The best illustration of this is the city of Pripyat near Chernobyl in Ukraine, which was abandoned after the nuclear disaster 20 years ago and remains deserted. "From a distance, you would still believe that Pripyat is a living city, but the buildings are slowly decaying," says Ronald Chesser, an environmental biologist at Texas Tech University in Lubbock who has worked extensively in the exclusion zone around Chernobyl. "The most pervasive thing you see are plants whose root systems get into the concrete and behind the bricks and into doorframes and so forth, and are rapidly breaking up the structure. You wouldn't think, as you walk around your house every day, that we have a big impact on keeping that from happening, but clearly we do. It's really sobering to see how the plant community invades every nook and cranny of a city."

With no one to make repairs, every storm, flood and frosty night gnaws away at abandoned buildings, and within a few decades roofs will begin to fall in and buildings collapse. This has already begun to happen in Pripyat. Wood-framed houses and other smaller structures, which are built to laxer standards, will be the first to go. Next down may be the glassy, soaring structures that tend to win acclaim these days. "The elegant suspension bridges, the lightweight forms, these are the kinds of structures that would be more vulnerable," says Masterton. "There's less reserve of strength built into the design, unlike solid masonry buildings and those using arches and vaults."

But even though buildings will crumble, their ruins—especially those made of stone or concrete—are likely to last thousands of years. "We still have records of civilisations that are 3000 years old," notes Masterton. "For many thousands of years there would still be some signs of the civilisations that we created. It's going to take a long time for a concrete road to disappear. It might be severely crumbling in many places, but it'll take a long time to become invisible."

The lack of maintenance will have especially dramatic effects at the 430 or so nuclear power plants now operating worldwide. Nuclear waste already consigned to long-term storage in air-cooled metal and concrete casks should be fine, since the containers are designed to survive thousands of years of neglect, by which time their radioactivity— mostly in the form of caesium-137 and strontium-90—will have dropped a thousandfold, says Rodney Ewing, a geologist at the University of Michigan who specialises in radioactive waste management. Active reactors will not fare so well. As cooling water evaporates or leaks away, reactor cores are likely to catch fire or melt down, releasing large amounts of radiation. The effects of such releases, however, may be less dire than most people suppose.

The area around Chernobyl has revealed just how fast nature can bounce back. "I really expected to see a nuclear desert there," says Chesser. "I was quite surprised. When you enter into the exclusion zone, it's a very thriving ecosystem."

The first few years after people evacuated the zone, rats and house mice flourished, and packs of feral dogs roamed the area despite efforts to exterminate them. But the heyday of these vermin proved to be short-lived, and already the native fauna has begun to take over. Wild boar are 10 to 15 times as common within the Chernobyl exclusion zone as outside it, and big predators are making a spectacular comeback. "I've never seen a wolf in the Ukraine outside the exclusion zone. I've seen many of them inside," says Chesser.

The same should be true for most other ecosystems once people disappear, though recovery rates will vary. Warmer, moister regions, where ecosystem processes tend to run more quickly in any case, will bounce back more quickly than cooler, more arid ones. Not surprisingly, areas still rich in native species will recover faster than more severely altered systems. In the boreal forests of northern Alberta, Canada, for example, human impact mostly consists of access roads, pipelines, and other narrow strips cut through the forest. In the absence of human activity, the forest will close over 80 per cent of these within 50 years, and all but 5 per cent within 200, according to simulations by Brad Stelfox, an independent land-use ecologist based in Bragg Creek, Alberta.

In contrast, places where native forests have been replaced by plantations of a single tree species may take several generations of trees—several centuries—to work their way back to a natural state. The vast expanses of rice, wheat and maize that cover the world's grain belts may also take quite some time to revert to mostly native species.

At the extreme, some ecosystems may never return to the way they were before humans interfered, because they have become locked into a new "stable state" that resists returning to the original. In Hawaii, for example, introduced grasses now generate frequent wild-fires that would prevent native forests from re-establishing themselves even if given free rein, says David Wilcove, a conservation biologist at Princeton University.

Feral descendants of domestic animals and plants, too, are likely to become permanent additions in many ecosystems, just as wild horses and feral pigs already have in some places. Highly domesticated species such as cattle, dogs and wheat, the products of centuries of artificial selection and inbreeding, will probably evolve back towards hardier, less specialised forms through random breeding. "If man disappears tomorrow, do you expect to see herds of poodles roaming the plains?" asks Chesser. Almost certainly not—but hardy mongrels will probably do just fine. Even cattle and other livestock, bred for meat or milk rather than hardiness, are likely to persist, though in much fewer numbers than today.

What about genetically modified crops? In August, Jay Reichman and colleagues at the US Environmental Protection Agency's labs in Corvallis, Oregon, reported that a GM version of a perennial called creeping bentgrass had established itself in the wild after escaping from an experimental plot in Oregon. Like most GM crops, however, the bentgrass is engineered to be resistant to a pesticide, which comes at a metabolic cost to the organism, so in the absence of spraying it will be at a disadvantage and will probably die out too.

Nor will our absence mean a reprieve for every species teetering on the brink of extinction. Biologists estimate that habitat loss is pivotal in about 85 per cent of cases where US species become endangered, so most such species will benefit once habitats begin to rebound. However, species in the direst straits may have already passed some critical threshold below which they lack the genetic diversity or the ecological critical mass they need to recover. These "dead species walking"—cheetahs and California condors, for example—are likely to slip away regardless.

Other causes of species becoming endangered may be harder to reverse than habitat loss. For example, about half of all endangered species are in trouble at least partly because of predation or competition from invasive introduced species. Some of these introduced species—house sparrows, for example, which are native to Eurasia but now dominate many cities in North America—will dwindle away once the gardens and bird feeders of suburban civilisation vanish. Others though, such as rabbits in Australia and cheat grass in the American west, do not need human help and will likely be around for the long haul and continue to edge out imperilled native species.

Ironically, a few endangered species—those charismatic enough to have attracted serious help from conservationists—will actually fare worse with people no longer around to protect them. Kirtland's warbler—one of the rarest birds in North America, once down to just a few hundred birds—suffers not only because of habitat loss near its Great Lakes breeding grounds but also thanks to brown-headed cowbirds, which lay their eggs in the warblers' nests and trick them into raising cowbird chicks instead of their own. Thanks to an aggressive programme to trap cowbirds, warbler numbers have rebounded, but once people disappear, the warblers could be in trouble, says Wilcove.

On the whole, though, a humanless Earth will likely be a safer place for threatened biodiversity. "I would expect the number of species that benefit to significantly exceed the number that suffer, at least globally," Wilcove says.

ON THE REBOUND

In the oceans, too, fish populations will gradually recover from drastic overfishing. The last time fishing more or less stopped—during the second world war, when few fishing vessels ventured far from port—cod populations in the North Sea skyrocketed. Today, however, populations of cod and other economically important fish have slumped much further than they did in the 1930s, and recovery may take significantly longer than five or so years.

The problem is that there are now so few cod and other large predatory fish that they can no longer keep populations of smaller fish such as gurnards in check. Instead, the smaller fish turn the tables and outcompete or eat tiny juvenile cod, thus keeping their erstwhile predators in check. The problem will only get worse in the first few years after fishing ceases, as populations of smaller, faster-breeding fish flourish like weeds in an abandoned field. Eventually, though, in the absence of fishing, enough large predators will reach maturity to restore the normal balance. Such a transition might take anywhere from a few years to a few decades, says Daniel Pauly, a fisheries biologist at the University of British Columbia in Vancouver.

With trawlers no longer churning up nutrients from the ocean floor, near-shore ecosystems will return to a relatively nutrient-poor state. This will be most apparent as a drop in the frequency of harmful algal blooms such as the red tides that often plague coastal areas today. Meanwhile, the tall, graceful corals and other bottom-dwelling organisms on deep-water reefs will gradually begin to regrow, restoring complex three-dimensional structure to ocean-floor habitats that are now largely flattened, featureless wastelands.

Long before any of this, however—in fact, the instant humans vanish from the Earth—pollutants will cease spewing from automobile tailpipes and the smokestacks and waste outlets of our factories. What happens next will depend on the chemistry of each particular pollutant. A few, such as oxides of nitrogen and sulphur and ozone (the ground-level pollutant, not the protective layer high in the stratosphere), will wash out of the atmosphere in a matter of a few weeks. Others, such as chlorofluorocarbons, dioxins and the pesticide DDT, take longer to break down. Some will last a few decades.

The excess nitrates and phosphates that can turn lakes and rivers into algae-choked soups will also clear away within a few decades, at least for surface waters. A little excess nitrate may persist for much longer within groundwater, where it is less subject to microbial conversion into atmospheric nitrogen. "Groundwater is the long-term memory in the system," says Kenneth Potter, a hydrologist at the University of Wisconsin at Madison.

Carbon dioxide, the biggest worry in today's world because of its leading role in global warming, will have a more complex fate. Most of the CO_2 emitted from burning fossil fuels is eventually absorbed into the ocean. This happens relatively quickly for surface waters—just a few decades—but the ocean depths will take about a thousand years to soak up their full share. Even when that equilibrium has been reached, though, about 15 per cent of the CO_2 from burning fossil fuels will remain in the atmosphere, leaving its concentration at about 300 parts per million compared with pre-industrial levels of 280 ppm. "There will be CO_2 left in the atmosphere, continuing to influence the climate, more than 1000 years after humans stop emitting it," says Susan Solomon, an atmospheric chemist with the US National Oceanic and Atmospheric Administration (NOAA) in Boulder, Colorado. Eventually calcium ions released from sea-bottom sediments will allow the sea to mop up the remaining excess over the next 20,000 years or so.

Even if CO_2 emissions stop tomorrow, though, global warming will continue for another century, boosting average temperatures by a further few tenths of a degree. Atmospheric scientists call this "committed warming," and it happens because the oceans take so long to warm up compared with the atmosphere. In essence, the oceans are acting as a giant air conditioner, keeping the atmosphere cooler than it would otherwise be for the present level of CO_2. Most policy-makers fail to take this committed warming into account, says Gerald Meehl, a climate modeller at the National Center for Atmospheric Research, also in Boulder. "They think if it gets bad enough we'll just put the brakes on, but we can't just stop and expect everything to be OK, because we're already committed to this warming."

That extra warming we have already ordered lends some uncertainty to the fate of another important greenhouse gas, methane, which produces about 20 per cent of our current global warming. Methane's chemical lifetime in the atmosphere is only about 10 years, so its concentration could rapidly return to pre-industrial levels if emissions cease. The wild card, though, is that there are massive reserves of methane in the form of methane hydrates on the sea floor and frozen into permafrost. Further temperature rises may destabilise these reserves and dump much of the methane into the atmosphere. "We may stop emitting methane ourselves, but we may already have triggered climate change to the point where methane may be released through other processes that we have no control over," says Pieter Tans, an atmospheric scientist at NOAA in Boulder.

No one knows how close the Earth is to that threshold. "We don't notice it yet in our global measurement network, but there is local evidence that there is some destabilisation going on of permafrost soils, and methane is being released," says Tans. Solomon, on the other hand, sees little evidence that a sharp global threshold is near.

All things considered, it will only take a few tens of thousands of years at most before almost every trace of our present dominance has vanished completely. Alien visitors coming to Earth 100,000 years hence will find no obvious signs that an advanced civilisation ever lived here.

Yet if the aliens had good enough scientific tools they could still find a few hints of our presence. For a start, the fossil record would show a mass extinction centred on the present day, including the sudden disappearance of large mammals across North America at the end of the last ice age. A little digging might also turn up intriguing signs of a long-lost intelligent civilisation, such as dense concentrations of skeletons of a large bipedal ape, clearly deliberately buried, some with gold teeth or grave goods such as jewelry.

And if the visitors chanced across one of today's landfills, they might still find fragments of glass and plastic—and maybe even paper—to bear witness to our presence. "I would virtually guarantee that there would be some," says William Rathje, an archaeologist at Stanford University in California who has excavated many landfills. "The preservation of things is really pretty amazing. We think of artifacts as being so impermanent, but in certain cases things are going to last a long time."

Ocean sediment cores will show a brief period during which massive amounts of heavy metals such as mercury were deposited, a relic of our fleeting industrial society. The same sediment band will also show a concentration of radioactive isotopes left by reactor meltdowns after our disappearance. The atmosphere will bear traces of a few gases that don't occur in nature, especially perfluorocarbons such as CF_4, which have a half-life of tens of thousands of years. Finally a brief, century-long pulse of radio waves will forever radiate out across the galaxy and beyond, proof—for anything that cares and is able to listen—that we once had something to say and a way to say it.

But these will be flimsy souvenirs, almost pathetic reminders of a civilisation that once thought itself the pinnacle of achievement. Within a few million years, erosion and possibly another ice age or two will have obliterated most of even these faint traces. If another intelligent species ever evolves on the Earth—and that is by no means certain, given how long life flourished before we came along—it may well have no inkling that we were ever here save for a few peculiar fossils and ossified relics. The humbling—and perversely comforting—reality is that the Earth will forget us remarkably quickly.

———

Bob Holmes wrote this piece for the October 14, 2006, issue of *New Scientist* <www. newscientist.com>.

Be It Ever So Homespun, There's Nothing Like Spin

BY KIM SEVERSON (2007)

Something made me uneasy when I dropped a box of gluten-free EnviroKidz organic Koala Crisp cereal in my shopping cart. But it's hard to suspect a cartoon koala, so I moved on.

The unsettling sensation came back when I bought a bag of my favorite organic frozen French fries. Why did the verdant fields in the Cascadian Farm logo make me feel so smug?

Then I got really suspicious. A bag of natural Cheetos seemed so much more appealing than the classic cheese puff. Why? Was it the image of a subdued Chester Cheetah rising gently from a farm field bathed in golden sunlight?

Like clues to a murder that suddenly point to a single culprit, the mystery in my shopping cart revealed itself. Wheat sheaf by wheat sheaf, sunrise by sunrise, the grocery store shelves had been greenwashed.

And I was falling for it.

The kind of greenwashing I'm talking about is not just a fake environmental ethos. Greenwashing, it seems to me, can also describe a pervasive genre of food packaging designed to make sure that manufacturers grab their slice of the $25 billion that American shoppers spend each year on natural or organic food.

As a design shorthand, it makes subtle use of specific colors, images, typefaces and the promise of what marketers call "an authentic narrative" to sell food. Especially in recent years, greenwashing has spilled out well past the organic section of the grocery store. Even the snack aisle at the gas station isn't immune.

"Somebody becomes successful with a specific point of view, and the consumer begins to identify with it and it spreads like a virus," said Paula Scher, a partner in Pentagram, an international design firm. From there it's only a matter of time before Cap'n Crunch shows up in a hemp jacket, raising money to save the manatees.

Buy a greenwashed product and you're buying a specific set of healthy environmental and socially correct values.

If the package does its work, then the food inside doesn't actually have to be organic, only organic-ish. The right cues on a package free mass-market consumers from doing any homework, said Elizabeth Talerman, a branding analyst. They can assume that a group she calls the green elite—those early adopters who pushed for organic food laws and who helped make Whole Foods markets a success—have done the work for them.

"The mass market wants an instant identifier," said Ms. Talerman, a longtime New York advertising consultant.

So what are the identifiers? After shopping for dozens of products in places as varied as food co-ops and convenience stores, I've uncovered the essential elements of a green-washed product. Start with a gentle image of a field or a farm to suggest an ample harvest gathered by an honest, hard-working family. To that end, strangely oversize vegetables or fruits are good. If they are dew-kissed and nestled in a basket, all the better. A little red tractor is O.K. Pesticide tanks and rows of immigrant farm laborers bent over in the hot sun are not.

Earth's Best, a baby and toddler food company, offers a delicious example. Its whole grain rice cereal features two babies working the rice fields. One is white and one is black. (A greenwashed package would never show the black child working in the fields alone.) A sign that looks hand-hewn declares "No GMO's." There is a barn, a butterfly and a typeface that could have come from the back room of a general store.

A good greenwashed product should show an animal displaying special skills or great emotional range. Some Organic Valley packages feature a sax-playing, environmentally friendly earthworm. Jaunty cows on Stonyfield Farm yogurt wear sunglasses and headbands. The cows on Horizon's milk cartons dance a bovine jig, despite challenges by organic purists that some Horizon cows see precious little pasture.

A little family history helps, too. My Family Farm of Fort Thomas, Ky., sells packaged cookies and crackers and promises to give some of the money to charity. On the back of the box is a story that begins, "With careers as licensed social workers, my sister and I are committed to improving the lives of children." A carton of Country Hen omega-3 eggs, which cost $3.69 for six, had a fuzzy black-and-white photograph inside showing the company's owner, George Bass, and the entire Country Hen family, along with their favorite eggnog recipe.

A cause is important. Nature's Path, the maker of Koala Crisp, promises that 1 percent of sales will be spent saving endangered species. Barbara's Bakery, maker of Puffins cereal, pays for the National Audubon Society's live "puffin cams" in the Gulf of Maine. Buy a box of Peace Cereal's raspberry ginger crisp, and a percentage of the profit helps pay for International Peace Prayer Day in New Mexico.

The actual health benefits of a product don't always matter. A package of organic Naturepops from College Farm shows a field of lollipops and a barn, suggesting a well-educated farmer tending her candy. The sugar might come from cane juice and tapioca syrup, but it's sugar just the same.

And although "organic" is losing its power as a code word for certain cultural values, it doesn't hurt to flaunt it if you've got it. The word appears 21 times on a box of Cascadian Farm Vanilla Almond Crunch.

Having established a design paradigm that succeeds in selling food that is often more expensive than conventional groceries, the design world should perhaps rejoice. This is not the case. Some top brand and package designers find the cartoonish animals and bad hippie typefaces as grating as a self-righteous vegan at a barbecue.

But then, they didn't like American food package design that much to begin with.

"It's the bottom of the barrel," said Ms. Scher, who works in the New York office of Pentagram design.

Riskier designs, like the clean lettering and curvy bottle of Pom Wonderful pome-granate juice, are rare. Food manufacturers usually agonize over changing the size of a box or shifting the background color from teal to aquamarine.

But when a trend starts to show success, it's a design pileup. That's what happened with the natural and organic category, which makes up about 10 percent of the food at the grocery store and has been growing by more than 20 percent a year since 2000. In the grocery business, a 4 percent jump is considered a victory.

"It's aisle after aisle of design desperation," said Brian Collins, chairman and chief creative officer of the design group at Ogilvy, the international advertising and public relations company. He called the look "phony naïveté" and predicted that its demise was close because consumers are wising up. There is value in telling a story, but it must be true, he said.

Merely dressing up the package is not enough, he said. Nonetheless, manufacturers are eager to project a wholesome image.

"It's the halo effect," said Caren Wilcox, executive director of the Organic Trade Association. "That's why we encourage consumers to look for the U.S.D.A. organic seal."

But even the organic seal doesn't necessarily offer assurances that the item is produced in a way that jibes with consumer expectations for something that comes in a green-washed package.

"All the ingredients being used in items with the organic seal are produced using the organic system," Ms. Wilcox said. "It doesn't mean they don't sometimes end up in products some people think other people shouldn't eat."

Design and packaging experts fix the start of sincerity and authenticity in food package design in the 1970s. Mo Siegel began selling Celestial Seasonings tea in boxes with sleepy bears. Tom and Kate Chappell gave up the corporate life to create Tom's of Maine toothpaste. Ben Cohen and Jerry Greenfield sold ice cream in Vermont, using goofy hand-rendered graphics to tell their story.

The trend grew in the 1980s, when corporate America entered a noncorporate phase. "Companies began to try to not look like big companies," Ms. Scher said.

By the late 1990s, anything with a hint of natural organic goodness sold in big numbers. Today, many companies that started with a humble story line have been purchased by larger interests. Unilever owns Ben and Jerry's, the Hain Celestial Group is traded on Nasdaq and Tom's of Maine is controlled by Colgate-Palmolive.

The kind of imagery that once marked a brand as an alternative to corporate food conglomerates has now been incorporated into Lay's potato chips. Consumers can buy classic Lay's in the shiny yellow bag, or Natural Lay's, with a thicker cut, expeller-pressed oil and sea salt. The package has a brown harvest graphic design, old-timey typefaces and a matte bag. The natural chips cost about 10 cents an ounce more than the classics. A handful of either still offers 150 calories and 10 grams of fat.

"When it gets to Lay's," Ms. Scher said, "its time to change."

Ms. Talerman, the New York advertising consultant, predicted that the fascination with what she called the green identifiers will last about five years longer. Then, she said, green-elite food consumers will push companies for even more information about environmental impact, labor practices and community involvement, and mass market consumers will start reading labels instead of just searching out easy identifiers.

Food manufacturers might begin to copy the new nutrition-style labels that Timberland is putting on its shoe boxes. Each one lists the amount of energy it took to make the shoes, how much of that was renewable, whether child labor was used and how many hours per pair Timberland dedicated to community service.

"As soon as the mass market starts to understand these issues more," Ms. Talerman predicted, "we'll get away from the fields and the giant vegetables and get back to better design."

———

Kim Severson wrote this piece for the January 3, 2007, edition of *The New York Times* <www.nytimes.com>.

Life in the Green Lane

BY JAMIE LINCOLN KITMAN (2006)

If you make your way over to the Javits Convention Center for the New York International Automobile Show—or if you've gone to any auto show in the last year or so—you'll know that hybrid cars are the hippest automotive fashion statement to come along in years. They've become synonymous with the worthy goal of reducing gasoline consumption and dependence on foreign oil and all that this means for a better environment and more stable geopolitics.

And yet like fat-free desserts, which sound healthy but can still make you fat, the hybrid car can make people feel as if they're doing something good, even when they're doing nothing special at all. As consumers and governments at every level climb onto the hybrid bandwagon, there is the very real danger of elevating the technology at the expense of the intended outcome—saving gas.

Few things these days say "environmentally aware consumer" so loudly as the fuel-sipping Toyota Prius. With its two power sources—one a gasoline-powered internal combustion engine, the other a battery-driven electric motor—the best-selling Prius (and other hybrids sold by Honda and Ford and due soon from several other car makers) can go further on a gallon and emit fewer pollutants in around-town use than most conventional automobiles because under certain circumstances they run on battery power and consume less fuel. For this reason, federal, state and local governments have been bending over backward to encourage the sale of hybrids, with a bewildering array of tax breaks, traffic lanes and parking spaces dedicated to hybrid owners.

But just because a car has so-called hybrid technology doesn't mean it's doing more to help the environment or to reduce the country's dependence on imported oil any more than a nonhybrid car. The truth is, it depends on the hybrid and the nonhybrid cars you are comparing, as well as on how you use the vehicles. There are good hybrids and bad ones. Fuel-efficient conventional cars are often better than hybrid S.U.V.'s — just look at how many miles per gallon the vehicle gets.

Being a professional car-tester, which is to say a person who gets asked for unpaid car-buying advice practically every day, I know these distinctions have already been lost on many car buyers. And I fear they're well on their way to being lost on our governments, too.

Lately, right-minded people have been calling me and telling me they're thinking about buying the Lexus 400H, a new hybrid S.U.V. When I tell them that they'd get better mileage in some conventional S.U.V.'s, and even better mileage with a passenger car, they protest, "But it's a hybrid!" I remind them that the 21 miles per gallon I saw while driving the Lexus is not particularly brilliant, efficiency-wise—hybrid or not. Because the Lexus 400H is a relatively heavy car and because its electric motor is deployed to provide speed more than efficiency, it will never be a mileage champ.

The car that started the hybrid craze, the Toyota Prius, is lauded for squeezing 40 or more miles out of a gallon of gas, and it really can. But only when it's being driven around town, where its electric motor does its best and most active work. On a cross-country excursion in a Prius, the staff of Automobile Magazine discovered mileage plummeted on the Interstate. In fact, the car's computer, which controls the engine and the motor, allowing them to run together or separately, was programmed to direct the Prius to spend most of its highway time running on gasoline because at higher speeds the batteries quickly get exhausted. Indeed, the gasoline engine worked so hard that we calculated we might have used less fuel on our journey if we had been driving Toyota's conventionally powered, similarly sized Corolla—which costs thousands less. For the owner who does the majority of her driving on the highway, the Prius's potential for fuel economy will never be realized and its price premium never recovered.

For years, most of the world's big car makers have shied away from building hybrids because while they are technologically intriguing, they are also an inelegant engineering solution—the use of two energy sources assures extra weight, extra complexity and extra expense (as much as $6,000 more per car.) The hybrid car's electric battery packs rob space from passengers and cargo and although they can be recycled, not every owner can be counted on to do the right thing at the end of their vehicle's service life. And an unrecycled hybrid battery pack, which weighs more than 100 pounds, poses a major environmental hazard.

So the ideal hybrid car is one that is used in town and carefully disposed of at the end of its days. Hybrid taxis and buses make enormous sense. But the market knows no such distinctions. People think they want hybrids and they'll buy them, even if a conventional car would make more sense for their pocketbook and for the environment. The danger is that the automakers will co-opt the hybrids' green mantle and, with the help of a government looking to bail out its troubled friends in Detroit, misguidedly encourage the sale of hybrids without reference to their actual effect on oil consumption.

Several bills floating around Congress, for instance, have proposed tax incentives to buyers of hybrid cars, irrespective of their gas mileage. Thus, under one failed but sure to resurface formulation, the suburbanite who buys a hypothetical hybrid Dodge Durango that gets 14 miles per gallon instead of 12 thanks to its second, electric power source would be entitled to a huge tax incentive, while the buyer of a conventional, gasoline-powered Honda Civic that delivers 40 miles per gallon on the open road gets none.

And under some imaginable patchwork of state and local ordinances, the Durango buyer might get a special parking space at the train station and the right to use a high occupancy vehicle lane, despite appalling fuel economy and a car full of empty seats, while the Honda driver will have to walk to the train from a distant parking lot after braving the worst of morning rush hour traffic on the highway just like everybody else.

Pro-hybrid laws and incentives sound nice, but they might just end up subsidizing companies that have failed to develop truly fuel-efficient vehicles at the expense of those that have had the foresight to design their cars right in the first place. And they may actually punish citizens who save fuel the old-fashioned way—by using less of it, with smaller, lighter and more efficient cars. All the while, they'll make a mockery of a potentially useful technology.

Jamie Lincoln Kitman is the New York bureau chief for *Automobile Magazine* and a columnist for *Top Gear,* a British magazine. This column appeared in the April 16, 2006, edition of *The New York Times* <www.nytimes.com>.

Going Nuclear: A Green Makes the Case

BY PATRICK MOORE (2006)

In the early 1970s when I helped found Greenpeace, I believed that nuclear energy was synonymous with nuclear holocaust, as did most of my compatriots. That's the conviction that inspired Greenpeace's first voyage up the spectacular rocky northwest coast to protest the testing of U.S. hydrogen bombs in Alaska's Aleutian Islands. Thirty years on, my views have changed, and the rest of the environmental movement needs to update its views, too, because nuclear energy may just be the energy source that can save our planet from another possible disaster: catastrophic climate change.

Look at it this way: More than 600 coal-fired electric plants in the United States produce 36 percent of U.S. emissions—or nearly 10 percent of global emissions—of CO_2, the primary greenhouse gas responsible for climate change. Nuclear energy is the only large-scale, cost-effective energy source that can reduce these emissions while continuing to satisfy a growing demand for power. And these days it can do so safely.

I say that guardedly, of course, just days after Iranian President Mahmoud Ahmadinejad announced that his country had enriched uranium. "The nuclear technology is only for the purpose of peace and nothing else," he said. But there is widespread speculation that, even though the process is ostensibly dedicated to producing electricity, it is in fact a cover for building nuclear weapons.

And although I don't want to underestimate the very real dangers of nuclear technology in the hands of rogue states, we cannot simply ban every technology that is dangerous. That was the all-or-nothing mentality at the height of the Cold War, when anything nuclear seemed to spell doom for humanity and the environment. In 1979, Jane Fonda and Jack Lemmon produced a frisson of fear with their starring roles in *The China Syndrome*, a fictional evocation of nuclear disaster in which a reactor meltdown threatens a city's survival. Less than two weeks after the blockbuster film opened, a reactor core meltdown at Pennsylvania's Three Mile Island nuclear power plant sent shivers of very real anguish throughout the country.

What nobody noticed at the time, though, was that Three Mile Island was in fact a success story: The concrete containment structure did just what it was designed to do—prevent radiation from escaping into the environment. And although the reactor itself was crippled, there was no injury or death among nuclear workers or nearby residents. Three Mile Island was the only serious accident in the history of nuclear energy generation in the United States, but it was enough to scare us away from further developing the technology: There hasn't been a nuclear plant ordered up since then.

Today, there are 103 nuclear reactors quietly delivering just 20 percent of America's electricity. Eighty percent of the people living within 10 miles of these plants approve of them (that's not including the nuclear workers). Although I don't live near a nuclear plant, I am now squarely in their camp.

And I am not alone among seasoned environmental activists in changing my mind on this subject. British atmospheric scientist James Lovelock, father of the Gaia theory, believes that nuclear energy is the only way to avoid catastrophic climate change. Stewart Brand, founder of the "Whole Earth Catalog," says the environmental movement must embrace nuclear energy to wean ourselves from fossil fuels. On occasion, such opinions have been met with excommunication from the anti-nuclear priesthood: The late British Bishop Hugh Montefiore, founder and director of Friends of the Earth, was forced to resign from the group's board after he wrote a pro-nuclear article in a church newsletter.

There are signs of a new willingness to listen, though, even among the staunchest anti-nuclear campaigners. When I attended the Kyoto climate meeting in Montreal last December, I spoke to a packed house on the question of a sustainable energy future. I argued that the only way to reduce fossil fuel emissions from electrical production is through an aggressive program of renewable energy sources (hydroelectric, geothermal heat pumps, wind, etc.) plus nuclear. The Greenpeace spokesperson was first at the mike for the question period, and I expected a tongue-lashing. Instead, he began by saying he agreed with much of what I said—not the nuclear bit, of course, but there was a clear feeling that all options must be explored.

Here's why: Wind and solar power have their place, but because they are intermittent and unpredictable they simply can't replace big baseload plants such as coal, nuclear and hydroelectric. Natural gas, a fossil fuel, is too expensive already, and its price is too volatile to risk building big baseload plants. Given that hydroelectric resources are built pretty much to capacity, nuclear is, by elimination, the only viable substitute for coal. It's that simple.

That's not to say that there aren't real problems—as well as various myths—associated with nuclear energy. Each concern deserves careful consideration:

- Nuclear energy is expensive. It is in fact one of the least expensive energy sources. In 2004, the average cost of producing nuclear energy in the United States was less than two cents per kilowatt-hour, comparable with coal and hydroelectric. Advances in technology will bring the cost down further in the future.
- Nuclear plants are not safe. Although Three Mile Island was a success story, the accident at Chernobyl, 20 years ago this month, was not. But Chernobyl was an accident waiting to happen. This early model of Soviet reactor had no containment vessel, was an inherently bad design and its operators literally blew it up. The multi-agency U.N. Chernobyl Forum reported last year that 56 deaths could be directly attributed to the accident, most of those from radiation or burns suffered while fighting the fire. Tragic as those deaths were, they pale in comparison to the more than 5,000 coal-mining deaths that occur worldwide every year. No one has died of a radiation-related accident in the history of the U.S. civilian nuclear reactor program. (And although hundreds of uranium mine workers did die from radiation exposure underground in the early years of that industry, that problem was long ago corrected.)
- Nuclear waste will be dangerous for thousands of years. Within 40 years, used fuel has less than one-thousandth of the radioactivity it had when it was removed from the reactor. And it is incorrect to call it waste, because 95 percent of the potential energy is still contained in the used fuel after the first cycle. Now that the United States has removed the ban on recycling used fuel, it will be possible to use that energy and to greatly reduce the amount of waste that needs treatment and disposal. Last month, Japan joined France, Britain and Russia in the nuclear-fuel-recycling business. The United States will not be far behind.
- Nuclear reactors are vulnerable to terrorist attack. The six-feet-thick reinforced concrete containment vessel protects the contents from the outside as well as the inside. And even if a jumbo jet did crash into a reactor and breach the containment, the reactor would not explode. There are many types of facilities that are far more vulnerable, including liquid natural gas plants, chemical plants and numerous political targets.

- Nuclear fuel can be diverted to make nuclear weapons. This is the most serious issue associated with nuclear energy and the most difficult to address, as the example of Iran shows. But just because nuclear technology can be put to evil purposes is not an argument to ban its use.

Over the past 20 years, one of the simplest tools—the machete—has been used to kill more than a million people in Africa, far more than were killed in the Hiroshima and Nagasaki nuclear bombings combined. What are car bombs made of? Diesel oil, fertilizer and cars. If we banned everything that can be used to kill people, we would never have harnessed fire.

The only practical approach to the issue of nuclear weapons proliferation is to put it higher on the international agenda and to use diplomacy and, where necessary, force to prevent countries or terrorists from using nuclear materials for destructive ends. And new technologies such as the reprocessing system recently introduced in Japan (in which the plutonium is never separated from the uranium) can make it much more difficult for terrorists or rogue states to use civilian materials to manufacture weapons.

The 600-plus coal-fired plants emit nearly 2 billion tons of CO_2 annually—the equivalent of the exhaust from about 300 million automobiles. In addition, the Clean Air Council reports that coal plants are responsible for 64 percent of sulfur dioxide emissions, 26 percent of nitrous oxides and 33 percent of mercury emissions. These pollutants are eroding the health of our environment, producing acid rain, smog, respiratory illness and mercury contamination.

Meanwhile, the 103 nuclear plants operating in the United States effectively avoid the release of 700 million tons of CO_2 emissions annually—the equivalent of the exhaust from more than 100 million automobiles. Imagine if the ratio of coal to nuclear were reversed so that only 20 percent of our electricity was generated from coal and 60 percent from nuclear. This would go a long way toward cleaning the air and reducing greenhouse gas emissions. Every responsible environmentalist should support a move in that direction.

———   .

Patrick Moore, co-founder of Greenpeace, is chairman and chief scientist of Greenspirit Strategies Ltd. <www.greenspirit.com>. This essay was published in the April 16, 2006, edition of *The Washington Post* <www.washingtonpost.com>.

FROM READING TO WRITING

1. After reading Jerry Adler's essay "The War of the Words," look on a few news media sites and blogs on the internet to see how people are referring to the global warming phenomenon. What do think is the most accurate term for the issue? Why?

2. In "Yelling 'Fire' on a Hot Planet," Andrew C. Revkin quotes *Americans and Climate Change* as saying that urgency, as a persuasive persona, is "prone to being discounted as unreasoned alarmism or even passion." Do you agree? Is passion necessarily unsuccessful in scientific arguments?

3. Characterize the ethos presented by three of the following writers, supporting your responses with evidence from the text. Which do you find most persuasive? Why?
   a. Jeffrey Kluger in "Be Worried, Be Very Worried."
   b. Richard Lindzen in "Climate of Fear: Global-Warming Alarmists Intimidate Dissenting Scientists into Silence."
   c. Greg Easterbrook in "Global Warming: Who Loses—and Who Wins?"
   d. Kim Severson in "Be It Ever So Homespun, There's Nothing Like Spin."
   e. Patrick Moore in "Going Nuclear: A Green Makes the Case."

4. Compare the causal chains in Jeffrey Kluger's and Richard Lindzen's essays. Analyze the arguments in each about global warming, paying particular attention to the causal links they present between carbon dioxide emissions and natural disasters. Whose do you find most persuasive? Cite specific passages that you find effective.

5. As people who support protecting the environment, Patrick Moore and Jamie Lincoln Kitman make surprising arguments in their essays concerning the effectiveness of hybrid vehicles and nuclear energy, respectively. Outline their arguments and responses to counterarguments. How do you think an author's biography influences his or her persuasiveness?

Eight

THAT'S ENTERTAINMENT

Watching TV Makes You Smarter

BY STEVEN JOHNSON (2005)

SCIENTIST A: *Has he asked for anything special?*

SCIENTIST B: *Yes, this morning for breakfast . . . he requested something called "wheat germ, organic honey and tiger's milk."*

SCIENTIST A: *Oh, yes. Those were the charmed substances that some years ago were felt to contain life-preserving properties.*

SCIENTIST B: *You mean there was no deep fat? No steak or cream pies or . . . hot fudge?*

SCIENTIST A: *Those were thought to be unhealthy.*

—from Woody Allen's Sleeper

On Jan. 24, the Fox network showed an episode of its hit drama 24, the real-time thriller known for its cliffhanger tension and often-gruesome violence. Over the preceding weeks, a number of public controversies had erupted around 24, mostly focused on its portrait of Muslim terrorists and its penchant for torture scenes. The episode that was shown on the 24th only fanned the flames higher: in one scene, a terrorist enlists a hit man to kill his child for not fully supporting the jihadist cause; in another scene, the secretary of defense authorizes the torture of his son to uncover evidence of a terrorist plot.

But the explicit violence and the post-9/11 terrorist anxiety are not the only elements of 24 that would have been unthinkable on prime-time network television 20 years ago. Alongside the notable change in content lies an equally notable change in form. During its 44 minutes—a real-time hour, minus 16 minutes for·commercials— the episode connects the lives of 21 distinct characters, each with a clearly defined "story arc," as the Hollywood jargon has it: a defined personality with motivations and obstacles and specific relationships with other characters. Nine primary narrative threads wind their way through those 44 minutes, each drawing extensively upon events and information revealed in earlier episodes. Draw a map of all those intersecting plots and personalities, and you get structure that—where formal complexity is concerned—more closely resembles *Middlemarch* than a hit TV drama of years past like *Bonanza*.

For decades, we've worked under the assumption that mass culture follows a path declining steadily toward lowest-common-denominator standards, presumably because the "masses" want dumb, simple pleasures and big media companies try to give the masses what they want. But as that 24 episode suggests, the exact opposite is happening: the culture is getting more cognitively demanding, not less. To make sense of an episode of 24, you have to integrate far more information than you would have a few decades ago watching a comparable show. Beneath the violence and the ethnic stereotypes, another trend appears: to keep up with entertainment like 24, you have to pay attention, make inferences, track shifting social relationships. This is what I call the Sleeper Curve: the most debased forms of mass diversion—video games and violent television dramas and juvenile sitcoms—turn out to be nutritional after all.

I believe that the Sleeper Curve is the single most important new force altering the mental development of young people today, and I believe it is largely a force for good: enhancing our cognitive faculties, not dumbing them down. And yet you almost never hear this story in popular accounts of today's media. Instead, you hear dire tales of addiction, violence, mindless escapism. It's assumed that shows that promote smoking or gratuitous violence are bad for us, while those that thunder against teen pregnancy or intolerance have a positive role in society. Judged by that morality-play standard, the story of popular culture over the past 50 years—if not 500—is a story of decline: the morals of the stories have grown darker and more ambiguous, and the antiheroes have multiplied.

The usual counterargument here is that what media have lost in moral clarity, they have gained in realism. The real world doesn't come in nicely packaged public-service announcements, and we're better off with entertainment like *The Sopranos* that reflects our fallen state with all its ethical ambiguity. I happen to be sympathetic to that argument, but it's not the one I want to make here. I think there is another way to assess the social virtue of pop culture, one that looks at media as a kind of cognitive workout, not as a series of life lessons. There may indeed be more "negative messages" in the mediasphere today. But that's not the only way to evaluate whether our television shows or video games are having a positive impact. Just as important—if not more important—is the kind of thinking you have to do to make sense of a cultural experience. That is where the Sleeper Curve becomes visible.

TELEVISED INTELLIGENCE

Consider the cognitive demands that televised narratives place on their viewers. With many shows that we associate with "quality" entertainment—*The Mary Tyler Moore Show, Murphy Brown, Frasier*—the intelligence arrives fully formed in the words and actions of the characters on-screen. They say witty things to one another and avoid lapsing into tired sitcom clichés, and we smile along in our living rooms, enjoying the company of these smart people. But assuming we're bright enough to understand the sentences they're saying, there's no intellectual labor involved in enjoying the show as a viewer. You no more challenge your mind by watching these intelligent shows than you challenge your body watching *Monday Night Football*. The intellectual work is happening on-screen, not off.

But another kind of televised intelligence is on the rise. Think of the cognitive benefits conventionally ascribed to reading: attention, patience, retention, the parsing of narrative threads. Over the last half-century, programming on TV has increased the demands it places on precisely these mental faculties. This growing complexity involves three primary elements: multiple threading, flashing arrows and social networks.

According to television lore, the age of multiple threads began with the arrival in 1981 of *Hill Street Blues*, the Steven Bochco police drama invariably praised for its "gritty realism." Watch an episode of *Hill Street Blues* side by side with any major drama from the preceding decades—*Starsky and Hutch*, for instance, or *Dragnet*—and the structural transformation will jump out at you. The earlier shows follow one or two lead characters, adhere to a single dominant plot and reach a decisive conclusion at the end of the episode. Draw an outline of the narrative threads in almost every *Dragnet* episode, and it will be a single line: from the initial crime scene, through the investigation, to the eventual cracking of the case. A typical *Starsky and Hutch* episode offers only the slightest variation on this linear formula: the introduction of a comic subplot that usually appears only at the tail end of the episode.

A *Hill Street Blues* episode complicates the picture in a number of profound ways. The narrative weaves together a collection of distinct strands—sometimes as many as 10, though at least half of the threads involve only a few quick scenes scattered through the episode. The number of primary characters—and not just bit parts—swells significantly. And the episode has fuzzy borders: picking up one or two threads from previous episodes at the outset and leaving one or two threads open at the end.

Critics generally cite *Hill Street Blues* as the beginning of "serious drama" native in the television medium—differentiating the series from the single-episode dramatic programs from the 50's, which were Broadway plays performed in front of a camera. But the *Hill Street* innovations weren't all that original; they'd long played a defining role in popular television, just not during the evening hours. The structure of a *Hill Street* episode—and indeed of all the critically acclaimed dramas that followed, from *thirtysomething* to *Six Feet Under*—is the structure of a soap opera. *Hill Street Blues* might have sparked a new golden age of television drama during its seven-year run, but it did so by using a few crucial tricks that *Guiding Light* and *General Hospital* mastered long before.

Bochco's genius with *Hill Street* was to marry complex narrative structure with complex subject matter. *Dallas* had already shown that the extended, interwoven threads of the soap-opera genre could survive the weeklong interruptions of a prime-time show, but the actual content of *Dallas* was fluff. (The most probing issue it addressed was the question, now folkloric, of who shot J.R.) *All in the Family* and *Rhoda* showed that you could tackle complex social issues, but they did their tackling in the comfort of the sitcom living room. *Hill Street* had richly drawn characters confronting difficult social issues and a narrative structure to match.

Since *Hill Street* appeared, the multi-threaded drama has become the most widespread fictional genre on prime time: *St. Elsewhere, L.A. Law, thirtysomething, Twin Peaks, N.Y.P.D. Blue, E.R., The West Wing, Alias, Lost.* (The only prominent holdouts in drama are shows like *Law and Order* that have essentially updated the venerable *Dragnet* format and thus remained anchored to a single narrative line.) Since the early 80's, however, there has been a noticeable increase in narrative complexity in these dramas. The most ambitious show on TV to date, *The Sopranos*, routinely follows up to a dozen distinct threads over the course of an episode, with more than 20 recurring characters.

The total number of active threads equals the multiple plots of "Hill Street," but on *The Sopranos* each thread is more substantial. The show doesn't offer a clear distinction between dominant and minor plots; each story line carries its weight in the mix. Episodes also display a chordal mode of storytelling entirely absent from *Hill Street*: a single scene in "The Sopranos" will often connect to three different threads at the same time, layering one plot atop another. And every single thread in many *Sopranos* episodes builds on events from previous episodes and continues on through the rest of the season and beyond.

Taken together, these programs show the Sleeper Curve rising over the past 30 years of popular television. In a sense, this is as much a map of cognitive changes in the popular mind as it is a map of on-screen developments, as if the media titans decided to condition our brains to follow ever-larger numbers of simultaneous threads. Before *Hill Street*, the conventional wisdom among television execs was that audiences wouldn't be comfortable following more than three plots in a single episode, and indeed, the *Hill Street* pilot, which was shown in January 1981, brought complaints from viewers that the show was too complicated. Fast-forward two decades, and shows like *The Sopranos* engage their audiences with narratives that make *Hill Street* look like *Three's Company*. Audiences happily embrace that complexity because they've been trained by two decades of multithreaded dramas.

Multi-threading is the most celebrated structural feature of the modern television drama, and it certainly deserves some of the honor that has been doled out to it. And yet multi-threading is only part of the story.

THE CASE FOR CONFUSION

Shortly after the arrival of the first-generation slasher movies—*Halloween, Friday the 13th*—Paramount released a mock-slasher flick called *Student Bodies*, parodying the genre just as the *Scream* series would do 15 years later. In one scene, the obligatory nubile teenage baby sitter hears a noise outside a suburban house; she opens the door to investigate, finds nothing and then goes back inside. As the door shuts behind her, the camera swoops in on the doorknob, and we see that she has left the door unlocked. The camera pulls back and then swoops down again for emphasis. And then a flashing arrow appears on the screen, with text that helpfully explains: *Unlocked!*

That flashing arrow is parody, of course, but it's merely an exaggerated version of a device popular stories use all the time. When a sci-fi script inserts into some advanced lab a nonscientist who keeps asking the science geeks to explain what they're doing with that particle accelerator, that's a flashing arrow that gives the audience precisely the information it needs in order to make sense of the ensuing plot. ("Whatever you do, don't spill water on it, or you'll set off a massive explosion!") These hints serve as a kind of narrative hand-holding. Implicitly, they say to the audience, "We realize you have no idea what a particle accelerator is, but here's the deal: all you need to know is that it's a big fancy thing that explodes when wet." They focus the mind on relevant details: "Don't worry about whether the baby sitter is going to break up with her boyfriend. Worry about that guy lurking in the bushes." They reduce the amount of analytic work you need to do to make sense of a story. All you have to do is follow the arrows.

By this standard, popular television has never been harder to follow. If narrative threads have experienced a population explosion over the past 20 years, flashing arrows have grown correspondingly scarce. Watching our pinnacle of early 80's TV drama, *Hill Street Blues*, we find there's an informational wholeness to each scene that differs markedly from what you see on shows like *The West Wing* or *The Sopranos* or *Alias* or *E.R.*

Hill Street has ambiguities about future events: will a convicted killer be executed? Will Furillo marry Joyce Davenport? Will Renko find it in himself to bust a favorite singer for cocaine possession? But the present-tense of each scene explains itself to the viewer with little ambiguity. There's an open question or a mystery driving each of these stories—how will it all turn out?—but there's no mystery about the immediate activity on the screen. A contemporary drama like *The West Wing*, on the other hand, constantly embeds mysteries into the present-tense events: you see characters performing actions or discussing events about which crucial information has been deliberately withheld. Anyone who has watched more than a handful of *The West Wing* episodes closely will know the feeling: scene after scene refers to some clearly crucial but unexplained piece of information, and after the sixth reference, you'll find yourself wishing you could rewind the tape to figure out what they're talking about, assuming you've missed something. And then you realize that you're supposed to be confused. The open question posed by these sequences is not "How will this turn out in the end?" The question is "What's happening right now?"

The deliberate lack of hand-holding extends down to the microlevel of dialogue as well. Popular entertainment that addresses technical issues—whether they are the intricacies of passing legislation, or of performing a heart bypass, or of operating a particle accelerator—conventionally switches between two modes of information in dialogue: texture and substance. Texture is all the arcane verbiage provided to convince the viewer that they're watching Actual Doctors at Work; substance is the material planted amid the background texture that the viewer needs make sense of the plot.

Conventionally, narratives demarcate the line between texture and substance by inserting cues that flag or translate the important data. There's an unintentionally comical moment in the 2004 blockbuster *The Day After Tomorrow* in which the beleaguered climatologist (played by Dennis Quaid) announces his theory about the imminent arrival of a new ice age to a gathering of government officials. In his speech, he warns that "we have hit a critical desalinization point!" At this moment, the writer-director Roland Emmerich—a master of brazen arrow-flashing—has an official follow with the obliging remark: "It would explain what's driving this extreme weather." They might as well have had a flashing "Unlocked!" arrow on the screen.

The dialogue on shows like *The West Wing* and *E.R.*, on the other hand, doesn't talk down to its audiences. It rushes by, the words accelerating in sync with the high-speed tracking shots that glide through the corridors and operating rooms. The characters talk faster in these shows, but the truly remarkable thing about the dialogue is not purely a matter of speed; it's the willingness to immerse the audience in information that most viewers won't understand. Here's a typical scene from *E.R.*:

[WEAVER AND WRIGHT push a gurney containing a 16-year-old girl. Her parents, JANNA AND FRANK MIKAMI, follow close behind. CARTER AND LUCY fall in.]

WEAVER:	16-year-old, unconscious, history of biliary atresia.
CARTER:	Hepatic coma?
WEAVER:	Looks like it.
MR. MIKAMI:	She was doing fine until six months ago.
CARTER:	What medication is she on?
MR. MIKAMI:	Ampicillin, tobramycin, vitamins a, d and k.
LUCY:	Skin's jaundiced.
WEAVER:	Same with the sclera. Breath smells sweet.
CARTER:	Fetor hepaticus?
WEAVER:	Yep.
LUCY:	What's that?

WEAVER:	Her liver's shut down. Let's dip a urine. *[To CARTER]* Guys, it's getting a little crowded in here, why don't you deal with the parents? Start lactulose, 30 cc's per NG.
CARTER:	We're giving medicine to clean her blood.
WEAVER:	Blood in the urine, two-plus.
CARTER:	The liver failure is causing her blood not to clot.
MR. MIKAMI:	Oh, God. . . .
CARTER:	Is she on the transplant list?
MR. MIKAMI:	She's been Status 2a for six months, but they haven't been able to find her a match.
CARTER:	Why? What's her blood type?
MR. MIKAMI:	ab.

[This hits CARTER like a lightning bolt. LUCY gets it, too. They share a look.]

There are flashing arrows here, of course—"The liver failure is causing her blood not to clot"—but the ratio of medical jargon to layperson translation is remarkably high. From a purely narrative point of view, the decisive line arrives at the very end: "AB." The 16-year-old's blood type connects her to an earlier plot line, involving a cerebral-hemorrhage victim who—after being dramatically revived in one of the opening scenes—ends up brain-dead. Far earlier, before the liver-failure scene above, Carter briefly discusses harvesting the hemorrhage victim's organs for transplants, and another doctor makes a passing reference to his blood type being the rare AB (thus making him an unlikely donor). The twist here revolves around a statistically unlikely event happening at the E.R.—an otherwise perfect liver donor showing up just in time to donate his liver to a recipient with the same rare blood type. But the show reveals this twist with remarkable subtlety. To make sense of that last "AB" line—and the look of disbelief on Carter's and Lucy's faces—you have to recall a passing remark uttered earlier regarding a character who belongs to a completely different thread. Shows like *E.R.* may have more blood and guts than popular TV had a generation ago, but when it comes to storytelling, they possess a quality that can only be described as subtlety and discretion.

EVEN BAD TV IS BETTER

Skeptics might argue that I have stacked the deck here by focusing on relatively high-brow titles like *The Sopranos* or *The West Wing*, when in fact the most significant change in the last five years of narrative entertainment involves reality TV. Does the contemporary pop cultural landscape look quite as promising if the representative show is *Joe Millionaire* instead of *The West Wing*?

I think it does, but to answer that question properly, you have to avoid the tendency to sentimentalize the past. When people talk about the golden age of television in the early 70's—invoking shows like *The Mary Tyler Moore Show* and *All in the Family*—they forget to mention how awful most television programming was during much of that decade. If you're going to look at pop-culture trends, you have to compare apples to apples, or in this case, lemons to lemons. The relevant comparison is not between *Joe Millionaire* and *MASH*; it's between *Joe Millionaire* and *The Newlywed Game*, or between *Survivor* and *The Love Boat*.

What you see when you make these head-to-head comparisons is that a rising tide of complexity has been lifting programming at the bottom of the quality spectrum and at the top. *The Sopranos* is several times more demanding of its audiences than *Hill Street* was, and *Joe Millionaire* has made comparable advances over *Battle of the Network Stars*. This is the ultimate test of the Sleeper Curve theory: even the junk has improved.

If early television took its cues from the stage, today's reality programming is reliably structured like a video game: a series of competitive tests, growing more challenging over time. Many reality shows borrow a subtler device from gaming culture as well: the rules aren't fully established at the outset. You learn as you play.

On a show like *Survivor* or *The Apprentice*, the participants—and the audience—know the general objective of the series, but each episode involves new challenges that haven't been ordained in advance. The final round of the first season of *The Apprentice*, for instance, threw a monkey wrench into the strategy that governed the play up to that point, when Trump announced that the two remaining apprentices would have to assemble and manage a team of subordinates who had already been fired in earlier episodes of the show. All of a sudden the overarching objective of the game—do anything to avoid being fired—presented a potential conflict to the remaining two contenders: the structure of the final round favored the survivor who had maintained the best relationships with his comrades. Suddenly, it wasn't enough just to have clawed your way to the top; you had to have made friends while clawing. The original *Joe Millionaire* went so far as to undermine the most fundamental convention of all—that the show's creators don't openly lie to the contestants about the prizes—by inducing a construction worker to pose as man of means while 20 women competed for his attention.

Reality programming borrowed another key ingredient from games: the intellectual labor of probing the system's rules for weak spots and opportunities. As each show discloses its conventions, and each participant reveals his or her personality traits and background, the intrigue in watching comes from figuring out how the participants should best navigate the environment that has been created for them. The pleasure in these shows comes not from watching other people being humiliated on national television; it comes from depositing other people in a complex, high-pressure environment where no established strategies exist and watching them find their bearings. That's why the water-cooler conversation about these shows invariably tracks in on the strategy displayed on the previous night's episode: why did Kwame pick Omarosa in that final round? What devious strategy is Richard Hatch concocting now?

When we watch these shows, the part of our brain that monitors the emotional lives of the people around us—the part that tracks subtle shifts in intonation and gesture and facial expression—scrutinizes the action on the screen, looking for clues. We trust certain characters implicitly and vote others off the island in a heartbeat. Traditional narrative shows also trigger emotional connections to the characters, but those connections don't have the same participatory effect, because traditional narratives aren't explicitly about strategy. The phrase "Monday-morning quarterbacking" describes the engaged feeling that spectators have in relation to games as opposed to stories. We absorb stories, but we second-guess games. Reality programming has brought that second-guessing to prime time, only the game in question revolves around social dexterity rather than the physical kind.

THE REWARDS OF SMART CULTURE

The quickest way to appreciate the Sleeper Curve's cognitive training is to sit down and watch a few hours of hit programming from the late 70's on Nick at Nite or the SOAPnet channel or on DVD. The modern viewer who watches a show like *Dallas* today will be bored by the content—not just because the show is less salacious than today's soap operas (which it is by a small margin) but also because the show contains far less information in each scene, despite the fact that its soap-opera structure made it one of the most complicated narratives on television in its prime. With *Dallas*, the modern viewer doesn't have to think to make sense of what's going on, and not having to think is boring. Many recent hit shows—*24*, *Survivor*, *The Sopranos*, *Alias*, *Lost*, *The Simpsons*, *E.R.*—take the opposite approach, layering each scene with a thick network of affiliations. You have to focus to follow the plot, and in focusing you're exercising the parts of your brain that map social networks, that fill in missing information, that connect multiple narrative threads.

Of course, the entertainment industry isn't increasing the cognitive complexity of its products for charitable reasons. The Sleeper Curve exists because there's money to be made by making culture smarter. The economics of television syndication and DVD sales mean that there's a tremendous financial pressure to make programs that can be watched multiple times, revealing new nuances and shadings on the third viewing. Meanwhile, the Web has created a forum for annotation and commentary that allows more complicated shows to prosper, thanks to the fan sites where each episode of shows like *Lost* or *Alias* is dissected with an intensity usually reserved for Talmud scholars. Finally, interactive games have trained a new generation of media consumers to probe complex environments and to think on their feet, and that gamer audience has now come to expect the same challenges from their television shows. In the end, the Sleeper Curve tells us something about the human mind. It may be drawn toward the sensational where content is concerned—sex does sell, after all. But the mind also likes to be challenged; there's real pleasure to be found in solving puzzles, detecting patterns or unpacking a complex narrative system.

In pointing out some of the ways that popular culture has improved our minds, I am not arguing that parents should stop paying attention to the way their children amuse themselves. What I am arguing for is a change in the criteria we use to determine what really is cognitive junk food and what is genuinely nourishing. Instead of a show's violent or tawdry content, instead of wardrobe malfunctions or the F-word, the true test should be whether a given show engages or sedates the mind. Is it a single thread strung together with predictable punch lines every 30 seconds? Or does it map a complex social network? Is your on-screen character running around shooting everything in sight, or is she trying to solve problems and manage resources? If your kids want to watch reality TV, encourage them to watch *Survivor* over *Fear Factor*. If they want to watch a mystery show, encourage 24 over *Law and Order*. If they want to play a violent game, encourage Grand Theft Auto over Quake. Indeed, it might be just as helpful to have a rating system that used mental labor and not obscenity and violence as its classification scheme for the world of mass culture.

Kids and grown-ups each can learn from their increasingly shared obsessions. Too often we imagine the blurring of kid and grown-up cultures as a series of violations: the 9-year-olds who have to have nipple broaches explained to them thanks to Janet Jackson; the middle-aged guy who can't wait to get home to his Xbox. But this demographic blur has a commendable side that we don't acknowledge enough. The kids are forced to think like grown-ups: analyzing complex social networks, managing resources, tracking subtle narrative intertwinings, recognizing long-term patterns. The grown-ups, in turn, get to learn from the kids: decoding each new technological wave, parsing the interfaces and discovering the intellectual rewards of play. Parents should see this as an opportunity, not a crisis. Smart culture is no longer something you force your kids to ingest, like green vegetables. It's something you share.

––––––

Steven Johnson's latest book is *Everything Bad Is Good for You: How Today's Popular Culture Is Actually Making Us Smarter,* from which this article is adapted. This piece was published in the April 24, 2005, edition of *The New York Times Magazine* <www.nytimes.com>.

The Case for Reality TV:
What the Snobs Don't Understand

BY MICHAEL HIRSCHORN (2007)

This past January, I had the pleasure of serving as official spear-catcher for a *CBS Evening News* report on the increasing levels of humiliation on *American Idol* and other reality-TV shows, including some on my channel, VH1. The segment featured snippets of our shows *I Love New York* (a dating competition with an urban vibe) and *Celebrity Fit Club* (which tracks the efforts of overweight singers and actors to get back in shape, and, by extension, reignite their careers). "VH1, among other things, show-cases faded celebrities who are fat," said the CBS correspondent Richard Schlesinger.

In between shots of me fake working at my computer and fake chatting with the amiable Schlesinger while fake strolling down our corporate-looking hallway, I took my best shot at defending the alleged horrors of *AI* and *Celebrity Fit Club*. But it was clear that CBS News was set on bemoaning what it saw as yet another outrage against the cul-ture. The central complaint, per Katie Couric's intro to the report, was that more peo-ple had watched *American Idol* the previous week than watched the State of the Union address on all the broadcast networks combined. When the segment ended, Couric signed off with an extravagant eye roll. "We're doing our part here at CBS News," she seemed to be saying, "but the barbarians are massing at the gates, people." A line had been drawn in the sand, as if the news were now akin to an evening at the Met.

Is there an easier position to take in polite society than to patronize reality TV? Even television programmers see the genre as a kind of visual Hamburger Helper: cheap filler that saves them money they can use elsewhere for more-worthy programming. Reality shows cost anywhere from a quarter to half as much to produce as scripted shows. The money saved on *Extreme Makeover: Home Edition*, the logic goes, allows ABC to pay for additional gruesome medical emergencies and exploding ferries on *Grey's Anatomy*. NBC's crappy *Fear Factor* pays for the classy *Heroes*.

As befits a form driven largely by speed and cost considerations, reality TV is not often formally daring. Fifteen years after MTV's *The Real World* set the template for contempo-rary reality TV by placing seven strangers in a downtown Manhattan loft, reality television has developed its own visual shorthand: short doses of documentary footage interspersed with testimonials (often called OTFs, for "on-the-fly" interviews) in which the partici-pants describe, ex post facto, what they were thinking during the action you are watching.

The current boom may be a product of the changing economics of the television business, but reality TV is also the liveliest genre on the set right now. It has engaged hot-button cultural issues—class, sex, race—that respectable television, including the august *CBS Evening News*, rarely touches. And it has addressed a visceral need for a dif-ferent kind of television at a time when the Web has made more traditionally produced video seem as stagy as Molière.

Reality TV may be an awkward admixture of documentary (with its connotations of thousands of hours of footage patiently gathered, redacted by monk-like figures into the purest expression of truth possible in 90 to 120 minutes) and scripted (with its auteurs and Emmys and noble overtones of craft). But this kludge also happens to have allowed reality shows to skim the best elements of scripted TV and documentaries while eschewing the problems of each. Reality shows steal the story structure and pacing of scripted television, but leave behind the canned plots and characters. They have the visceral impact of documentary reportage without the self-importance and general lugubriousness. Where documentaries must construct their narratives from found matter, reality TV can place real people in artificial surroundings designed for maximum emotional impact.

Scripted television is supposedly showing new ambition these days, particularly in the hour-long drama form. *Studio 60 on the Sunset Strip* was going to bring the chatty intelligence of *The West Wing* back to prime time. *Lost* was going to challenge network audiences like never before, with complex plots, dozens of recurring characters, and movie-level production values. Shows are bigger now: On *24* this season, a nuclear bomb exploded. But network prime-time television remains dominated by variants on the police procedural (*Law & Order, CSI, Criminal Minds*), in which a stock group of characters (ethnically, sexually, and generationally diverse) grapples with endless versions of the same dilemma. The episodes have all the ritual predictability of Japanese Noh theater: Crimes are solved, lessons are learned, order is restored.

Reality shows have leaped into this imaginative void. Discovery's *Deadliest Catch*, which began its third season in April, is an oddly transfixing series about . . . crab fishermen in the Bering Sea. As a straightforward documentary, *Catch* would have been worthy fodder, but the producers have made it riveting by formatting the whole season as a sporting event, with crab tallies for each of the half dozen or so boats and a race-against-the-clock urgency that, for all its contrivance, gives structure and meaning to the fishermen's efforts.

Narrative vibrancy is not the only thing that electrifies these shows. Reality TV presents some of the most vital political debate in America, particularly about class and race. Fox's *Nanny 911* and ABC's *Supernanny* each offer object lessons on the hazards of parenting in an age of instant gratification and endless digital diversion. ABC's *Extreme Makeover: Home Edition* features intensely emotional tales of people who have fallen through the cracks of Bush-era America—often blue-collar families ravaged by disease, health-care costs, insurance loopholes, layoffs, and so forth. My channel's *The (White) Rapper Show* turned into a running debate among the aspiring white MCs over cultural authenticity—whether it is more properly bestowed by class or race.

Class realities are plumbed to remarkable effect on *The Real Housewives of Orange County,* a "docu soap" that completed its second season on Bravo this spring. The show is inspired by a trio of suburban dramas: *The O.C., Desperate Housewives,* and the 1999 movie *American Beauty.* Lacking the visual panache, or the budgets, of its scripted forebears, *Real Housewives* nonetheless goes deeper, charting the spiritual decay of life in gated communities, where financial anxieties, fraying families, and fear of aging leave inhabitants grasping for meaning and happiness as they steer their Escalades across Southern California's perfectly buffed, featureless landscape. *Crash,* the 2006 Oscar winner, trafficked in similar white California dread, but with all the nuance of a two-by-four to the face.

In *Real Housewives,* businessman Lou Knickerbocker stages a photo shoot to promote his new "highly oxygenated" water, variously called "Aqua Air" and "O.C. Energy Drink" ("We have patented technology that produces water from air"). The models are attractive-ish teen and 20-something girls: Lou's daughter Lindsey, by ex-wife Tammy; a few other daughters of O.C. housewives; and a newcomer whom Lou apparently found waitressing at a local restaurant.

Lou and Tammy made piles of money—it's not clear how—but their finances seem to have fractured along with their marriage. The photo shoot, therefore, is throwing off more than the normal amount of flop sweat. Lou apparently has personally selected the girls, which means he has declined to showcase his other daughter, Megan, because of her tattoos and lack of physical fitness. Lou believes the "Aqua Air Angels" should embody the Aqua Air ideal, which is why they can't drink or smoke and must have grade-point averages higher than 3.5. "This is a photo shoot," he barks after a fight breaks out between one of the girls and the waitress, "not a gang bang, for chrissakes."

The detail is what puts the scene over: Lou's lip-smacking focus on the girls, the girls' bland acquiescence. "That's it, baby, smile," Lou urges his daughter. "Show those teeth," says Tammy. A similar scenario on *Desperate Housewives* could never have been quite this preposterous, quite this blandly amoral. The characters would have been scripted with softening, redeeming qualities, or been rendered comically evil. Lou would've gotten his comeuppance, like Wallace Shawn's money-siphoning literary agent in that series. Here, the apparent willingness of the young women and at least some of the parents to indulge Lou's bottom-of-the-barrel scheming outlines, in a few short brushstrokes, a community's shared value system.

Value systems are smashed into each other, like atoms in an accelerator, on ABC's *Wife Swap,* where the producers find the most extreme pairings possible: lesbian mommies with bigots, godless cosmopolites with Bible thumpers. On one February show, a Pentacostal family, the Hoovers, was paired with the family of a former pastor, Tony Meeks, who has turned from God to follow his rock-and-roll dreams (mom Tish rocks out as well). "I feel by being there," Kristin Hoover said, "I was able to remind Tony that God still loves him and is not finished with him." The episode took seriously the Hoovers' commitment to homeschooling and their rejection of contemporary culture (a rejection not taken to the extreme of declining an invitation to appear on reality TV). Compare this with the tokenism of "born-again Christian" Harriet Hayes on NBC's dramedy *Studio 60 on the Sunset Strip*. Harriet's but a cipher, a rhetorical backboard against which ex-boyfriend Matt Albie can thwack his heathen wisecracks.

The competitions and elimination shows are latter-day Milgram experiments that place real people in artificial situations to see what happens. *The Apprentice* is Darwinism set loose inside an entrepreneurial Habitrail. Post-9/11, *Survivor* became less a fantasy and more a metaphor for an imagined postapocalyptic future. What happens on these shows might be a Technicolor version of how we behave in real life, but so is most fiction. Creative endeavors—written, scripted, or produced—should be measured not by how literally they replicate actual life but by how effectively they render emotional truths. The best moments found on reality TV are unscriptable, or beyond the grasp of most scriptwriters. It's no coincidence that 2006's best scripted dramas—*The Wire*, HBO's multi-season epic of inner-city Baltimore; and *Children of Men*, Alfonso Cuarón's futuristic thriller—were studies in meticulously crafted "realness," deploying naturalistic dialogue, decentered and chaotic action, stutter-step pacing, and a reporter's eye for the telling detail. *The Wire*'s season and Cuarón's movie both ended on semi-resolved novelistic notes, scorning the tendency in current television and cinema toward easy narrative closure. Watching them only threw into higher relief the inability of so much other scripted product to get beyond stock characterizations and pat narrative.

For all the snobbism in the doc community, reality TV has actually contributed to the recent boom in documentary filmmaking. The most successful docs of recent vintage have broken through in part by drawing heavily from reality television's bag of tricks, dropping the form's canonical insistence on pure observation. In *Fahrenheit 9/11*, Michael Moore brings an Army recruiter with him to confront legislators and urge them to enlist their children in the Iraq War effort. In *Bowling for Columbine*, Moore takes children who were shot at Columbine to a Kmart, where they ask for a refund on the bullets that are still lodged in their bodies. Of course, Moore's never been a doc purist. *TV Nation*, his short-lived 1994 television series, prefigured a long line of gonzo reality, from *Joe Millionaire* to *Punk'd*. Having the Serbian ambassador sing along to the Barney theme song ("I love you, you love me") while statistics about the number of Bosnians killed during the breakup of Yugoslavia appeared on the screen was not only ur-reality; it was ur-Borat. And speaking of talking animals, *March of the Penguins* turned stunning footage of mating and migrating penguins into an utterly contrived Antarctic version of *Love Story*.

The resistance to reality TV ultimately comes down to snobbery, usually of the generational variety. People under 30, in my experience, tend to embrace this programming; they're happy to be entertained, never mind the purity of conception. As an unapologetic producer of reality shows, I'm obviously biased, but I also know that any genre that provokes such howls of protest is doing something interesting. Try the crab.

Michael Hirschorn, VH1's executive vice president for original programming and production, wrote this piece for the May 2007 issue of *The Atlantic Monthly* <www.theatlantic.com>.

My Plan to Save Network Television
BY CHARLIE HAUCK (2006)

Let's say you've created a network television series for the 2006–2007 season. It's beautifully calibrated to appeal to the only viewers of any value to advertisers: young people. It's about a family of migrant lifeguards. They travel to beaches all over the world in revealing swimwear, saving lives and drinking popular beverages. They have a soon-to-be-famous catch phrase, which they use in the face of any adversity: "You can't stop progress."

The attractive brothers and sisters are in their late teens and early 20's. Mom is played by a movie hottie still in her 30's whose film career has stalled. Dad's reserve unit was called to Iraq. He can come home during sweeps week.

But after your premiere the Nielsen ratings bring distressing news: old people are watching your show. Maybe they like the family's pet cockatiel. Maybe one of the lifeguards reminds them of the young Alan Ladd. But they are wreaking havoc on your demographics, the lifeblood of a series. Your show is "skewing old."

Many assume that mature viewers, with their $2 trillion a year in spending power, would be welcomed by the networks. Well, they aren't. Advertisers want to lock in viewers' buying habits early in life, not struggle with them to change brands in their last few decades. The key demographic in the weekly Nielsen ratings report is 18-49. Anyone outside that range is undesirable. People over 49 do not buy interesting products. They detract from the hip environment advertisers seek. The shows they watch tend not to become "water cooler" shows. They are not, as one media buyer puts it, "an opportunity audience."

The majestic glacier that is network television is very gradually melting. Many young viewers, particularly males in their 20's, have been stolen away by such lures as the Internet, iPods, the Xbox and opera. This makes the young people who do watch all the more valuable to advertisers. They have far greater disposable income than older people, and they actually dispose of it. Advertisers gladly pay steep premiums for those young eyes. But it is more difficult to single them out when older viewers clutter the demographics.

The fact is, mature viewers are threatening the well-being of network television. I have a bold but common-sense suggestion: old people should not be allowed to watch TV.

I anticipate the predictable charges of "discriminatory," "unfair," "idiotic." Well, millions of elderly people live in age-restricted retirement communities, and you don't hear young people whining about that. Right-thinking older Americans will see this as a chance to do something for their country. Nurturing a nation's consumer base is as vital as protecting its streams and forests. It's time for people over 49 to "take one for the team." Besides, it's really not such a terrible sacrifice; they have Sudoku now.

Once the necessary "49 and Out" federal legislation is enacted, we'll need a system in place to block older viewers' network access. Fingerprinting, iris scans, re-purposed V-chips, psychoacoustic masking? Perhaps it would be possible to borrow some of the amazing technology being developed in the Transportation Security Administration's laboratories; they aren't using it at the airports.

Boomers will feel they should be exempt from this law. They're "younger" than previous old people. They're in tune with contemporary culture. If you're a boomer and thinking along those lines, take this simple test:

"They combed out Ann Miller's hair and found the Lindbergh baby."

If you laughed at that, if you understood the references, you have no business in front of a television set.

This ban applies only to the Big Four broadcast networks. Older viewers would still be free to tune into the many cable channels. At programs like "The O'Reilly Factor," an onslaught of people still in their 50's will be greeted with flowers.

A warning to certain lobbyists for the elderly, who may resort to selfish interpretations of the Constitution to thwart this needed legislation: beware the backlash. Nielsen Media Research, the keeper of the ratings, is owned by VNU, an increasingly powerful media conglomerate headquartered in the Netherlands. The Netherlands, where laws governing euthanasia are extremely lenient. "You can't stop progress." I'm just saying.

———

Charlie Hauck is a television writer and producer. He wrote this piece for the September 16, 2006, edition of *The New York Times* <www.nytimes.com>.

Rosie the Riveter

Why do right-wing pundits hate Rosie O'Donnell so much? Because she was the lone ardently progressive voice in corporate news programming.
BY JENNIFER L. POZNER (2007)

"Boy, I'm going to miss attacking her," quipped MSNBC's Tucker Carlson after Rosie O'Donnell announced that she will leave The View in June over a contract dispute with ABC.

Carlson isn't the only journalist who will miss the woman who served as conservative cable news hosts' favorite punching bag for the past year. "I could always count on Rosie O'Donnell saying something completely out of her mind insane every day," Glenn Beck, CNN's resident anti-Rosie ranter, mused, "And for a guy who does three hours of radio every day, do you know how much money I've made off of that?"

Indeed, Beck and his bombastic broadcast buddies have spent the last year bashing the mouthy talk show host all the way to the bank. During her eight-month tenure on The View, a Nexis search shows O'Donnell was berated 186 times by Bill O'Reilly, 91 times by Sean Hannity on Fox News, 41 times by the now-wistful Carlson, and 71 times by MSNBC's Joe Scarborough—who once called her a "fat, ugly, bully, pimp, loser, ignorant, terrible person, animal. Did I say fat?" If that's not bad enough, a whopping 2,911 local, national network and cable news stories have quoted Donald Trump trash-talking O'Donnell, calling her "disgusting," "crude," "arrogant," "pushy," "self-destructive," "a degenerate," "a stone-cold loser" and so hideous that her wife must be grossed out "having to kiss that every night."

Considering this collective vendetta, it's no surprise that O'Donnell turned down a reported $30 million rather than commit to three more years of this treatment—nor that the news of her departure was greeted with a rousing chorus of "Ding dong, the witch is dead." But while the rumor mill is buzzing about why she's moving on, the more compelling question is why she aroused such agita in the zeitgeist from the moment she began offering her uncompromising views.

It's tempting to write off the media's ridiculously vehement reaction to O'Donnell as solely the result of good old-fashioned sexism on the part of arrogant boys who aren't accustomed to sharing their celluloid sandbox with a girl—especially a non-girlie girl who cares more about what comes out of her mouth than what color lip-gloss adorns it. That bias has absolutely been in play—but there's more beneath the rage of her detractors than simple macho hazing.

The anti-Rosie backlash is indicative of nothing so much as the stiflingly limited range of debate allowed within the corporate media, whose gatekeepers want to erase true leftist dissent in America. Over the past year, O'Donnell has brought a consistently progressive, feminist voice to ABC's kaffeeklatsch and, in doing so, allowed daily television viewers entree into discussions wholly missing from the mainstream media lineup. She burst onto the public stage like a lefty tornado, loud and insistent, using her daytime post like a bullhorn at a peace march. (Who else on network television would have allowed actress Olympia Dukakis to declare that "The world can't wait to drive out the Bush regime" during an interview about her latest romantic comedy?)

O'Donnell has regularly denounced the Iraq war, blasted government-sanctioned torture, and spoken out adamantly against the president not only for the war but for what she considers his racist failure during Hurricane Katrina, his corrupt ties to corporate string-pullers, and his stoking of anti-Americanism abroad. And she says this at a time when opponents of the Bush administration are still being branded "un-American." Indeed, on Scarborough Country last month, guest Danny Bonaduce actually suggested that, "If anybody had a rope thick enough, I think that Rosie should be strung up for treason."

But unlike MSNBC's Keith Olbermann, whose ballyhooed liberal ire is mostly targeted at Bush's war, O'Donnell has also been an outspoken advocate for women's reproductive freedom, gay rights, gun control, mental health care, and a variety of other issues rarely discussed on TV from a feminist perspective. Besides, have you ever heard a prominent media figure declare, "I'm fat and I'm gay" in the same blithe manner as she trades parenting tips or ponders who should be booted off American Idol?

O'Donnell was an instantly controversial figure because she dared to upset the traditional TV balance of fiery conservatives debating centrists and, occasionally, tepid liberals (think The McLaughlin Group, or actually, the pre-Rosie View). In this climate, the talking heads treated O'Donnell's daily ruminations as if she was speaking in some sort of Martian code, rather than recognizing her simply as a passionate progressive woman who advocates her beliefs with the same vociferous zeal as do right-leaning O'Reilly, Scarborough, Hannity, Beck, Carlson, Rush Limbaugh, Ann Coulter and many other network news show hosts and pundits every single day.

Despite their dominance over the journalistic landscape, the overwhelmingly male punditocracy were so threatened by intellectual competition that they began gunning for O'Donnell's job shortly after her View debut. Back in September—her second week on the air—two Scarborough Country episodes encouraged ABC to censor or even fire her for saying that radical Christianity is as dangerous as radical Islam. Guests like GOP strategist Jack Burkman called O'Donnell's comment "one of the most mindless and terrible things ever said on American television! I think this is so serious, I'm shocked that she's still on the air." MSNBC's faux-liberal media analyst, Steve Adubato, insisted that O'Donnell "cannot be allowed to get away with saying that . . . she has to be held accountable," while Scarborough echoed: "if she does not back off of her statement, she needs to be forced from The View. That is not free speech. That is lunacy. And it is dangerous and it spreads hatred."

Their overwrought reaction lays bare the hollow yet persistent myth that the media are liberal. Put one actual feminist on TV—even on a women's chat show—and all the blustering boob tube boys line up to run off the radical interloper. If O'Donnell had a modicum of political company anywhere in mainstream corporate news programming, the reception to her would never have been so extreme.

Nor would such double standards have abounded. I was a recent guest on Fox's Hannity & Colmes to discuss O'Donnell's right to talk about gun control in the wake of the Virginia Tech shootings. The segment opened with Sean Hannity saying that O'Donnell's "immediate rush to politicize something for an agenda is so offensive to me." What viewers couldn't have known was that I initially declined the appearance, offering to connect producers with gun control experts who could offer insights into reducing violent crime in America, but all they wanted to discuss was Rosie. Who, would you say, was pushing their agenda?

The hypocrisy here is laughable. The name of O'Donnell's show explicitly delineates her views as subjective. She's an entertainer, albeit a politically-minded one, with a very different mandate than the responsibilities of journalists to present the news-viewing public with factual information and well-researched opinion. Yet the same news wonks who have ranted about the "hateful," "irresponsible" and "inaccurate" opinions O'Donnell expressed on The View have been guilty of far worse under the guise of informed journalism. Bill O'Reilly, of all people, complained that she "does not feel the responsibility to back up her statements with facts, and she feels personal attacks on people are fine"— this from a guy who misled his viewers about non-existent weapons of mass destruction in Iraq, called Katrina victims "drug-addicted . . . thugs," and blamed an 18-year-old girl who was raped and murdered for being "moronic" and inciting her killer by wearing a miniskirt. Joe Scarborough lambasted O'Donnell for being mean-spirited and misrepresentative, yet he devoted an entire segment to the housekeeping skills of Sen. Hillary Clinton and once used his show to allow Arnold Schwarzenegger's gubernatorial campaign to smear a woman who accused him of sexual assault, falsely claiming she had a record for prostitution and narcotics. And where does Glenn Beck—who has called Hillary Clinton a "bitch," Katrina survivors "scumbags," and suggested that "good Muslims" should "shoot the bad Muslims in the head"—get off critiquing anyone's on-air behavior?

Yet Rosie O'Donnell has uttered "the most mindless and terrible things ever said on American television."

I didn't always agree with O'Donnell (all feminists don't all think alike, after all). I was certainly disappointed by her over-the-top 9/11 conspiracy theories, and her indefensible, racist mocking ("ching chong, ching chong") of Asian accents. I was also surprised that she defended Don Imus in the wake his "nappy-headed hos" controversy. Sure, comedians tend to stick together, but Imus hasn't been spewing "humorous" hate speech in some dank basement with a two-drink minimum—this was a guy who admitted hiring a producer to do "nigger jokes" on a show featuring political and journalistic bigwigs.

But I greatly appreciated O'Donnell's fearlessness. I was often pleasantly surprised to find her far more well-informed than I expected a celebrity comic to be. Though she isn't a journalist or a scholar, she took her platform seriously and turned a fluffy morning show without much information, interest, or disagreement into a real forum for hard-hitting discussion about the pressing issues of the day . . . at least, as hard-hitting as one can expect in between segments about where to buy the latest product-placement Capri pants. That's why women loved watching her—because she spoke her mind, and because she treated her female viewers as if they had more than three brain cells to rub together at any given point.

This is all very confusing to the beltway boys. On the night she announced her departure, I appeared on Scarborough Country, the only woman among four men scratching their heads about why O'Donnell was so popular in the first place. How was she able to bring up "very, very heavy issues" on "a women's talk show, a gabfest," Scarborough asked. MSNBC's Steve Adubato, Newsweek's Richard Wolffe, and Los Angeles Times online columnist Tom O'Neil joined him in wondering why O'Donnell had been able to bring "a pretty tough brand of political dogma" about such serious topics to daytime television. They never did come up with an answer.

Scarborough wouldn't let me into that part of the conversation (why ask the woman about what women watch?), but I was dying to expose the elephant in the room: Daytime audiences are predominately female, while cable news commentators are predominately male. If certain media men don't understand O'Donnell's popularity, it's not just because they're out of touch with millions of liberal and progressive Americans—it's also because they thoroughly underestimate the intelligence of the female viewing public. Underneath their bewilderment is the ugly belief that women who watch daytime television are mostly stupid, concerned only with the latest fashions, celebrity gossip, and sex tips, while men are interested in the "hard news" of politics, economics, labor, science, and world events.

In fact, female daytime viewers are just as concerned about most of the same issues as nighttime (assumed to be male) viewers. More women than men report to pollsters their desire for peace and an end to the Iraq war—and issues such as gun control, abortion, health care and the environment resonate extremely strongly for women. So it was hardly a surprise that The View's ratings skyrocketed when O'Donnell elevated the discussion with real content. As I told Scarborough, we should seek to foster more debate, not less. O'Donnell's departure will leave a gaping hole, as discussions she initiated during the day often sparked nightly news stories about progressive topics otherwise marginalized on in corporate media. Without her, next year's TV news lineup promises to be extremely boring—at all times of the day.

Jennifer L. Pozner is founder and executive director of Women In Media & News, a women's media analysis, education and advocacy group, and manages WIMN's Voices, a women's media monitoring group blog. She lectures on women and the media at colleges and communities across the country, and is working on a book about reality TV as cultural backlash against women. She wrote this piece, posted on May 1, 2007, for the online edition of *The American Prospect* <www.prospect.org>.

Cut Buster Loose

BY GEORGE F. WILL (2005)

In 1967 Lyndon Johnson added yet another piece to the jigsaw puzzle of national perfection: The Corporation for Public Broadcasting was born. Public television was a dubious idea even when concocted as a filigree on the Great Society. Why should government subsidize the production and distribution of entertainment and, even worse, journalism? Even if there were—has there ever been?—a shortage of either in America, is it government's duty to address all cultural shortages?

Today, with iPod earphone cords dangling from millions of heads, and movies flooding into homes where they jostle for plasma screen time with video games, Americans are entertaining themselves into inanition. Furthermore, journalism and imitations of it have become social smog. Even in airport concourses you are bombarded by televised human volcanoes verbally assaulting each other about the "news," broadly—very broadly—defined to include Kobe Bryant's presence on Michael Jackson's witness list.

In 1967 public television did at least increase, for many, the basic television choices from three—CBS, NBC, ABC—to four. Not that achieving some supposedly essential minimum was, or is, the government's business. In today's 500-channel environment, public television is a preposterous relic.

Not too long ago the Public Broadcasting Service tried an amazingly obtuse and arrogant slogan: "If PBS doesn't do it, who will?" What was the antecedent of the pronoun "it"? Presumably "culture" or "seriousness" or "relevance." Or something. But in a television universe that includes the History Channel, Biography, A&E, Bravo, National Geographic, Disney, TNT, BBC America, Animal Planet, the Learning Channel, the Outdoor Channel, Noggin, Nickelodeon, and scads of other cultural and information channels, what is the antecedent?

Now PBS is airing some HBO films. There is a nifty use of tax dollars—showing HBO reruns. Which contribute how to "diversity"?

In 1967 public television's enthusiasts were ahead of the curve of cultural inanity, making frequent use of the d-word, which required decades more to become the great signifier of cultural correctness. The chairman of the Federal Communications Commission hailed public television's promise of "more diversity," and a Carnegie report foresaw increased "diversities." Thirty-eight years later, 500 channels mock public television as crucial to diversity.

The recent spat about Buster, PBS's cartoon rabbit, visiting two lesbian parents quickly became a second spat about the Education Department's threat to stop financing Buster. But a third spat should have been about why the Education Department (a fourth spat: Is that department necessary?) is paying for any of Buster's adventures. Is there a desperate shortage of television cartoons? Is Buster to other cartoons as Beethoven is to Bon Jovi?

Public television, its supporters say, is especially important for people who cannot afford cable or satellite television. But 62 percent of poor households have cable or satellite television, and 78 percent have a VCR or DVD player.

Public television is akin to the body politic's appendix: It is vestigial, purposeless and occasionally troublesome. Of the two arguments for it, one is impervious to refutation and the other refutes itself.

The impervious argument is: The small size of the audiences for most of public television's programming proves how necessary public television is. The big networks gather big audiences by catering to vulgar cultural tastes, leaving the refined minority an orphan, because any demand the private market satisfies must be tacky.

The self-refuting argument is: Big Bird. Never mind that the average age of PBS viewers is 58. "Sesame Street"—see how its merchandise sells, and Barney's, too—supposedly proves that public television can find mass audiences.

But the refined minority, as it sees itself, now has ample television choices for the rare moments when it is not rereading Proust. And successes such as "Sesame Street" could easily find private, taxpaying broadcast entities to sell them.

President Johnson, no slouch at the "progressive" rhetoric of platitudinous gush, said the prospect of public television should fill Americans with "the same awe and wonderment" that caused Samuel Morse, when he successfully tested his telegraph, to exclaim, "What hath God wrought?" But by 2002 PBS President Pat Mitchell was warning: "We are dangerously close in our overall prime-time numbers to falling below the relevance quotient."

Public television's survival, with no remaining rationale, should fill students of government with awe, wonderment and melancholy. Would it vanish without the 15 percent of its revenue it gets from government? Let's find out.

———

Syndicated columnist George Will wrote this essay for the March 3, 2005, edition of *The Washington Post* <www.washingtonpost.com>.

The Imus Fallout: Who Can Say What?

BY JAMES PONIEWOZIK (2007)

Say this for Don Imus: the man knows how to turn an economical phrase. When the radio shock jock described the Rutgers women's basketball team, on the April 4 Imus in the Morning, as "nappy-headed hos," he packed so many layers of offense into the statement that it was like a perfect little diamond of insult. There was a racial element, a gender element and even a class element (the joke implied that the Scarlet Knights were thuggish and ghetto compared with the Tennessee Lady Vols).

Imus was a famous, rich, old white man picking on a bunch of young, mostly black college women. So it seemed pretty cut-and-dried that his bosses at CBS Radio would suspend his show—half frat party, half political salon for the Beltway elite—for two weeks, and that MSNBC would cancel the TV simulcast. And that Imus would plan to meet with the students he offended. Case closed, justice served, lesson—possibly—learned. Move on.

But a reasonable person could ask, What was the big deal? And I don't mean the lots-of-black-rappers-say-"hos" argument, though we'll get to that. Rather, I mean, what celebrity isn't slurring some group nowadays?

I exaggerate slightly. But our culture has experienced an almost psychotic outburst of -isms in the past year. Michael Richards and "nigger." Isaiah Washington and "faggot." Senator George Allen and "macaca." Mel Gibson and "f__ing Jews."

But we also live in a culture in which racially and sexually edgy material is often—legitimately—considered brilliant comment, even art. Last year's most critically praised comedy, *Borat: Cultural Learnings of America for Make Benefit Glorious Nation of Kazakhstan*, won Sacha Baron Cohen a Golden Globe for playing a Kazakh journalist who calls Alan Keyes a "genuine chocolate face" and asks a gun-shop owner to suggest a good piece for killing a Jew. Quentin Tarantino has made a career borrowing tropes from blaxploitation movies. In the critics-favorite sitcom *The Sarah Silverman Program*, the star sleeps with God, who is African American and who she assumes is "God's black friend." And the current season of *South Park* opened with an episode about a Michael Richards-esque controversy erupting when a character blurts the word niggers on *Wheel of Fortune*. (He answers a puzzle—N-GGERS—for which the clue is "People who annoy you"; the correct answer is "naggers.")

This is not to say that *Borat* made Imus do it or to make excuses for Imus. Even in the midst of his apology tour last week, Imus did enough of that for himself, citing his charity work, his support of black Senate candidate Harold Ford Jr., even his booking the black singing group Blind Boys of Alabama on his show. (He didn't mention how, last fall, he groused about persuading the "money grubbing" "Jewish management" to okay the booking.)

But in the middle of his stunning medley of sneer, apology and rationalization, Imus asked a pretty good question: "This phrase that I use, it originated in the black community.

That didn't give me a right to use it, but that's where it originated. Who calls who that and why? We need to know that. I need to know that."

So let's ask.

Imus crossed a line, boorishly, creepily, paleolithically. But where is that line nowadays? In a way, the question is an outgrowth of something healthy in our society: the assumption that there is a diverse audience that is willing to talk about previously taboo social distinctions more openly, frankly and daringly than before. It used to be assumed that people were free to joke about their own kind (with some license for black comedians to talk about how white people dance). Crossing those lines was the province of the occasional "socially conscious artist," like Dick Gregory or Lenny Bruce, who was explicit about his goals: in Bruce's words, to repeat "'niggerniggernigger' until the word [didn't] mean anything anymore."

Now, however, we live in a mash-up world, where people—especially young people—feel free to borrow one another's cultural signifiers. In a now classic episode of *Chappelle's Show*, comic Dave Chappelle plays a blind, black white supremacist who inadvertently calls a carload of rap-listening white boys "niggers." The kids' reaction: "Did he just call us niggers? Awesome!" The country is, at least, more pop-culturally integrated—one nation under Jessica Alba, J. Lo and Harold & Kumar—and with that comes greater comfort in talking about differences.

But that's a harder attitude for older people—who grew up with more cultural and actual segregation—to accept or to mimic. Part of the problem with Imus' joke was that it was so tone-deaf. "That's some rough girls from Rutgers," he said. "Man, they got tattoos . . . That's some nappy-headed hos there." The joke played badly in every community, raising memories of beauty bias (against darker skin and kinkier hair) that dates back to slavery. Tracy Riley, 37, of Des Moines, Iowa, who is of mixed race, said the incident was among her four kids' first exposures to overt racism. "Our kids don't see color the way we do," she said. "They don't see it as much. 'You're my friend or not,' but it's not about race.'"

The line was as damning as anything for what it suggested about Imus' thought process: a 66-year-old white male country-music fan rummaging in his subconscious for something to suggest that some young black women looked scary, and coming up with a reference to African-American hair and a random piece of rap slang. (Maybe because older, male media honchos are more conscious of—and thus fixated on—race than gender, much of the coverage of Imus ignored the sexual part of the slur on a show with a locker-room vibe and a mostly male guest list. If Imus had said "niggas" rather than "hos," would his bosses have waited as long to act?)

So who gets to say "ho," in an age when *Pimp My Ride* is an innocent car show and "It's Hard Out Here for a Pimp" is an Oscar-winning song? As even Essence Carlson, one of the Rutgers students Imus insulted, acknowledged at a press conference, black rap artists labeled young black women as "hos" long before Imus did. And while straight people may not be able to say "faggot," *Queer Eye for the Straight Guy* and *Will & Grace* helped mainstream the nonhostile gay joke for straight people. But all this reappropriation and blurring—distinguishing a good-natured "That's so gay!" from a homophobic one—has created a situation in which, when Richards went off on his Laugh Factory rant, it was possible to wonder if he was playing a character.

The license to borrow terms other people have taken back can worry even edgy comics. A few months ago, I interviewed Silverman, who argued that her material was not racist but about racism (and I agree). But she added something that surprised me, coming from her: "I'm not saying 'I can say nigger because I'm liberal.' There is a certain aspect of that that I'm starting to get grossed out by. 'Oh, we're not racist. We can say it.'"

Comedians work through these danger zones in the presence of other comics. In a comedians' get-together or a TV writers' room, nothing is off-limits: without airing the joke that goes too far, you can never get to the joke that flies in front of an audience. Trouble might come if material meant for that smaller audience went public, as in 1993, when Ted Danson got in trouble after word got out of a Friars Club routine he did in blackface, though his jokes were defended—and reportedly written by—his then girlfriend Whoopi Goldberg.

Today, because of cable and YouTube, because of a media culture that rewards the fastest, least censoring mouth, we are all in the writers' room. (Friars Club roasts are now televised on Comedy Central.) Punditry and gonzo comedy have become less and less distinguishable. (And I'm not talking here about *The Daily Show*, whose host Jon Stewart is, ironically, one of the most conservative defenders of the idea of sober, evenhanded news—see his 2004 tirade against Tucker Carlson.) Got something on your mind? Say it! Don't think about it! If you don't, the next guy in the greenroom will! C'mon, it'll kill!

Right-wing pundit Ann Coulter is probably the best example of this, playing a constant game of "Can you top this?" with herself, as in March, when she told the Conservative Political Action Conference that she would have a comment on Senator John Edwards, "but it turns out that you have to go into rehab if you use the word faggot." Coulter is only the most egregious example—from Bill O'Reilly on Fox to Glenn Beck on CNN, offense is the coin of the cable realm.

The flip side of the instant-attention era is the gotcha era. We may be more inured to shock than ever, but when someone manages to find and cross a line, we're better able to generate, spread and sustain offense. You get eaten by the same tiger that you train. Imus got special love from the media over the years because his show was such a media hangout. But when the controversy erupted, it snowballed in part because the media love to cover the media.

Every public figure—athlete, pundit, actor—now has two audiences: the one he or she is addressing and the one that will eventually read the blogs or see the viral video. A few have adapted, like Stephen Colbert, whose routine at last year's White House Correspondents' Association dinner was decried by attendees as rude and shrill—but made him a hero to his YouTube audience. Imus, a 30-plus-year veteran of radio shock, seemed to underestimate the power of the modern umbrage-amplification machine. The day after his remarks, Imus said dismissively on air that people needed to relax about "some idiot comment meant to be amusing." Shockingly, they did not, and by the next day, Imus had tapped an inner wellspring of deepest regret.

As in so many scandals, the first response may have been the most authentic—at least we're inclined to take it that way because the contrition cycle has become so familiar. You blurt. You deny. You apologize. You visit the rehab center or speak with the Official Minority Spokesperson of your choice and go on with your life. Although—or maybe because—it's so easy to get caught today, it's also easier to get forgiven. In 1988 Jimmy (the Greek) Snyder was fired by CBS for saying black athletes were "bred" to be better than whites. In 1996 CBS golf analyst Ben Wright was suspended indefinitely after he was quoted as saying that lesbians had hurt the sport.

To his credit, Imus never played the "I'm sick" card. Perhaps he felt confident because he had been legitimized by his high-profile guests. Imus could have made a remark just as bad years ago and suffered few if any consequences. Scratch that: Imus did make remarks as bad or worse for years. Speaking about Gwen Ifill, the African-American PBS anchor who was then White House correspondent for the *New York Times*, he said, "Isn't the *Times* wonderful? It lets the cleaning lady cover the White House." He called a *Washington Post* writer a "boner-nosed, beanie-wearing Jewboy" and Arabs "towelheads."

Yet politicians and journalists (including TIME writers) still went on his show to plug their candidacies and books because Imus knew how to sell. "If Don Imus likes a book," says Katie Wainwright, executive director of publicity at publisher Hyperion, "not only does he have the author on, he will talk about it before, during and after, often for weeks afterwards." The price: implicitly telling America that the mostly white male Beltway elite is cool with looking the other way at racism. They compartmentalized the lengthy interviews he did with them from the "bad" parts of the show, though the boundary was always a little porous. And evidently many still do. "Solidarity forever," pledged *Boston Globe* columnist Tom Oliphant in a phone interview with Imus on April 9. Senator John McCain and Rudolph Giuliani said they would return to the show. "I called him a little while ago to talk to him about it personally," Giuliani told the *New York Times*. "And I believe that he understands that he made a very big mistake." (Senator Barack Obama, who appeared on the show once, has said he will not go back; other politicians have hedged.)

In fact, while there might be more media and blogger scrutiny of Imus' future guests, his suspension may have inoculated them—if his radio show survives. The show draws 2 million daily listeners, and it's a more valuable property on radio than it was on TV. (It brings in about $15 million annually for CBS Radio compared with several million for MSNBC.) But the show has already lost advertisers, including American Express, Staples and Procter & Gamble. [CBS Radio and MSNBC canceled the show after this article went to press.]

Imus argued repeatedly that his critics should consider the "context" of his larger life, including the formidable work for sick children he does through his Imus Ranch charity. But it's not Imus Ranch he broadcasts from 20 hours a week. You can't totally separate the lives of celebrities from their work—it didn't excuse Gibson that he attacked the Jews in his free time—but finally what determines who can make what jokes is the context of their work: the tone of their acts, the personas they present, the vehicles they create for their work.

That context is not as kind to Imus. He comes out of the shock jock tradition, but all shock jocks are not created equal. If Opie & Anthony or Mancow had made the "nappy-headed" comment, it wouldn't have been a blip because future Presidents do not do cable-news interviews with Opie & Anthony and Mancow.

Then there's personality, or at least persona. Compared with Imus, for instance, his rival Howard Stern may be offensive, but he's also self-deprecating, making fun of his own satyrism, looks and even manly endowment. Imus doesn't take it nearly as well as he dishes it out. His shtick is all cowboy-hatted swagger, and his insults set him up as superior to his targets and the alpha dog to his supplicant guests.

Imus uses jokes to establish his power, in other words. He's hardly the only humorist to do that. But making jokes about difference—race, gender, sexual orientation, the whole list—is ultimately about power. You need to purchase the right to do it through some form of vulnerability, especially if you happen to be a rich, famous white man. But the I-Man—his radio persona, anyway—is not about vulnerability. (The nickname, for Pete's sake: I, Man!) That's creepy enough when he's having a big-name columnist kiss his ring; when he hurled his tinfoil thunderbolts at a team of college kids, it was too much. "Some people have said, 'Well, he says this all the time,'" Rutgers' team captain Carson told TIME. "But does that justify the remarks he's made about anyone?"

Of course, assessing Imus' show is a subjective judgment, and setting these boundaries is as much an aesthetic call as a moral one. It's arbitrary, nebulous and, yes, unfair. Who doesn't have a list of artists or leaders whose sins they rationalize: Elvis Costello for calling Ray Charles a "blind, ignorant nigger," Eminem for peppering his lyrics with "faggot," Jesse Jackson for "Hymietown," D.W. Griffith for lionizing the Klan or T.S. Eliot for maligning Jews?

You might say that there's no excuse and that I'm as big a hypocrite as Imus' defenders for suggesting that there is one. Which may be true. That's finally why "Where's the line?" is a misleading question. There are as many lines as there are people. We draw and redraw them by constantly arguing them. This is how we avoid throwing out the brilliance of a Sacha Baron Cohen—who offends us to point out absurdities in our society, not just to make "idiot comments meant to be amusing"—with a shock jock's dirty bathwater. It's a draining, polarizing but necessary process.

Which may be why it was such a catharsis to see the Rutgers players respond to Imus at their press conference in their own words. "I'm a woman, and I'm someone's child," said Kia Vaughn. "I achieve a lot. And unless they've given this name, a 'ho,' a new definition, then that is not what I am." She stood with her teammates, a row of unbowed, confident women. For a few minutes, anyway, they drew a line we could all agree on and formed a line we could all get behind.

—With reporting by Jeremy Caplan, Lina Lofaro and
Andrea Sachs/New York and Betsy Rubiner/Des Moines.

———

James Poniewozik wrote this piece for the April 12, 2007, issue of *Time* magazine <www.time.com>.

Our Prejudices, Ourselves

BY HARVEY FIERSTEIN (2007)

America is watching Don Imus's self-immolation in a state of shock and awe. And I'm watching America with wry amusement.

Since I'm a second-class citizen—a gay man—my seats for the ballgame of American discourse are way back in the bleachers. I don't have to wait long for a shock jock or stand-up comedian to slip up with hateful epithets aimed at me and mine. Hate speak against homosexuals is as commonplace as spam. It's daily traffic for those who profess themselves to be regular Joes, men of God, public servants who live off my tax dollars, as well as any number of celebrities.

In fact, I get a good chuckle whenever someone refers to "the media" as an agent of "the gay agenda." There are entire channels, like Spike TV, that couldn't fill an hour of programming if required to remove their sexist and homophobic content. We've got a president and a large part of Congress willing to change the Constitution so they can deprive of us our rights because they feel we are not "normal."

So I'm used to catching foul balls up here in the cheap seats. What I am really enjoying is watching the rest of you act as if you had no idea that prejudice was alive and well in your hearts and minds.

For the past two decades political correctness has been derided as a surrender to thin-skinned, humorless, uptight oversensitive sissies. Well, you anti-politically correct people have won the battle, and we're all now feasting on the spoils of your victory. During the last few months alone we've had a few comedians spout racism, a basketball coach put forth anti-Semitism and several high-profile spoutings of anti-gay epithets.

What surprises me, I guess, is how choosy the anti-P.C. crowd is about which hate speech it will not tolerate. Sure, there were voices of protest when the TV actor Isaiah Washington called a gay colleague a "faggot." But corporate America didn't pull its advertising from "Grey's Anatomy," as it did with Mr. Imus, did it? And when Ann Coulter likewise tagged a presidential candidate last month, she paid no real price.

In fact, when Bill Maher discussed Ms. Coulter's remarks on his HBO show, he repeated the slur no fewer than four times himself; each mention, I must note, solicited a laugh from his audience. No one called for any sort of apology from him. (Well, actually, I did, so the following week he only used it once.)

Face it, if a Pentagon general, his salary paid with my tax dollars, can label homosexual acts as "immoral" without a call for his dismissal, who are the moral high and mighty kidding?

Our nation, historically bursting with generosity toward strangers, remains remarkably unkind toward its own. Just under our gleaming patina of inclusiveness, we harbor corroding guts. America, I tell you that it doesn't matter how many times you brush your teeth. If your insides are rotting your breath will stink. So, how do you people choose which hate to embrace, which to forgive with a wink and a week in rehab, and which to protest? Where's my copy of that rule book?

Let me cite a non-volatile example of how prejudice can cohabit unchecked with good intentions. I am a huge fan of David Letterman's. I watch the opening of his show a couple of times a week and have done so for decades. Without fail, in his opening monologue or skit Mr. Letterman makes a joke about someone being fat. I kid you not. Will that destroy our nation? Should he be fired or lose his sponsors? Obviously not.

But I think that there is something deeper going on at the Letterman studio than coincidence. And, as I've said, I cite this example simply to illustrate that all kinds of prejudice exist in the human heart. Some are harmless. Some not so harmless. But we need to understand who we are if we wish to change. (In the interest of full disclosure, I should confess to not only being a gay American, but also a fat one. Yes, I'm a double winner.)

I urge you to look around, or better yet, listen around and become aware of the prejudice in everyday life. We are so surrounded by expressions of intolerance that I am in shock and awe that anyone noticed all these recent high-profile instances. Still, I'm gladdened because our no longer being deaf to them may signal their eventual eradication.

The real point is that you cannot harbor malice toward others and then cry foul when someone displays intolerance against you. Prejudice tolerated is intolerance encouraged. Rise up in righteousness when you witness the words and deeds of hate, but only if you are willing to rise up against them all, including your own. Otherwise suffer the slings and arrows of disrespect silently.

––––––

Harvey Fierstein is an actor and playwright. He wrote this piece for the April 13, 2007, edition of *The New York Times* <www.nytimes.com>.

Which Came First: The Lyrics or Libidos?

BY MARK MORFORD (2006)

Let's just say it outright: AC/DC is God's most beautiful and significant gift to humankind.

Hey, it's a fact. I personally spent upward of 3.6 billion hours (give or take) as a happy, rebellious, well-fed, surly, middle-class teen pounding my delicate eardrums and grinding my nerves to this glorious Aussie rock band's dizzy, brain-churning music, shaking my pale fist to its monster-arena blues and soaking my burgeoning id in the profound lyrics of songs like "Dirty Deeds Done Dirt Cheap" and "What Do You Do for Money Honey." To their giant slab of divine truth, I hereby testify.

Around the time of my initial AC/DC affection, I also had sex. And like many of the male teen persuasion, I enjoyed it quite a lot. So much so that—also like many of the male teen persuasion—I became passionately enamored of and reverential about the female gender, not to mention convinced that the overwhelming, mind-altering, time-space-bending force of my newfound enjoyment of this wondrous activity might somehow cause me to levitate and spontaneously combust and go absolutely insane. Simultaneously.

This did not happen. At least, not yet. But the feeling, I have to say, remains to this day.

But now I have a new understanding. Now I can attribute at least part of this mad hot desire, this otherworldly adoration, to my beloved AC/DC. In fact, I might even go so far as to claim that the Aussie rock gods added serious fuel to my lubricious fire, transformed my bones and shaped the arc of my life. Without them, I might never have evolved into the calm and Hitachi-advocating lightworker I am today. I am considering sending them a gift basket.

See, there is this new study, yet another one that says teens who listen to lots of sexually explicit music full of "degrading" lyrics are much more likely to have sex sooner than those who listen to, say, church hymns and banjo music and Carrie Underwood preening her way through "Jesus Take the Wheel." I know, it's shocking.

The study, from the nonprofit Rand think tank in Philly, surveyed about 1,200 kids who listen to hours upon hours of hip-hop, R&B and rock on their iPods. Apparently, among "heavy listeners" of raunchy and "degrading" songs, 51 percent started having sex within a couple years, versus only 29 percent who listened to, say, Coldplay. Or Beyoncé. George Benson. Whatever.

But the study might as well be referring to AC/DC. Or Elvis. Or the Starland Vocal Band belting out "Afternoon Delight." Hey, it's all devil music, right? It all objectifies women as sex objects and reduces men to dumb superstuds, and it all makes you want to have sex and do drugs and light stuff on fire and eat your own flesh and laugh maniacally. You know, same as it ever was.

Now, you may jump up and down and call this study silly, revealing nothing and only reminding you of the old days when networks refused to show Elvis from the waist down lest an entire nation quiver and explode and start grinding their pelvises against the TV. You may say it tries—and fails—to make a tenuous causal connection, isolating one influence on teens amid an ocean of frenzied influences, from music to TV to peer pressure to sexually terrified parents to MySpace to Internet porn to Red Bull to thong underwear. And you would be quite correct.

Let's flip it around: What would you have thought if it had concluded that listening to thousands of hours of raunchy lyrics had zero effect on teen attitudes and behaviors? "Those sure are some inept teens," you might've said, recalling how good it was to get it on in the backseat of that Trans Am to the dulcet sounds of, say, Van Halen's "Ice Cream Man." "Bring me my 'Sticky Fingers' LP and a hookah and a bottle of Goldschlager, stat!" you might've cried, revealing a bit too much information.

But aren't you also thinking, Wait, don't they have it exactly backward? Doesn't the fact that you're a sexually desperate, hormone-blasted teen make you that much more likely to crave music that reflects your surging desires?

Are you not, after all, just another misinformed and misled American teenager, weaned on a sickly diet of insidious abstinence programs, lousy sex ed and horribly mixed messages about sex and love and your body? But it does not matter, because all of that is easily crushed by a pile of hormones so raging you think you will jump out of your skin at any moment.

Hence, are you not merely seeking music to match this feeling? Is it not a case of which came first, the eager chicken or the throbbing, groovy egg? Of course it is.

From what I can recall, the music I loved (and still love) was as much a balm and mirror and therapist for my pimpled and tormented young soul as it was any sort of motivation or shaper of sexual attitude. And truly, the music was a minor accomplice when compared with, say, those early Penthouse Forum letters. Or the existence of tight jeans. Or Denet Whitaker's skin. Note to researchers: Isolate one aspect at your peril. If you divorce one random influence from the context of a teen's manic life, the significance of your point simply collapses.

But there is another tragedy hidden in this rather silly study, slipping away unnoticed. The report implies that the lyrics to many hip-hop and rock songs have become grossly raunchy, straight pornography, stripped entirely of even the playful and juvenile double-entendres of AC/DC, Zeppelin and Run-DMC. And it's true.

There is no more "Squeeze my lemon till the juice runs down my leg." There is no more "She was holding a pair, but I had to try/ Her deuce was wild, but my ace was high." There is no "The men don't know, but the little girls understand." There is only, well, the unprintable straight-porn versions thereof.

It is a case of kids being regularly assaulted by, well, really lousy lyrics. It is a heart-breaking case of songwriters with zero imagination, with a lack of appreciation for the craft of penning a cunning, puerile lyric that will attach itself like a sloppy kiss to the budding libidos of an entire generation.

Forget the problem of myopic adults who generate silly, brow-furrowed studies on teen behavior. Where is the next generation of lyrical pun masters? Whither double entendres and sticky innuendo with more than one layer? Who, pray who, will teach our children about, say, "giving the dog a bone"? It's an unsung tragedy is what it is.

———

Mark Morford wrote this piece for the August 11, 2006, edition of the *San Francisco Chronicle* <www.sfconfonicle.com>.

The Rap against Rockism

BY KELEFA SANNEH (2004)

Bad news travels fast, and an embarrassing video travels even faster. By last Sunday morning, one of the Internet's most popular downloads was the hours-old 60-second .wmv file of Ashlee Simpson on *Saturday Night Live*. As she and her band stood onstage, her own prerecorded vocals—from the wrong song—came blaring through the speakers, and it was too late to start mouthing the words. So she performed a now-infamous little jig, then skulked offstage, while the band (were a few members smirking?) played on. One of 2004's most popular new stars had been exposed as. . . .

As what, exactly? The online verdict came fast and harsh, the way online verdicts usually do. A typical post on her Web site bore the headline, "Ashlee you are a no talent fraud!" After that night, everyone knew that Jessica Simpson's telegenic sister was no rock 'n' roll hero—she wasn't even a rock 'n' roll also-ran. She was merely a lip-synching pop star.

Music critics have a word for this kind of verdict, this knee-jerk backlash against producer-powered idols who didn't spend years touring dive bars. Not a very elegant word, but a useful one. The word is rockism, and among the small but extraordinarily pesky group of people who obsess over this stuff, rockism is a word meant to start fights. The rockism debate began in earnest in the early 1980's, but over the past few years it has heated up, and today, in certain impassioned circles, there is simply nothing worse than a rockist.

A rockist isn't just someone who loves rock 'n' roll, who goes on and on about Bruce Springsteen, who champions ragged-voiced singer-songwriters no one has ever heard of. A rockist is someone who reduces rock 'n' roll to a caricature, then uses that caricature as a weapon. Rockism means idolizing the authentic old legend (or underground hero) while mocking the latest pop star; lionizing punk while barely tolerating disco; loving the live show and hating the music video; extolling the growling performer while hating the lip-syncher.

Over the past decades, these tendencies have congealed into an ugly sort of common sense. Rock bands record classic albums, while pop stars create "guilty pleasure" singles. It's supposed to be self-evident: U2's entire oeuvre deserves respectful consideration, while a spookily seductive song by an R&B singer named Tweet can only be, in the smug words of a recent VH1 special, "awesomely bad."

Like rock 'n' roll itself, rockism is full of contradictions: it could mean loving the Strokes (a scruffy guitar band!) or hating them (image-conscious poseurs!) or ignoring them entirely (since everyone knows that music isn't as good as it used to be). But it almost certainly means disdaining not just Ms. Simpson but also Christina Aguilera and Usher and most of the rest of them, grousing about a pop landscape dominated by big-budget spectacles and high-concept photo shoots, reminiscing about a time when the charts were packed with people who had something to say, and meant it, even if that time never actually existed. If this sounds like you, then take a long look in the mirror: you might be a rockist.

Countless critics assail pop stars for not being rock 'n' roll enough, without stopping to wonder why that should be everybody's goal. Or they reward them disproportionately for making rock 'n' roll gestures. Writing in *The Chicago Sun-Times* this summer, Jim DeRogatis grudgingly praised Ms. Lavigne as "a teen-pop phenom that discerning adult rock fans can actually admire without feeling (too) guilty," partly because Ms. Lavigne "plays a passable rhythm guitar" and "has a hand in writing" her songs.

Rockism isn't unrelated to older, more familiar prejudices—that's part of why it's so powerful, and so worth arguing about. The pop star, the disco diva, the lip-syncher, the "awesomely bad" hit maker: could it really be a coincidence that rockist complaints often pit straight white men against the rest of the world? Like the anti-disco backlash of 25 years ago, the current rockist consensus seems to reflect not just an idea of how music should be made but also an idea about who should be making it.

If you're interested in—O.K., mildly obsessed with—rockism, you can find traces of it just about everywhere. Notice how those tributes to "Women Who Rock" sneakily transform "rock" from a genre to a verb to a catch-all term of praise. Ever wonder why OutKast and the Roots and Mos Def and the Beastie Boys get taken so much more seriously than other rappers? Maybe because rockist critics love it when hip-hop acts impersonate rock 'n' roll bands. (A recent *Rolling Stone* review praised the Beastie Boys for scruffily resisting "the gold-plated phooey currently passing for gangsta.")

From punk-rock rags to handsomely illustrated journals, rockism permeates the way we think about music. This summer, the literary zine *The Believer* published a music issue devoted to almost nothing but indie-rock. Two weeks ago, in *The New York Times Book Review*, Sarah Vowell approvingly recalled Nirvana's rise: "a group with loud guitars and louder drums knocking the whimpering Mariah Carey off the top of the charts." Why did the changing of the guard sound so much like a sexual assault? And when did we all agree that Nirvana's neo-punk was more respectable than Ms. Carey's neo-disco?

Rockism is imperial: it claims the entire musical world as its own. Rock 'n' roll is the unmarked section in the record store, a vague pop-music category that swallows all the others. If you write about music, you're presumed to be a rock critic. There's a place in the Rock and Roll Hall of Fame for doo-wop groups and folk singers and disco queens and even rappers—just so long as they, y'know, rock.

Rockism just won't go away. The rockism debate began when British bands questioned whether the search for raw, guitar-driven authenticity wasn't part of rock 'n' roll's problem, instead of its solution; some new-wave bands emphasized synthesizers and drum machines and makeup and hairspray, instead. "Rockist" became for them a term of abuse, and the anti-rockists embraced the inclusive possibilities of a once-derided term: pop. Americans found other terms, but "rockist" seems the best way to describe the ugly anti-disco backlash of the late 1970's, which culminated in a full-blown anti-disco rally and the burning of thousands of disco records at Comiskey Park in Chicago in 1979: the Boston Tea Party of rockism.

That was a quarter of a century and many genres ago. By the 1990's, the American musical landscape was no longer a battleground between Nirvana and Mariah (if indeed it ever was); it was a fractured, hyper-vivid fantasy of teen-pop stars and R&B pillow-talkers and arena-filling country singers and, above all, rappers. Rock 'n' roll was just one more genre alongside the rest.

Yet many critics failed to notice. Rock 'n' roll doesn't rule the world anymore, but lots of writers still act as if it does. The rules, even today, are: concentrate on making albums, not singles; portray yourself as a rebellious individualist, not an industry pro; give listeners the uncomfortable truth, instead of pandering to their tastes. Overnight celebrities, one-hit-wonders and lip-synchers, step aside.

And just as the anti-disco partisans of a quarter-century ago railed against a bewildering new pop order (partly because disco was so closely associated with black culture and gay culture), current critics rail against a world hopelessly corrupted by hip-hop excess.

Since before Sean Combs became Puff Daddy, we've been hearing that mainstream hip-hop was too flashy, too crass, too violent, too ridiculous, unlike those hard-working rock 'n' roll stars we used to have. (This, of course, is one of the most pernicious things about rockism: it finds a way to make rock 'n' roll seem boring.)

Much of the most energetic resistance to rockism can be found online, in blogs and on critic-infested sites like I Love Music <ilx.wh3rd.net>, where debates about rockism have become so common that the term itself is something of a running joke. When the editors of a blog called Rockcritics Daily noted that rockism was "all the rage again," they posted dozens of contradictory citations, proving that no one really agrees on what the term means. (By the time you read this article, a slew of indignant refutations and addenda will probably be available online.)

But as more than one online ranter has discovered, it's easier to complain about rockism than it is to get rid of it. You literally can't fight rockism, because the language of righteous struggle is the language of rockism itself. You can argue that the shape-shifting feminist hip-pop of Ms. Aguilera is every bit as radical as the punk rock of the 1970's (and it is), but then you haven't challenged any of the old rockist questions (starting with: Who's more radical?), you've just scribbled in some new answers.

The challenge isn't merely to replace the old list of Great Rock Albums with a new list of Great Pop Songs—although that would, at the very least, be a nice change of pace. It's to find a way to think about a fluid musical world where it's impossible to separate classics from guilty pleasures. The challenge is to acknowledge that music videos and reality shows and glamorous layouts can be as interesting—and as influential—as an old-fashioned album.

In the end, the problem with rockism isn't that it's wrong: all critics are wrong sometimes, and some critics (now doesn't seem like the right time to name names) are wrong almost all the time.

The problem with rockism is that it seems increasingly far removed from the way most people actually listen to music.

Are you really pondering the phony distinction between "great art" and a "guilty pleasure" when you're humming along to the radio? In an era when listeners routinely—and fearlessly—pick music by putting a 40-gig iPod on shuffle, surely we have more interesting things to worry about than that someone might be lip-synching on *Saturday Night Live* or that some rappers gild their phooey. Good critics are good listeners, and the problem with rockism is that it gets in the way of listening. If you're waiting for some song that conjures up soul or honesty or grit or rebellion, you might miss out on Ciara's ecstatic electro-pop, or Alan Jackson's sly country ballads, or Lloyd Banks's felonious purr.

Rockism makes it hard to hear the glorious, incoherent, corporate-financed, audience-tested mess that passes for popular music these days. To glorify only performers who write their own songs and play their own guitars is to ignore the marketplace that helps create the music we hear in the first place, with its checkbook-chasing superproducers, its audience-obsessed executives and its cred-hungry performers. To obsess over old-fashioned stand-alone geniuses is to forget that lots of the most memorable music is created despite multimillion-dollar deals and spur- of-the-moment collaborations and murky commercial forces. In fact, a lot of great music is created because of those things. And let's stop pretending that serious rock songs will last forever, as if anything could, and that shiny pop songs are inherently disposable, as if that were necessarily a bad thing. Van Morrison's "Into the Music" was released the same year as the Sugarhill Gang's "Rapper's Delight"; which do you hear more often?

That doesn't mean we should stop arguing about Ms. Simpson, or even that we should stop sharing the 60-second clip that may just be this year's best music video. But it does mean we should stop taking it for granted that music isn't as good as it used to be, and it means we should stop being shocked that the rock rules of the 1970's are no longer the law of the land. No doubt our current obsessions and comparisons will come to seem hopelessly blinkered as popular music mutates some more—listeners and critics alike can't do much more than struggle to keep up. But let's stop trying to hammer young stars into old categories. We have lots of new music to choose from—we deserve some new prejudices, too.

———

Kelefa Sanneh is a music writer and critic for *The New York Times* <www.nytimes.com>, where this essay was published on October 31, 2004.

An Apology for Rockism

BY ADAM ELLWANGER (2007)

In the middle of an essay condemning the discriminating tastes of rock music fans, Kelefa Sanneh suggests that rockists think too much about what they listen to: he asks "Are you really pondering the phony distinction between 'great art' and a 'guilty pleasure' when you're humming along to the radio?" Despite what he wants us to believe, it is clear that Sanneh is mulling over that very distinction as he tries to hum along to Lil Jon on his way to work: people who don't obsess over this problem don't write articles like "The Rap Against Rockism."

Although rockism is a notoriously hard concept to define, it is typically used to describe a certain way of listening to popular music. For listeners who believe that rock music is generally better than other genres, the title of "rockist" can be worn as a badge of honor to indicate a superior aesthetic taste and sensibility. For some fans of performers like Christina Aguilera, Usher, and BBMak, the rockist is the jerk with the arched eyebrow and the sour look who unfairly ensures that these acts will continue to struggle for artistic legitimacy. "The Rap Against Rockism" proposes establishing a new hierarchy of popular music that would in part entail "replac[ing] the old list of Great Rock Albums with a new list of Great Pop Songs." Like Sanneh, I believe that rockism is an important topic of discussion. The political interests that motivate each side of the debate over rockism also animate the national discourse on issues of considerably greater concern than rock 'n' roll. Sanneh's essay is a much more vicious attack on rockists than he seems willing to concede, but his gross misunderstanding and misrepresentation of the rockist position is not the central problem with the revaluation he proposes. More important is that Sanneh's blind and enthusiastic endorsement of commercialized, over-produced pop music is socially irresponsible.

Sanneh's essay implicitly furthers one of the subtler projects of American leftist politics, namely undermining the right of the individual to pass judgment. One word is repeated throughout "The Rap Against Rockism": *prejudice*. As a society, we largely agree that to pass judgment before one has the necessary information and experience to do so is wrong. We should not tolerate prejudice. According to Sanneh, rockists are inherently prejudiced, and thus they should not be tolerated. Here his misunderstanding of rockism is made clear. He seems unaware that rockists don't *pre*-judge music, they merely judge it. Simply because I think Nelly's "Hot in Herre" is terrible doesn't mean I've had the "knee-jerk" reaction Sanneh suggests I've had. On the contrary, my judgment of Nelly is very well-informed. I've endured the song countless times over the past few years at the drive-thru, in the bowling alley, at the basketball game, on the Fourth of July, in TV commercials, etc., etc., etc. —and in this way I've come to an intimate understanding of its crappiness.

At some point in the past few decades, judgment, prejudice, and discrimination became interchangeable in the public vocabulary, and this is a dangerous conflation. Citizens in democracies need to be able to judge and discriminate (or recognize differences) in order to engage in conversations about the best courses of action for the nation. We rely on our ability to judge and discriminate to understand and evaluate those conversations. I am a discriminator: I think cake is better than pie because it tastes better to me. I think ibuprofen is better than aspirin because it works faster on my headache. And I think Richard Wright is a better writer than John Grisham because I think *Black Boy* is a better book than *The Firm*. I am also a rockist. I *do* think that The Boss is better than the Black Eyed Peas, because "Jungleland" *is* a better song than "My Humps" or anything Black Eyed Peas have or ever will put out. The qualitative difference between the songs is clear, and if other listeners can't grasp this then it can only be because of the bad taste and atrophied aesthetic sensibility that pop radio encourages. It is my right to make these judgments that drives Kelefa Sanneh crazy: he wants me to lighten up, stop thinking about it, learn to shake my ass. But to me, this decade doesn't seem very conducive to ass-shaking, and I want music that has meaning outside the confines of the dance floor.

Sanneh is not ignorant of the wider implications of his critique of judgment. He seems a little too at ease with the term *rockism* itself. It is a convenient one for his political enterprise, sounding so similar to the other, more insidious, "isms" that have plagued our society since its inception—racism, sexism, ageism, classism, speciesism. And sure enough, he painstakingly links rockism to those prejudices, explicitly characterizing rockists as sexist, racist homophobes. But rockism is not racism, nor is it sexism or homophobia. In fact, throughout its existence rock music has played a small but significant role in fighting those prejudices and the social structures that enable them. Further, women and minorities who create rock music are readily embraced by fans (think Hendrix, Heart, Fleetwood Mac, Bad Brains, The Slits, The Mars Volta, Pansy Division). Rock 'n' roll is much more inclusive than Sanneh suggests, and it has a tradition of progressivism that he willfully ignores. But if rockism isn't simply an exclusionary politics based in conservative and nostalgic prejudices, then what is it?

The rockist position is the belief that rock 'n' roll is superior to other types of popular music in the ways that it sounds, the ways it is created, the ways it is produced, the ways it is distributed, and in the ways it is performed. Rockists do privilege the visceral rawness of electric guitars. They prefer individuals who write and perform their own songs and producers who ensure that the bands are recorded in such a way that the spirit of the band is not violated by the sound of the record. Rockists champion the independent labels that support artists who demonstrate creativity and innovation rather than commercial viability. They enjoy the intimate setting of a club for a live show rather than the 683rd row of the impersonal AOL Time-Life Warner Megalosseum. Sanneh is correct when he recounts these preferences, but he doesn't understand that they amount to a political statement about how individuals relate to their culture and what functions that culture ought to perform. Taken together, the tenets of rockism are a way individuals can inhabit a materialistic society that is obsessed with the idea of newness. This hunger for the new is satisfied by art that is mostly vapid and totally transitory, and that is a trade-off rockists are unwilling to accept. Rockism gives people a means to resist the dark commercial forces that have seeped into the fabric of the culture, enabling them to retain a sense of identity and community that is made coherent by a collective devotion to rigid aesthetic standards.

Americans are increasingly titillated by the disposability of culture. A plethora of items for one-time use has hit the market: disposable bibs for babies, disposable cameras, prepackaged single servings of salsa. Verizon recently even introduced a disposable cell phone. In contrast to the consumers of such products, rockists are on the righteous quest for the timeless cultural artifact. The rock concept album is the highest prize, a sustained and unified musical and lyrical statement that helps us understand something about living in a certain time and place. Rockism implies an ambivalent and antagonistic relation to commodity culture and the disposability it holds up as an ideal. Undertaking the revaluation that Sanneh suggests by subordinating the rock tradition to the "incoherent, corporate-financed, audience-tested mess that passes for popular music" would be to abandon all resistance to disposable culture. It is the rockist position that the "overnight celebrities, one-hit wonders and lip-synchers" that Sanneh fetishizes are merely new instantiations of this disposability, and as such must be resisted. This project is propagated by a constant reaffirmation of the passion and authenticity of rock music. Is the battle against the disposability of culture one that can be won by making sure you buy the latest releases by Sufjan Stevens or The Hold Steady? Probably not. The simple fact that audiophiles must now convert their record collections to audio files suggests that rockists will ultimately lose. But there's not much rock fans enjoy more than a lost cause and fighting against seemingly unconquerable forces, and it is that fight that is at the center of the rockist program.

I believe that all music fans (rockist and popist) search out music that reflects back to them some truth about their lives and the world in which they live. Can Usher's repetition of "Yeah! Yeah!" over a loop of four synthesized notes bring someone to a deeper understanding of contemporary life? I suppose. But it doesn't tell *me* anything about *my* life. And neither does Fergie's ode to her lady-lumps. However, Radiohead *has* helped me to think about the existential anxiety that seemed to be intensified by the beginning of the new millennium. The lyrics on Pavement's albums *do* seem to echo some of the banality I felt growing up as a middle-class suburban kid in the mid-1990s. And it is here that I most strongly resent Sanneh's agenda—why should I be under an obligation to be inspired by Justin Timberlake? Is anyone imploring Lil Wayne's fans to listen to more Dinosaur Jr.? Sanneh's pop music world would disable us from making the sorts of judgments that define our identities, hindering our capacities to be good citizens in a diverse democratic society. Further, his complacency in the face of the commercial interests that dictate the production of pop music encourages total surrender to the logic of the commodity and the disposability of culture. Perhaps rockists do think too much about the music they listen to, but until Britney does something more artistic than forget her panties, I'm sticking with my rock 'n' roll.

———

Adam Ellwanger, who is from Rochester, N.Y., thinks your favorite band sucks. He is also pursuing a Ph.D. in rhetoric at the University of South Carolina, where he teaches courses in composition, literature, and speech.

FROM READING TO WRITING

1. Compare the television essays by Steven Johnson and Michael Hirschorn. Which writer presents a more effective argument? Why? How do you think Johnson would respond to Hirschorn's central argument about reality TV?

2. Discuss the following quotation from "Watching TV Makes You Smarter," and explain how it contributes to the author's larger argument: "Of course, the entertainment industry isn't increasing the cognitive complexity of its products for charitable reasons. The Sleeper Curve exists because there's money to be made by making culture smarter."

3. In her essay "Rosie the Riveter," Jennifer L. Pozner claims that the "anti-Rosie backlash is indicative of nothing so much as the stiflingly limited range of debate allowed within the corporate media, whose gatekeepers want to erase true leftist dissent in America." Explain what Pozner means by this, citing specific evidence from her essay. What do you think of this claim?

4. Are you a "rockist"? Explain, using Kelefa Sanneh's definition and Adam Ellwanger's response as starting points.

5. Choose one of the essays from the list below and do the following: summarize the argument (include the author's central claim and the evidence he or she provides); discuss the intended audience and how the author appeals to that audience; and evaluate the effectiveness of the argument (is it a strong argument or not? Why?).

    a. "The Case for Reality TV: What the Snobs Don't Understand"

    b. "Rosie the Riveter"

    c. "My Plan to Save Network Television"

    d. "Cut Buster Loose"

6. Summarize the central arguments that James Poniewozik presents in "The Imus Fallout: Who Can Say What?" and that Harvey Fierstein presents in "Our Prejudices, Ourselves." Whose position is presented more effectively? Explain.

Nine

WHAT'S SO FUNNY?

PAY ATTENTION!

If you can, that is. It's not easy if you suffer from ADD, better known as a children's condition but now afflicting more and more adults—including our author.

I need to tell you this: While writing this article, I panicked. I hit the "on" button on my computer and nothing happened. Frantic, I unplugged the thing and drove to the local college, where I ran to the tech-support department cradling my computer like a sick infant and begged for help.

"There's nothing wrong with it," they told me. I'd simply been pressing the wrong key. I stood there, rooted to the floor, wanting to will myself out of existence, cringing with embarrassment. This was the computer I'd used on a daily basis for six years. I'd suddenly, inexplicably forgotten how to turn it on, and my calamity button had gone off once again. You see, if everything in my life starts going too well for too long—it had been a fairly calm week—I start thinking, "Uh-oh. What scary thing is going to happen now?" And I brace for the onslaught.

Some would label me a "drama queen," a "career ditz," a "perennial screw-up." I wish it were that simple. I have Attention Deficit Disorder. I've had it all my life, although I don't really believe ADD is something you have so much as something you are.

Children have it; adults have it. For many, it's a cradle-to-grave deal, and there's no time off for good behavior (whatever the heck that is). My ADD brain is apparently missing vital chemicals that sort of "glue" thoughts together; it is physiologically different from what's considered "normal." This thing I have is neurobiological; it has nothing to do with my attitude.

Got that?

See, I receive lectures from other adults on a fairly regular basis on how I could "pull my life together" if I just dug in. If I just concentrated. If I just followed a handy system to be determined, in most cases, by the person delivering the lecture.

"HEY! FOCUS!" I hear all the time. And I want to say, "HEY! LOSE 10 POUNDS, PORKCHOP! How dare you tell me how to be?"

In most states, ADD is considered a (manageable) disability. In other words, I am not a "mentally ill" or "nuts" individual who deserves to be thrown in a loony bin any more than a dyslexic person or someone in a wheelchair. But political correctness is not often practiced around me. I don't imagine you'd make silly faces at a blind person for your own amusement. But people let fly with the "blonde jokes" around me every day because I have a hard time concentrating and seem always to be in three places at once.

I found my phone bill in the freezer one time, and I don't really believe I put it there on purpose, though you never know. I sometimes find myself brushing my teeth and getting so distracted halfway through that I may not finish the job until an hour or so later, though I may have sat down at the piano and written a song in the meantime; or logged on and sent a couple of e-mails; or figured out the distance from Seattle to Portland by car in case I ever want to have the gas money saved in advance for a road trip I may or may not take in the next decade.

My mind works very, very well, actually. And I probably do not ever do anything in any kind of sequence that makes sense to you. My internal alphabet starts at "P" and moves on to "L" and goes on to "T," and then maybe jump-starts at "ABCDE" just to confound other people, then probably starts inventing other "experimental" letters you've never, ever heard of. And then the did-I-pay-my-phone-bill voices start up in my head, and I get overwhelmed and need to go lie down for a while. It's funny. No, it's scary. No, funny. No, scary—except when it's tragically, wrenchingly, stomach-churningly funny.

So many wonderful ideas float around in my head every day. I call them my "dead babies"—a gruesome image, I'll grant you. My brain utterly lacks the organizational skills to bring these "lost" ideas to fruition, is the thing. I know my (real) goal in life is to be a singer, or an actress, or a political cartoonist, or an educator, or a children's book illustrator, or a geologist, or a motivational speaker, or a novelist, or a makeup artist. (Luckily, I'm over 40 now; I have that list narrowed down to a manageable size.)

A psychiatrist once told me I needed a husband to keep me on track, and I thought, "I'd need to give the guy combat pay. Not to mention weekends and holidays off." When I meet a man, he often thinks that I'm not interested in him because, if I am, I often get nervous and start fidgeting. It makes for an uncomfortable first date—and it's unusual I get asked out for a second. When I see a "JUST MARRIED" procession passing on the street, I think, "How the heck did they do that?"

As a child, I got yelled at a lot for not finishing things I'd started, though I was not considered hyperactive. (Hyperactivity may or may not accompany ADD.) Since I spent so much time in my private inner world, I missed out on developing a lot of social skills children need. I heard (through third parties) that boys found me "weird" or "twisted" or "stuck-up" or "from a solar system other than our own." Everyone said I was really creative. I never wore "outfits" to school; it was more like "costumes." I'd show up wearing ski knickers, construction boots and earrings I had made out of discarded office supplies. (This inventiveness, this "power-of-synthesis" talent, by the way, is a hallmark of ADD.) Nowadays, they simply put kids on Ritalin.

I bring up medication because it's such a flash point in any discussion of ADD. It's never had any effect on me, personally, though I have taken antidepressants, just to keep my frustration levels manageable. I believe in medication as an option, certainly, but I think it's important to try all the options available, because each ADDer's brain chemistry is unique.

I have friends with ADD who say, "There's no way I'd want to be any different. I'm cool just like this." I'd give anything to be normal, though, or closer to it. I wouldn't have asked for this thing. I die from shame each time I make a simple error. I probably try 10 times harder than the average person to get it right, and take 10 times longer to finish a job, frantically checking for errors that, ironically, often aren't even there.

I'll give you an example: I recently worked as a temp at a real-estate firm. (Financially, I always seem to be on the edge of a yawning precipice with komodo dragons at the bottom.) I spent the week squirting out faxes, filing invoices, routing phone calls, even sorting soft drinks alphabetically in the company refrigerator. At the end of the week, I had not made a single error. But when it came time to call up the payroll system to log in my hours, I simply forgot all about it. I literally forgot to get paid that week. I had put so much energy into not letting anybody else down (and I was exhausted at the end of every day) that I let down myself.

That's one reason I avoid having a "real" job. I prefer not to inflict my blunder-ready nature on any poor, unsuspecting, profit-minded organization, not to mention I also have a tough time reading the subtle signals of human behavior that are the bread and butter of office politics. Plus, my sense of humor usually terrifies anyone over the age of 5.

People tell me, "Grow up." Indeed, there's some controversy over whether people do, in fact, grow out of ADD. I say the very idea is hogwash; it's like saying you can grow out of being left-handed, or being tall, or having brown eyes. What an ADD person becomes adept at, rather, is "passing." Just as light-skinned African Americans "passed" as white not long ago, and just as many gays and lesbians have hidden their true identities, a lot of ADD people are "in the closet."

At the moment, I'm working as a temp in a bank, pasting colored labels on file folders, then lining up the folders, one by one. I make up little stories in my head about the people whose names are on the folders. They're pretty good stories, actually. By day's end, the folders are all perfectly arranged. Everyone says I'm doing a bang-up job. By the time I get home, though, I have usually forgotten all the stories. If I thought about it, I imagine this would be depressing.

Oh, yeah . . . this article is by Stephanie Brush

Stephanie Brush wrote this piece for the July 15, 2001, edition of *USA Today Weekend* <www.usatoday.com>.

Rachael Ray, My Dinner Hooker
BY MARY ELIZABETH WILLIAMS (2006)

There is an entire industry built around the loathing of peppy media chef-phenomenon Rachael Ray. Google up "Rachael Ray" and "hate" and you'll uncover an enthusiastic community devoting considerable energy to "Raytard's" manic je ne sais quoi and dubious fashion sense. But does the "Joker faced" celebrity chef really merit that much scorn? This is a woman who, as far as we know, has never thrown a phone at an assistant, evaded her taxes, launched into any unfortunate, blood-alcohol-elevated tirades, or rapped at the Teen Choice Awards. If there ever comes a day that Rachael Ray is hospitalized for exhaustion, it'll be a safe bet that she really is exhausted. Why then is there such a thriving cult of antipathy toward the woman *Forbes* recently identified as the second most trusted person in America?

Because there are two kinds of people in the world. There are those who leap out of bed smiling and eager to start the day, the kind who come up with team-building exercises for their departments, who stay out late into the evening line dancing because it's just so darn fun, and who wake up again the next morning still smiling and eager to start the day. These are the kind of people who sell T-shirts on their Web sites that say "Yum-O." Then there are the rest of us, the ones who see people like that and want to barf-o.

Rachael Ray, the turbocharged personality who has built an entire career on the notion that anyone can pull dinner out of their ass in under a half-hour, has, in the past year, gone from high-profile basic cable star to full-blown media juggernaut. She is the face of her own magazine, the author of a string of bestselling cookbooks, and the host of approximately a bazillion Food Network series. In September, her eponymously named daytime talk show launched with the highest ratings for a syndicated debut since Dr. Phil hit the airwaves four years ago. Earlier this year, *Time* named Ray one of the 100 most influential people in the world. She has become, to crib from her bottomless supply of stock phrases, a big ta-da.

Hers is a quintessentially self-made American success story. Small-town girl and specialty food buyer hits upon the idea to teach "30 Minute Meal" classes as a way of moving the merchandise. The classes lead to TV appearances, which lead to cookbooks and a Food Network gig, which lead to guesting on "Oprah" and subsequent total media domination. Ray has no formal culinary training, and a brash willingness to embrace pre-washed produce and canned broth. She has boasted that she's completely unqualified for every job she's ever had. Unsurprisingly, she pisses a lot of people off.

Unlike some of her other Food Network compatriots, Ray brings no seductive charge, no "food porn" element to her work. Jamie Oliver, Tyler Florence, Giada De Laurentiis and their ilk infuse their personas with the erotic decadence that comes from good cooking. Their newest colleague, Nigella Lawson, owes much of her fame to languorous finger licking. Ray, in contrast, is all brisk and bouncy. Even when she posed for FHM a few years ago in a series of skimpy outfits, her wholesome smile, her cheerful lack of subtext when nibbling a strawberry, remained firmly intact.

Ray does not exist to wine you and dine you. She is here to wham-bam thank-you-ma'am you, an abundantly useful strategy. I may find her personality considerably off-putting. I may feel guilty for turning to her again and again at that certain hour of the evening when I need gratification. Rachael Ray is my dinner hooker—fast, reliable, a sure bet. Her critics can bemoan the meteoric rise of the warp-speed dinner; they can turn up their noses at her "sammies" and burgers. But not every meal can be a truffle-infused work of art. Most nights, you're just grateful for a little culinary reach-around.

Therein lies the secret of her success. Perhaps she's a star because that breakneck energy and interjection-riddled vocabulary are genuinely appealing, although if that's the case I may have to move to another, far more dour corner of the globe. I prefer to believe she's made it despite the relentless ebullience, that she connects because she understands that for a whole lot of people, getting dinner on the table is a major accomplishment. You work late, you take care of your kids, you have no time to shop. You contemplate choking down a solitary Luna Bar or picking up a supersize bucket of trans fats at the drive-through. Rachael Ray says there's another option, and with her chipper, can-do attitude, she demystifies cooking. If she weren't sugarcoated to the gills, her message would be almost too tough to take. Suck it up, she's saying. If I can do it, you can to it. Take one lousy half-hour and get a hot meal together, for yourself and for your family. A real meal, preferably the kind with some lean meat and fresh vegetables. No expensive equipment or specialty store ingredients; no fancy French terms or techniques. No excuses.

My own relationship with Ray began in her early days on Food Network, when I was a frazzled new mother and the sight of watching people cook was the most soothing thing I could imagine. Her "30 Minute Meals" offered a warm and accessible personality, a regular gal who, like me, was just trying to get dinner made without having a nervous breakdown. I enjoyed the repetitive lull of her drizzling "EVOO" (that's extra virgin olive oil to you and me) "twice around the pan" night after night after night, even as her patter about Grandpa Emmanuel and Daddy's Cajun cred wore thin. Our bond was truly fixed, however, when I was pregnant with my second child, and I was helpfully gifted with one of her cookbooks.

It was a fascinating read. On the one hand, what legitimate cookbook author uses more exclamation points than a month's worth of Craigslist postings? Who in her right mind actually writes out phrases like "h-e-double-hockey-sticks" or "WHOA! I can't find the time to do all that!"? I, a semi-competent, fairly snobby home chef with a subscription to *Cooks Illustrated*, was appalled. On the other hand, the annoying chick delivered. Mere speed and convenience alone do not a successful recipe make, as anyone who's ever watched the Cool Whip-wielding nightmare that is Sandra Lee will attest. In contrast, Ray's roast leg of lamb was a crusty, garlicky hit, and her rosemary grilled chicken was, according to my mate, "restaurant quality." The last thing I made before going into labor was Rachael Ray's green minestrone. In the weeks and months that followed, her other cookbooks appeared on the shelf, and became battered and grease-spattered from constant abuse. She may grate on my nerves like a block of Parmesan on a blade, but dammit, she's my fix.

She wasn't always this irritating. Take a gander at the early episodes of "30 Minute Meals" that air regularly on Food Network, and you'll find a coherent personality putting together some pretty decent dinners. As her star has risen, so, apparently, has Ray's energy level and fondness for cutesy phrasing. The woman who could once do the "chop and drop" with a reasonable amount of serenity has been replaced by something resembling a hyperactive Red Bull addict going through a speed drill while delivering a stream of consciousness. Case in point: Her laid-back howdy-do of yore has been obliterated on her new show, which opens with a large metal gate parting to unleash Ray, bat-out-of-hell-style, upon the masses. As she patters a mile a minute and announces she's heading into her kitchen (emblazoned, à la Mary Richards, with the star's trademark monogram) to grab a cup of coffee, one can only pray that it's decaf. During the course of a recent episode, I heard the 38-year-old use the phrase "back in the day" twice in one minute, "awesome" in four staccato repetitions, and "girl" what felt like roughly 9,000 times. And when she settled down to nervously interrupt and giggle her way through the next interview, somewhere, I could hear the sound of a blogger's hands rubbing gleefully together.

But consider this: 66 percent of Americans are overweight or obese, while fast food and takeout consumption and portion sizes have ballooned. It's estimated that less than half of American families sit down to eat together every night. It doesn't take a genius to figure out how these things are related. So if the woman that Anthony Bourdain is not unjustified in referring to as a bobble-head can make dinner a little less intimidating, I can admit she may not be the antichrist. If she understands the vicissitudes of the dinner hour well enough to divide a recent tome into "Meals for the Exhausted," "Meals for the Not Too Tired" and "Bring It On! (But Be Gentle)," she can girlishly giggle herself all the way to the bank. And if, most important of all, a fair share of her recipes actually pass the taste test, she's welcome on my shelf any day.

Do the meals that have become my weeknight staples actually get made in under 30 minutes? Sometimes. My husband has been known to hopefully flip open a Ray recipe 30 minutes before he expects to eat, only to emerge considerably later, bathed in flop sweat and exasperation. But as Ray "eyeballs" her measurements, I do likewise with my time, and I can usually hit pretty close to her mark. The timing is realistically livable, and I'm not dialing for takeout or beating myself for not having a pot roast-compatible lifestyle. Our family sits down together. We eat our vegetables. We have time for the rest of the evening. The most frantic woman in America, ironically, brings a measure of peace and pleasure into my hummingbird-paced day. So I'll keep making Ray's seafood stew, her veal involtini, and, when the fear of a lingering, E. coli-related death leaves me, her spinach rolls. Just don't expect me to ever call them yum-o.

———

Mary Elizabeth Williams wrote this piece for the Oct. 14, 2006, issue of *Salon* <www.salon.com>.

Antarctic Story: Why Human Beings Like "March of the Penguins"

BY JOE QUEENAN (2005)

Innumerable theories (well, let's say six) have been put forth to explain the phenomenal success of the documentary *March of the Penguins*. The most obvious is that everyone loves penguins, as opposed to wolves, deer, or mandrills. A recent film by the revered German auteur Werner Herzog, about a man who befriended an ingrate grizzly bear that eventually ate him, did not fare nearly as well at the box office, and sharks, rats, and anacondas have been in a serious commercial slump for some time.

It is not true, however, that affection for penguins is universal. When I suggested to my 85-year-old mother, who had not been to the movies since *The Mask of Zorro* came out in 1998, that we take in *March of the Penguins*, she politely declined, saying that she would rather wait for *The Legend of Zorro*, as she much preferred the way Antonio Banderas carried himself to the clumsy waddling of the self-absorbed denizens of the Antarctic who, at least in her view, may only clamber about in that cunningly maladroit way when they know the camera is on them. (Of course, she is a typically contrary native Philadelphian, and may only be saying this to be mean.)

The heat wave that coincided with the release of the film may also explain why it did so well at the box office, as would the Schadenfreudic delight derived by Americans once they found out that the miserable camera crew that spent 13 months documenting the penguins' herculean mating rituals in the most brutal temperatures known to man — very nearly perishing in the process — were French. Nor can we overlook the fact that, at just 85 minutes, *March of the Penguins* is the perfect chick flick, providing men with a rare opportunity to accompany their spouses, girlfriends, or mistresses to a film they would probably not see if left to their own devices, but that at least will not make them ill. (The last film meeting these criteria was the 2002 comedy *Bend It Like Beckham*, which featured cute English girls in shorts.)

Yet another explanation for the success of the film is the notion that it supports the theory of intelligent design. Penguins clamber out of the water, waddle 70 miles to a mysterious, preordained mating ground, pair off with a suitable member of the opposite sex, and procreate. Then the winter sets in and the animals suffer prodigiously. Once the eggs appear, the males cover them with their fur, incubating them for four months while the females stagger back to the water, eat everything that isn't nailed down, then waddle back to feed the chicks. George Will, among others, has questioned how such a cumbersome, often fatal, procedure could possibly affirm the hidden hand of a wise, all-knowing creator. Frankly, a case can be made that the whole thing suggests that Mother Nature is sometimes asleep at the wheel.

Certainly, the fashion in which the film has been edited for release in America has contributed to its wide appeal. Shot and released by a French producer, the film originally featured talking penguins trying to make themselves heard above a lethal French soundtrack. But when it was repackaged by National Geographic, the cute dialogue got deep-sixed, a generic New Age nature film soundtrack was substituted, and the narration of Morgan "The Voice of God" Freeman was imposed over the proceedings. Narration is becoming terribly fashionable in films these days, as it liberates directors from the cumbersome duty of actually having to shoot their films. If you don't believe me, check out *Million Dollar Baby*. Or *Sin City*. Or *Good Bye, Lenin!* Or any other film released in the past three years.

My own theory about the film's popularity is much simpler. Initially, I subscribed to the belief that the public deliberately made a hit out of *March of the Penguins* just to punish Hollywood for continuing to release cynical trash like *The Island*, *Bewitched*, and *Stealth*. The public, an ornery lot, has done this sort of thing before, capriciously voting thumbs-down to industry-designated blockbusters, and transforming demure charmers like *Sideways* or cornpone like *My Big Fat Greek Wedding* into preposterously huge hits.

But at long last, I no longer think this is the case. Speaking for myself and, therefore, as a proxy for most redblooded males, I now believe that the appeal of the film abides in its deceptively ambiguous sexual politics. Just as women have always flocked to Cary Grant, Gregory Peck, and even Hugh Grant movies because they secretly wish they were married to debonair sophisticates instead of the tattooed psychopaths into whose hands Fate has delivered them, many women seem to be smitten by the selfless behavior of the male penguins, who not only help out with the kids, but do it in subfreezing weather where their very survival is at stake. It probably also helps that penguins have more hair than most American men past the age of 35.

Ironically, the film's appeal to men also relates to child-rearing, but for exactly the opposite reason. A male penguin spends four months on the edge of death in Antarctica, but after that has no other responsibilities to his offspring. He doesn't have to feed them. He doesn't have to nurture them. He doesn't have to raise the cash to send them to college. Medical coverage is not an issue. Hand-holding sessions are not required. This is why men draw exactly the opposite conclusion from the film than women: Most men would willingly suffer hideous deprivation for four months during a savage Antarctic winter if it would free them from any further responsibilities to their progeny.

Speaking personally, with two kids at expensive colleges, the whole thing strikes me as a win-win proposition. So next reincarnation, I'm coming back as a penguin. Sounds like an intelligent design to me.

Joe Queenan is author, most recently, of *Queenan Country: A Reluctant Anglophile's Pilgrimage to the Mother Country*. He wrote this piece for the November 7, 2005, edition of *The Weekly Standard* <www.weeklystandard.com>.

Chicken in the Henhouse

BY DAVID SEDARIS (2004)

It was one of those hotels without room service, the type you wouldn't mind if you were paying your own bill but would complain about if someone else was paying. I was not paying my own bill, and so the deficiencies stuck out and were taken as evidence of my host's indifference. There was no tub, just a plastic shower stall, and the soap was brittle and smelled like dishwashing detergent. The bedside lamp was missing a bulb, but that could have been remedied easily enough. I could have asked for one at the front desk, but I didn't want a lightbulb. I just wanted to feel put-upon.

It started when the airline lost my luggage. Time was lost filling out forms, and I'd had to go directly from the airport to a college an hour north of Manchester, where I gave a talk to a group of students. Then there was a reception and a forty-five-minute drive to the hotel, which was out in the middle of nowhere. I arrived at one A.M. and found they had booked me into a basement room. Late at night it didn't much matter, but in the morning it did. To open the curtains was to invite scrutiny, and the people of New Hampshire stared in without a hint of shame. There wasn't much to look at, just me, sitting on the edge of the bed with a phone to my ear. The airline had sworn my suitcase would arrive overnight, and when it didn't, I called the 800 number printed on the inside of my ticket jacket. My choices were either to speak to a machine or to wait for an available human. I chose the human, and after eight minutes on hold I hung up and started looking for someone to blame.

"I don't care if it's my son, my congressman, what have you. I just don't approve of that lifestyle." The speaker was a woman named Audrey who'd called the local talk-radio station to offer her opinion. The Catholic Church scandal had been front-page news for over a week, and when the priest angle had been exhausted, the discussion filtered down to pedophilia in general and then, homosexual pedophilia, which was commonly agreed to be the worst kind. It was, for talk radio, one of those easy topics, like tax hikes or mass murder. "What do you think of full-grown men practicing sodomy on children?"

"Well, I'm *against* it!" This was always said as if it was somehow startling, a minority position no one had yet dared lay claim to.

I'd been traveling around the country for the past ten days, and everywhere I went I heard the same thing. The host would congratulate the caller on his or her moral fortitude, and wanting to feel that approval again, the person would rephrase the original statement, freshening it up with an adverb or qualifier. "Call me old-fashioned, but I just hugely think it's wrong." Then, little by little, they'd begin interchanging the words *homosexual* and *pedophile*, speaking as if they were one and the same. "Now they've even got them on TV," Audrey said. "And in the schools! Talk about the proverbial chicken in the henhouse."

"Fox," the host said.

"Oh, they're the worst," Audrey said. "*The Simpsons* and such—I never watch that station."

"I meant in the henhouse," the host said. "I believe the saying is 'the fox in the henhouse,' not 'the chicken in the henhouse.'"

Audrey regrouped. "Did I say chicken? Well, you get my point. These homosexuals can't reproduce themselves, and so they go into the schools and try to recruit our young people."

It was nothing I hadn't heard before, but I was crankier than usual and found myself in the middle of the room, one sock on and one sock off, shouting at the clock radio. "Nobody recruited *me*, Audrey. And I *begged* for it."

It was *her* fault I was stuck in a basement room with no luggage, her and all the people just like her: the satisfied families trotting from the parking lot to the first-floor restaurant, the hotel guests with whirlpool baths and rooms overlooking the surrounding forest. *Why waste the view on a homosexual? He only looks at schoolboys' rectums. And a suitcase? Please! We all know what they do with those.* They might not have come out and said it, but they were sure thinking it. I could tell.

It stood to reason that if the world was conspiring against me, my Mr. Coffee machine was broken. It sat on the bathroom counter, dribbling cold water, and after a brief, completely unsatisfying cry, I finished getting dressed and left the room. There was a staircase at the end of the hall, and beside it a little cleared area where a dozen or so elderly women knelt upon the carpet, piecing together a patchwork quilt. They looked up as I passed, one of them turning to ask me a question. "Yoin' shurch?" Her mouth was full of pins and it took me a moment to realize what she was saying—You going to church? It was an odd question, but then I remembered that it was a Sunday, and I was wearing a tie. Someone at the college had loaned it to me the night before, and I'd put it on in hopes it might distract from my shirt, which was wrinkled and discolored beneath the arms. "No," I told her, "I am *not* going to church." Oh, I was in a horrible mood. Midway up the stairs I stopped and turned back around. "I *never* go to church," I said. "Never. And I'm not about to start *now*."

"Shute shelf," she said.

Past the restaurant and gift shop, in the center of the lobby, was a complimentary beverage stand. I thought I'd get a coffee and take it outdoors, but just as I approached, a boy swooped in and began mixing himself a cup of hot chocolate. He looked like all of the kids I'd been seeing lately, in airports, in parking lots: the oversize sweatshirts stamped with team emblems, the baggy jeans and jazzy sneakers. His watch was fat and plastic, like a yo-yo strapped to his wrist, and his hair looked as if it had been cut with the lid of a can, the irregular hanks stiffened with gel and coaxed to stand at peculiar angles.

It was a complicated business, mixing a cup of hot chocolate. You had to spread the powdered cocoa from one end of the table to the other and use as many stirrers as possible, making sure to thoroughly chew the wetted ends before tossing them upon the stack of unused napkins. This is what I like about children: complete attention to one detail and complete disregard of another. When finally finished, he scooted over to the coffee urn, filling two cups, black, and fitting them with lids. The drinks were stacked into a tower, then tentatively lifted off the table. "Whoa," he whispered. Hot chocolate seeped from beneath the lid of the bottom cup and ran down his hand.

"Do you need some help with those?" I asked.

The boy looked at me for a moment. "Yeah," he said. "Carry these upstairs." There was no *please* or *thank you*, just "I'll take the hot chocolate myself."

He set the coffees back on the table, and as I reached for them it occurred to me that maybe this was not such a good idea. I was a stranger, an admitted homosexual traveling through a small town, and he was, like, ten. And alone. The voice of reason whispered in my ear. *Don't do it, buster. You're playing with fire.*

I withdrew my hands, then stopped, thinking, *Wait a minute. That's not reason. It's Audrey, that crackpot from the radio.* The real voice of reason sounds like Bea Arthur, and when it failed to pipe up, I lifted the coffees off the table and carried them toward the elevator, where the boy stood mashing the call button with his chocolate-coated fingers.

A maid passed and rolled her eyes at the desk clerk. "Cute kid."

Before the church scandal I might have said the same thing, only without the sarcasm. Now, though, any such observation seemed suspect. Though Audrey would never believe it, I am not physically attracted to children. They're like animals to me, fun to watch but beyond the bounds of my sexual imagination. That said, I am a person who feels guilty for crimes I have not committed, or have not committed in years. The police search the train station for a serial rapist and I cover my face with a newspaper, wondering if maybe I did it in my sleep. The last thing I stole was an eight-track tape, but to this day I'm unable to enter a store without feeling like a shoplifter. It's all the anxiety with none of the free stuff. To make things just that much worse, I seem to have developed a remarkable perspiration problem. My conscience is cross-wired with my sweat glands, but there's a short in the system and I break out over things I didn't do, which only makes me look more suspect. Innocently helping to lighten a child's burden was a *good* thing—I knew this—yet moments after lifting the coffees off the table I was soaking wet. As usual, the sweat was fiercest on my forehead, under my arms, and, cruelly, on my ass, which is a great mystery to me. If the stress is prolonged, I'll feel the droplets inching down the back of my legs, trapped, finally, by my socks, which are cotton and bought expressly for their absorbent powers.

If there was a security camera in the lobby, this is what it would have shown: A four-and-a-half-foot-tall boy stands mashing and then pounding the elevator call button. Beside him is a man, maybe a foot taller, dressed in a shirt and tie and holding a lidded cup in each hand. Is it raining outside? If not, perhaps he just stepped from the shower and threw on his clothes without drying himself. His eyes shift this way and that, giving the impression that he is searching for somebody. Could it be this silver-haired gentleman? He's just walked up, looking very dapper in his tweed jacket and matching cap. He talks to the boy and lays a hand on the back of his head, scolding him probably, which is good, as somebody needed to. The other man, the wet one, is just standing there, holding the cups and trying to wipe his forehead with his sleeve at the same time. A lid pops off and something—it looks like coffee—spills down the front of his shirt. He leaps about, prancing almost, and pulls the fabric away from his skin. The boy seems angry now and says something. The older gentleman offers a handkerchief, and the man sets down one of his cups and runs—literally runs, panting—off camera, returning thirty seconds later with another lidded cup, a replacement. By this time the elevator has arrived. The gentleman holds open the door, and he and the boy wait as the man picks the other cup off the floor and joins them. Then the door closes, and they are gone.

"So, who have we got here?" the gentleman asked. His voice was jovial and enthusiastic. "What do you call yourself, big fella?"

"Michael," the boy said.

'Well, that's a grown-up name, isn't it."

Michael guessed that it was, and the man caught my eye and winked, the way people do when they're establishing a partnership. *We'll just put on the small fry, what do you say?* "I bet a big guy like you must have a lot of girlfriends," he said. "Is that true?"

"No."

"You *don't?* Well, what's the problem?"

"I don't know. I just don't have one. That's all," Michael said.

I had always hated it when men asked the girlfriend question. Not only was it corny, but it set you in their imaginations in a way that seemed private to me. Answer yes and they'd picture your wee courtship: the candlelit dinner of hot dogs and potato chips, the rumpled Snoopy sheets. Answer no and you were blue-balled, the frustrated bachelor of the second grade. It was an idea of children as miniature adults, which was about as funny to me as a dog in sunglasses.

"Well, there must be *someone* you have your eye on."

The boy did not answer, but the man persisted in trying to draw him out. "Is Mommy sleeping in this morning?"

Again, nothing.

The man gave up and turned to me. "Your wife," he said. "I take it she's still in bed?"

He thought I was Michael's father, and I did not correct him. "Yes," I said. "She's upstairs. . . passed out." I don't know why I said this, or then again, maybe I do. The man had constructed a little family portrait, and there was a pleasure in defacing it. Here was Michael, here was Michael's dad, and now, here was Mom, lying facedown on the bathroom floor.

The elevator stopped on three, and the man tipped his hat. "All right, then," he said. "You two enjoy the rest of the morning." Michael had pressed the button for the fifth floor no less than twenty times, and now he gave it an extra few jabs just for good measure. We were alone now, and something unpleasant entered my mind.

Sometimes when I'm in a tight situation, I'll feel a need to touch somebody's head. It happens a lot on airplanes. I'll look at the person seated in front of me, and within a moment the idea will have grown from a possibility to a compulsion. There is no option—I simply have to do it. The easiest method is to make like I'm getting up, to grab the forward seat for support and just sort of pat the person's hair with my fingers. "Oh, I'm sorry," I say.

"No problem."

Most often I'll continue getting out of my seat, then walk to the back of the plane or go to the bathroom and stand there for a few minutes, trying to fight off what I know is inevitable: I need to touch the person's head again. Experience has taught me that you can do this three times before the head's owner either yells at you or rings for the flight attendant. "Is something wrong?" she'll ask.

"I don't think so, no."

"What do you mean 'no,'" the passenger will say. "This freak keeps touching my head."

"Is that true, sir?"

It's not always a head. Sometimes I need to touch a particular purse or briefcase. When I was a child this sort of compulsive behavior was my life, but now I practice it only if I'm in a situation where I can't smoke: planes—as I mentioned—and elevators.

Just touch the boy's head, I thought. The old man did it, so why can't you?

To remind myself that this is inappropriate only makes the voice more insistent. The thing must be done *because* it is inappropriate. If it weren't, there'd be no point in bothering with it.

He won't even notice it. Touch him now, quick.

Were we traveling a long distance, I would have lost the battle, but fortunately we weren't going far. The elevator arrived on the fifth floor and I scrambled out the door, set the coffees on the carpet, and lit a cigarette. "You're going to have to give me a minute here," I said.

"But my room's just down the hall. And this is nonsmoking."

"I know, I know."

"It's not good for you," he said.

"That's true for a lot of people," I told him. "But it *really is* good for me. Take my word for it."

He leaned against a door and removed the DO NOT DISTURB sign, studying it for a moment before sticking it in his back pocket.

I only needed to smoke for a minute, but realized when I was finished that there was no ashtray. Beside the elevator was a window, but of course it was sealed shut. Hotels.

They do everything in their power to make you want to jump to your death, and then they make certain that you can't do it. "Are you finished with your cocoa?" I asked.

"No."

"Well, are you finished with the lid?"

"I guess so."

He handed it to me and I spit into the center—no easy task, as my mouth was completely dry. Fifty percent of my body water was seeping out my ass, and the other half was in transit.

"That's gross," he said.

"Yeah, well, you're just going to have to forgive me." I stubbed the cigarette into the spit, set the lid on the carpet, and picked up the coffees. "Okay. Where to?"

He pointed down a long corridor and I followed him, gnawing on a question that's been troubling me for years. What if you had a baby and you just . . . you just needed to touch it where you knew you shouldn't. I don't mean that you'd want to. You wouldn't *desire* the baby any more than you desire a person whose head you've just touched. The act would be compulsive rather than sexual, and while to you there'd be a big difference, you couldn't expect a prosecutor, much less an infant, to recognize it. You'd be a bad parent, and once the child could talk and you told it not to tell anyone, you would become a manipulator—a monster, basically—and the reason behind your actions would no longer matter.

The closer we got to the end of the hall, the more anxious I became. I had not laid a finger on the boy's head. I have never poked or prodded either a baby or a child, so why did I feel so dirty? Part of it was just my makeup, the deep-seated belief that I deserve a basement room, but a larger, uglier part had to do with the voices I hear on talk radio, and my tendency, in spite of myself, to pay them heed. The man in the elevator had not thought twice about asking Michael personal questions or about laying a hand on the back of his head. Because he was neither a priest nor a homosexual, he hadn't felt the need to watch himself, worrying that every word or gesture might be misinterpreted. He could unthinkingly wander the halls with a strange boy, while for me it amounted to a political act—an insistence that I was as good as the next guy. Yes, I am a homosexual; yes, I am soaking wet; yes, I sometimes feel an urge to touch people's heads, but still I can safely see a ten-year-old back to his room. It bothered me that I needed to prove something this elementary. And prove it to people whom I could never hope to convince.

"This is it," Michael said. From the other side of the door I heard the sound of a television. It was one of those Sunday-morning magazine programs, a weekly hour where all news is good news. Blind Jimmy Henderson coaches a volleyball team. An ailing groundhog is fitted for a back brace. That type of thing. The boy inserted his card key into the slot, and the door opened onto a bright, well-furnished room. It was twice the size of mine, with higher ceilings and a sitting area. One window framed a view of the lake, and the other a stand of scarlet maples.

"Oh, you're back," a woman said. She was clearly the boy's mother, as their profiles were identical, the foreheads easing almost imperceptibly into blunt freckled noses. Both too had spiky blond hair, though for her I imagined the style was accidental, the result of the pillows piled behind her head. She was lying beneath the covers of a canopy bed, examining one of the many brochures scattered across the comforter. A man slept beside her, and when she spoke, he shifted slightly and covered his face with the crook of his arm. "What took you so long?" She looked toward the open door, and her eyes widened as they met mine. "What the . . ."

There was a yellow robe at the foot of the bed, and the woman turned her back to me as she got up and stepped into it. Her son reached for the coffees, and I tightened my grip, unwilling to surrender what I'd come to think of as my props. They turned me from a stranger to a kindly stranger, and I'd seen myself holding them as his parents rounded on me, demanding to know what was going on.

"Give them to me," he said, and rather than making a scene, I relaxed my grip. The coffees were taken, and I felt my resolve starting to crumble. Empty-handed, I was just a creep, the spooky wet guy who'd crawled up from the basement. The woman crossed to the dresser, and as the door started to close she called out to me. "Hey," she said. "Wait a minute." I turned, ready to begin the fight of my life, and she stepped forward and pressed a dollar into my hand. "You people run a very nice hotel," she told me. "I just wish we could stay longer."

The door closed and I stood alone in the empty corridor, examining my tip and thinking, *Is that all?*

Mommie Fearest

I'm due in four weeks and if the predictions of my mother friends are accurate,
I should feel like a total impostor, a crappy mom, a complete failure.
BY HEATHER HAVRILESKY (2006)

The joys of motherhood await me! In about a month, if all goes well, I'll be the first-time mother of a newborn. According to my friends who are mothers, this means that the healthy glow and abnormally cheerful moods of pregnancy will soon be gone, replaced by a sallow zombie mask. I'll have trouble running a brush through my hair, my stomach will sag like an empty duffel bag, there will be big, dark circles under my eyes, and acquaintances will speculate as to the severity of my postpartum depression—which will be very, very severe indeed.

Of course I'll try my best to do everything I've been told—I'll try not to "overthink" breast-feeding but will aim to achieve a "good latch," I'll try to pump early and often, I'll nap when my baby is napping, I'll make my husband change every single diaper and walk the baby in a million little circles, I'll treat motherhood as my brand-new, overtime, around-the-clock job, I won't attempt to vacuum or shower or pay bills, I won't guilt myself into thinking I should be back at work prematurely—but even so, I'm told that I'll feel angry and sullen and overwhelmed. I'll cry over nothing, or over the fact that there's a lamprey-like beast sucking my will to live straight out of my sore breasts.

Yes, just four weeks from now, if the predictions of my mother friends are accurate, I should feel like a total impostor, a crappy mom, a complete failure at my "new career," but I'll also be so spaced out and slow that I'll wonder if I can ever return to my old career again. I'll have to let my husband wash the lamprey, just in case I turn into Andrea Yates in a weak moment. I'll be just like Brooke Shields was after her first baby was born, except that I'll look like shit and I won't have the energy to write a book about it—and even if I do, no one will buy it.

Occasionally, I'll make desperate, weepy calls to friends, barely able to string enough words together to describe the feeling of walking around underwater, spaced out, stuck in some hazy existential crisis. My closest friends, who are childless, will sigh sympathetically, then hurry off the phone, depressed by the prospect of procreating. My friends who are moms will chuckle sympathetically, then hurry off the phone to prevent their toddler from sticking a fork into the nearest electrical outlet.

Now and then, I'll go out for a walk, lamprey in tow, just like I'm supposed to do. My lamprey will whine and then explode into tears, but I'll sally forth, determined to make it to the local coffee joint, even though I can't actually drink any coffee, since I'm breast-feeding and the caffeine is sure to give my lamprey ADHD or autism or asthma. I'll stumble over to the "child play area," which always seemed to be full of moms trading epidural stories when I worked there on my laptop—you know, back when I was a successful writer with a flourishing career and a life of endless promise stretching out before me. There'll be one mom there with a toddler and a camera-ready model baby, sleeping in its expensive stroller. She'll point out that I have my Baby Bjorn strapped on incorrectly, in a way that's known to increase the risk of suffocation. While she readjusts my Bjorn, she'll ask me polite questions about the lamprey sucking the life blood out of me, as if it's not strange at all, as if I'm not clearly starring in some sci-fi horror flick that ends badly.

Then she'll launch into her enthusiastic views of attachment parenting and other all-consuming child-rearing techniques that I know nothing about, other than the fact that they demand that mothers annihilate their egos and bend the laws of space and time in order to accommodate their children. While she talks, she'll begin unpacking a seemingly endless array of tiny Tupperware containers from her leather diaper bag, each housing a different organic, wheat-free, lactose-free snack, and she'll pull out several scent-free sanitary wipes and a sippy cup full of juice and a very expensive breast pump, and she'll (very discreetly) feed her very attractive baby with one breast while (efficiently and effectively) pumping the other breast, and she'll hand out small, tasty chunks of food to her toddler, all of them rich in Omega-3 and iron and vitamin C. Watching her will suddenly make me feel very faint, and my lamprey and I will hit the floor with a sickening thud that causes everyone in the entire coffee joint to turn their heads and gasp and vow never, ever to forsake their very promising and brilliant writing careers in order to procreate.

But things will get better for me a few months later, don't you worry! The lamprey will start sleeping for two-hour stretches at a time (What a luxury!), enough time for me to actually call my few remaining friends and tell them I can't make it to whatever fun-sounding event they're planning. I'll blame it all on the lamprey, of course, and I'll describe, in excruciating detail, how cute the lamprey's expressions are these days, especially when it has gas. I'll even check my e-mail, just like I did in the old days! Of course, once I get tired of reading old messages, I'll just delete them all and send out a group e-mail announcing that I can no longer be expected to return calls or e-mails in a timely fashion and I can't drive for more than three minutes without the lamprey crying (unless I sing "Farmer in the Dell" in a very happy, high voice, but that only buys me another two minutes), so anyone who wants to talk to me or see me will have to come to my house, where I'll be distracted constantly and will have one or the other of my bloated, pale, blue-vein-covered boobs out at all times.

In my e-mail, I'll explain that, yes, I recognize that some women in Africa only pause for half a second to give birth, and then they return to toil in the fields while their baby is raised by their 3-year-old or their grandmother or their dog, but that's only because those women have very mellow babies, not colicky, fussy little creatures like my lamprey, and besides, studies have shown that babies in Africa often develop emotional insecurity from being raised by their 3-year-old siblings, who also don't tend to notice when they're getting loose stools or eczema or painful rashes from their non-hypoallergenic burlap bedding. I will remind my friends that American children have the distinct advantage of being the center of their parents' universes, and without overzealous, overbearing helpings of attention and care, they'll never grow up to be neurotic, overachieving, ulcerous mutants that fit neatly into our society's soulless, workaholic culture.

It will feel good to reconnect with my dear friends through the convenience of a mass e-mail! But best of all, every week or so, I'll venture out of the house *without the lamprey*! I'll get to take luxurious half-hour strolls down to the pharmacy for more diaper rash cream. It will feel so nice to get away from home, every corner of which is now filled with brightly colored plastic devices and discarded butt wipes and little radios that play happy baby songs that make you want to beat someone's head in with a tire iron.

Sure, I'll sometimes wonder if the lamprey is still breathing without me there, watching it closely, monitoring its every breath. I'll picture my husband, dropping the lamprey on the floor and then tripping over it. I'll picture the dogs, fighting over the lamprey like a chew toy. And then, while I'm in line for the cashier, I'll catch a glimpse of that Vanity

Fair cover with Katie Holmes and Tom Cruise and that creepy, overstyled, wise little elf Suri tucked between them, the whole family looking painfully smug and rich and scary, and I'll break down sobbing and I won't be able to stop. I'll rush back home to the lamprey and I'll feel relieved that it's still alive, but I'll notice that it's got spit-up on its onesie and its diaper hasn't been changed, and I'll fly into a rage and accuse my husband of being a shitty father.

But things will get better after that, don't you worry! Eventually, I'll get divorced, and the lamprey will start to talk, babbling on about Teletubbies and Pokemon and other really tedious stuff, and then the lamprey will become a sullen big kid who proclaims that it's "bored" all the time, so I'll rush around to keep it busy and happy, and sooner than you know it, the lamprey will be an angry, temperamental teenager with a seriously overblown sense of its own importance. Finally, one day in the not-so-distant future, maybe after it has a particularly helpful therapy session, the lamprey will call me to tell me that, as part of its "healing process" it needs for me to understand that I was a crappy mother. On top of being seriously stupid and uncool, I was incredibly injurious to its sense of self, and I would've been a way better parent if I hadn't worried about it so much or driven it to piano lessons (which it fucking *hated*), because all of my energy and focus on it were just a total *nightmare* and *that's* why it was driven to drink and drive and shoot drugs and shoplift and catch venereal diseases from scary losers with gun collections and bad hair and corn-chip breath. When I start to get defensive, saying that maybe I made some mistakes, but really, all I wanted was to do my best and love my kid with all of my heart, the lamprey will scream that I don't understand anything—I never understood anything!—and then it'll hang up on me.

Several birthdays and holidays and Mother's Days will go by, unmarked, as I hobble around my cluttered, dusty, cat-filled house, but don't worry! Things will get better when I go to live in a nursing home, and my lamprey comes by one afternoon to introduce me to its lampreys (all grown up now), who seem to hate its guts almost as much as it hates my guts. And when the little (full-grown) lampreys cringe as they watch me unwrap and eat my apple sauce out of its plastic cup without the aid of my dentures, which are disinfecting in a glass by my adjustable bed, my lamprey will shoot me a sympathetic look. No, my darling lamprey won't say, "I'm sorry" or "I love you, Mom" or anything like that, but that look it gives me will more than make up for all of the pain and sacrifices I went through as a mother! I'll get a warm glow deep down inside, and I won't even feel bad later, when I discover that my antique gold watch and the roll of $20 bills I save for Bingo are both missing from my sock drawer.

To think, in just one month, the joys of motherhood begin at last! How blessed I feel, to be poised on the precipice of this wonderful new adventure!

———

Heather Havrilesky wrote this piece for the October 2, 2006, issue of *Salon* <www.salon.com>.

New Bill Would Defend Marriage from Sharks
FROM *THE ONION*

Senator Bill Frist (R-TN) introduced a controversial new bill Tuesday that would severely limit the ability of sharks to "mutilate the institution of marriage until it is completely unrecognizable."

"For too long, we've stood by as our most sacred institution has been thrashed, bit by bit, by these amoral predators," said Frist at a press conference, standing in front of a detailed diagram of a great white shark. "Marriage is a union between one man and one woman, and no shark should come between them with its powerful jaws and massive dorsal fin."

Bill S-691, also known as The Protection Of Marital Extremities Act, was co-sponsored by Mel Martinez (R-FL), who said that, as a devoted husband, he would not want his own 25-year marriage to be split to pieces by a shark, and hinted that opponents of the bill were in fact aiding the fish in their "murderous ways."

"Liberals and Democrats would have you believe that sharks pose no threat to married couples," Martinez said. "They tell us that sharks should just be left alone to mind their own business, and they won't do anyone any harm. But we say it's time for those of us with backbone to stand up for what we believe in—before that backbone is torn violently from our torsos by these soulless, underwater killers."

Added Martinez: "Marriage is a sacred institution, but it is also very fragile, especially when coming into contact with the saw-edged teeth of a bloodthirsty bull shark."

Frist said it was vital that Congress act sooner than later.

"Sharks can smell a healthy, vibrant marriage from miles away, and it doesn't matter whether the couple are celebrating their 50th anniversary or are on their honeymoon—no one is safe," Frist said. He then held up a photo of a lifeless, newly caught shark hanging behind a happily married couple, which he said was meant to show sharks everywhere that the U.S. government "means business."

"It's simply a matter of faith," Frist added. "And I have absolute faith that, if we do nothing, we'll see many more families torn apart."

Despite the fact that the bill calls for mandatory fines of up to $100,000 and a permanent designation on the Marriage Offenders National Registry for any shark found guilty under the new guidelines, some conservative groups still complain that it does not go far enough.

"This bill focuses too much on the species who have attacked marriage in the past, such as the hammerhead, oceanic whitetip, and tiger sharks, but we need protection against all sharks," said Nathan Comino, president of The Quint Group, a conservative anti-shark think tank. "Scientific evidence shows that the once-indifferent whale shark is now angrier than ever over holy matrimony. We can't afford to ignore the facts."

Critics also complained that the language in the bill regarding jellyfish was too vague, leaving a number of loopholes whereby they could escape prosecution.

According to recent polls, only 22 percent of voters who live in shark-infested areas on either of the country's coasts say they are "very worried" about the damage sharks could wreak on married couples, while that number jumps to 86 percent in more conservative, landlocked, regions of the South and Midwest—a statistic that opponents of the new bill are using to bolster their argument.

"Republicans are once again playing the fear card, squashing the potential progress this country could make by accepting sharks into the mainstream," said Eli Pariser, a member of the liberal group Move On. "Yes, sharks look different and act different. But that doesn't mean they shouldn't have the right to choose their own lifestyles and swim with married couples."

While opponents of anti-shark legislation have been vocal, some Democrats who say they support sharks' rights have been careful not to oppose the bill outright.

"I believe they should be able to swim and feed as they always have, but I do not condone sharks attacking marriage," Sen. John Kerry (D-MA) said. "This is an issue best left up to the individual states, whose residents know better than anyone which of their waters are safe to be married in."

Frist remained confident, however, that the bill would have support in the Senate.

"The endless onslaught from activist judges, liberal media, and sharks ends today," Frist said. "Nor have we forgotten the other threats marriage faces, and this bill sends an unmistakable message to rattlesnakes, mountain lions, and lightning that we are dead serious about protecting marriage."

This piece was published in the September 19, 2006, issue of the satirical newspaper *The Onion* <www.theonion.com>.

My Amendment

BY GEORGE SAUNDERS (2004)

As an obscure, middle-aged, heterosexual short-story writer, I am often asked, George, do you have any feelings about Same-Sex Marriage?

To which I answer, Actually, yes, I do.

Like any sane person, I am against Same-Sex Marriage, and in favor of a constitutional amendment to ban it.

To tell the truth, I feel that, in the interest of moral rigor, it is necessary for us to go a step further, which is why I would like to propose a supplementary constitutional amendment.

In the town where I live, I have frequently observed a phenomenon I have come to think of as Samish-Sex Marriage. Take, for example, K, a male friend of mine, of slight build, with a ponytail. K is married to S, a tall, stocky female with extremely short hair, almost a crewcut. Often, while watching K play with his own ponytail as S towers over him, I have wondered, Isn't it odd that this somewhat effeminate man should be married to this somewhat masculine woman? Is K not, on some level, imperfectly expressing a slight latent desire to be married to a man? And is not S, on some level, imperfectly expressing a slight latent desire to be married to a woman?

Then I ask myself, Is this truly what God had in mind?

Take the case of L, a female friend with a deep, booming voice. I have often found myself looking askance at her husband, H. Though H is basically pretty masculine, having neither a ponytail nor a tight feminine derriere like K, still I wonder: H, when you are having marital relations with L, and she calls out your name in that deep, booming, nearly male voice, and you continue having marital relations with her (i.e., you are not "turned off"), does this not imply that you, H, are, in fact, still "turned on"? And doesn't this indicate that, on some level, you, H, have a slight latent desire to make love to a man?

Or consider the case of T, a male friend with an extremely small penis. (We attend the same gym.) He is married to O, an average-looking woman who knows how to fix cars. I wonder about O. How does she know so much about cars? Is she not, by tolerating this non-car-fixing, short-penised friend of mine, indicating that, on some level, she wouldn't mind being married to a woman, and is therefore, perhaps, a tiny bit functionally gay?

And what about T? Doesn't the fact that T can stand there in the shower room at our gym, confidently towelling off his tiny unit, while O is at home changing their sparkplugs with alacrity, indicate that it is only a short stroll down a slippery slope before he is completely happy being the "girl" in their relationship, from which it is only a small fey hop down the same slope before T is happily married to another man, perhaps my car mechanic, a handsome Portuguese fellow I shall refer to as J?

Because my feeling is, when God made man and woman He had something very specific in mind. It goes without saying that He did not want men marrying men, or women marrying women, but also what He did not want, in my view, was feminine men marrying masculine women.

Which is why I developed my Manly Scale of Absolute Gender.

Using my Scale, which assigns numerical values according to a set of masculine and feminine characteristics, it is now easy to determine how Manly a man is and how Fem a woman is, and therefore how close to a Samish-Sex Marriage a given marriage is.

Here's how it works. Say we determine that a man is an 8 on the Manly Scale, with 10 being the most Manly of all and 0 basically a Neuter. And say we determine that his fiancee is a –6 on the Manly Scale, with a –10 being the most Fem of all. Calculating the difference between the man's rating and the woman's rating—the Gender Differential—

we see that this proposed union is not, in fact, a Samish-Sex Marriage, which I have defined as "any marriage for which the Gender Differential is less than or equal to 10 points."

Friends whom I have identified as being in Samish-Sex Marriages often ask me, George, given that we have scored poorly, what exactly would you have us do about it?

Well, one solution I have proposed is divorce—divorce followed by remarriage to a more suitable partner. K, for example, could marry a voluptuous high-voiced N.F.L. cheerleader, who would more than offset his tight feminine derriere, while his ex-wife, S, might choose to become involved with a lumberjack with very large arms, thereby neutralizing her thick calves and faint mustache.

Another, and of course preferable, solution would be to repair the existing marriage, converting it from a Samish-Sex Marriage to a healthy Normal Marriage, by having the feminine man become more masculine and/or the masculine woman become more feminine.

Often, when I propose this, my friends become surly. How dare I, they ask. What business is it of mine? Do I think it is easy to change in such a profound way?

To which I say, It is not easy to change, but it is possible.

I know, because I have done it.

When young, I had a tendency to speak too quickly, while gesturing too much with my hands. Also, my opinions were unfirm. I was constantly contradicting myself in that fast voice, while gesturing like a girl. Also, I cried often. Things seemed so sad. I had long blond hair, and liked it. My hair was layered and fell down across my shoulders, and, I admit it, I would sometimes slow down when passing a shop window to look at it, to look at my hair! I had a strange constant feeling of being happy to be alive. This feeling of infinite possibility sometimes caused me to laugh when alone, or even, on occasion, to literally skip down the street, before pausing in front of a shop window and giving my beautiful hair a cavalier toss.

To tell the truth, I do not think I would have scored very high on my Manly Scale, if the Scale had been invented at that time, by me. I suspect I would have scored so Fem on the test that I would have been prohibited from marrying my wife, P, the love of my life. And I think, somewhere in my heart, I knew that.

I knew I was too Fem.

So what did I do about it? Did I complain? Did I whine? Did I expect activist judges to step in on my behalf, manipulating the system to accommodate my peculiarity?

No, I did not.

What I did was I changed. I undertook what I like to think of as a classic American project of self-improvement. I made videos of myself talking, and studied these, and in time succeeded in training myself to speak more slowly, while almost never moving my hands. Now, if you ever meet me, you will observe that I always speak in an extremely slow and manly and almost painfully deliberate way, with my hands either driven deep into my pockets or held stock-still at the ends of my arms, which are bent slightly at the elbows, as if I were ready to respond to the slightest provocation by punching you in the face. As for my opinions, they are very firm. I rarely change them. When I feel like skipping, I absolutely do not skip. As for my long beautiful hair—well, I am lucky, in that I am rapidly going bald. Every month, when I recalculate my ranking on the Manly Scale, I find myself becoming more and more Manly, as my hair gets thinner and my girth increases, thickening my once lithe, almost girlish physique, thus insuring the continuing morality and legality of my marriage to P.

My point is simply this: If I was able to effect these tremendous positive changes in my life, to avoid finding myself in the moral/legal quagmire of a Samish-Sex Marriage, why can't K, S, L, H, T, and O do the same?

I implore any of my readers who find themselves in a Samish-Sex Marriage: Change. If you are a feminine man, become more manly. If you are a masculine woman, become more feminine. If you are a woman and are thick-necked or lumbering, or have ever had the slightest feeling of attraction to a man who is somewhat pale and fey, deny these feelings and, in a spirit of self-correction, try to become more thin-necked and light-footed, while, if you find it helpful, watching videos of naked masculine men, to sort of retrain yourself in the proper mode of attraction. If you are a man and, upon seeing a thick-waisted, athletic young woman walking with a quasi-mannish gait through your local grocery, you imagine yourself in a passionate embrace with her, in your car, a car that is parked just outside, and which is suddenly, in your imagination, full of the smell of her fresh young breath—well, stop thinking that! Are you a man or not?

I, for one, am sick and tired of this creeping national tendency to let certain types of people take advantage of our national good nature by marrying individuals who are essentially of their own gender. If this trend continues, before long our towns and cities will be full of people like K, S, L, H, T, and O, people "asserting their rights" by dating, falling in love with, marrying, and spending the rest of their lives with whomever they please.

I, for one, am not about to stand by and let that happen.

Because then what will we have? A nation ruled by the anarchy of unconstrained desire. A nation of willful human hearts, each lurching this way and that and reaching out for whatever it spontaneously desires, trying desperately to find some comforting temporary shred of warmth in a mostly cold world, totally unconcerned about the external form in which that other, long-desired heart is embodied.

That is not the kind of world in which I wish to live.

I, for one, intend to become ever more firmly male, enjoying my golden years, while watching P become ever more female, each of us vigilant for any hint of ambiguity in the other.

And as our children grow, should they begin to show the slightest hint of some lingering residue of the opposite gender, P and I will lovingly pull them aside and list all the particulars by which we were able to identify their unintentional deficiency.

Then, together, we will devise a suitable correction.

And, in this way, the race will go on.

George Saunders, who teaches creative writing at Syracuse University, has published two collections of stories, *Pastoralia* and *CivilWarLand in Bad Decline,* and a children's story, *The Very Persistent Gappers of Frip.* This essay appeared in the March 8, 2004, edition of *The New Yorker* <www.newyorker.com>.

Dropping the F-Bomb

BY JOEL ACHENBACH (2006)

The most versatile word in our language can do almost anything, other than be printed in a family newspaper. It can be a noun, a verb, a gerund, an adjective or just an expletive. It can be literal or figurative. Although it has an explicit sexual meaning, it's usually used figuratively these days, as an all-purpose intensifier.

The F-word remains taboo. But just barely. We may be entering an era in which this fabled vulgarity is on its way to becoming just another word—its transgressive energy steadily sapped by overuse.

From hip-hop artists to bloggers to the vice president of the United States, everyone's dropping the F-bomb. Young people in particular may not grasp how special this word has been in the past. They may not realize how, like an old sourdough starter, the word has been lovingly preserved over the centuries and passed from generation to generation. For the good of human communication we must come together, as a people, to protect this word, and ensure that, years from now, it remains obscene.

Our leaders aren't helping. Before he was elected president, George W. Bush used the word repeatedly during an interview with Tucker Carlson. Dick Cheney on the Senate floor told a Democratic senator to *eff* himself. Presidential candidate John F. Kerry said of Bush and the war, "Did I expect George Bush to [mess] it up as badly as he did? I don't think anybody did." No one is shocked that these people use such language, but as statesmanship it's not exactly Lincolnesque.

More generally, the word is imperiled by the profusion of communications technologies. Everyone's talking, e-mailing, blogging and commenting on everyone else's comments. Combine that with partisan rancor and a general desperation to get one's message across, and naturally the word gets overtaxed. In Blogworld there are no idiots anymore, only [blithering] idiots. The most opportunistic move in the corporate realm may have been the decision by a retailer to call itself French Connection United Kingdom, which allowed it to put the company's initials on T-shirts everywhere. Jeepers, that's clever!

I don't want to make a federal case out of all of this—but that's what the government is doing. The Federal Communications Commission in recent years has cracked down on "indecency" in general and this word specifically. The FCC's fines for indecency have risen steadily: a mere $4,000 in 1995, then $48,000 in 2000, then $440,000 in 2003 and finally a whopping $7.9 million in 2004. President Bush signed a bill last week increasing by tenfold the maximum fine for indecency on radio or TV, to $325,000. Broadcasters have sued to overturn recent FCC rulings, arguing that broadcasters shouldn't have to abide by laws that don't affect cable and satellite providers (which is why HBO's "Deadwood" can clock, by one Web site's calculation, 1.48 F-words per minute). The inability to be indecent is, for broadcasters, a competitive disadvantage.

In any case, government fines for indecency are something of a rearguard action, unlikely to stem the tide. It's like trying to fight rising sea levels one sandbag at a time.

A landmark case revolves around the word used by Bono, the rock star, at the 2003 Golden Globe Awards. He blurted out that winning an award was "[bleepin'] brilliant." The FCC first ruled that his comment wasn't indecent, because it didn't describe a sexual act. But in 2004, after the Janet Jackson breast exposure during the Super Bowl half-time show, the commission reversed the Bono ruling, saying the singer's comment was indeed profane and indecent.

The FCC's logic, however, was a stretch. It argued that any use of the word "inherently has a sexual connotation." But that's just not true. In fact, the reason it is used so often is because it has escaped the bonds of its sexual origin. It's now used as a generic intensifier. It makes plain language more colorful and emphatic.

The reason it must be suppressed in polite society is not because it's a bad word, but because, in certain circumstances, it is a very good word. It is a solidly built word of just four letters, bracketed by rock-hard consonants. It is not a mushy word, but one with sharp edges. Consider how clunky the term "the F-word" is. The authentic article, by contrast, explodes into space from a gate formed by the upper incisors and the lower lip. Then it slams to a dramatic glottal cough.

I'd even argue that it has therapeutic properties. Ponder, if you will, how critically important this word can be when you stub a toe. It serves as an instant palliative. It's like verbal morphine. You can't hop around the dining room, holding your foot, shouting "Drat!" or "Dagnabbit!" or "Heavens to Betsy!" Those words don't work.

"It's a sexual word in origin but it's not used that way very often," says Jesse Sheidlower, editor at large of the Oxford English Dictionary and editor of the 1995 book "The F-Word," a 224-page dictionary in which some of the permutations of the word are absofreakin'lutely ridiculous.

"It does not have the sting that it used to," he says. "For young people, it just doesn't have that much power for them."

The word has been around since at least the 15th century. The English word with which we are familiar is related to similar words found in the Germanic languages, such as Dutch, Norwegian, Swedish and German. These words meant "to thrust" or "to strike" or "to copulate." The first known printed appearance, Sheidlower says, comes from a text around 1475, in a poem that more or less said the monks of Cambridge did not go to heaven because of their sexual dalliances with women. For the next four centuries it was almost always used in a literal sexual sense. The figurative uses so common today didn't arise until the late 19th century, Sheidlower says.

The word was not openly printed in the United States until 1926, when it appeared once in Howard Vincent O'Brien's memoir "Wine, Women and War," according to Sheidlower's book. After World War II, writer Norman Mailer negotiated his way around the taboo by using the made-up word "fug" in the dialogue of the book "The Naked and the Dead." This spring, Andrew Crocker, a Harvard senior, turned in his thesis on the use of the word in post-World War II America, and he relates the famous story that Tallulah Bankhead (or, in some tellings, Dorothy Parker, or Mae West) said to Mailer at a cocktail party, "So you're the man who can't spell f—." Nice line, though Crocker says it's apocryphal.

James Jones used the word in his 1951 novel "From Here to Eternity." Like Mailer, Jones was reflecting the speech of American soldiers during the war. This point is key: The word was routinely used by real people, it just was rarely published and never broadcast. It was still taboo.

Liberating the word became a dubious triumph of the 1960s counterculture. At Woodstock, Country Joe and the Fish led a rousing cheer that began with "Give me an F!" and continued on through "K," finally asking, "What's that spell?" Now it sounds silly. Wow. They said a bad word out loud! What revolutionaries!

Soon, the word became common in popular culture, but still retained some of its sizzle. Consider the classic line by Otter in the 1978 movie "Animal House" after the fraternity brothers have wrecked Flounder's car: "Flounder, you can't spend your whole life worrying about your mistakes! You [effed] up—you trusted us!" Drift a few years forward to 1989, and Spike Lee's "Do the Right Thing," and the word gets a real workout in the mouth of Sal, who at one point uses it six times in the space of five sentences.

Today it still has enough power to be memorable, as when Jack and Miles in the movie "Sideways" discuss the possibility of drinking merlot:

Jack: "If they want to drink merlot, we're drinking merlot."

Miles: "No, if anyone orders merlot, I'm leaving. I am NOT drinking any [expletive deleted] merlot!"

Just to clarify: This is funny not because Miles used a bad word, but because of the juxtaposition of the bad word with the one that follows. We do not expect to hear a person express such strong feelings—to the point of vulgarity—when discussing a particular kind of grape.

We must not overharvest the swear words that are part of the commons of our language. It is an adults-only commons, of course. Kids need to be told that they still can't use it. How can a 13-year-old be transgressively vulgar with the word if his 5-year-old sister already uses it? This word is supposed to be a reward of adulthood. We have to conserve it, so that our children and our children's children can use it when we're gone.

There is a wonderful scene in the 1987 movie "Hope and Glory." A gang of boys is rambling through the rubble of London during the Blitz. The new boy, Bill, wants to join. They ask if he knows any swear words. He says he does. Say them, the boys insist. He hesitates. He admits finally that he knows only one swear word. After much delay and agonizing, he says it, loudly.

The word.

The other boys are shocked into silence. "That word is special," the gang leader finally says. "That word is only for something really important."

Precisely.

———

Joel Achenbach is a staff writer for the *Washington Post* magazine. This piece appeared in the June 25, 2006, edition of the *Post* <www.washingtonpost.com>.

Swearing Off Swearing

BY RICK REILLY (2006)

You and I have the same problem. We swear too goddam much.

Growing up, the worst my mom ever said was, "Crying in the beer bucket!" Still have no idea what it meant, but it was serious. She said cursing was "for the locker room." Man, she wouldn't believe how big the locker room is now.

I realized it a couple of weeks ago at the Colorado-Colorado State football game. The two student sections cursed like teamsters in two-sizes-too-small thongs.

They yelled, "F— 'em up! F— 'em up! Go CU!" They sang, "Bullllls—!" at a ref's call. And they chanted, "F–you, CSU!" (Clap-clap, clap-clap-clap!) And that was their clever stuff.

No student seemed to be able to pass a rival in the concourse without hurling a "F— you!" in the other's ear, accompanied by twin birds and projectile spittle. (And, really, some of the men were just as bad.)

It's not just Colorado. We have become a nation of !@#$%&ers. Michigan hockey fans serenade each opponent sent to the penalty box with a dozen elegant words: "Chump! D—! Wuss! Douche bag! A—— ! P— ! Cheater! Bitch! Whore! Slut! C———!"

Higher education at its finest.

That's why I'm all for what they're doing at Boston University. Beginning this season, anybody who cusses at a BU home athletic event gets pitched out of the arena. "We had to do something," says hockey coach Jack Parker. "People are telling me they're afraid to bring their kids to games."

It's not going to be easy making BU hockey fans give up swearing. It's like asking frogs to give up flies or R Kelly 15-year-olds. Not only that, but how will the Terriers play games with only three players left on the ice? "I just hope an usher doesn't come down and get me," says Parker.

Athletic director Mike Lynch and dean of students Kenneth Elmore decided something had to be done after BU fans cursed a blue streak during last spring's NCAA hockey tournament. Now the school will station cuss cops—officials, ushers, even Lynch—all over Agganis Arena's infamous section 118. "They're trying to censor us," says Nick Williams, sports editor of the student paper. "I feel like it limits my freedom of speech."

What the students are mad about is losing their favorite chant, which they yell 25 times a game, no matter whom they're playing: "F— 'em up! F— 'em up! BC sucks!" That's a speech?

Besides, until the last decade, it was "Rough 'em up! Rough 'em up! BC sucks!" according to former BU and Olympic star Mike Eruzione, who asks, "Is it too much to show a little class?"

At least BU has the guts to do something. Maryland's students would make George Carlin blush, but the university still lets them work blue. The best university president C.D. Mote could do was write a sternly worded letter to the student paper that said: "Use of profanity will change when our students decide to change it." Great point, C.D.! Even better, let's make the little darlings drop a nickel in a jar every time they swear!

I'm no better. I'm cursed with cursing. I hate myself for it not just because it's disgusting but also because it's just so unimaginative. When I shank one, I yell, "Son of a f— whore!" I wish I could be like my buddy, who yells, "My heinous cousin!" Only his cousin can take offense.

Isn't it more fun to spew something fresher than the same old, "Go f— yourself!"? Any Raiders fan could've scrawled that on his cell wall. Why not, "May you suffer a severe groin injury not covered in your workman's compensation package!"

Thanks to the book *Cuss Control*, by James V. O'Connor, director of (this is true) the Cuss Control Academy, I'm making progress. According to O'Connor, I should use words that sound like cusses but aren't. I've tried "That was Bolshevik, pal!" and "You nickerfutz, ref!" and "Sock-chucker!" People look at you as if they've been stabbed but can't find any blood.

You could always unearth a dead language, like Sanskrit or Latin: illigitimi! (Bastards!) Or steal from the 1920s: "Great oogoly moogoly!" Or go edgy Amish: "You son of a biscuit!"

If those don't work, O'Connor says to pretend your grandma is listening. Hey, Michigan students, would you repeat what you just said? Your granny missed it.

Anyway, the world is ugly enough without us turning on each other. So good for you, BU. Because, really, this s— has got to stop.

(Oops. Sorry, Mom.)

Rick Reilly wrote this piece for the September 25, 2006, issue of *Sports Illustrated* <www. si.com>.

The Lady or the Tiger
BY CHUCK KLOSTERMAN (2003)

It's no secret that cold cereal was invented to help nineteenth-century Victorians stifle their rampant sexual desires. Any breakfast historian can tell you that. Sylvester Graham (1794–1851), a so-called "philosopher and nutrition crusader," was the kind of forward-thinking wackmobile who saw an indisputable connection between a person's decadence and their eating habits; this was partially augmented by his perception that the medical profession was wicked. "Disease is never the legitimate result of the normal operations of any of our organs," he wrote, a sentiment that would eventually spawn the creation of Quisp.

Mr. Graham suspected that bad food and inappropriate sexual desires—particularly masturbation—were the true cause of every major illness. This made the cure for all sickness relatively simple: sexual moderation (i.e., less than thirteen orgasms a year for married couples, which actually seems reasonable), daily exercise, and a proper diet.

By 1840, Graham's career was in shambles; this does not seem altogether surprising, considering he was insane. However, his well-argued insanity influenced a New Yorker named James Caleb Jackson, and Jackson embraced Graham's philosophy on his way toward creating a bad-tasting wafer out of graham flour and water. He called his food "Granula" (a precursor to Granola). Jackson was force-feeding his wretched Granula in his Dansville, New York, sanitarium when it was discovered by Ellen Harmon White, a Seventh-Day Adventist. She adopted the idea and started her own sanitarium in Battle Creek, Michigan, in 1866. In need of a staff doctor, White hired a scrappy young physician named John Harvey Kellogg. John hired his brother, William, as clerk of the institute.

John Kellogg was also a disciple of the Graham philosophy and agreed that a flavorless, grain-based food was precisely what America needed. By 1902, he had conjured a way to produce flake cereal—the ideal medium for a crunchy, soulless pabulum. He tried to make wheat flakes, but the technology for such a innovation did not yet exist. Corn flakes, however, worked swimmingly.

Initially developed for scientific purposes, corn flakes struck the brothers Kellogg as a savvy business opportunity. This crispy treat seemed perfect for a society assumedly filled with oversexed, disease-ridden lunatics. And while selling cereal made money, it also raised ethical dilemmas: The angelic White was devastated that the Kelloggs were making money from a food designed to improve human purity. Meanwhile, John Kellogg was upset that his brother added sugar to the flake recipe to improve sales, a supplement he believed would liberate the public libido and turn every corn flake aficionado into a raging sexaholic. The Kellogg brothers eventually sued one another. After winning the lawsuit, William Kellogg took control of the enterprise; his puritan brother remained a stockholder.

Years later, a trio of Rastafarian elves would promote puffed rice.

Today, few members of the scientific community see a close connection between cold cereal and sex, although advertisers still did in the 1950s. Early Corn Flakes commercials showed Superman eating cereal with Jimmy Olsen, but never with Lois Lane; this was to keep viewers from inferring that Superman and Lois Lane had spent the night together (evidently, the notion of Superman and Jimmy Olsen having a homosexual relationship was not a concern). However, sex is not the central theme to modern cereal advertising. In fact, selling cereal is not the central theme to cereal advertising. Saturday morning commercials for all the best cereals are teaching kids how to figure out what's cool. They're the first step in the indoctrination of future hipsters: Cereal commercials teach us that anything desirable is supposed to be exclusionary.

An inordinate number of cereal commercials are based on the premise that a given cereal is so delicious that a fictional creature would want to steal it. We are presented with this scenario time and time again. The most obvious is the Trix Rabbit, a tragic figure whose doomed existence is not unlike that of Sisyphus. Since the cereal's inception, the rabbit—often marginalized as "silly"—has never been allowed to enjoy even one bowl of his favorite foodstuff, and the explanation for this embargo smacks of both age discrimination and racism (we are to accept that Trix is reserved exclusively "for kids").[1]

An even sadder illustration of cereal segregation is Sonny the Cuckoo Bird, arguably the most tortured member of the advertising community. Sonny is plagued with self-loathing; though outspokenly *otaku* for Cocoa Puffs, he doesn't feel he deserves to consume them. Sonny will do anything to escape from his jones, including (but not limited to) locking himself into a primitive skycycle and shooting himself into outer space. To make matters worse, he is bombarded by temptation: Random children endlessly taunt him with heaping bowls of C-Puffs, almost like street junkies waving heroin needles in the face of William S. Burroughs. The kids have cereal, and Sonny does not. Translation: The kids are cool, and Sonny's an extremist and a failure. And as long as they possess what he does not, Sonny shall remain a second-class phoenix, doomed by his own maniacal ambition for breakfast.

Commercials for Lucky Charms star a leprechaun who replaced the pot of gold at the end of the rainbow with a bowl of marshmallow-laden cereal, a narrative device that

---

1. Proof that America is ultimately a sympathetic nation surfaced in 1976, when a consumer election sponsored by General Mills indicated that over 99 percent of Trix eaters felt the flamboyant six-foot rabbit deserved a bowl of Trix, which places his approval rating on par with Colin Powell in 1996.

slightly overstated the value of the actual product. The Cookie Crisp[2] mascot was a masked rapscallion named "Crook," whose whole self-identity was built on stealing cereal. In ads for both Cocoa and Fruity Pebbles, Barney Rubble went to ridiculous lengths in the hope of shoplifting Fred Flintstone's breakfast, occasionally dressing like a woman and/or rapping like Ghostface Killah. Time and time again, commercials for cereal assault children with the same theme: A product's exclusivity is directly proportional to its social cachet, which is the definition of calculated adult coolness.

When I say *calculated adult coolness*, I'm referring to the kind of coolness that generally applies to people between the ages of nineteen and thirty-six. This is different than *mainstream teen coolness* and *aging hipster default coolness*, both of which reflect an opposing (and sort of pathetic) consumer aesthetic. Cereal ads are directed at kids, but they barely work on young people; the kind of advertising that works on a teenager are bandwagon spots for things like Trident and khaki Gap pants. Those ads imply that these are products everybody else already owns. Teenagers claim they want to be cool, but they mostly just want to avoid being uncool. It's the same for aging hipsters, an equally terrified class of Americans who slowly conclude that the key to staying relevant is by exhibiting default appreciation for the most obvious youth culture entities; this is why you often hear forty-seven-year-old men with ponytails saying things like, "Oh, I'm totally into the new stuff. That new Nickelback record is just terrific." Aging hipsters and corduroy-clad high school sophomores are both primarily concerned with dodging lameness. However, there is a stretch in everyone's early adulthood where they can choose (or choose against) creating their own personalized version of nonpopulist cool, which may (or may not) succeed. This is accomplished by embracing semioriginal, semielitist cultural artifacts that remain just out of reach to those who desire them—the so-called "Cocoa Puffs of Power."

We all relate to Sonny the Cuckoo Bird. We pursue that which retreats from us, and coolness is always a bear market. Coolness is always what others seem to have naturally—an unspecific, delicious, chocolately paradigm we must pilfer through subterfuge. It drives us, for lack of a better term, coo coo. And part of the reason we struggle is because there is no hard-and-fast clarity about what qualifies anything as *cool*. It needs to be original, but only semioriginal: It would be legitimately inventive (and kind of "out there") to

---

2. This is not to be confused with the short-lived Oatmeal Cookie Crisp, a cereal fronted by the good-natured wizard "Cookie Jarvis."

casually walk around with the petrified skull of a orangutan under your arm for no obvious reason, but this would only seem cool to a select class of performance artist. A better choice would be a T-shirt featuring the cast of *After M*A*S*H*. A cool image also needs to be semielitist, but it can't be *wholly* elitist: What you display should be extremely hard to find, yet could have been *theoretically* found by absolutely *anyone* six months ago (had they possessed the foresight). This is why calculated adult coolness would reward the possession of, say, a can of Elf soda pop, yet frown upon the possession of, say, four ounces of weapons-grade uranium.[3]

The impact of this understanding comes later in life, usually at college, and usually around the point when being "weird" starts to be periodically interpreted by others as "charming" and/or "sexually intriguing." As noted earlier, kids don't really understand the nuance of cereal advertising until they reach their twenties; this is when characters like the Trix Rabbit evolve into understated Christ figures. And though the plot is not purposeful on the behalf of cereal makers, it's also not accidental. Cereal mascots are generally associated with sugared cereals—while a box of Wheaties might feature anyone from Bruce Jenner to Michelle Kwan, Count Chocula sticks with its mischievous vampire. Super Golden Crisp sells itself with the portrait of a laid-back bear wearing a mock turtleneck; Grape Nuts sells itself with a photograph of Grape Nuts. And this is more proof of cereal's overlooked relationship to American cool: Being cool is mostly ridiculous, and so is sugared cereal. That's why we like it.

I eat sugared cereal almost exclusively. This is because I'm the opposite of a "no-nonsense" guy. I'm an "all-nonsense" guy. Every time I drive a long distance, I'm hounded by the fear that I will get a flat tire and be unable to change it. When a button falls off one of my dress shirts, I immediately throw away the entire garment and buy a new one. I can't swim; to me, twelve feet of water is no different than twelve feet of hydrochloric acid (it will kill me just as dead). However, I *can* stay awake for seventy-two straight hours. I *can* immediately memorize phone numbers without writing them down. When flipping channels during commercial breaks in televised sporting events, I *can* innately sense the perfect moment to return to what I was watching originally. So the rub is that I have these semicritical flaws and I have these weirdly specific gifts, and it seems like most Americans are similarly polarized by what they can (and cannot) do. There are

---

3. Although this would make you very cool in Syria.

no-nonsense people, and there are nonsense people. And it's been my experience that nonsense people tend to consume Cocoa Krispies and Lucky Charms and Cap'n Crunch ("nonsense food," if you will). Consequently, we nonsense types spend hours and hours staring at cardboard creatures like the Trix Rabbit and absorbing his ethos, slowly ingesting the principles of exclusionary coolness while rapidly ingesting sugar-saturated spoonfuls of Vitamin B-12.

The desire to be cool is—ultimately—the desire to be rescued. It's the desire to be pulled from the unwashed masses of society. It's the desire to be advanced beyond the faceless humanoid robots who will die unheralded deaths and never truly matter, mostly because they all lived the same pedestrian life. Without the spoils of exclusionary coolness, we're just cogs in the struggle. We're like a little kid trying to kayak (or perhaps freestyle rock climb), and all the older kids keep mocking our efforts, openly implying that we cannot compete. But if we can just find that one cool thing that nobody else has—that gregarious, nine-foot animated jungle cat who can provide a glimmer of hope and a balanced breakfast—we can be better than ourselves. *We can be tigers.* 'Atta boy.

FROM READING TO WRITING

1. What makes humor a useful tool for getting people to think and talk about difficult or uncomfortable subjects? Are there issues that we should never use humor to discuss? Explain, using at least two of the essays from this chapter in your response.

2. Define "satire" and explain why satirical writing lends itself so well to discussions of public issues. What makes a satire effective?

3. Choose one essay in this chapter that you found to be funny and explain why it was humorous. Be specific in your response.

4. Choose one of the following essays and answer these questions about it: what is the author's argument? How does humor work in the essay? Is the argument is effective? Refer to specific passages from the essay in your response.
   a. "Pay Attention"
   b. "Chicken in the Henhouse"
   c. "My Amendment"
   d. "Dropping the F-Bomb"
   e. "The Lady or the Tiger"

5. Is "Mommy Fearest" funny? Explain.

Chapter 10

ARGUMENTS BY GENRE

A Matter of Definition: What Makes a Civil War, and Who Declares It So?

BY EDWARD WONG (2006)

Is Iraq in a civil war?

Though the Bush administration continues to insist that it is not, a growing number of American and Iraqi scholars, leaders and policy analysts say the fighting in Iraq meets the standard definition of civil war.

The common scholarly definition has two main criteria. The first says that the warring groups must be from the same country and fighting for control of the political center, control over a separatist state or to force a major change in policy. The second says that at least 1,000 people must have been killed in total, with at least 100 from each side.

American professors who specialize in the study of civil wars say that most of their number are in agreement that Iraq's conflict is a civil war.

"I think that at this time, and for some time now, the level of violence in Iraq meets the definition of civil war that any reasonable person would have," said James Fearon, a political scientist at Stanford.

While the term is broad enough to include many kinds of conflicts, one of the sides in a civil war is almost always a sovereign government. So some scholars now say civil war began when the Americans transferred sovereignty to an appointed Iraqi government in

June 2004. That officially transformed the anti-American war into one of insurgent groups seeking to regain power for disenfranchised Sunni Arabs against an Iraqi government led by Prime Minister Ayad Allawi and increasingly dominated by Shiites.

Others say the civil war began this year, after the bombing of a revered Shiite shrine in Samarra set off a chain of revenge killings that left hundreds dead over five days and has yet to end. Mr. Allawi proclaimed a month after that bombing that Iraq was mired in a civil war. "If this is not civil war, then God knows what civil war is," he said.

Many insurgencies and ethnic or sectarian wars are also civil wars. Vietnam and Lebanon are examples. Scholars say the Iraq civil war has elements of both an insurgency—one side is struggling to topple what it sees as an illegitimate national government—and a sectarian war—the besieged government is ruled by Shiites and opposed by Sunni Arabs.

In Iraq, sectarian purges and Sunni-Shiite revenge killings have become a hallmark of the fighting, but the cycles of violence are ignited by militia leaders who have political goals. The former Yugoslav president, Slobodan Milosovic, did this during the wars in the Balkans.

The civil strife in Iraq largely takes place in mixed Sunni-Shiite areas that include the cities of Baghdad, Mosul and Baquba. In Anbar Province, which is overwhelming Sunni Arab, much of the violence is aimed at American troops. Large swaths of Iraq have little violence, but those areas are relatively homogenous and have few people.

Governments and people embroiled in a civil war often do not want to label it as such. In Colombia, officials insisted for years that the rebels there were merely bandits.

Some Bush administration officials have argued that there is no obvious political vision on the part of the Sunni-led insurgent groups, so "civil war" does not apply.

In the United States, the debate over the term rages because many politicians, especially those who support the war, believe there would be domestic political implications to declaring it a civil war. They fear that an acknowledgment by the White House and its allies would be seen as an admission of a failure of President Bush's Iraq policy.

They also worry that the American people might not see a role for American troops in an Iraqi civil war and would more loudly demand a withdrawal.

But in fact, many scholars say the bloodshed here already puts Iraq in the top ranks of the civil wars of the last half-century. The carnage of recent days—beginning with bombings on Thursday in a Shiite district of Baghdad that killed more than 200 people—reinforces their assertion.

Mr. Fearon and a colleague at Stanford, David D. Laitin, say the deaths per year in Iraq, with at least 50,000 reportedly killed since March 2003, place this conflict on par with wars in Burundi and Bosnia.

Iraq's president and prime minister avoid using the term, but many Iraqis say extremists have thrust the country into civil war, even as moderates have struggled to pull back from the brink.

"You need to let the world know there's a civil war here in Iraq," said Adel Ibrahim, 44, a sheik in the Subiah tribe, which is mostly Shiite. "It's a crushing civil war. Mortars kill children in our neighborhoods. We're afraid to travel anywhere because we'll be killed in buses. We don't know who is our enemy and who is our friend."

The spiraling bloodshed here bolsters arguments that this is a civil war. A United Nations report released Wednesday said at least 3,709 Iraqis were killed in October, the highest of any month since the American-led invasion. More than 100,000 Iraqis a month are fleeing to Syria and Jordan.

"It's stunning; it should have been called a civil war a long time ago, but now I don't see how people can avoid calling it a civil war," said Nicholas Sambanis, a political scientist at Yale who co-edited "Understanding Civil War: Evidence and Analysis," published by the World Bank in 2005. "The level of violence is so extreme that it far surpasses most civil wars since 1945."

Among scholars, "there's a consensus," Mr. Sambanis said. Scholars in the United States generally agree that there have been at least 100 civil wars since 1945. At the smaller end of the scale is the war in Northern Ireland. Measured by total killed, the largest modern civil wars were in Angola, Afghanistan, Nigeria, China and Rwanda.

However, there are some dissenting historians on the definition of civil war, and whether it applies to Iraq. John Keegan, the British writer of war histories, finds only five clear-cut cases, starting with the English civil war of the 17th century through to the Lebanese war of the 20th century. His criteria are that the feuding groups must be vying for national authority, have leaders who publicly announce what they are fighting for and clash in set-piece battles while wearing uniforms, among other things. He argues in the December issue of Prospect magazine that Iraq is therefore not in civil war.

On Friday, Scott Stanzel, a White House spokesman, insisted that the Iraq conflict was not civil war, noting that Iraq's top leaders had agreed with that assessment. Last month, Tony Snow, the chief spokesman for President Bush, acknowledged that there were many groups trying to undermine the government, but said that there was no civil war because "it's not clear that they are operating as a unified force. You don't have a clearly identifiable leader."

By contrast, Sen. Joseph R. Biden Jr., the top Democrat on the Senate Foreign Relations Committee, said on Fox News in September that "a political solution is necessary to end the civil war in Iraq."

In 2003, at the start of the Sunni-led insurgency, Bush administration officials called the guerrillas "dead-enders" and insisted their only goal was to sow chaos. Now, American commanders acknowledge that political dominance is at the heart of this conflict.

In Congressional testimony this month, Lt. Gen. Michael D. Maples of the Defense Intelligence Agency characterized the situation as an "ongoing, violent struggle for power" and said the country was moving closer to a "significant breakdown of central authority."

Many Iraqis and Americans who have tracked the insurgency say it has been strongly shaped by former Baath Party members who want to keep Shiites from taking power. Even the newer jihadist groups have articulated political goals on Web sites—most notably to establish a Sunni-ruled Islamic caliphate.

"There was a whole regime that ruled this country for 35 years," said Mahmoud Othman, a senior Kurdish legislator. "Now they've gone underground. This is the main body of the resistance."

Scholars say it is crucial that policy makers and news media organizations recognize the Iraq conflict as a civil war.

"Why should we care how it is defined, if we all agree that the violence is unacceptable?" asked Mr. Laitin, the Stanford professor. "Here is my answer: There is a scientific community that studies civil wars, and understands their dynamics and how they, in general, end. This research is valuable to our nation's security."

—Reporting was contributed by Qais Mizher from Baghdad,
and by Mark Mazzetti, Jim Rutenberg and Kate Zernike from Washington.

————

Edward Wong wrote this piece for the November 26, 2006, edition of *The New York Times* <www.nytimes.com>.

DEFINITIONAL ARGUMENT

Planet Politics: How I Tried—and Failed—to Save Pluto

BY OWEN GINGERICH (2006)

Naming has always been a tricky business in astronomy. When Galileo discovered four "planets" accompanying Jupiter, he intended to name them "Medicean stars," after his hoped-for patron. He got the job, but lost on the names. Kepler introduced the word "satellites," and Medicean never stuck.

William Herschel tried to name his new planet "Georgium Sidus" for King George III, but the international astronomy community would have none of that, calling it Uranus instead.

Lowell Observatory in Flagstaff, Ariz., was luckier with Pluto, which was discovered there in 1930. The name, suggested by an 11-year-old Oxford school girl, incorporated the initials of Boston Brahmin Percival Lowell, who had initiated the search for the object decades earlier.

Yet controversy finally caught up with Pluto in 2006. Pluto, it had turned out, was not a massive object influencing Uranus and Neptune in their courses, as Lowell and his contemporaries had assumed. It was a dwarf, smaller than our moon, and 400 times less massive than the earth. The supposed wobbles in Neptune's positions resulted from using an incorrect mass for Neptune itself when calculating its orbit. Had these facts been known in 1930, Pluto's planetary status would have been disputed at the outset.

The International Astronomical Union has for 80-odd years been naming comets and asteroids without controversy, but when Mike Brown of Cal Tech and his colleagues recently found an object even bigger than Pluto plying the frozen reaches beyond Neptune, it ignited a crisis of nomenclature. Had he found a 10th planet? And were there more candidates waiting to be discovered among the numerous icy chunks in the so-called Kuiper belt?

In a quandary, the IAU decided to appoint a small but broadly based committee to look into the matter. As both an astrophysicist and historian of science, I was tapped to chair it.

There are two distinct scientific ways to approach the problem of defining planet-hood. One is extrinsic, to define a planet in terms of its neighbors and its interactions with its environment. This route would select the dominant bodies in the solar system, the ones whose gravity perturbs one another.

It was the flash of insight that not only the sun holds the planets in orbit, but that each planet attracts each other one, that led Isaac Newton to the concept of universal gravitation. Neptune attracts Pluto, locking it into a resonant orbit so that in the time Neptune takes to round the sun three times, Pluto revolves exactly twice. But Pluto is too lightweight to have an observable effect on giant Neptune. The eight dominant heavyweights, from Mercury to Neptune, are big enough to rule their zones and swallow up most of the smaller bodies or kick them out of the way.

Choosing such dominance is a comfortable way to go when defining what constitutes a planet: While it would dismiss Pluto, it would forever place the other eight planets in an exclusive club. An alternative way to define a planet, however, is intrinsic—that is, by the properties of the body itself, more or less independent of its environment. This is the way planetary geologists look at the problem, and pretty much the way astronomers looking at the hundred-plus planets circling other stars do. The idea of using the basic physics of the object appealed to our committee as the forward-looking way to define planets, for it could apply not only to the far stretches of the solar system, but to the objects being found around distant stars as well.

Rather than arbitrarily drawing a line in the sand that would either include or exclude Pluto, we opted to let nature pick a dividing line between planets and the hundreds of thousands of lumpy asteroids now known—nearly 140,000 numbered objects and an equal number awaiting their catalog numbers. If a body is massive enough, with enough self-gravity to pull itself into a ball, let it be a planet. If it's just a lump, let it be an asteroid or a comet.

Of course, the roundness definition could open the gates to a dozen or more snowballs in the Kuiper belt, and we were quite aware that these bodies would be minor lightweights in a system of traditional heavyweights. So we decided to distinguish the eight classical planets from the Kuiper belt planets. As a group, these Kuiper belt planets needed a name, something that gave a tip of the hat to the longstanding eminence of

Pluto. We eventually backed the name "plutonian." Thus Pluto, while being demoted, would be cast in the position of being a group leader and would still be a planet, though of a different sort.

In August our committee took this recommendation to Prague, to the triennial IAU congress, where it became the most-talked-about issue of the meeting. (I recently put "Pluto" and "Gingerich" into Google and got 41,000 hits!) The media there had two questions: Was Pluto still a planet? And how many planets would there be?

In the committee it had never occurred to us to count the current number, because we knew the tally of plutonians would rapidly grow. We also knew that the Hubble Space Telescope had recently shown that the earliest known asteroid, Ceres, was round. Ceres would thus fit our definition of a planet, though it would be in a category of its own, being neither a heavyweight nor a plutonian—a term we reserved for the lightweight planets beyond Neptune.

All this was more complexity than could be accounted for in any handy mnemonic phrase. We felt, however, that our definition reflected the new-found diversity in our solar system, which modern science shows is far more complex than dreamt of by Percival Lowell. Our definition suggested the growing richness of our environment. But it also proved to be the Achilles' heel of our proposal.

The media, eager to promote controversy, quickly found vocal critics to say that the whole business was too complicated. In the final days of the congress, a group of astronomers persuaded enough of their colleagues that a simpler result was desirable (even if it required a more complicated definition), and the intrinsic approach was voted down.

The IAU thereafter defined a planet in our solar system as an object large enough to clear the smaller bodies from its orbit, a definition just murky enough to give teachers a considerable challenge to explain precisely what this means. Taking the exclusive club approach for the heavyweights, the IAU went on to create a class of "dwarf planets," including Pluto, that by definition are not planets. To me this is a linguistic absurdity, a contradiction that could have been avoided if they had chosen to define only the eight classical planets as the basic type of planets, allowing dwarf planets to be considered planets too, albeit of a different kind. But this cultural compromise was specifically rejected.

In their muddled wisdom, the IAU members did at least vote to make Pluto the prototype object for a new category. Ceres will stand alone as a dwarf planet in the asteroid belt while Pluto will be the charter member of a new class of dwarf planets beyond Neptune, much as our committee originally proposed. But, by a virtual tie vote, the IAU decided not to adopt the obvious name "plutonians" for that category. The name awaits in the wings.

———

Owen Gingerich is professor emeritus of astronomy and history of science at the Harvard-Smithsonian Center for Astrophysics and the author of *God's Universe*, to be published this month. This essay was first published in the September 3, 2006, edition of *The Boston Globe*.

EVALUATIVE ARGUMENT (CATEGORICAL)

"From Justin to Kelly": A Criminally Misguided Musical

BY HEATHER HAVRILESKY (2003)

This "American Idol" spinoff musical is one of the worst movies you'll ever see—but it's still not worth seeing.

Remember, girls, when you were 10 or 11, and you made your Barbie dolls go on dates, even if they had to stoop to dating your brother's G.I. Joe? Remember the kind of dialogue you'd dream up for your dolls, gleaned from years of watching washed-up stars romance each other on "The Love Boat"? Well, those early Barbie-improv experiences might just qualify you to write the screenplay of a $12 million summer movie.

If you don't believe me, feast your eyes on this scene from "From Justin to Kelly," in which Justin (Justin Guarini) and Kelly (Kelly Clarkson) putter around in a motorboat at sunset, alternately bellowing a song about how madly in love they are, and quietly, awkwardly discussing their budding romance.

Kelly: "So, do you bring all your girls out here?"

Justin: "No, I mostly come out here to think."

Kelly: "What are you thinking about now?"

Justin: "Thinking about how glad I am that you gave me a second chance."

My brother's G.I. Joe was always going places alone to think, too, probably because I already suspected that most guys spent far less time in quiet contemplation than I had hoped. Even so, I was a little disappointed that Kelly gave Justin a second chance, since it would've been more entertaining to watch Kelly sit around her hotel room eating corn dogs and painting her toenails than it was to witness a romance so unconvincing and leaden, you'd think both Justin and Kelly were gay and incredibly seasick.

But maybe they were still queasy from the first half-hour of the film, in which most of the scenes are less dynamic and original than a 6-year-old's puppet show. "Dude, this year, spring break is gonna rock!" proclaims one of Justin's two nondescript sidekicks. "We are going to go to the best parties and meet the hottest guys!" squeals one of Kelly's bland pals. Like strangers stuck on a crowded, smelly bus, Kelly and Justin don't meet but rather apprehend each other on the beach in one of the most awkward, badly choreographed, terribly edited party scenes ever made. In the unlucky couple's first moments dancing together, they look about as swept away as they might while pulling a wad of hair from a shower drain. The music is mixed badly and sounds flat and distant from the scene, and the camera seems to capture the dancing crowds at all the wrong moments, making every move look clumsy and out of sync with the music.

The horrible lighting and crappy makeup certainly don't help matters much. Despite the fun-in-the-sun theme, the entire movie seems to be shot under overcast skies, and the interior scenes are so badly lit, you probably have home movies that look a lot better. (The director here is Robert Iscove, previously in charge of such teen romances as "She's All That" and "Boys and Girls.") Kelly Clarkson is an attractive enough woman who can look beautiful with the proper makeup and lighting, but in this movie, she looks like somebody's frumpy cousin they were forced to bring to the party. Justin Guarini rings about as false as he did in the latter stages of last year's "American Idol" finals, and inexplicably strides around among the bare-chested men on the beach wearing cargo pants and long-sleeved shirts.

What's amazing is that a scripted, choreographed musical could be this bad, when party scenes from the flawed but enjoyable reality-movie flop "The Real Cancun" could lure a nun into the spirit of spring-break insanity. The producers of that movie took hours of footage of untrained dancers and random bystanders at clubs, and made them look like movie stars. The makers of "From Justin to Kelly" took two talented vocalists who are also able enough dancers, and made them look like "Fame" rejects. The bland lines that drop from their mouths make the drunken blatherings of the stars of "The Real Cancun" sound like snippets of Shakespeare.

But let's not forget the story, which brings us back to the days when Barbie's conniving best friend Superstar Barbie cheated with G.I. Joe in the Barbie Dreamhouse. You'll recall that Kelly and Justin meet and fall madly in love while pulling hair from a shower drain. Afterward Kelly's like, "So, do you really think he was looking at me?" and Kelly's nice friend Kaya (Anika Noni Rose) says that he totally was, but Kelly's evil friend Alexa (Katherine Bailess) gives Justin her cell number instead of Kelly's, and then enters Kelly in a whipped-cream bikini contest (Kelly's reaction: "You entered me in a whipped-cream bikini contest?!"), knowing that Justin is one of the contest's organizers and judges. Kelly thinks that is totally gross and there is, like, no way she's going to participate, which she demonstrates by shoving whipped cream in Justin's face. Burn! So then, Justin keeps messaging Kelly, but he's, like, messaging the wrong number the whole time, and Alexa keeps messaging back stuff like, "Sorry, not intrsted"! So Kelly tries to meet Justin but Alexa keeps changing the plans and not telling Kelly, but they do get to go on the boat ride and that's when they both start to bellow and swoon without looking at each other.

Which is pretty sly, since every time these two look at each other, they seem to be either stifling laughter or trying not to vomit all over each other's sneakers. And it would all be funny, if this weren't one of the worst ways you could possibly blow $12 million.

I know what you're thinking, though: "That sounds really bad, incredibly bad, so bad, in fact . . . that it's good!" And I don't blame you for getting your hopes so high. After all, there weren't any press screenings for the movie, and Clarkson openly proclaimed that critics wouldn't like it. "They like stuff like 'In the Bedroom,'" she told TV Guide Online. "They're gonna want to tear into it because all people like to do is build something up to tear it down. This movie shouldn't be screened by the critics because it's not for them—it's for the fans."

Clarkson should have known she'd send our expectations soaring with such comments. And maybe she did believe her movie might be the so-bad-it's-good hit of the season, a classic in the exalted tradition of "Crossroads" or "The Apple" or "Lambada: The Forbidden Dance."

But when Kelly sings an entire melodramatic ballad while walking zombie-like through an unattractive swatch of sand and trees, all emotionless and scrub-faced, as if she just rose from bed, and then Justin appears in the background like the villain in that scene in "Halloween II," only this scene really isn't supposed to be horrifying, it's just painful and no, it doesn't hurt so good. These two have incredible, soaring voices, and maybe they're not movie stars, but it might have been nice if some modicum of skill had been applied to making them look like they could be movie stars, instead of extras from "Night of the Living Dead." Justin and Kelly both looked a million times better sweating under the lights on "American Idol," and even their most tedious performances were far more entertaining than the endless boat ride and hideous beach march of "From Justin to Kelly."

Forget the critics. This movie doesn't just do a disservice to the fans, it does a horrible disservice to Justin and Kelly, manufactured stars who are new to the game and have to rely on their supposedly expert handlers to make them look good. America is more than willing to embrace manufactured celebrity, but part of the fun is seeing how the magic can transform a talented but ordinary kid into something larger than life. The makers of "From Justin to Kelly" didn't even bother to break out the pixie dust.

———

This review was first published on June 25, 2003, at Salon.com.

EVALUATIVE ARGUMENT (ETHICAL)

Are We Really So Fearful?

BY ARIEL DORFMAN (2006)

It still haunts me, the first time—it was in Chile, in October of 1973—that I met someone who had been tortured. To save my life, I had sought refuge in the Argentine Embassy some weeks after the coup that had toppled the democratically elected government of Salvador Allende, a government for which I had worked. And then, suddenly, one afternoon, there he was. A large-boned man, gaunt and yet strangely flabby, with eyes like a child, eyes that could not stop blinking and a body that could not stop shivering.

That is what stays with me—that he was cold under the balmy afternoon sun of Santiago de Chile, trembling as though he would never be warm again, as though the electric current was still coursing through him. Still possessed, somehow still inhabited by his captors, still imprisoned in that cell in the National Stadium, his hands disobeying the orders from his brain to quell the shuddering, his body unable to forget what had been done to it just as, nearly 33 years later, I, too, cannot banish that devastated life from my memory.

It was his image, in fact, that swirled up from the past as I pondered the current political debate in the United States about the practicality of torture. Something in me must have needed to resurrect that victim, force my fellow citizens here to spend a few minutes with the eternal iciness that had settled into that man's heart and flesh, and demand that they take a good hard look at him before anyone dare maintain that, to save lives, it might be necessary to inflict unbearable pain on a fellow human being. Perhaps the optimist in me hoped that this damaged Argentine man could, all these decades later, help shatter the perverse innocence of contemporary Americans, just as he had burst the bubble of ignorance protecting the young Chilean I used to be, someone who back then had encountered torture mainly through books and movies and newspaper reports.

That is not, however, the only lesson that today's ruthless world can learn from that distant man condemned to shiver forever.

All those years ago, that torture victim kept moving his lips, trying to articulate an explanation, muttering the same words over and over. "It was a mistake," he repeated, and in the next few days I pieced together his sad and foolish tale. He was an Argentine revolutionary who had fled his homeland and, as soon as he had crossed the mountains into Chile, had begun to boast about what he would do to the military there if it staged a coup, about his expertise with arms of every sort, about his colossal stash of weapons. Bluster and braggadocio—and every word of it false.

But how could he convince those men who were beating him, hooking his penis to electric wires and waterboarding him? How could he prove to them that he had been lying, prancing in front of his Chilean comrades, just trying to impress the ladies with his fraudulent insurgent persona?

Of course, he couldn't. He confessed to anything and everything they wanted to drag from his hoarse, howling throat; he invented accomplices and addresses and culprits; and then, when it became apparent that all this was imaginary, he was subjected to further ordeals.

There was no escape.

That is the hideous predicament of the torture victim. It was always the same story, what I discovered in the ensuing years, as I became an unwilling expert on all manner of torments and degradations, my life and my writing overflowing with grief from every continent. Each of those mutilated spines and fractured lives—Chinese, Guatemalan, Egyptian, Indonesian, Iranian, Uzbek, need I go on?—all of them, men and women alike, surrendered the same story of essential asymmetry, where one man has all the power in the world and the other has nothing but pain, where one man can decree death at the flick of a wrist and the other can only pray that the wrist will be flicked soon.

It is a story that our species has listened to with mounting revulsion, a horror that has led almost every nation to sign treaties over the past decades declaring these abominations as crimes against humanity, transgressions interdicted all across the earth. That is the wisdom, national and international, that has taken us thousands of years of tribulation and shame to achieve. That is the wisdom we are being asked to throw away when we formulate the question—Does torture work?—when we allow ourselves to ask whether we can afford to outlaw torture if we want to defeat terrorism.

I will leave others to claim that torture, in fact, does not work, that confessions obtained under duress—such as that extracted from the heaving body of that poor Argentine braggart in some Santiago cesspool in 1973—are useless. Or to contend that the United States had better not do that to anyone in our custody lest someday another nation or entity or group decides to treat our prisoners the same way.

I find these arguments—and there are many more—to be irrefutable. But I cannot bring myself to use them, for fear of honoring the debate by participating in it.

Can't the United States see that when we allow someone to be tortured by our agents, it is not only the victim and the perpetrator who are corrupted, not only the "intelligence" that is contaminated, but also everyone who looked away and said they did not know, everyone who consented tacitly to that outrage so they could sleep a little safer at night, all the citizens who did not march in the streets by the millions to demand the resignation of whoever suggested, even whispered, that torture is inevitable in our day and age, that we must embrace its darkness?

Are we so morally sick, so deaf and dumb and blind, that we do not understand this? Are we so fearful, so in love with our own security and steeped in our own pain, that we are really willing to let people be tortured in the name of America? Have we so lost our bearings that we do not realize that each of us could be that hapless Argentine who sat under the Santiago sun, so possessed by the evil done to him that he could not stop shivering?

Ariel Dorfman, a Chilean American writer and professor at Duke University, is author of "Death and the Maiden." He wrote this piece for the September 24, 2006, edition of The Washington Post <www.washingtonpost.com>.

CAUSAL ARGUMENT

A Bargain at 77 Cents to a Dollar

BY CARRIE LUKAS (2007)

Why are politicians again championing the Equal Rights Amendment—newly minted as the Women's Equality Amendment—when the speaker of the House, secretary of state and the Democratic presidential front-runner are women, and when women are making gains in education and the workforce? One reason is that many claim women are systematically discriminated against at work, as the existence of the so-called wage gap proves.

Talking about wage discrimination against women is a political mainstay. Last month, Sen. Hillary Clinton expressed consternation that women continue to make "just 77 cents for every dollar that a man makes" and reintroduced legislation, the Paycheck Fairness Act, that would give the government more power to make "an equal paycheck for equal work" a reality.

This statistic—probably the most frequently cited of the Labor Department's data— is also its most misused.

Yes, the Labor Department regularly issues new data comparing the median wage of women who work full time with the median wage of men who work full time, and women's earnings bob at around three-quarters those of men. But this statistic says little about women's compensation and the influence of discrimination on men's and women's earnings. All the relevant factors that affect pay—occupation, experience, seniority, education and hours worked—are ignored. This sound-bite statistic fails to take into account the different roles that work tends to play in men's and women's lives.

In truth, I'm the cause of the wage gap—I and hundreds of thousands of women like me. I have a good education and have worked full time for 10 years. Yet throughout my career, I've made things other than money a priority. I chose to work in the nonprofit world because I find it fulfilling. I sought out a specialty and employer that seemed best suited to balancing my work and family life. When I had my daughter, I took time off and then opted to stay home full time and telecommute. I'm not making as much money as I could, but I'm compensated by having the best working arrangement I could hope for.

Women make similar trade-offs all the time. Surveys have shown for years that women tend to place a higher priority on flexibility and personal fulfillment than do men, who focus more on pay. Women tend to avoid jobs that require travel or relocation, and they take more time off and spend fewer hours in the office than men do. Men disproportionately take on the dirtiest, most dangerous and depressing jobs.

When these kinds of differences are taken into account and the comparison is truly between men and women in equivalent roles, the wage gap shrinks. In his book "Why Men Earn More," Warren Farrell—a former board member of the National Organization for Women in New York—identifies more than three dozen professions in which women out-earn men (including engineering management, aerospace engineering, radiation therapy and speech-language pathology). Farrell seeks to empower women with this information. Discrimination certainly plays a role in some workplaces, but individual preferences are the real root of the wage gap.

When women realize that it isn't systemic bias but the choices they make that determine their earnings, they can make better-informed decisions. Many women may not want to follow the path toward higher pay—which often requires more time on the road, more hours in the office or less comfortable and less interesting work—but they're better off not feeling like victims.

Government attempts to "solve" the problem of the wage gap may in fact exacerbate some of the challenges women face, particularly in balancing work and family. Clinton's legislation would give Washington bureaucrats more power to oversee how wages are determined, which might prompt businesses to make employment options more rigid. Flexible job structures such as the one I enjoy today would probably become scarcer. Why would companies offer employees a variety of work situations and compensation packages if doing so puts them at risk of being sued?

Women hearing Clinton's pledge to solve their problems and increase their pay should think hard about the choices they have made. They should think about the women they know and about their career paths. I bet they'll find that maximizing pay hasn't always been the top priority. Eliminating the wage gap may sound like a good campaign promise, but since the wage gap mostly reflects individual differences in priorities, it's a promise that we should hope a President Hillary Clinton wouldn't try to keep.

———

Carrie Lukas is vice president for policy and economics at the Independent Women's Forum and the author of *The Politically Incorrect Guide to Women, Sex, and Feminism*. This column was published on April 3, 2007, in *The Washington Post*.

CAUSAL ARGUMENT

Where Have All the Criminals Gone?

From *Freakonomics: A Rogue Economist Explores the Hidden Side of Everything*
BY STEVEN D. LEVITT AND STEPHEN J. DUBNER (2005)

In 1966, one year after Nicolae Ceausescu became the Communist dictator of Romania, he made abortion illegal. "The fetus is the property of the entire society," he proclaimed. "Anyone who avoids having children is a deserter who abandons the laws of national continuity."

Such grandiose declarations were commonplace during Ceausescu's reign, for his master plan—to create a nation worthy of the New Socialist Man—was an exercise in grandiosity. He built palaces for himself while alternately brutalizing and neglecting his citizens. Abandoning agriculture in favor of manufacturing, he forced many of the nation's rural dwellers into unheated apartment buildings. He gave government positions to forty family members including his wife, Elena, who required forty homes and a commensurate supply of fur and jewels. Madame Ceausescu, known officially as the Best Mother Romania Could Have, was not particularly maternal. "The worms never get satisfied, regardless of how much food you give them," she said when Romanians complained about the food shortages brought on by her husband's mismanagement. She had her own children bugged to ensure their loyalty.

Ceausescu's ban on abortion was designed to achieve one of his major aims: to rapidly strengthen Romania by boosting its population. Until 1966, Romania had had one of the most liberal abortion policies in the world. Abortion was in fact the main form of birth control, with four abortions for every live birth. Now, virtually overnight, abortion was forbidden. The only exemptions were mothers who already had four children or women with significant standing in the Communist Party. At the same time, all contraception and sex education were banned. Government agents sardonically known as the Menstrual Police regularly rounded up women in their workplaces to administer pregnancy tests. If a woman repeatedly failed to conceive, she was forced to pay a steep "celibacy tax."

Ceausescu's incentives produced the desired effect. Within one year of the abortion ban, the Romanian birth rate had doubled. These babies were born into a country where, unless you belonged to the Ceausescu clan or the Communist elite, life was miserable. But these children would turn out to have particularly miserable lives. Compared to Romanian children born just a year earlier, the cohort of children born after the abortion ban would do worse in every measurable way: they would test lower in school, they would have less success in the labor market, and they would also prove much more likely to become criminals.

The abortion ban stayed in effect until Ceausescu finally lost his grip on Romania. On December 16, 1989, thousands of people took to the streets of Timisoara to protest his corrosive regime. Many of the protestors were teenagers and college students. The police killed dozens of them. One of the opposition leaders, a forty-one-year-old professor, later said it was his thirteen-year-old daughter who insisted he attend the protest, despite his fear. "What is most interesting is that we learned not to be afraid from our children," he said. "Most were aged thirteen to twenty." A few days after the massacre in Timisoara, Ceausescu gave a speech in Bucharest before one hundred thousand people. Again the young people were out in force. They shouted down Ceausescu with cries of "Timisoara!" and "Down with the murderers!" His time had come. He and Elena tried to escape the country with $1 billion, but they were captured, given a crude trial, and, on Christmas Day, executed by firing squad.

Of all the Communist leaders deposed in the years bracketing the collapse of the Soviet Union, only Nicolae Ceausescu met a violent death. It should not be overlooked that his demise was precipitated in large measure by the youth of Romania—a great number of whom, were it not for his abortion ban, would never have been born at all.

. . .

The story of abortion in Romania might seem an odd way to begin telling the story of American crime in the 1990s. But it's not. In one important way, the Romanian abortion story is a reverse image of the American crime story. The point of overlap was on that Christmas Day of 1989, when Nicolae Ceausescu learned the hard way—with a bullet to the head—that his abortion ban had much deeper implications than he knew.

On that day, crime was just about at its peak in the United States. In the previous fifteen years, violent crime had risen 80 percent. It was crime that led the nightly news and the national conversation.

When the crime rate began falling in the early 1990s, it did so with such speed and suddenness that it surprised everyone. It took some experts many years to even recognize that crime was falling, so confident had they been of its continuing rise. Long after crime had peaked, in fact, some of them continued to predict ever darker scenarios. But the evidence was irrefutable: the long and brutal spike in crime was moving in the opposite direction, and it wouldn't stop until the crime rate had fallen back to the levels of forty years earlier.

Now the experts hustled to explain their faulty forecasting. The criminologist James Alan Fox explained that his warning of a "bloodbath" was in fact an intentional over-statement. "I never said there would be blood flowing in the streets," he said, "but I used strong terms like 'bloodbath' to get people's attention. And it did. I don't apologize for using alarmist terms." (If Fox seems to be offering a distinction without a difference — "bloodbath" versus "blood flowing in the streets" — we should remember that even in retreat mode, experts can be self-serving.)

After the relief had settled in, after people remembered how to go about their lives without the pressing fear of crime, there arose a natural question: just where did all those criminals go?

At one level, the answer seemed puzzling. After all, if none of the criminologists, police officials, economists, politicians, or others who traffic in such matters had foreseen the crime decline, how could they suddenly identify its causes?

But this diverse army of experts now marched out a phalanx of hypotheses to explain the drop in crime. A great many newspaper articles would be written on the subject. Their conclusions often hinged on which expert had most recently spoken to which reporter. Here, ranked by frequency of mention, are the crime-drop explanations cited in articles published from 1991 to 2001 in the ten largest circulation papers in the LexisNexis database:

Explanation	Citations
1. Innovative policing strategies	52
2. Increased reliance on prisons	47
3. Changes in crack, other drug markets	33
4. Aging of the population	32
5. Tougher gun control laws	32
6. Strong economy	28

7. Increased number of police   26
8. All other explanations (increased use of capital
    punishment, concealed-weapons laws, gun buybacks,
    and others)   34

If you are the sort of person who likes guessing games, you may wish to spend the next few moments pondering which of the preceding explanations seem to have merit and which don't. Hint: of the seven major explanations on the list, only three can be shown to have contributed to the drop in crime. The others are, for the most part, figments of someone's imagination, self-interest, or wishful thinking. Further hint: one of the greatest measurable causes of the crime drop does not appear on the list at all, for it didn't receive a single newspaper mention.

. . .

Let's begin with a fairly uncontroversial one: *the strong economy*. The decline in crime that began in the early 1990s was accompanied by a blistering national economy and a significant drop in unemployment. It might seem to follow that the economy was a hammer that helped beat down crime. But a closer look at the data destroys this theory. It is true that a stronger job market may make certain crimes relatively less attractive. But that is only the case for crimes with a direct financial motivation—burglary, robbery, and auto theft—as opposed to violent crimes like homicide, assault, and rape. Moreover, studies have shown that an unemployment decline of 1 percentage point accounts for a 1 percent drop in nonviolent crime. During the 1990s, the unemployment rate fell by 2 percentage points; nonviolent crime, meanwhile, fell by roughly 40 percent. But an even bigger flaw in the strong-economy theory concerns violent crime. Homicide fell at a greater rate during the 1990s than any other sort of crime, and a number of reliable studies have shown virtually no link between the economy and violent crime. This weak link is made even weaker by glancing back to a recent decade, the 1960s, when the economy went on a wild growth spurt—as did violent crime. So while a strong 1990s economy might have seemed, on the surface, a likely explanation for the drop in crime, it almost certainly didn't affect criminal behavior in any significant way.

Unless, that is, "the economy" is construed in a broader sense—as a means to build and maintain hundreds of prisons. Let's now consider another crime-drop explanation: *increased reliance on prisons*. It might help to start by flipping the crime question around.

Instead of wondering what made crime fall, think about this: why had it risen so dramatically in the first place?

During the first half of the twentieth century, the incidence of violent crime in the United States was, for the most part, fairly steady. But in the early 1960s, it began to climb. In retrospect, it is clear that one of the major factors pushing this trend was a more lenient justice system. Conviction rates declined during the 1960s, and criminals who were convicted served shorter sentences. This trend was driven in part by an expansion in the rights of people accused of crimes—a long overdue expansion, some would argue. (Others would argue that the expansion went too far.) At the same time, politicians were growing increasingly softer on crime—"for fear of sounding racist," as the economist Gary Becker has written, "since African-Americans and Hispanics commit a disproportionate share of felonies." So if you were the kind of person who might want to commit a crime, the incentives were lining up in your favor: a slimmer likelihood of being convicted and, if convicted, a shorter prison term. Because criminals respond to incentives as readily as anyone, the result was a surge in crime.

It took some time, and a great deal of political turmoil, but these incentives were eventually curtailed. Criminals who would have previously been set free—for drug-related offenses and parole revocation in particular—were instead locked up. Between 1980 and 2000, there was a fifteenfold increase in the number of people sent to prison on drug charges. Many other sentences, especially for violent crime, were lengthened. The total effect was dramatic. By 2000, more than two million people were in prison, roughly four times the number as of 1972. Fully half of that increase took place during the 1990s.

The evidence linking increased punishment with lower crime rates is very strong. Harsh prison terms have been shown to act as both deterrent (for the would-be criminal on the street) and prophylactic (for the would-be criminal who is already locked up). Logical as this may sound, some criminologists have fought the logic. A 1977 academic study called "On Behalf of a Moratorium on Prison Construction" noted that crime rates tend to be high when imprisonment rates are high, and concluded that crime would fall if imprisonment rates could only be lowered. (Fortunately, jailers did not suddenly turn loose their wards and sit back waiting for crime to fall. As the political scientist John J. DiIulio Jr. later commented, "Apparently, it takes a Ph.D. in criminology to doubt that keeping dangerous criminals incarcerated cuts crime.") The "Moratorium" argument rests on a fundamental confusion of correlation and causality. Consider a parallel argument. The mayor of a city sees that his citizens celebrate wildly when their team wins the World Series. He is intrigued by this correlation but, like the "Moratorium" author, fails to see the direction in which the correlation runs. So the following year, the mayor decrees that his citizens start celebrating the World Series before the first pitch is thrown — an act that, in his confused mind, will ensure a victory.

There are certainly plenty of reasons to dislike the huge surge in the prison population. Not everyone is pleased that such a significant fraction of Americans, especially black Americans, live behind bars. Nor does prison even begin to address the root causes of crime, which are diverse and complex. Lastly, prison is hardly a cheap solution: it costs about $25,000 a year to keep someone incarcerated. But if the goal here is to explain the drop in crime in the 1990s, imprisonment is certainly one of the key answers. It accounts for roughly one-third of the drop in crime.

Another crime-drop explanation is often cited in tandem with imprisonment: *the increased use of capital punishment*. The number of executions in the United States quadrupled between the 1980s and the1990s, leading many people to conclude — in the context of a debate that has been going on for decades — that capital punishment helped drive down crime. Lost in the debate, however, are two important facts.

First, given the rarity with which executions are carried out in this country and the long delays in doing so, no reasonable criminal should be deterred by the threat of execution. Even though capital punishment quadrupled within a decade, there were still only 478 executions in the entire United States during the 1990s. Any parent who has ever said to a recalcitrant child, "Okay, I'm going to count to ten and this time I'm really going to punish you," knows the difference between deterrent and empty threat. New York State, for instance, has not as of this writing executed a single criminal since reinstituting its death penalty in 1995. Even among prisoners on death row, the annual execution rate is only 2 percent — compared with the 7 percent annual chance of dying faced by a member of the Black Gangster Disciple Nation crack gang. If life on death row is safer than life on the streets, it's hard to believe that the fear of execution is a driving force in a criminal's calculus. [. . .] The negative incentive of capital punishment simply isn't serious enough for a criminal to change his behavior.

The second flaw in the capital punishment argument is even more obvious. Assume for a moment that the death penalty is a deterrent. How much crime does it actually deter? The economist Isaac Ehrlich, in an oft-cited 1975 paper, put forth an estimate that is generally considered optimistic: executing 1 criminal translates into 7 fewer homicides that the criminal might have committed. Now do the math. In 1991, there were 14 executions in the United States; in 2001, there were 66. According to Ehrlich's calculation, those 52 additional executions would have accounted for 364 fewer homicides in 2001—not a small drop, to be sure, but less than 4 percent of the actual decrease in homicides that year. So even in a death penalty advocate's best-case scenario, capital punishment could explain only one twenty-fifth of the drop in homicides in the 1990s. And because the death penalty is rarely given for crimes other than homicide, its deterrent effect cannot account for a speck of decline in other violent crimes.

It is extremely unlikely, therefore, that the death penalty, as currently practiced in the United States, exerts any real influence on crime rates. Even many of its onetime supporters have come to this conclusion. "I feel morally and intellectually obligated simply to concede that the death penalty experiment has failed," said U.S. Supreme Court Justice Harry A. Blackmun in 1994, nearly twenty years after he had voted for its reinstatement. "I no longer shall tinker with the machinery of death."

. . .

So it wasn't capital punishment that drove crime down, nor was it the booming economy. But higher rates of imprisonment did have a lot to do with it. All those criminals didn't march into jail by themselves, of course. Someone had to investigate the crime, catch the bad guy, and put together the case that would get him convicted. Which naturally leads to a related pair of crime-drop explanations: innovative policing strategies and increased number of police.

Let's address the second one first. The number of police officers per capita in the United States rose about 14 percent during the 1990s. Does merely increasing the number of police, however, reduce crime? The answer would seem obvious—yes—but proving that answer isn't so easy. That's because when crime is rising, people clamor for protection, and invariably more money is found for cops. So if you just look at raw correlations between police and crime, you will find that when there are more police, there tends to be more crime. That doesn't mean, of course, that the police are causing the crime, just as it doesn't mean, as some criminologists have argued, that crime will fall if criminals are released from prison.

To show causality, we need a scenario in which more police are hired for reasons completely unrelated to rising crime. If, for instance, police were randomly sprinkled in some cities and not in others, we could look to see whether crime declines in the cities where the police happen to land.

As it turns out, that exact scenario is often created by vote-hungry politicians. In the months leading up to Election Day, incumbent mayors routinely try to lock up the law-and-order vote by hiring more police—even when the crime rate is standing still. So by comparing the crime rate in one set of cities that have recently had an election (and which therefore hired extra police) with another set of cities that had no election (and therefore no extra police), it's possible to tease out the effect of the extra police on crime. The answer: yes indeed, additional police substantially lower the crime rate.

Again, it may help to look backward and see why crime had risen so much in the first place. From 1960 to 1985, the number of police officers *fell* more than 50 percent relative to the number of crimes. In some cases, hiring additional police was considered a violation of the era's liberal aesthetic; in others, it was simply considered too expensive. This 50 percent decline in police translated into a roughly equal decline in the probability that a given criminal would be caught. Coupled with the above-cited leniency in the other half of the criminal justice system, the courtrooms, this decrease in policing created a strong positive incentive for criminals.

By the 1990s, philosophies—and necessities—had changed. The policing trend was put in reverse, with wide-scale hiring in cities across the country. Not only did all those police act as a deterrent, but they also provided the manpower to imprison criminals who might have otherwise gone uncaught. The hiring of additional police accounted for roughly 10 percent of the 1990s crime drop.

But it wasn't only the number of police that changed in the 1990s; consider the most commonly cited crime-drop explanation of all: *innovative policing strategies*.

There was perhaps no more attractive theory than the belief that smart policing stops crime. It offered a set of bona fide heroes rather than simply a dearth of villains. This theory rapidly became an article of faith because it appealed to the factors that, according to John Kenneth Galbraith, most contribute to the formation of conventional wisdom: the ease with which an idea may be understood and the degree to which it affects our personal well-being.

The story played out most dramatically in New York City, where newly elected mayor Rudolph Giuliani and his handpicked police commissioner, William Bratton, vowed to fix the city's desperate crime situation. Bratton took a novel approach to policing. He ushered the NYPD into what one senior police official later called "our Athenian period," in which new ideas were given weight over calcified practices. Instead of coddling his precinct commanders, Bratton demanded accountability. Instead of relying solely on old-fashioned cop know-how, he introduced technological solutions like CompStat, a computerized method of addressing crime hot spots.

The most compelling new idea that Bratton brought to life stemmed from the broken window theory, which was conceived by the criminologists James Q. Wilson and George Kelling. The broken window theory argues that minor nuisances, if left unchecked, turn into major nuisances: that is, if someone breaks a window and sees it isn't fixed immediately, he gets the signal that it's all right to break the rest of the windows and maybe set the building afire too.

So with murder raging all around, Bill Bratton's cops began to police the sort of deeds that used to go unpoliced: jumping a subway turnstile, panhandling too aggressively, urinating in the streets, swabbing a filthy squeegee across a car's windshield unless the driver made an appropriate "donation."

Most New Yorkers loved this crackdown on its own merit. But they particularly loved the idea, as stoutly preached by Bratton and Giuliani, that choking off these small crimes was like choking off the criminal element's oxygen supply. Today's turnstile jumper might easily be wanted for yesterday's murder. That junkie peeing in an alley might have been on his way to a robbery. As violent crime began to fall dramatically, New Yorkers were more than happy to heap laurels on their operatic, Brooklyn-bred mayor and his hatchet-faced police chief with the big Boston accent. But the two strong-willed men weren't very good at sharing the glory. Soon after the city's crime turnaround landed Bratton—and not Giuliani—on the cover of *Time*, Bratton was pushed to resign. He had been police commissioner for just twenty-seven months.

New York City was a clear innovator in police strategies during the 1990s crime drop, and it also enjoyed the greatest decline in crime of any large American city. Homicide rates fell from 30.7 per 100,000 people in 1990 to 8.4 per 100,000 people in 2000, a change of 73.6 percent. But a careful analysis of the facts shows that the innovative policing strategies probably had little effect on this huge decline.

First, the drop in crime in New York began in 1990. By the end of 1993, the rate of property crime and violent crime, including homicides, had already fallen nearly 20 percent. Rudolph Giuliani, however, did not become mayor—and install Bratton—until early 1994. Crime was well on its way down before either man arrived. And it would continue to fall long after Bratton was bumped from office.

Second, the new police strategies were accompanied by a much more significant change within the police force: a hiring binge. Between 1991 and 2001, the NYPD grew by 45 percent, more than three times the national average. As argued above, an increase in the number of police, regardless of new strategies, has been proven to reduce crime. By a conservative calculation, this huge expansion of New York's police force would be expected to reduce crime in New York by 18 percent relative to the national average. If you subtract that 18 percent from New York's homicide reduction, thereby discounting the effect of the police-hiring surge, New York no longer leads the nation with its 73.6 percent drop; it goes straight to the middle of the pack. Many of those new police were in fact hired by David Dinkins, the mayor whom Giuliani defeated. Dinkins had been desperate to secure the law-and-order vote, having known all along that his opponent would be Giuliani, a former federal prosecutor. (The two men had run against each other four years earlier as well.) So those who wish to credit Giuliani with the crime drop may still do so, for it was his own law- and-order reputation that made Dinkins hire all those police. In the end, of course, the police increase helped everyone—but it helped Giuliani a lot more than Dinkins.

Most damaging to the claim that New York's police innovations radically lowered crime is one zsimple and often overlooked fact: crime went down everywhere during the 1990s, not only in New York. Few other cities tried the kind of strategies that New York did, and certainly none with the same zeal. But even in Los Angeles, a city notorious for bad policing, crime fell at about the same rate as it did in New York once the growth in New York's police force is accounted for.

It would be churlish to argue that smart policing isn't a good thing. Bill Bratton certainly deserves credit for invigorating New York's police force. But there is frighteningly little evidence that his strategy was the crime panacea that he and the media deemed it. The next step will be to continue measuring the impact of police innovations—in Los Angeles, for instance, where Bratton himself became police chief in late 2002. While he duly instituted some of the innovations that were his hallmark in New York, Bratton announced that his highest priority was a more basic one: finding the money to hire thousands of new police officers.

. . .

Now to explore another pair of common crime-drop explanations: tougher gun laws and changes in crack and other drug markets.

First, the guns. Debates on this subject are rarely coolheaded. Gun advocates believe that gun laws are too strict; opponents believe exactly the opposite. How can intelligent people view the world so differently? Because a gun raises a complex set of issues that change according to one factor: whose hand happens to be holding the gun.

It might be worthwhile to take a step back and ask a rudimentary question: what is a gun? It's a tool that can be used to kill someone, of course, but more significantly, a gun is a great disrupter of the natural order.

A gun scrambles the outcome of any dispute. Let's say that a tough guy and a not-so-tough guy exchange words in a bar, which leads to a fight. It's pretty obvious to the not-so-tough guy that he'll be beaten, so why bother fighting? The pecking order remains intact. But if the not-so-tough guy happens to have a gun, he stands a good chance of winning. In this scenario, the introduction of a gun may well lead to more violence.

Now instead of the tough guy and the not-so-tough guy, picture a high-school girl out for a nighttime stroll when she is suddenly set upon by a mugger. What if only the mugger is armed? What if only the girl is armed? What if both are armed? A gun opponent might argue that the gun has to be kept out of the mugger's hands in the first place. A gun advocate might argue that the high-school girl needs to have a gun to disrupt what has become the natural order: it's the bad guys that have the guns. (If the girl scares off the mugger, then the introduction of a gun in this case may lead to *less* violence.) Any mugger with even a little initiative is bound to be armed, for in a country like the United States, with a thriving black market in guns, anyone can get hold of one.

There are enough guns in the United States that if you gave one to every adult, you would run out of adults before you ran out of guns. Nearly two-thirds of U.S. homicides involve a gun, a far greater fraction than in other industrialized countries. Our homicide rate is also much higher than in those countries. It would therefore seem likely that our homicide rate is so high in part because guns are so easily available. Research indeed shows this to be true.

But guns are not the whole story. In Switzerland, every adult male is issued an assault rifle for militia duty and is allowed to keep the gun at home. On a per capita basis, Switzerland has more firearms than just about any other country, and yet it is one of the safest places in the world. In other words, guns do not cause crime. That said, the established U.S. methods of keeping guns away from the people who *do* cause crime are, at best, feeble. And since a gun—unlike a bag of cocaine or a car or a pair of pants—lasts pretty much forever, even turning off the spigot of new guns still leaves an ocean of available ones.

So bearing all this in mind, let's consider a variety of recent gun initiatives to see the impact they may have had on crime in the 1990s.

The most famous gun-control law is the Brady Act, passed in 1993, which requires a criminal check and a waiting period before a person can purchase a handgun. This solution may have seemed appealing to politicians, but to an economist it doesn't make much sense. Why? Because regulation of a legal market is bound to fail when a healthy black market exists for the same product. With guns so cheap and so easy to get, the standard criminal has no incentive to fill out a firearms application at his local gun shop and then wait a week. The Brady Act, accordingly, has proven to be practically impotent in lowering crime. (A study of imprisoned felons showed that even before the Brady Act, only about one-fifth of the criminals had bought their guns through a licensed dealer.) Various local gun-control laws have also failed. Washington, D.C., and Chicago both instituted handgun bans well before crime began to fall across the country in the 1990s, and yet those two cities were laggards, not leaders, in the national reduction in crime. One deterrent that has proven moderately effective is a stiff increase in prison time for anyone caught in possession of an illegal gun. But there is plenty of room for improvement. Not that this is likely, but if the death penalty were assessed to anyone carrying an illegal gun, and if the penalty were actually enforced, gun crimes would surely plunge.

Another staple of 1990s crime fighting—and of the evening news—was the gun buyback. You remember the image: a menacing, glistening heap of firearms surrounded by the mayor, the police chief, the neighborhood activists. It made for a nice photo op, but that's about as meaningful as a gun buyback is. The guns that get turned in are generally heirlooms or junk. The payoff to the gun seller—usually $50 or $100, but in one California buyback, three free hours of psychotherapy—isn't an adequate incentive for anyone who actually plans to use his gun. And the number of surrendered guns is no match for even the number of new guns simultaneously coming to market. Given the number of handguns in the United States and the number of homicides each year, the likelihood that a particular gun was used to kill someone that year is 1 in 10,000. The typical gun buyback program yields fewer than 1,000 guns—which translates into an expectation of less than one-tenth of one homicide per buyback. Not enough, that is, to make even a sliver of impact on the fall of crime.

Then there is an opposite argument—that we need more guns on the street, but in the hands of the right people (like the high-school girl above, instead of her mugger). The economist John R. Lott Jr. is the main champion of this idea. His calling card is the book *More Guns, Less Crime*, in which he argues that violent crime has decreased in areas where law-abiding citizens are allowed to carry concealed weapons. His theory might be surprising, but it is sensible. If a criminal thinks his potential victim may be armed, he may be deterred from committing the crime. Handgun opponents call Lott a pro-gun ideologue, and Lott let himself become a lightning rod for gun controversy. He exacerbated his trouble by creating a pseudonym, "Mary Rosh," to defend his theory in online debates. Rosh, identifying herself as a former student of Lott's, praised her teacher's intellect, his evenhandedness, his charisma. "I have to say that he was the best professor that I ever had," s/he wrote. "You wouldn't know that he was a 'right-wing' ideologue from the class. . . . There were a group of us students who would try to take any class that he taught. Lott finally had to tell us that it was best for us to try and take classes from other professors more to be exposed to other ways of teaching graduate material." Then there was the troubling allegation that Lott actually invented some of the survey data that support his more-guns/less-crime theory. Regardless of whether the data were faked, Lott's admittedly intriguing hypothesis doesn't seem to be true. When other scholars have tried to replicate his results, they found that right-to-carry laws simply don't bring down crime.

. . .

Consider the next crime-drop explanation: *the bursting of the crack bubble*. Crack cocaine was such a potent, addictive drug that a hugely profitable market had been created practically overnight. True, it was only the leaders of the crack gangs who were getting rich. But that only made the street-level dealers all the more desperate to advance. Many of them were willing to kill their rivals to do so, whether the rival belonged to the same gang or a different one. There were also gun battles over valuable drug-selling corners. The typical crack murder involved one crack dealer shooting another (or two of them, or three) and not, contrary to conventional wisdom, some bug-eyed crackhead shooting a shopkeeper over a few dollars. The result was a huge increase in violent crime. One study found that more than 25 percent of the homicides in New York City in 1988 were crack-related.

The violence associated with crack began to ebb in about 1991. This has led many people to think that crack itself went away. It didn't. Smoking crack remains much more popular today than most people realize. Nearly 5 percent of all arrests in the United States are still related to cocaine (as against 6 percent at crack's peak); nor have emergency room visits for crack users diminished all that much.

What did go away were the huge profits for selling crack. The price of cocaine had been falling for years, and it got only cheaper as crack grew more popular. Dealers began to underprice one another; profits vanished. The crack bubble burst as dramatically as the Nasdaq bubble would eventually burst. (Think of the first generation of crack dealers as the Microsoft millionaires; think of the second generation as Pets.com.) As veteran crack dealers were killed or sent to prison, younger dealers decided that the smaller profits didn't justify the risk. The tournament had lost its allure. It was no longer worth killing someone to steal their crack turf, and certainly not worth being killed.

So the violence abated. From 1991 to 2001, the homicide rate among young black men—who were disproportionately represented among crack dealers—fell 48 percent, compared to 30 percent for older black men and older white men. (Another minor contributor to the falling homicide rate is the fact that some crack dealers took to shooting their enemies in the buttocks rather than murdering them; this method of violent insult was considered more degrading—and was obviously less severely punished—than murder.) All told, the crash of the crack market accounted for roughly 15 percent of the crime drop of the 1990s—a substantial factor, to be sure, though it should be noted that crack was responsible for far more than 15 percent of the crime increase of the 1980s. In other words, the net effect of crack is still being felt in the form of violent crime, to say nothing of the miseries the drug itself continues to cause.

. . .

The final pair of crime-drop explanations concern two demographic trends. The first one received many media citations: *aging of the population*.

Until crime fell so drastically, no one talked about this theory at all. In fact, the "bloodbath" school of criminology was touting exactly the opposite theory—that an increase in the teenage share of the population would produce a crop of superpredators who would lay the nation low. "Just beyond the horizon, there lurks a cloud that the winds will soon bring over us," James Q. Wilson wrote in 1995. "The population will start getting younger again . . . Get ready."

But overall, the teenage share of the population wasn't getting much bigger. Criminologists like Wilson and James Alan Fox had badly misread the demographic data. The real population growth in the 1990s was in fact among the elderly. While this may have been scary news in terms of Medicare and Social Security, the average American had little to fear from the growing horde of oldsters. It shouldn't be surprising to learn that elderly people are not very criminally intent; the average sixty-five-year-old is about one-fiftieth as likely to be arrested as the average teenager. That is what makes this aging-of-the-population theory of crime reduction so appealingly tidy: since people mellow out as they get older, more older people must lead to less crime. But a thorough look at the data reveals that the graying of America did nothing to bring down crime in the 1990s. Demographic change is too slow and subtle a process—you don't graduate from teenage hoodlum to senior citizen in just a few years to even begin to explain the suddenness of the crime decline.

There was another demographic change, however, unforeseen and long-gestating, that did drastically reduce crime in the 1990s.

Think back for a moment to Romania in 1966. Suddenly and without warning, Nicolae Ceausescu declared abortion illegal. The children born in the wake of the abortion ban were much more likely to become criminals than children born earlier. Why was that? Studies in other parts of Eastern Europe and in Scandinavia from the 1930s through the 1960s reveal a similar trend. In most of these cases, abortion was not forbidden outright, but a woman had to receive permission from a judge in order to obtain one. Researchers found that in the instances where the woman was denied an abortion, she often resented her baby and failed to provide it with a good home. Even when controlling for the income, age, education, and health of the mother, the researchers found that these children too were more likely to become criminals.

The United States, meanwhile, has had a different abortion history than Europe. In the early days of the nation, it was permissible to have an abortion prior to "quickening"— when the first movements of the fetus could be felt, usually around the sixteenth to eighteenth week. In 1828, New York became the first state to restrict abortion; by 1900 it had been made illegal throughout the country. Abortion in the twentieth century was often dangerous and usually expensive. Fewer poor women, therefore, had abortions. They also had less access to birth control. What they did have, accordingly, was a lot more babies.

In the late 1960s, several states began to allow abortion under extreme circumstances: rape, incest, or danger to the mother. By 1970 five states had made abortion entirely legal and broadly available: New York, California, Washington, Alaska, and Hawaii. On January 22, 1973, legalized abortion was suddenly extended to the entire country with the U.S. Supreme Court's ruling in Roe v. Wade. The majority opinion, written by Justice Harry Blackmun, spoke specifically to the would-be mother's predicament:

The detriment that the State would impose upon the pregnant woman by denying this
choice altogether is apparent. . . . Maternity, or additional offspring, may force upon
the woman a distressful life and future. Psychological harm may be imminent. Mental
and physical health may be taxed by child care. There is also the distress, for all con-
cerned, associated with the unwanted child, and there is the problem of bringing a
child into a family already unable, psychologically and otherwise, to care for it.

The Supreme Court gave voice to what the mothers in Romania and Scandinavia—
and elsewhere—had long known: when a woman does not want to have a child, she
usually has good reason. She may be unmarried or in a bad marriage. She may consider
herself too poor to raise a child. She may think her life is too unstable or unhappy, or
she may think that her drinking or drug use will damage the baby's health. She may
believe that she is too young or hasn't yet received enough education. She may want a
child badly but in a few years, not now. For any of a hundred reasons, she may feel that
she cannot provide a home environment that is conducive to raising a healthy and productive child.

In the first year after Roe v. Wade, some 750,000 women had abortions in the United
States (representing one abortion for every 4 live births). By 1980 the number of abortions
reached 1.6 million (one for every 2.25 live births), where it leveled off. In a country of
225 million people, 1.6 million abortions per year—one for every 140 Americans—may
not have seemed so dramatic. In the first year after Nicolae Ceausescu's death, when
abortion was reinstated in Romania, there was one abortion for every twenty-two Romanians. But still: 1.6 million American women a year who got pregnant were suddenly not
having those babies.

Before Roe v. Wade, it was predominantly the daughters of middle- or upper-class
families who could arrange and afford a safe illegal abortion. Now, instead of an illegal
procedure that might cost $500, any woman could easily obtain an abortion, often for
less than $100.

What sort of woman was most likely to take advantage of Roe v. Wade? Very often
she was unmarried or in her teens or poor, and sometimes all three. What sort of future
might her child have had? One study has shown that the typical child who went unborn
in the earliest years of legalized abortion would have been 50 percent more likely than
average to live in poverty; he would have also been 60 percent more likely to grow up with
just one parent. These two factors—childhood poverty and a single-parent household—

are among the strongest predictors that a child will have a criminal future. Growing up in a single-parent home roughly doubles a child's propensity to commit crime. So does having a teenage mother. Another study has shown that low maternal education is the single most powerful factor leading to criminality.

In other words, the very factors that drove millions of American women to have an abortion also seemed to predict that their children, had they been born, would have led unhappy and possibly criminal lives.

To be sure, the legalization of abortion in the United States had myriad consequences. Infanticide fell dramatically. So did shotgun marriages, as well as the number of babies put up for adoption (which has led to the boom in the adoption of foreign babies). Conceptions rose by nearly 30 percent, but births actually fell by 6 percent, indicating that many women were using abortion as a method of birth control, a crude and drastic sort of insurance policy.

Perhaps the most dramatic effect of legalized abortion, however, and one that would take years to reveal itself, was its impact on crime. In the early 1990s, just as the first cohort of children born after Roe v. Wade was hitting its late teen years—the years during which young men enter their criminal prime—the rate of crime began to fall. What this cohort was missing, of course, were the children who stood the greatest chance of becoming criminals. And the crime rate continued to fall as an entire generation came of age minus the children whose mothers had not wanted to bring a child into the world. Legalized abortion led to less unwantedness; unwantedness leads to high crime; legalized abortion, therefore, led to less crime.

This theory is bound to provoke a variety of reactions, ranging from disbelief to revulsion, and a variety of objections, ranging from the quotidian to the moral. The likeliest first objection is the most straightforward one: is the theory true? Perhaps abortion and crime are merely correlated and not causal.

It may be more comforting to believe what the newspapers say, that the drop in crime was due to brilliant policing and clever gun control and a surging economy. We have evolved with a tendency to link causality to things we can touch or feel, not to some distant or difficult phenomenon. We believe especially in near-term causes: a snake bites your friend, he screams with pain, and he dies. The snakebite, you conclude, must have killed him. Most of the time, such a reckoning is correct. But when it comes to cause and effect, there is often a trap in such open-and-shut thinking. We smirk now when we think of ancient cultures that embraced faulty causes—the warriors who believed, for instance, that it was their raping of a virgin that brought them victory on the battlefield. But we too embrace faulty causes, usually at the urging of an expert proclaiming a truth in which he has a vested interest.

How, then, can we tell if the abortion-crime link is a case of causality rather than simply correlation?

One way to test the effect of abortion on crime would be to measure crime data in the five states where abortion was made legal before the Supreme Court extended abortion rights to the rest of the country. In New York, California, Washington, Alaska, and Hawaii, a woman had been able to obtain a legal abortion for at least two years before Roe v. Wade. And indeed, those early-legalizing states saw crime begin to fall earlier than the other forty-five states and the District of Columbia. Between 1988 and 1994, violent crime in the early legalizing states fell 13 percent compared to the other states; between 1994 and 1997, their murder rates fell 23 percent more than those of the other states.

But what if those early legalizers simply got lucky? What else might we look for in the data to establish an abortion-crime link? One factor to look for would be a correlation between each state's abortion rate and its crime rate. Sure enough, the states with the highest abortion rates in the 1970s experienced the greatest crime drops in the 1990s, while states with low abortion rates experienced smaller crime drops. (This correlation exists even when controlling for a variety of factors that influence crime: a state's level of incarceration, number of police, and its economic situation.) Since 1985, states with high abortion rates have experienced a roughly 30 percent drop in crime relative to low-abortion states. (New York City had high abortion rates and lay within an early-legalizing state, a pair of facts that further dampen the claim that innovative policing caused the crime drop.) Moreover, there was no link between a given state's abortion rate and its crime rate before the late 1980s—when the first cohort affected by legalized abortion was reaching its criminal prime—which is yet another indication that Roe v. Wade was indeed the event that tipped the crime scale.

There are even more correlations, positive and negative, that shore up the abortion-crime link. In states with high abortion rates, the entire decline in crime was among the post-Roe cohort as opposed to older criminals. Also, studies of Australia and Canada have since established a similar link between legalized abortion and crime. And the post-Roe cohort was not only missing thousands of young male criminals but also thousands of single, teenage mothers—for many of the aborted baby girls would have been the children most likely to replicate their own mothers' tendencies.

To discover that abortion was one of the greatest crime-lowering factors in American history is, needless to say, jarring. It feels less Darwinian than Swiftian; it calls to mind a long ago dart attributed to G. K. Chesterton: when there aren't enough hats to go around, the problem isn't solved by lopping off some heads. The crime drop was, in the language of economists, an "unintended benefit" of legalized abortion. But one need not oppose abortion on moral or religious grounds to feel shaken by the notion of a private sadness being converted into a public good.

Indeed, there are plenty of people who consider abortion itself to be a violent crime. One legal scholar called legalized abortion worse than either slavery (since it routinely involves death) or the Holocaust (since the number of post-Roe abortions in the United States, roughly thirty-seven million as of 2004, outnumber the six million Jews killed in Europe). Whether or not one feels so strongly about abortion, it remains a singularly charged issue. Anthony V. Bouza, a former top police official in both the Bronx and Minneapolis, discovered this when he ran for Minnesota governor in 1994. A few years earlier, Bouza had written a book in which he called abortion "arguably the only effective crime-prevention device adopted in this nation since the late 1960s." When Bouza's opinion was publicized just before the election, he fell sharply in the polls. And then he lost.

However a person feels about abortion, a question is likely to come to mind: what are we to make of the trade-off of more abortion for less crime? Is it even possible to put a number on such a complicated transaction?

As it happens, economists have a curious habit of affixing numbers to complicated transactions. Consider the effort to save the northern spotted owl from extinction. One economic study found that in order to protect roughly five thousand owls, the opportunity costs—that is, the income surrendered by the logging industry and others—would be $46 billion, or just over $9 million per owl. After the Exxon Valdez oil spill in 1989, another study estimated the amount that the typical American household would be willing to pay to avoid another such disaster: $31. An economist can affix a value even to a particular body part. Consider the schedule that the state of Connecticut uses to compensate for work-related injuries.

Lost or Damaged Body Part	Compensated Weeks of Pay
Finger (first)	36
Finger (second)	29
Finger (third)	21
Finger (fourth)	17
Thumb (master hand)	63
Thumb (other hand)	54
Hand (master)	168
Hand (other)	155
Arm (master)	208
Arm (other)	194
Toe (great)	28
Toe (any other)	9
Foot	125
Nose	35
Eye	157
Kidney	117
Liver	347
Pancreas	416
Heart	520
Mammary	35
Ovary	35
Testis	35
Penis	35–104
Vagina	35–104

Now, for the sake of argument, let's ask an outrageous question: what is the relative value between a fetus and a newborn? If faced with the Solomonic task of sacrificing the life of one newborn for an indeterminate number of fetuses, what number might you choose?

This is nothing but a thought exercise—obviously there is no right answer but it may help clarify the impact of abortion on crime.

For a person who is either resolutely pro-life or resolutely pro-choice, this is a simple calculation. The first, believing that life begins at conception, would likely consider the value of a newborn versus the value of a fetus to be 1:1. The second person, believing that a woman's right to an abortion trumps any other factor, would likely argue that no number of fetuses can equal even one newborn.

But let's consider a third person. (If you identify strongly with either person number one or person number two, the following exercise might strike you as offensive, and you may want to skip this paragraph and the next.) This third person does not believe that a fetus is the 1:1 equivalent of a newborn, yet neither does he believe that a fetus has no relative value. Let's say that he is forced, for the sake of argument, to affix a relative value, and he decides that 1 newborn is worth 100 fetuses.

There are roughly 1.5 million abortions in the United States every year. For a person who believes that 1 newborn is worth 100 fetuses, those 1.5 million abortions would translate—dividing 1.5 million by 100—into the equivalent of a loss of 15,000 human lives. Fifteen thousand lives: that happens to be about the same number of people who die in homicides in the United States every year. And it is far more than the number of homicides eliminated each year due to legalized abortion. So even for someone who considers a fetus to be worth only one one-hundredth of a human being, the trade-off between higher abortion and lower crime is, by an economist's reckoning, terribly inefficient.

What the link between abortion and crime does say is this: when the government gives a woman the opportunity to make her own decision about abortion, she generally does a good job of figuring out if she is in a position to raise the baby well. If she decides she can't, she often chooses the abortion.

Steven D. Levitt, who teaches at the University of Chicago, recently received the John Bates Clark Medal, awarded every two years to the best American economist under 40. Stephen J. Dubner writes for *The New York Times* and *The New Yorker* and is the author of *Turbulent Souls and Confessions of a Hero-Worshiper*. This piece is excerpted from their 2005 book *Freakonomics: A Rogue Economist Explores the Hidden Side of Everything*.

POLICY ARGUMENT

Bigotry That Hurts Our Military

BY ALAN K. SIMPSON (2007)

As a lifelong Republican who served in the Army in Germany, I believe it is critical that we review—and overturn—the ban on gay service in the military. I voted for "don't ask, don't tell." But much has changed since 1993.

My thinking shifted when I read that the military was firing translators because they are gay. According to the Government Accountability Office, more than 300 language experts have been fired under "don't ask, don't tell," including more than 50 who are fluent in Arabic. This when even Secretary of State Condoleezza Rice recently acknowledged the nation's "foreign language deficit" and how much our government needs Farsi and Arabic speakers. Is there a "straight" way to translate Arabic? Is there a "gay" Farsi? My God, we'd better start talking sense before it is too late. We need every able-bodied, smart patriot to help us win this war.

In today's perilous global security situation, the real question is whether allowing homosexuals to serve openly would enhance or degrade our readiness. The best way to answer this is to reconsider the original points of opposition to open service.

First, America's views on homosexuals serving openly in the military have changed dramatically. The percentage of Americans in favor has grown from 57 percent in 1993 to a whopping 91 percent of 18- to 29-year-olds surveyed in a Gallup poll in 2003.

Military attitudes have also shifted. Fully three-quarters of 500 vets returning from Iraq and Afghanistan said in a December Zogby poll that they were comfortable interacting with gay people. Also last year, a Zogby poll showed that a majority of service members who knew a gay member in their unit said the person's presence had no negative impact on the unit or personal morale. Senior leaders such as retired Gen. John Shalikashvili and Lt. Gen. Daniel Christman, a former West Point superintendent, are calling for a second look.

Second, 24 nations, including 12 in Operation Enduring Freedom and nine in Operation Iraqi Freedom, permit open service. Despite controversy surrounding the policy change, it has had no negative impact on morale, cohesion, readiness or recruitment. Our allies did not display such acceptance back when we voted on "don't ask, don't tell," but we should consider their common-sense example.

Third, there are not enough troops to perform the required mission. The Army is "about broken," in the words of Colin Powell. The Army's chief of staff, Gen. Peter Schoomaker, told the House Armed Services Committee in December that "the active-duty Army of 507,000 will break unless the force is expanded by 7,000 more soldiers a year." To fill its needs, the Army is granting a record number of "moral waivers," allowing even felons to enlist. Yet we turn away patriotic gay and lesbian citizens.

The Urban Institute estimates that 65,000 gays are serving and that there are 1 million gay veterans. These gay vets include Capt. Cholene Espinoza, a former U-2 pilot who logged more than 200 combat hours over Iraq, and Marine Staff Sgt. Eric Alva, who lost his right leg to an Iraqi land mine. Since 2005, more than 800 personnel have been discharged from "critical fields"—jobs considered essential but difficult in terms of training or retraining, such as linguists, medical personnel and combat engineers. Aside from allowing us to recruit and retain more personnel, permitting gays to serve openly would enhance the quality of the armed forces.

In World War II, a British mathematician named Alan Turing led the effort to crack the Nazis' communication code. He mastered the complex German enciphering machine, helping to save the world, and his work laid the basis for modern computer science. Does it matter that Turing was gay? This week, Gen. Peter Pace, chairman of the Joint Chiefs, said that homosexuality is "immoral" and that the ban on open service should therefore not be changed. Would Pace call Turing "immoral"?

Since 1993, I have had the rich satisfaction of knowing and working with many openly gay and lesbian Americans, and I have come to realize that "gay" is an artificial category when it comes to measuring a man or woman's on-the-job performance or commitment to shared goals. It says little about the person. Our differences and prejudices pale next to our historic challenge. Gen. Pace is entitled, like anyone, to his personal opinion, even if it is completely out of the mainstream of American thinking. But he should know better than to assert this opinion as the basis for policy of a military that represents and serves an entire nation. Let us end "don't ask, don't tell." This policy has become a serious detriment to the readiness of America's forces as they attempt to accomplish what is arguably the most challenging mission in our long and cherished history.

———

Alan K. Simpson, a Republican senator from Wyoming from 1979 to 1997, wrote this piece for the March 14, 2007, edition of *The Washington Post* <www.washingtonpost.com>.

POLICY ARGUMENT

A Christian View of War

BY OLIVER "BUZZ" THOMAS (2006)

"Pray for our troops."

Millions of signs and bumper stickers carry the message, and part of me likes it. But part of me keeps waiting for another bumper sticker—the one I still haven't seen. Whether Jesus would drive an SUV, I'm still not sure. Truth is he'd probably ride the bus. Or the subway. But if he had money for a car and didn't give it all away to the hookers and the homeless before he got to the used-car lot, I'm pretty sure that his bumper sticker would say "pray for our enemies."

Before you write me off as a left-wing crackpot, consider what we know. During his famous Sermon on the Mount, Jesus said three things relevant to the subject of war:

- Blessed are the peacemakers.
- Turn the other cheek.
- Pray for your enemies.

Here's something else we know. Three-quarters of the U.S. population consider themselves Christian. That translates into about 224 million Americans.

So why are so few of us taking the teachings of Jesus seriously when it comes to this latest war? Out here in the heartland, only a handful of churches are even talking about it.

CHRISTIAN OBLIGATIONS

The most plausible explanation is that we're scared. Some things, it seems, may trump religion. Fear is one of them. If Christians are afraid (and who could blame them after 9/11?), it's not surprising that they're listening to other voices besides Jesus' when it comes to the war in Iraq. So what should the three-fourths of Americans who identify themselves as "Christian" make of the Iraq war?

We could spend a lot of time debating whether St. Augustine's "Just War Theory" can be stretched to accommodate our invasion of Iraq, but at this late date it really doesn't matter. We invaded. And, if the Just War Theory means anything, it means that we shouldn't leave Iraq in a bigger mess than we found it. Americans of faith, it would seem, are obligated to do at least the following:

- Express concern for all suffering, including that of our enemies. That means more than paying lip service. As James, the brother of Jesus, said, it does not suffice to tell a hungry man "God bless you!" or "We will pray for you!" We must address his hunger. The same can be said for the additional food, health care, police and countless other things the Iraqi people need. And, though an immediate withdrawal would be precipitous, we must work diligently to respond to the Iraqis' desire that our troops leave as quickly as possible.

- Recommit ourselves to the fundamental principles of justice and human rights that have been a hallmark of our faith, as well as of our nation. That means no more secret prisons, no more secret trials and no more torture. America cannot resort to the worst practices of the Gulag (where citizens were declared "enemies of the state" and whisked away to Siberian work camps without the benefit of a fair trial or the assistance of counsel) and expect to be an accepted member of the world community, much less a leader of it.

- Repudiate the statements of any religious or political leader who suggests that America has a special claim on God. He may have a special claim on us, but we do not have a special claim on him. Our beloved nation is a civil state, not a religious one. There are no references to God in our Constitution. The only reference to religion—other than in the First Amendment—is found in Article VI, which proclaims that there will be no religious test for public office in the USA. The Founding Fathers gave us a secular state in which all religions are free to flourish or flounder on their own initiative without interference by the government. Those running around claiming we are "in the army of God" or slapping up copies of the Ten Commandments on government buildings threaten to turn us into the very sort of society we are fighting against in this new war.

- Force our elected officials to address the conditions that have given rise to global terrorism in the first place. Terrorism exists for a reason. One of those reasons is that our society has been far too unconcerned about the plight of Muslim people around the world. Why, for example, have we not instituted a mini-Marshall Plan for the millions of Palestinians who have often gone without adequate land, roads, hospitals and schools since the 1967 war with Israel? Corruption among Palestinian leaders has squandered billions in the past, but responsible partners on the ground can and must be found. Private foundations with a long history of engagement might be a good place to start.

TACKLING TERRORISM'S ROOTS

We need not and should not repudiate our long-standing alliance with Israel to accomplish this. It's simply that our religious traditions teach us that to whom much is given, much is required. The irony, of course, is that it's in our best interest to relieve Palestinian suffering. True, some terrorist leaders come from affluent families and cite Western worldliness and decadence as their motivation for jihad, but the economic factor cannot be ignored. There is no better recruiting ground for the troops of terror than the maddening monotony and grinding poverty of a refugee camp.

In ancient times, particular gods were associated with particular nations. "Tribal deities," we call them. Today we know better. God is not the mascot of Republicans, Democrats or, for that matter, Americans. God transcends all national and political affiliations. His precinct is the universe.

America is in the deep woods. Never have we been less popular in the eyes of the world. Never have we faced so unsettling an enemy. But before we circle the wagons, Christians should get serious about following the teachings of the one by whose name we are called. He might just know the way out.

Oliver "Buzz" Thomas is a minister in Tennessee and author of *10 Things Your Minister Wants to Tell You (But Can't Because He Needs the Job)*. He wrote this column for the September 18, 2006, edition of *USA Today*.

INDEXES

INDEXES

Name Index

Title Index

ACADEMIC RESPONSIBILITY STATEMENT

In addition to my teacher's syllabus and course policies, I have read the "Policies and Procedures" and "Academic Responsibility" sections of The Student's Guide to First-Year English online at <www.cas.sc.edu/engl/fye/students/index.html>. I understand the information provided, specifically the attendance and plagiarism policies. I also understand that I can find further information about academic responsibility through USC's Office of Academic Integrity <http://www.sc.edu/academicintegrity>.

Name (please print): _____

Course and section number: _____   Instructor: _____

Signature: _____   Date: _____